The complete annotated
Grateful dead
Lyrics

The Collected Lyrics of Robert Hunter and John Barlow,
Lyrics to All Original Songs, with Selected
Traditional and Cover Songs

Annotations by David Dodd

Illustrated by Jim Carpenter
Edited by Alan Trist and David Dodd

FREE PRESS
New York   London   Toronto   Sydney

FREE PRESS
A Division of Simon & Schuster, Inc.
1230 Avenue of the Americas
New York, NY 10020

By arrangement with Ice Nine Publishing Company, Inc.

FREE PRESS and colophon are trademarks
of Simon & Schuster, Inc.

For information about special discounts for bulk purchases,
please contact Simon & Schuster Special Sales at
1-800-456-6798 or business@simonandschuster.com

Cover illustration and design: Jim Carpenter
Interior design: Harry Choron, Sandy Choron, March Tenth, Inc.

Manufactured in the United States of America

10 9 8 7 6 5 4 3 2 1

Library of Congress Cataloging-in-Publication Data is available

ISBN-13: 978-0-7432-7747-1
ISBN-10:   0-7432-7747-3

Diana, Rosemary, and Alexander: I love you more than words can tell.
—David Dodd

It's a hand-me-down
The thoughts are broken
Perhaps they're better left unsung
I don't know
Don't really care
Let there be songs to fill the air

—Robert Hunter, "Ripple"

contents

the Lyrics 1965-1995

(Songs are listed by date of first performance or, if never
in the live repertoire, by date of studio recording,
whichever comes first. An alphabetical list of songs is
included in the index.)

foreword

hat, after all, is the point of a compendium of scatology and ontology viz the lyrics of the Grateful Dead? When fans hear a song they like, they internalize it, dance to it, sing along. Tape it, collect it, trade it. When scholars hear a song they like, they annotate it. There is more than one way to love a song. There are as many ways as there are listeners.

The songlist of the Grateful Dead has achieved an anomalous status within the archives of current pop culture. It begins to appear that our output embodied the summation and close of a musical era, rather than heralding the bright new beginning devoutly wished for. But it bears mentioning that our work was a natural and inevitable blending of rock and roll, jazz, and traditional folk culture. It

was, in its day, as shockingly innovative as the music of mounting urban psychosis that was to displace it. Its verbal and musical complexity offer little of overwhelming market value to a more intensely stratified current musical culture. I'm optimistically uncertain as to whether it is a dead issue or a ticking time bomb set to detonate long after its progenitors have quit this sphere of commercial sorrow. My own improbable dream was to aid and abet a unified indigenous American, or at least Western, music, drawing on all bona fide traditional currents including pop. Tall order for a bunch of white kids. Big dreams. But jazz wasn't talking to pop, and bluegrass wasn't talking to the blues—experimental postclassic soundscape wasn't talking to anybody.

Most bands can be copied, but bands that have tried to mimic the Grateful Dead in a creative way, other than note-by-note reproduction, tend to fall short of the mark because there is no specific style to mimic, rather a range of styles that the band members have individually mastered and integrated into the music. Pigpen played blues and was accepted as a regular in the black nightclubs of East Palo Alto in his early teens. Phil studied composition with the great Italian avant-garde composer Luciano Berio to augment his classical training. Garcia's knowledge and facility with American folk forms and instrumental styles was compendious. Mickey Hart was a titled world-champion rudimental drummer from a family of drummers and studied Indian rhythmic intricacies with Zakir Hussein and Ali Akbar Khan. Several of us were veterans of regular jazz sessions by sterling musicians such as Lester Hellum, Bob Pringle, Rudy Jackson, and Dan Barnett while living at the Chateau. My particular strength was a good memory. I knew the words to most of the popular songs of the forties and fifties and to most of the classics of the swing era, through my parents' record collection (also strong in folk music) and through playing through "fake books" of the era on my trumpet. I also absorbed the lyrics to an untold number of folk songs during the folk revival of the sixties. Just a knack, but it's small wonder that my songs are often fraught with allusions.

I believe that the lyrics themselves say all that wants saying but acknowledge that scholastic exegesis has a momentum of its own and it's not my business to impede it, though I always believed we were "historicized" too early for comfort. I also believe, through experience, that beneath the window dressing of metaphor and rhyme, song is a naked, living, and amorphous creature. Where some assume that song is the transcription of self, my more intimate belief is that one goes out in the woods and *ketches* one, dresses it up, and trains it to talk. How the brute is trained is a matter of personal style, but beneath the window dressing, the song remains elusively itself, prevented from full expression by the limits of its intended use. The writer's prejudices, blindsides, and occasional strengths are all utilized in the disguising of the primordial beast into form adequate to its specific purpose.

Scatology is the activity of tracking the spoor of the song, detecting borrowings, influences, and/or outright thefts; of uncovering, through internal evidence, the parentage of a particular song, or of repetitive tendencies throughout a body of work—of actual or imagined contingent sources. It is evidence for induction, building a hypothetical dinosaur from fossil traces. Looking for what species of fire causes such and such a spiral of smoke. Sometimes, there is indeed a flame; other times, the writer was just

stretching for a rhyme, accepting something conven-
ient with a deadline impending, no further significance intended. At other times, evidence is ironically
removed from normal context and bespeaks *influence*
less than sheer serendipitous proximity. All practice
is acceptable practice! Who arbitrates this stuff anyway? It isn't the artist's sworn duty to be easily or
accurately traceable. I grudgingly admit that prior
knowledge of select sources can establish a context
for a song that might positively increase the effec-
tiveness of the allusions. One of my conscious goals
as a songwriter is to provide a connective thread to
the ongoing project of Western music, when and if
it feels natural and right.

Ontology is an examination of causative factors, of
intent. What was the *impulse* that seemed to require
certain images to be duly expressed? Love, carnal or
spiritual? Irony? Sentiment? Contempt? Patriotism?
Existential devaluation? Self-advertisement? Revenge?
Paranoia? Romance? Annoyance? Deconstruction?
Revolution? Peer status? Exuberance? Broken-heart-
edness? Grief? Indomitability? Salvation? Sales?
Sacrilege? Inanity? Responsibility or the lack of?
Need of another song for the album? Discontent?
Protest? Inspiration from another song? Disaster,
personal or worldwide? There are prime models for
each of these impulses in the literature of song, in
the musical ocean in which we swim.

Who stands behind the mask of a song? Anyone
willing and able to provide the voice can wear the
mask and intone the metaphors. Song, a series of
tones enhanced by metaphor, coalesces into a visage
in the act of performance. Why just exactly
metaphor? What is metaphor? Metaphor is that
which stands for something that cannot stand for
itself, since all else stands upon it. Philosophy is
metaphor, war is metaphor, and, oh yes, dear sweet
love itself. A broad term. What lies outside the
capacity of imagining, by way of metaphor, is unde-
fined because indefinable. The something I speak of
is evocable, in a limited sense of emotional repercus-
sion, by appropriate metaphor. It is *surmisable* though
not contained by it. The juxtaposition of one
metaphor to another yields relation; a juxtaposition
of relations, a situation. A juxtaposition of
situations provides narrative. Is music also
metaphor? Yes, but you lose the value of both words
by saying so. Invocation and evocation are classically
terms of magic. You don't evoke your dog, you call
him. Spirit, however, you must invoke, coax with
metaphor. A song, successfully invoked, evokes person, place, time, and condition.

Sometimes the singer becomes the song. This can
be dangerous because the metaphoric mask, fitting

too well, can be difficult to remove. Hans Christian Andersen's tale of "The Red Shoes" is the scarifying metaphor of this situation. But when the metaphor supplants the mediator in less than tragic circumstances, mere make-believe becomes magic theater. We buy our tickets hoping this will happen and are disappointed when it doesn't. But when it does—the audience, as well as the artist, assimilated by metaphor exalted by music—performance becomes ceremony. Words are no longer strictly necessary, they have done their duty toward the primary evocation; rhythm and tonality alone prolong the experience until it's time to haul it back down to earth and bid you goodnight.

The Grateful Dead was, is, the master metaphor for our group situation. And yes, the shoes have run away with the feet at times. The evocative power of that strange, not at all comical name is considerable, for grace and ill. I know that my own input into the scene, my words, were heavily conditioned by that powerful name. It called sheaves of spirits down on us all. It expressed a deep and mystic hope about the nature of eternity. Our shows were ceremonies and our people, celebrants, in the most archaic sense of the term. There was no place else on God's green earth that I, for one, fitted. Now that it is gone, there is no place else I fit so exactly as to shape and size. But that I fit once, and well, into something that fit me, that had a piece exactly my size missing, gives hope, in that such things may be at all, that thus it may be so again. Madly in love with metaphor, I took a lover's liberties with it, crushing unlikely relations into strange situations, letting it summon a sense of its own, or none, or to be continued. . . . Crazy? By all means, whatever that peculiar metaphor of relative sanity portends. The attempt to speak on as many levels at once as is humanly possible, considering the limitations of language (which is also its condition of freedom), can invite the worried concern of more orderly minds.

The components of metaphor that can't be so easily isolated or identified are those that have nothing to do with image per se, but rather the arrangement of the articles of the image. Say the image of the metaphor is, for example, *a red silk banner in the rain.* The same metaphor can be expressed as: *in the rain, a silken banner of red.* Or: *silken, red, a banner in the rain.* Same metaphor, different emphases and rhythmic pulses. In the context of rhyme, the same metaphor in different inversions could provoke many different shades of feeling.

Weeping tears of crimson pain
silken, red, a banner in the rain.

A certain elegance is provided by rhythmic contrast that would be lost in the doggerel rhythm of:

Weeping tears of crimson pain

a red silk banner in the rain.

All I mean to imply by examining this scrap of suspect metaphor is that there is a point where we leave scatology and ontology behind and enter the sphere of poetics, the land of measured feet, onomatopoeia, and rhythmic accent.

There are songs of such enduring stature that they have become part of the common mind, from "Row, Row, Row Your Boat" to "Happy Birthday to You," from "Stardust" to "Auld Lang Syne," from "Subterranean Homesick Blues" to "(I Can't Get No) Satisfaction." They seem like natural forces (as indeed they are)—unequivocal as the moon and perennial as grass—but in each case, oddly enough, somebody *wrote* the piece, wrote it or made it up, and passed it along, always around a fire—somebody whose name has come down through the ages along with his song, somebody like King David or Cab Calloway, or, more commonly, somebody forgotten. I like to acknowledge some of these works (it's called allusion), borrowing a bit of their pizzazz or charm, certain of their authority if not my own. People ask me who my major influences are, and I have to smile, thinking, "You mean other than Walt Disney?" All qualitative assumptions aside, what music first moved us? Got down deep in there before we'd

erected any barriers of taste and sophistication? An apt allusion can act like a magnet among the iron filings of a verse, making them all coalesce and decisively point north. One seeks the point in the soul that has already been touched in an undeniable way, only to proceed in directions of one's own. A four-leaf clover on Mars is the desired item. A scrap of Stephen Foster or a bow to Mother Goose pleases the Muse who watches over such things. She likes us when we borrow, loves us when we steal. All of what song is ventures from and flies home to the same place: soul to soul. Copyright is an interesting and fairly new idea, but I don't think it'll ever rule the creative sphere where all things interpenetrate and cross-fertilize. A song is only eveb fully realized when it belongs to everyone whose language it inhabits. Which is as much as to say: Few songs are ever fully realized. More than simple creative acts, they are acts of accretion, moss-covered and lichen-bearing bits of interstellar matter, living beings of word and harmony.

There is an approach that allows a song to achieve multiple personal evocations of déjà vu. Not amenable to recognizable formulation (like metric, rhyme, or allusion), it fits the facts of many lives, typifying a variety of situations, and seems to each of many listeners as though written for them alone. I mean specifically written for them, not just generically, but personally. I've run across too many testimonials to the phenomenon regarding my own work to doubt it—and have experienced it myself (who hasn't?) in the lyric works of others that touch me most. A lyric that places its situation too restrictively in a particular time and place may fail in this regard but, on the other hand, might just redouble in such associative power to the ears of those from the same time and place. Usually New York City in the not-too-distant past. Mostly it's the trusty love song, specifically new love and love disappointed, that takes you there. When the parallels get a little too exact, it's just uncanny, and there's not much more to say about that. It's a bit more difficult to find subjects other than romantic love that partake of the particular and the universal at the same time, which is what a song must do to make any difference in the life of the listener. By report, I've done this with a few songs, such as "Ripple" and "Box of Rain" (neither love songs in the conventional sense), but I can't tell how it's done, only how it feels: like I've just spoken clearly to myself and survived the experience. Exalted. Satisfied. Though the facts of the writing of many lyrics are forgotten, I don't forget the moments that define and validate my choice of professions.

The truths of song are not the truths of prose or those of nonlyric poetry. Poetry much finer than your garden-variety song lyric can fail entirely to accomplish what rhymed couplets of suspiciously nil content can pull off with mere emotional conviction. Denigrate the art of Hank Williams who dare! What speaks to the head most often misses the heart, since song is above all else and beyond all else, a language of direct emotion, which to be powerful must be simple. Elements of abstraction are added at peril, but in the instances where a mix of brain and heart doesn't flat-out fail, it can work memorably well. Most studied attempts provide satisfactory fodder for neither mind nor heart; successful linkage is a gift of the moment's Muse—it comes out of the blue or it doesn't come.

The sheer dinkiness of rhyming (which the heart enjoys), besides providing an easy key to memorization for the performer, can be a distinct impediment to the free exercise of poetic flexibility. One of the great free-verse poets of our time, Allen Ginsberg (whose attempts at song lyric suffer from the constriction of a vast soul into iambic pentameter) asked me, "Does a song lyric have to rhyme?" I answered impulsively from the apparent truth of the matter that, yes, it must. He didn't ask for elucidation but nodded gravely and simply accepted the pronouncement. I've made a kind of trademark of seeing how far I could push lyric into abstraction without losing touch with the heart. Just so far and no further. I've pushed it too far several times and lived to lick my critical bruises. To test the limit and miss, should the work suffer recording and release, is to be labeled pretentious and henceforth beneath notice. "Too bad," they shake their heads, "he almost had us fooled." The best way past that misfortune is to collaborate with someone with strong populist instincts. A song needn't be bone-dumb, mind you, but it must strike past its quanta of intellection to the quiddity (thatness, thereness, suchness) of feeling, music itself being the most direct route to the big red pump.

The extasis of a song lyric is not particularly evident on the printed page, though I confess to being more attentive than strictly necessary about how my work appears to the eye, what's called symmetry and enjambment, but this is just a personal foible that has no bearing whatsoever on the viability of a lyric, which must be sounded and settled into the nest of its melody, serving not only exposition but the chords and pulses of the arrangement.

At best, it should seem like a tune could have no other words and the words, no other tune. In most cases, that's probably a delusion, as I've discovered by hearing hard-core rap lyrics set to Grateful Dead records with the original words electronically erased. The thought that someday my version of how those fine old tracks go will be only *one of many* that gives pause to consider.

Songwriting is 51 percent craft and 49 percent feel. After a few years in the business, I developed a rhyming dictionary in my head and didn't even bother to write an end word that would provide a too-limited scope and palette of rhyme. One learns early to tuck the word *love* into the middle of the line rather than deal with *shove, glove, dove, of,* and *above. Wind* is one of the most beautiful and multi-expressive words in the language, but has no usable consonant word except the false rhyme *begin.* So engrained is this acquired facility that I can literally listen to nearly any modern pop song and tell you what the next line will be more than 50 percent of the time. Most lyric writers telegraph their punches, especially when plowing over well-turned fields for the first time. But hey, it's all good. There are so many aspects involved in successfully matching a lyric to a set track, it's a wonder when it expresses anything coherent at all. There's more liberty to writing a lyric destined to be set to music than in "scoring." Then the struggle is on the musician's side, but at least there's a framework for composition rather than raw air and the buzz of an amp. Since I write faster than most musicians compose, I generally got my way if only because I had something to present and they didn't. For most full-time musicians, composition is the most dreaded thing of all. I reckon three-quarters of the collaborative output I've been involved in originated in my own head. In my experience, it's much easier to write a lyric than to create a supple and convincing tune. But the only way to write a song is to begin. No songs, to my knowledge, were ever performed that were not first begun. Small point, but not all that obvious. It could be that songs whose lyrics originated in my head are better in sum than those written for the compositions of others, though that is far from a safe generalization and I wouldn't like to put it to the test. Insofar as writing to composed music can utilize the music's own juice, the words are subordinated to the composer's intent. For a lyric to be interesting enough in its own right, to tempt a composer to score, a lot of juice must be present in the words to begin with.

I wonder if there are half a dozen other people in the English-speaking world who've made their long-term living solely as lyricists. Pretty small fraternity this. I was granted a rare chance to develop my craft in the public eye, in conjunction with a band of rare longevity. Fortunately, I had a lot to say and, equally fortunate, in retrospect, there was not enough "profile" to the shadowy writer's gig to turn my head. Not too much anyway. I lived lyric year in and year out for decades and never lost my taste for it. I ascribe this less to raw talent than to a fortuitous pairing of coincidences: suitable cohorts and the unique cultural ferment of the sixties. I don't know how many songs I wrote, thousands; they were forever getting lost, snatched up by pixies and transported to the land of lost socks or folded in somebody's back pocket and put through the wash with no duplicate copy. And I wrote reams of bad songs, bitching about everything under the sun, which I kept to myself: Cast not thy swines before pearls. And once in a while something would sort of pop out of nowhere. The sunny London afternoon I wrote "Brokedown Palace," "To Lay Me Down," and "Ripple," all keepers, was in no way typical, but it remains in my mind as the personal quintessence of the union between writer and Muse, a promising past and bright future prospects melding into one great glowing apocatastasis in South Kensington, writing words that seemed to flow like molten gold onto parchment paper. The only similar moment came while conceiving "Terrapin Station" in a lightning-split thunderstorm overlooking the lashing bay at China Camp. That I spent so many sessions trying to add to "Terrapin" in subsequent years was perhaps more an effort to recapture the magic of the moment than because the piece really needed completion. The moment lives on in the song; there's no need to repeat it. One would think that the culminating moment of a song's creation would culminate in hearing it performed for the first time, but in my experience this is seldom so; the nexus of eternity achieved in instants of assured and fluent creation reign supreme. The pudding is in the proof, so to speak.

Back in the day, I didn't allow my lyrics to be published with the recordings so people could dub in their own misdhearings, adding a bit of themselves to the song. Stone Age recording technique assured a certain amount of verbal blur, particularly if the band was dynamic in the mid and bass ranges. Though the recordings of the Grateful Dead have been remastered so that lyrics can be heard without suppressing the bass drum, there was a time when the words could be accurately deciphered neither on record nor in concert. Since they weren't printed, very few people other than the singers knew what I

was saying in any detail. Not that this state of things influenced my writing, but I've generally found that the words to songs I *thought* I heard in the works of others were more colorful and enigmatically apt than the words I eventually discovered *were* intended. More to my personal taste. I assume the same is true of my own work. Mishearing can be as much a strength as a liability. People, accidentally overhearing their own thoughts, are inclined to like what they hear, self-recognized at a distance and mistaken for another.

My purpose in writing song lyrics, besides having nothing better to do and making a living, is the exaltation of my spirit through the exaltation of other spirits. Traditional tools and forms are often apt for the purpose, such as the "Come All Ye" form so popular in sailor songs and union ballads. When I recommend others "come hear Uncle John's Band," I verbalize, in a way deeply meaningful to me, one of the ongoing agendas of life, the coaxing and cajoling of the forces of generational unity. I don't say *we*, the purveyors of the song, are Uncle John's Band (though anything was possible on a good night in the late sixties)—the truth is that we as a group also wanted to come hear "UJB," and to come home, too, if it's not too much to ask. When I'm lucky, what is meant to me by the gnomic phrases that rise from the reverie of writing is found equally meaningful to others. When asked who specifically Uncle John—or St. Stephen—is, I have to think someone's missed the point. They're you or they're no one. I once got a midnight phone call on my listed number from Uncle John and St. Stephen, which caused me to yank the cord out of the wall and go phoneless for the next year. I can't tell you why my reaction was so severe—I only know that it was.

The images and themes of "Uncle John's Band" are more than normally allusive, even for me. It was, incidentally, the first lyric I wrote with the aid of that newfangled gadget, the cassette tape recorder. I taped the band playing the arrangement and was able to score lyrics at leisure rather than scratch away hurriedly at rehearsals, waiting for particular sections to come around again. Few of their songs ("Box of Rain" is an exception) were so fully realized as "UJB" before the incorporation of lyrics. "UJB" (many Grateful Dead songs are known to fans by their initials) is a celebration of folk themes played "down by the riverside," hailing from a peculiar place where Appalachia met immigrant Scottish, English, Welsh, and Irish folk traditions, to my mind the mythic territory of Fennario, where Sweet William courted "Pretty Peggy-O" with such romantically disastrous consequences. I wanted to supercharge that ethos as something of ultimate value into the public consciousness. You can swallow a song like "UJB" whole for what it evokes in you, mystery and all—or you can track down the resources I selected while stumbling through the dark of composition, toward some kind of light, and achieve a gnostic synthesis of the song that may forever change the way you hear it. It may deepen the experience, or just explain it away. As with the language of love, the meaning of a song often lies less in what is said than in how it's said, the scan of the rhythm relative to counterweight of color and image. And mystery has a color all its own. But there's something other than those retrievable devices that's necessary: a uniqueness of overall character— that the song be *that* song, borrowings and all, and not any other. Not a copy of anything. A representative example of a genre that doesn't even exist, if it comes to that! A China Cat Sunflower. Avoidance of popular genres does not make for a commercially successful music; there's no formula for the cultural froth to fix on, but it does invite a long-term following. With only one hit in thirty years, I'm not even sure the Grateful Dead belong in the pop music section of the record store. But it definitely found its domain in the tape machines of an army of bootleggers. Due to the setlist–free creative variety of the performances, there are probably more hours in private circulation, of taped Grateful Dead music than of any musical group in history. What you lose on one side, you gain on another.

I realized some time ago that I've unwittingly given myself to the world. Maybe that's why the phone call from my characters disturbed me so deeply. The keys to my cloud are out there, and almost anybody can know more about me than I'll ever know about them. I don't think that thought often; it's a bit too uncanny for comfort. Obversely, it can lead to a feeling that anybody but me has a right to interpret the meanings of the songs. Well, yes, I know exactly what every line of my work was meant to mean, its sources or lack of them, and what it's trying to prove—if not the subconscious motivations all artists keep hidden from themselves, the tinder to ignite their dreams. So why don't I say it all for once and for good, and fatten this book up a bit? I'll say it again: The songs themselves say everything I personally want to say about them. The melodies of the unstrung harp are meant to be felt, not heard.

There were other lyricists involved in the writing of the Grateful Dead canon. Had I not joined, by invitation, as *lyricist in residence* a year after they chose the name and nailed down the job through sheer

prolixity, the band would have developed differently. It might have been less odd and more popular, for one thing. It would likely have remained more blues-based. The passing rage of psychedelia would have happened regardless. "The Other One" is a band-generated example of that, lyrics by Jerry Garcia and Bob Weir. In flipping through the draft pages of this book, I was surprised at the number of early lyrics by Garcia and by Ron "Pigpen" McKernan, songs that got an airing or two but apparently rang no bells for them. Both writers show distinct lyric promise. Their skills would have developed in proportion to the effort they exerted in songwriting, though both were first and foremost musicians. Words tend to be a chore when your first love is the performing of music. Penning and chord-combing don't have the same charge. I know from personal experience that when I perform much, my writing dwindles. In my opinion, most bands could benefit from a lyricist able to devote full time to the task. Musicianship and lyric acuity seldom dwell in the same body—different brain configurations, I figure. There are, of course, profound exceptions to this rule.

Another scenario might have found the weight put on Bobby Petersen and Peter Zimels, aka Peter Monk, both literate, interested, and available. Peter, once a Zen monk, was spiritual, political, and properly pissed off, lyrically articulate. Not a bad combination. Bobby was a masterfully poetic outlaw and a man of vast experience, much behind bars of both sorts. Both were gifted and serious poets trying their hand at lyric. I never considered myself a poet. I was into literature (as awed by James Joyce as were my friends by Coltrane), novel-writing, and folk music. Previous to "Alligator," I'd written only three songs, in 1957, for a rock-and-roll quartet I had in high school, but they were pop-style dreck with no resources beyond the pop-culture mind of the day, just something to sing. In 1967, I mailed to my old chum and fellow folkie Garcia three lyrics from New Mexico, extracted from songs I wrote and played at parties with some success, expecting no reply. I got the first and only letter I ever received from him, almost by return mail, asking me to come out and join the band. The lyrics were "Saint Stephen," "China Cat Sunflower," and "Alligator."

Bobby Petersen said to me, near the end of his life, "I could have done what you did." I wouldn't be qualified to judge, since fate granted me the chance to develop my craft in the public arena and denied it to him by penal circumstance and a savagely prodigious thirst that took its toll on health and ability. As testament to what might have been, he bequeathed the band "New Potato Caboose" and "Unbroken Chain," the latter a delicately beautiful poetic evocation of sorrow and loss. His youthful poetic prowess is demonstrated in his posthumous book of poetry, *Alleys of the Heart.* Had circumstance allowed, his old friend Phil would probably have come more forward in the solo vocal output, though this was something Phil didn't seem particularly keen to do, not liking the sound of his own voice, which is unfortunate because, given confidence, he would have been just dandy, as his vocal on our cowritten "Box of Rain" demonstrates. His tenor harmonies define the GD vocal blend.

In different circumstances, Bob Weir's collaboration with his school friend John Barlow might have begun earlier. Weir himself was capable of writing a nice breezy lyric to witness "Born Cross-eyed" and his part of "The Other One" lyrics—but had no confidence in his abilities and didn't develop the talent. The folk elements that characterized the recorded output were a function of Garcia and my mutual deep and tolerably well-informed interests, developed by having played as a folk duet, Bob & Jerry (with matching shirts!), and later in several old-timey and bluegrass bands prior to Mother McCree's Uptown Jug Champions, which transmogrified into the Warlocks, which became, and stayed, the Grateful Dead. Invited to play jug in Mother McCree's, I just couldn't get a sound out of the damned thing and dropped out of the band scene to pursue my novel- writing. Fate apparently had plans for me other than musicianship, or I would have made that jug ring! In the end, all those mutual folk elements got me the job of providing Garcia with the type of song he could sing with righteous authority. The others were a little worried about the folk direction, but agreeable; the band was, after all, desperate for material and, wonder of wonders, it clicked! Our albums went from the bottom of the charts to the upper reaches, consistently. Folk-biased music would never top the charts; that was for the Beatles, the Captain and Tennille, James Brown, the Monkees, and the Rolling Stones (Dylan had sort of disappeared from public view at this time due to his accident), but we did pretty well. We would have done better with a hit, three of which we had until they got banned from the airwaves by FCC warning, and two for mentioning cocaine: "Truckin'" (later declared "a national treasure" by an act of Congress—some Deadhead in the House, no doubt) and "Casey Jones." "Uncle John's Band" got kicked off the airwaves for swearing "God Damn! I declare / Have you seen the like?" Strangled in our infant cradle by the evil Nixon! He'll never know what a

favor he did us. We needed another decade of hard-work-just-to-survive to temper our metal. Burnout was providentially deferred.

As I see it, in my absence the Grateful Dead would have tended toward a balance between the Garcia, McKernan, Weir, and Lesh vocal and writing base, drawing moderately from outside the group for lyric material, most likely supplied by Barlow, Petersen, Zimmels, and, not inconceivably by Richard Brautigan, Lew Welch, and, Allen Ginsberg, requiring, as the band did, a dozen or more new songs a year to record. Folk-style repertoire would still have been evident, as with "Viola Lee Blues," but it would more likely have been covers than originals. But as it actually happened, my affinity with Garcia's interest in Americana conspired to provide the band with a resource not easily laid aside. The songs fit the times and helped to define them. For several years, the Garcia-Hunter song machine dominated the proceedings, with perhaps predictable results. With the impetus of *Rolling Stone's* decision to recast the GD as "Jerry & his band" with two big cover shots of his truly and interviews, not all of which were flattering to the band, Garcia's public persona decisively overshadowed his band-mates. McKernan's presence dwindled to feature spots, and Weir began to stand uncomfortably in the big guy's increasingly solid shadow. The drummers didn't care one way or another, but Phil's progressive tastes, at a guess, might well have been hampered by the verse-chorus-bridge song oriented approach so suitable to the 33 $^1/_3$ RPM, double-sided record format. Whatever the details, and there were many, the "resource not easily laid aside" showed signs of becoming "the monster who ate the band," and I felt conflicting pressures directed at my role, Garcia's position of eminence being unassailable. Weir voiced a desire, in collaboration, to have my words be more textural and less central to his compositions. Lyrics that didn't call attention to themselves. "The sound of thick air," as he once requested from engineer Dave Hassinger, who promptly quit. Probably a reasonable enough request, but I wasn't prone to minimize my skills, nor he to be overridden in matters of his own musical inclinations. Truth is, I wrote the same for him as I did for Garcia. It was *how* I wrote; I wasn't involved in a program of putting words in singers' mouths or defining their personae; I was simply expressing my own creative daemon. But it was the first indication that my little boat was shipping water and that continued clear sailing might not be in the cards.

I'm often asked what it takes to become a songwriter. Either those who write the majority of memorable songs are hypocrites or this is pretty much the recipe. No one ever said it'd be easy. You can either get a guitar, a pencil, and some paper and do it, or proceed to violate your mind and body to a certain degree to prove the worth of your salt as an artist. You should maybe stop short of running right over a cliff, though one or two major falls do you no harm if you survive intact. Beware creative-writing programs. It is well if you have your heart broken many times and break the hearts of others through your creative self-indulgence. It's de rigueur to do a certain number of foolhardy things with a fair degree of regularity, or, if a coward by nature (which is perfectly fine), you should learn to cringe at things that cannot possibly harm you and to fear where there is no reason to fear. If you are so base as to have money, it is recommended you spend it foolishly and make no provision whatsoever for your old age, unlikely as it is you'll have one. Above all, recognize that everything you know is a flat-out lie or only relatively true in certain restricted and unpleasant situations. Trust only in how you feel about things, not in their so-called reality. Love God ferociously and live like the very devil. Always count your chickens before they've hatched. Compromise on the larger picture but never on details. Remember that deadlines are for dummies. If you can't neglect an appointment, at least be late. Be of good cheer where others moan, and strike a glum face in the midst of merriment. Remember, you're an artist and it's your proud tradition to be difficult.

An explosion of unresolved ambition and creatively frustrating circumstances loomed over us like a cloud of dirty dishwater. Enter John Barlow in Pecos Bill getup, silk kerchief, and Stetson hat, as befit a Wyoming ranch boss and author of the lyrics to "Mexicali Blues." Billy goats together, only he knew Weir well enough to butt horns with him, part friends, and do it again. Barlow didn't want to write thick air, either. Nor did he make an attempt to aid Weir in developing his own sense of direction. He rejected, as soundly as I had, Weir's tendency to wantonly rewrite the fruits of your Muse. It was good to see that road show at a distance, realizing they would both survive and even come up with some tunes that would be a credit to the repertoire. Though less than delighted at relinquishing part of my hard-earned dominion to another, becoming Garcia's lyricist rather than lyricist to the Grateful Dead, catastrophe was averted. In hindsight, any more time spent as sovereign wordbird of the immense lyrical heights of all Deaddom might have melted the wax in my wings. As it was, the jolt of the landing only fired my Muse to react with

"Promontory Rider" and "Terrapin," where I make my stand upon the promontories of my own heart, in the shadow of the moon, and recover meaning. Deep down, Weir made the only choice both of us could live with, and there are no hard feelings on either side. He remains my brother, but creatively we were just oil and water, "Truckin'," "Sugar Magnolia," "Jack Straw," and "Playing in the Band" notwithstanding.

With songwriting to spare, enter Weir's vehicle Kingfish and a string of Garcia solo bands. Phil and Ned Lagin's sophisticated sound sculpture *Seastones* was miles ahead of its time and decidedly not geared to a pop audience. So much music from so few. My usual prolixity unabated, I wrote more songs than I knew what to do with and began handing them out to solo projects, notably Mickey Hart's tremendously enjoyable house parties on record, such as *Rolling Thunder.* A stream of Garcia solo albums took up more of the slack. I even began putting out records of my own: *Tales of the Great Rumrunners* and *Tiger Rose,* thanks to Mickey, who generously provided unlimited freedom of his studio and infectious creative input. Fortunately, none of the side projects bid seriously to displace the parent project. Through one accommodation or another, we managed to keep the group going as an active entity for an unheard-of three decades with only one year-long vacation from touring. The critics of the 1980s were not well disposed to like anything but the dynamically emerging sound of punk; whatever we created was *old-school* by definition. Despite them, and punk's rendezvous with musical history, we continued to accumulate the biggest steady draw in rock-and-roll history. We weathered the tides of reggae, new wave, goth, glam glitter, Madonna, and rap and resolved the internal difficulties that destroy other bands in short order. How? Because we made a solemn, spoken agreement early on that we were in this for life. Come what may. We pledged.

After 1974's *From the Mars Hotel*, more Garcia-Hunter material ended up on Jerry's solo albums than on the Grateful Dead song list, as he relinquished compositional tasks to others. This culminated in the 1980 *Go to Heaven* album (originally titled *Go to Hell*) which contained only two of our collaborations, featuring instead the driving songs of new keyboard player Brent Mydland.

The Garcia-Hunter songwriting flower put forth its last bloom in 1987. Though only four of our songs appeared on the album *In the Dark*, one was our first hit single, "Touch of Grey." Though there were still good songs to come, they were fewer as Garcia's dwindling interest in songwriting turned to painting. During the recording of *In the Dark*, something extremely uncharacteristic of the Grateful Dead—and deeply meaningful to me—happened. Bill Kreutzmann took me aside and said, "We love you. Don't ever leave us." The only acknowledgment that ever equaled that in my heart of hearts came one August afternoon, when Garcia called me, out of the blue, to say, "Your lyrics never once stuck in my throat." Cool.

Been there, done that, wrote about it. What else? Glance over the shoulder. Next? Ever wonder what thick air in the words to a song might actually sound like? Hasn't been done yet, to my knowledge. . . .

—Robert Hunter
San Rafael, California
March 2005

preface

*"No poet, no artist of any art, has his complete meaning alone. His significance, his appreciation
is the appreciation of his relationship to the dead poets and artists."*
— T. S. Eliot, "Tradition and Individual Talent" in *Selected Essays*

In his Foreword, Hunter addresses the tradition deeply, illuminating for us the inspiration of his own songwriting. He defines the musical innovations of the Grateful Dead as blending and building upon genres of music from classical to the American songbook. And he allows that David Dodd's annotations are another way to draw our attention to the cultural heritage of the West. We glimpse the hunting grounds of creativity through reference in literature, history, folklore, folk song, contemporary writing, Americana, biblical narrative. Where it can be done because a prior published source can be tracked down and cited, he has done it. He has not been rigorous in restricting citation to eminent tomes, for the playful influence of his web-site correspondents is evident. He has let them in to enliven his scholarly apparatus. Who is to say that these connections, seen in some gold band or dark hollow of concert experience, are not essential? No creative mystery has been violated in David's work, and perhaps it could not be.

My own part in this story began in 1961 in a bookstore with coffee tables in Palo Alto, Keplers, where the sources, the books in the then-new paper-bound form, ranged like wizened fruit along crowded shelves. These we devoured to the sounds of Garcia's daily practice. He sang to us—Hunter, Petersen, Lesh, Laird, Christie, Legate, and others, some of whom later fell off the bus or are no longer with us. A growing extension of this living room has been home ever since, with ever-new family members joining till we are legion. The art arising from those beginnings and their maturity is now itself becoming part of the tradition, entering a new room with new players, a new world being born.

It has been my fortune to have maintained these old connections and to have been steward of the Grateful Dead's song catalog for most of the time since the founding of Ice Nine Publishing Company, in 1970. It is a rare privilege to have the opportunity to bring such a body of work to publication.

To Robert Hunter, to the Grateful Dead in the immediate and largest sense, to John Barlow, Bobby Petersen, and Peter Monk, to all those with the Free Press and March Tenth who have put up with our strictures, to my loving family, and to our illustrator, Jim Carpenter, who has brought a subtle humor to the work, thank you.

—Alan Trist
Ice Nine Publishing Company
San Rafael, California
March 2005

introduction

"A scrap of age-old Lullabye down some forgotten street . . ."
—Robert Hunter, "Standing on the Moon"

rateful Dead lyrics can contain the world. I've worked on the annotations found attached to the collected lyrics in this book for more than ten years, and I'm always finding new references, resonances, and refractions. They change as I change. The shades of meaning correspond to my age, the state of the world, the context of our times. After September 11, 2001, Robert Hunter, whose daughter lost a dear friend in the disaster in New York City, wrote movingly in his online journal about playing "Terrapin Station" and repeating the line "hold away despair" over and over again. So, even for their author, these words can capture new meaning as change arises in our lives and in our world.

Twenty years ago, I set out to discover who Crazy Otto was. That's all, I swear. I didn't mean to wind up annotating the entire body of lyrics. But Crazy Otto led to Billy Sunday. And then I started to wonder about the whole song, "Ramble On Rose." Nonsense? Profundity? I submitted my annotated version of the song to Blair Jackson, hoping for publication in his magazine for Grateful Dead fans, *Golden Road.* He kindly but firmly refused me. I set the project aside, but then I started to wonder about Mr. Benson, from "Candyman." Who was he? And what about "China Cat Sunflower?" Robert Hunter, in the interviews I could track down, dropped clues here and there about his songwriting, but he was absolute in his refusal to state, for the record, what any given song meant. This intrigued me. I felt that I had found a poet who acknowledged that meaning accrues as much according to individual readings, hearings, and perceptions as from the authority of the author. I made notes on piles of discarded catalog cards—a handy side product of the automation of library catalogs.

When the World Wide Web hit, in 1994 or so, I was working as a cataloger at the University of Colorado in Colorado Springs. I was an academic by default, in a tenure-track faculty position. I needed a research project, and it occurred to me that the web was wonderfully suited to literary annotation—as far as I know, *The Annotated Grateful Dead Lyrics,* the website I began, was the first use of hypertext to annotate any kind of literary text. I spent an ungodly number of hours putting the site together. The book you hold in your hands is the result, though perhaps not the end result. And while *The Annotated Grateful Dead Lyrics* website may have been the first of its kind, it certainly wasn't the last, as other annotated-lyrics projects sprang up on the web, including sites for the lyrics of Van Morrison, the Beastie Boys, R.E.M., the Pogues, and Jethro Tull, among others.

Early on, I realized that the project was not mine alone. Over the past ten years, I've probably averaged five emails per day from people weighing in on the lyrics in one form or another. I began to incorporate these readers' comments into the site. I started the ball rolling, and I've been running along after it ever since, trying to keep up. It's hopeless. There are many more thoughts and theories out there than I can ever hope to capture or do justice to on the website. Many of them are included in this book, and they'll continue to come. I hope the margins are big enough for readers to add their own notes.

My work area at home is itself an illustration of the nature of the process of compiling this book. Two shelves of books directly relating to the Grateful Dead are supplemented by stacks of books haphazardly piled on the floor, on the computer desk, and on any other available surface, including atop the two-volume compact edition of the *Oxford English Dictionary.* They include an edition of *Hoyle's Rules of Games,* a United States gazetteer, books on native plants of California, Grzimek's encyclopedia volumes relating to birds, dictionaries of phrases and allusions, quotation books, and an early edition of *Hortus,* the definitive reference on gardening. Several shelves of poetry are also near at hand, and across the room, piled on top of and beside my piano, are stacks of songbooks. It is a highly untidy library, but I know where everything is. From these sources I extract most of what I need for the annotations. It's not a neat or straightforward process. I've also had to spend considerable time (in addition to my work time as a librarian) in actual libraries, and that has been a joy.

There are two guiding metaphors for the project: First, if you ever went to see the Grateful Dead at

Winterland, you'll remember the revolving mirrored ball hanging from the ceiling, which was turned on at high points in any given show. It scattered light around the room but never really illuminated anything. That's one metaphor for the annotations: a mirror ball. The other is more of a notion than a metaphor: What if, when you started to read something, you came upon a reference or a phrase or a concept that you didn't fully understand, and before you could continue, you had to go and read up on that? And if in reading the next thing, you again came across something new and unfamiliar, and you then had to research that before proceeding? Would you ever finish the first thing you started reading? Hypertext is like that to me. I fear for our ability to read in a sustained fashion any longer. We're distractible. We jump around a lot on the Internet, and the neurological implications are probably greater than we realize. The upcoming generations may not be able to read in the way that our and earlier generations think of reading. That doesn't mean they won't be gaining knowledge and adding to the incremental increase of knowledge in coming generations—it'll just be different.

So: My intent here is to allow for an expanded experience of the lyrics of the Grateful Dead, without providing interpretation. If there's a reference to an old folk song, I want to provide some information about that song. You should be able to track down real people mentioned in the songs. Same with places. Occasionally, I'll talk about a particular symbol, but that's bordering on interpretation, so I don't do that too much. The symbols that recur throughout the lyrics (roses, trains, cats, cards . . .) receive annotations as they come up, as needed.

What's included? All of the original lyrics written for the Grateful Dead. A small subset of the traditional tunes and covers performed by the band are also included, because they play a large part in giving context to the other songs. I wish I could have included them all, but that would have proved impractical. Some songs are heavily annotated; some are not. I hope that the level of annotation is appropriate to each song—some simply don't require elucidation.

We settled, after some deliberation, on the sidenote style of annotation, which is a common and respected format. It's also the style used in one of my own favorite examples of the art of the book, in San Francisco printer John Henry Nash's edition of Dante's *Divine Comedy*.

Working on the project with Alan Trist, the Grateful Dead's publisher, has been a privilege and a pleasure. His long experience with the catalog, and his thoughtful editing, added a missing perspective. We had definite ideas on how the book should be presented, and I trust our vision comes through enough that you now hold in your hands a book for the ages. The lyrics, of course, varied at times from performance to performance, but the versions here may be considered "standard," which means you might settle the occasional bar bet. Or not! Where brackets are found in the lyrics, we have been unable to be absolutely certain about the words, so you can fill them in yourself.

I don't want it to go without saying that the words of Robert Hunter, John Barlow, and all the others who wrote lyrics for the Grateful Dead are the primary inspiration for this book: Thank you to all the wordsmiths. To the Grateful Dead, thanks for bringing this music to us all.

Elizabeth Stein and Dominick Anfuso of Free Press deserve special thanks for their almost unbelievable patience in working with what must have seemed at times like a herd of kitty-cats, any of whom might, at any given moment, show claws. Thank you, Sandy Choron, my agent, and her husband, Harry Choron, who designed the book. To my long-suffering colleagues at the Kraemer Family Library at the University of Colorado in Colorado Springs: Thank you, Rita Hug, Laurie Williams, and everyone else at UCCS. Professor Fred Lieberman of the University of California at Santa Cruz arranged for the website to be hosted by UCSC and has been a supporter of my work for a long time. Steve Silberman, who weighed in early and enthusiastically, gave me a big boost. Thanks to David Gans, Mary Eisenhart, and everyone at the WELL, especially those on the Deadlit and Deadsongs conferences. Thanks to Blair Jackson, whose work permeates these pages. Thank you to Robert Weiner, my co-author and friend, who published an early version of "The Annotated 'Ramble on Rose'." Thanks to Alex Allan, for his indispensable Lyric and Song-Finder website and for his frequent contributions to my own site. Mary Minow, lawyer and librarian extraordinaire, has provided counsel regarding permissions. Also, thanks to my friend Joe Cochrane, a reference librarian's reference librarian, for his careful reading of this work in draft. (All errors are mine, though!) The staff of San Rafael's Panama Hotel were very tolerant of our long sessions at their tables. Diana Spaulding, my wife, you make it all worthwhile.

—David Dodd
Petaluma, California
May 2005

The complete annotated
Grateful dead
Lyrics

can't come down

I'm flying down deserted streets
Wrapped in mother's winding sheets
Asbestos boots on flaming feet
Dreaming of forbidden treats
When uniforms on nighttime beats
Ask me where I'm going and what I eat
I answer them with a voice so sweet

I can't come down, it's plain to see
I can't come down, I've been set free
Who you are and what you do don't make no
   difference to me

Well someone trying to tell me where it's at
And how I do this and why I do that
1 With secret smiles like a Cheshire cat
2 And leather wings like a vampire bat
I fly away to my cold-water flat
And eat my way through a bowl of fat
And I say to the man with the funny hat

I can't come down, it's plain to see
I can't come down, I've been set free
Who you are and what you do don't make no
   difference to me

They say I've begun to lose my grip
My hold on reality is starting to slip
They tell me to get off this trip
They say that it's like a sinking ship
Life's sweet wine's too warm to sip
And if I drink I'll surely flip
I just say as I take a nip

1 **cheshire cat**
A reference to the Cheshire Cat of Lewis Carroll's *Alice's Adventures in Wonderland* (1865): We first meet the Cheshire Cat in the Duchess's kitchen. She is nursing a baby:

> The only two creatures in the kitchen, that did *not* sneeze, were the cook, and a large cat, which was lying on the hearth and grinning from ear to ear.
> "Please would you tell me," said Alice, a little timidly, for she was not quite sure whether it was good manners for her to speak first, "why your cat grins like that?"
> "It's a Cheshire Cat," said the Duchess, "and that's why."

And a little later, she meets the cat again:

> . . . when she was a little startled by seeing the Cheshire-Cat sitting on a bough of a tree a few yards off.
> The Cat only grinned when it saw Alice. It looked good-natured, she thought: still it had *very* long claws and a great many teeth, so she felt that it ought to be treated with respect.
> "Cheshire-Puss," she began, rather timidly, as she did not at all know whether it would like the name: however, it only grinned a little wider. "Come, it's pleased so far," thought Alice, and she went on. "Would you tell me, please, which way I ought to go from here?"
> "That depends a good deal on where you want to get to," said the Cat.
> "I don't much care where—" said Alice.
> "Then it doesn't matter which way you go," said the Cat.

"—so long as I get *somewhere*," Alice added as an explanation.

And later,

"By-the-bye, what became of the baby?" [ed. note: See "What's Become of the Baby?"] said the Cat. "I'd nearly forgotten to ask."

"It turned into a pig," Alice answered very quietly, just as if the Cat had come back in a natural way.

"I thought it would," said the Cat, and vanished again.

The cat makes one more (partial) appearance, at the Queen's croquet game. She orders him beheaded, but the executioner says he can't behead the cat, since only the head is visible.

A footnote in the wonderful *The Annotated Alice* speculates on the origin of the Cheshire Cat:

"Grin like a Cheshire cat" was a common phrase in Carroll's day. Its origin is not known. The two leading theories are: (1) A sign painter in Cheshire (the county, by the way, where Carroll was born) painted grinning lions on the signboards of inns in the area (see *Notes and Queries,* no. 130, April 24, 1852, p. 402), (2) Cheshire cheeses were at one time molded in the shape of a grinning cat (see  *Notes and Queries,* no. 55, Nov. 16, 1850, p. 412). "This has a peculiar Carrollian appeal," writes Dr. Phyllis Greenacre in her psychoanalytic study of Carroll, "as it provokes the fantasy that the cheesy cat may eat the rat that would eat the cheese." The Cheshire Cat is not

I can't come down, it's plain to see
I can't come down, I've been set free
Who you are and what you do don't make no
    difference to me

So as I dream of forgotten seas
And granite halls and redwood trees
And of the eye that only sees
Endless mirrors and infinite me's
About the winter's coming freeze
This afterthought I say with ease
To all of you who made your pleas

I can't come down, it's plain to see
I can't come down, I've been set free
Who you are and what you do don't make no
    difference to me

Words by Jerry Garcia
Music by the Grateful Dead

in the original manuscript, *Alice's Adventures Underground.* [1]

Other references to the Cheshire cat in Grateful Dead and related lyrics include "China Cat Sunflower" and "Down the Road," with its image of Garcia disappearing in the sky, leaving just "a smile in empty space."

The evocations brought out by the use of the word *Cheshire* include all the wonderful characters and situations of the Alice stories, which were widely evoked in rock lyrics of the late sixties, most notably in the Jefferson Airplane's "White Rabbit." A case could be made for the Beatles' "I Am the Walrus" as well.

2 vampire bat

Bram Stoker's classic 1897 horror tale, *Dracula,* is set in Transylvania and features an evil count who seems to have been based on the historical Vlad V of Wallachia, aka Vlad the Impaler. Count Dracula assumes the guise of a bat and sucks the blood of unsuspecting victims, who then in turn become vampires themselves.

From Lord George Gordon Byron's 1813 *The Giaour: A Fragment of a Turkish Tale:*

> But first on earth, as vampire sent,
> Thy corse shall from its tomb be rent,
> Then ghastly haunt thy native place
> And suck the blood of all thy race.

Notes:
Studio recording: November 3, 1965. Played 1965–66, then dropped from the repertoire. Released in the box set *So Many Roads.*

First performance: The only live performance documented in *DeadBase* is from January 7, 1966, at the Matrix in San Francisco.

Bob Weir described the writing of the song in an interview: "Well, we wrote all the music and Jerry wrote the lyrics. Jerry excused himself for a moment and went off. He came back with a couple of verses and we put together a chorus."

caution (do not stop on tracks)

1 gypsy woman
A reference to a fortune-teller or to a traditional healer who is a member of the people known as the Rom. Still a people of mystery to the *gaje* ("outsiders"), they take care to preserve their closed society

from outside scrutiny. They have traditionally occupied positions at the fringes of Western society, as fortune-tellers, tinkers, musicians, animal trainers, etc.

2 mojo hand
The title of a song recorded by Lightnin' Hopkins.

Mojo is magic—the ability to cast spells, probably deriving from the Gullah dialect, in which *moco* means "witchcraft" or "magic." *Lucky hand* is a synonym for *mojo,* and *mojo* is also a slang term for morphine.

According to *Hoodoo—Conjuration—Witchcraft—Rootwork: Beliefs Accepted by Many Negroes and White Persons, These Being Orally Recorded Among Blacks and Whites by Harry Middleton Hyatt* (Hannibal, Mo.: Alma Egan Hyatt Foundation, 1970):

> A *hand* is a magic helper, an object or act, which aids a person in obtaining a desire. *Hand* has other names, among them—*toby, guide, shield, roots, mojo, jomo* (transposition of syllables in mojo), and *hoodoo bag.*

I went down one day
I went down to see a gypsy woman just one day, yes I did   1
I wanna find out
What's wrong with me and my baby
We ain't been getting down like we used to do
I mean it's pretty good now
But there was a time when it didn't work out too well
I went down to see this gypsy woman, you understand
And I told her my story
I told her what was going on
And she turned to me and she said
All you need
All you gotta have
Just a touch, that's all you gotta have
Just a touch of mojo hand   2
And it feels pretty good

Words and music by Ron McKernan

Notes:

Studio recording: *Anthem of the Sun* (July 18, 1968).

First known performance: November 3, 1965, at Mother's in San Francisco.

Pigpen's improvisatory style made for many variations on the lyrics.

This version is the one performed on *Anthem of the Sun*.

From Phil Lesh's autobiography:

> At one point, we were standing out there, entranced by the rhythm of the wheels clickety-clacking over the welds in the rails; Billy and I looked at each other and just knew—we simultaneously burst out, "We can play this!" "This" later turned into "Caution (Do Not Stop on Tracks)," one of our simplest yet farthest-reaching musical explorations. Based on the train rhythm, it had only one chord and was played at a blistering tempo. . . . [95]

mindbender

If I could only be less blind
If only I knew what to find,
Everywhere and all of the time—
It's bending my mind.   1

Confusion's prince is at my door.
The crown I wear's the one he wore
He's here to bring me down some more
And bend my mind.

The friendly stranger called my name
He only wants me for his game
But it don't matter, just the same
I'll bend his mind.

I've waved my flags into the sun
I've fought my wars, and now they're won
And I don't need nobody's gun
I bent their mind.

If I could only be less blind
If only I knew what to find,
Everywhere and all of the time—
It's bending my mind

Words and music by Jerry Garcia and Phil Lesh

The OnLy Time IS NOW

Oh I know there is no place you can go to
And I know you don't know anyone at all
So come walking in the sun with me my
   little one
And remember that the only time is now

Well strange is the story your eyes tell me
And quiet all the few words that you say
So come and hold my hand, for you see I'd
   understand
And remember that the only time is now

Oh I come to you a ragged laughing stranger
And you come to me an angel of the night
So I'll dance and we will sing, for it doesn't
   mean a thing
To remember that the only time is now

So forget about your yesterdays of sorrow
And forget about the darkness you have seen
For there's only you and me at the edge of an
   endless sea
And remember that the only time is now

Words by Jerry Garcia
Music by the Grateful Dead

Notes:

Studio recording: November 3, 1965. Released on *The Golden Road* box set. Sung by Lesh.

Only documented performance: January 7, 1966, at the Matrix in San Francisco.

cold rain and snow

Notes:
Studio recording: *Grateful Dead* (March 17, 1967).

First documented performance: February 23, 1966, location unknown. The song became a staple of the repertoire thereafter.

This tune comes from the Eastern-mountain music tradition, most likely the Blue Ridge Mountains of North Carolina or Virginia. Rarely recorded, this white blues has long been popular among old-timey music groups. Pegging an "original" version is impossible, since it dates back (at least) to the nineteenth century and is "folk" music in the truest sense. Perhaps the best-known recording of the tune among country aficionados is one by Obray Ramsey on his *Obray Ramsey Sings Folksong from Three Laurels.* (Jackson: *Goin' Down the Road*) 94

Well she's coming down the stairs, combing
  back her yellow hair
And I ain't gonna be treated this-a-way
This-a-way
And I ain't gonna be treated this-a-way

Well she went up to her room and she sang a
  fateful tune
And I'm going where those chilly winds
  don't blow
Winds don't blow
And I'm going where those chilly winds
  don't blow

Well I married me a wife, she's been trouble
  all my life
Run me out in the cold rain and snow
Rain and snow
Run me out in the cold rain and snow

Words and music: traditional
Arranged by the Grateful Dead

I Know You Rider

I know you rider, gonna miss me when I'm gone
I know you rider, gonna miss me when I'm gone
Gonna miss your baby, from rolling in your arms

Lay down last night, Lord, I could not take
    my rest
Lay down last night, Lord, I could not take
    my rest
My mind was wandering like the wild geese in
    the West

The sun will shine in my back door some day
The sun will shine in my back door some day
March winds will blow all my troubles away

1   I wish I was a headlight on a north-bound train
    I wish I was a headlight on a north-bound train
    I'd shine my light through the cool Colorado rain

I know you rider, gonna miss me when I'm gone
I know you rider, gonna miss me when I'm gone
Gonna miss your baby, from rolling in your arms

I know you rider, gonna miss me when I'm gone
I know you rider, gonna miss me when I'm gone
Gonna miss your baby, from rolling in your arms

Words and music: traditional
Arranged by the Grateful Dead

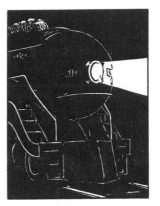

**1 I wish I was a
headlight . . .**
Garcia's portrait is included
as the headlight on a train
on the album cover of his
solo work *Reflections.*

Notes:
Recording: *Europe '72*
(November 1972).

Performances: Played from
very early days onward
and usually paired with "China Cat Sunflower."

This traditional black song has been passed
around in different versions (with different
verses added and subtracted) for over a century, though it has been recorded relatively few
times. The term *rider* comes up often in early
blues, usually to talk about a woman, but in
this case the song is popularly sung from each
gender's perspective. One example of a verse
from a woman's point of view: "Lovin' you,
baby, just as easy as rollin' off a log / But if I
can't be your woman / I sure ain't gonna be
your dog." The Dead used to sing a verse
(pre-1971) that included a few key words from
the above—"I'd rather drink muddy water,
sleep in a hollow log / Than stay here in
Frisco, be treated like a dog."
   According to Bruce Jackson, author of
Wake Up Dead Man, a book about early Texas
prison songs, *rider* was also slang for the
guards on horseback who would supervise
prison laborers. The term found its way into
some prison blues, almost as a code word
that the guards wouldn't understand.
(Jackson. *Goin' Down the Road*) 94

you see a Broken Heart

Notes:

Recording: Released on *Rare Cuts and Oddities, 1966* (2005).

Only known performance thought to have been March 12, 1966, at the Danish Center in Los Angeles.

You see a broken heart
My baby's 'bout to set me free

I said look, look, look at me
I said what, what, what do you see
I said look, look, look at me
I said what, what, what do you see
You see a broken heart
My baby's 'bout to set me free

I got tears, tears, tears in my eyes
And I got pain, pain, pain in my heart
I got tears, tears, tears in my eyes
And I got pain, pain, pain in my heart
You see a broken heart
My baby's 'bout to set me free

Well just a little bit softer now
Well just a little bit softer now
Well just a little bit louder now

Words and music by Ron McKernan

Beat It on Down the Line

Well this job I got is just a little too hard
Running out of money, Lord, I need more pay
I'm gonna wake up in the morning, Lord
I'm gonna pack up my bags
I'm gonna beat it on down the line

Goin' down the line *(goin' down the line)*
Goin' down the line *(goin' down the line)*
Goin' down the line *(goin' down the line)*
Goin' down the line *(goin' down the line)*
Goin' down the line *(goin' down the line)*
Goin' down the line *(goin' down the line)*
Beat it on down the line

Yes and I'll be waiting at the station, Lord,
    when that train pulls on by
I'm going back where I belong
Yes and I'm goin' north to my same old used to
    be

1 Down in Joe Brown's coal mine
Coal mine *(coal mine)*
Coal mine *(coal mine)*
Coal mine *(coal mine)*
Coal mine *(coal mine)*
Coal mine *(coal mine)*
Coal mine *(coal mine)*
Down in Joe Brown's coal mine

Yes I'm goin' back to that shack way across the
    railroad track
That's where I think I belong
Yes I got a sweet woman, Lord, she's waiting
    there for me

1 joe brown's coal mine
Also mentioned in Joshua "Peg Leg" Howell's
(1888–1966) 1929 song "Rolling Mill Blues"
(which is a version of "Corinne") and in some
versions of the traditional tune "In the Pines."

Joseph Emerson Brown (1821–1894), elected
four times as governor of Georgia, was president
of the Dade Coal Company, which had extensive
coalmine holdings in that state.

Notes:
Studio recording: *Grateful Dead* (March 17,
1967).

First documented performance: March 12, 1966,
at the Danish Center, Los Angeles. A steady number in the repertoire thereafter.

A feature of this tune in concert was the
drum-beat introduction and the fact that
the number of beats would vary from concert
to concert. The particular meaning of the
number of beats is not always obvious; it
often matches the day of the month. The
most beats on record is forty-two, in honor of
Mickey Hart's forty-second birthday, while
some versions omit the intro beats entirely.
(Jackson, Randy)

The original recording of this one appears on a
1961 album called *The Lone Cat* by the song's
author, Jesse Fuller. Fuller was a fixture on the
Bay Area blues scene for many years, and the
Dead were familiar with his records and local
live performances.
    Born into extreme poverty in Jonesboro,
Georgia, in 1896, Fuller never really knew his
natural parents. He was instead brought up by
a couple who treated him "worse than a dog,"
until he managed to get out of the house at
age nine and work as a cow grazer outside of
Atlanta. Throughout his teens, he worked for

next to nothing in a lumber camp. He went west in the early twenties, taking odd jobs and singing along the way. After a stay of several years in Los Angeles (he ran a hot dog stand inside the United Artists film lot and even appeared as an extra in a few films), he moved to Oakland, where he lived until he died in 1976. During those decades, he worked variously as a laborer for the Southern Pacific Railroad (hence the train imagery that fills so many of his songs), a shipbuilder, and a farm laborer. He was "discovered" in the mid-fifties, playing in Bay Area clubs and bars, and recorded his first record in 1955. Never particularly well-known, Fuller was nonetheless a fine songwriter and interpreter whose songs vividly speak of a life of hard times and hard work while still exhibiting great spirit and even humor.

An interesting aspect of his talent (and Weir even alludes to this before the May 5, 1970, version of Fuller's "The Monkey and the Engineer") was that he made some of his own musical instruments, including a huge stand-up bass, called a fotdella, which he would play with his right foot in solo performances. (Jackson: *Goin' Down the Road*) 94

That's where I'm gonna make my happy home

Happy home *(happy home)*
Happy home *(happy home)*
Happy home *(happy home)*
Happy home *(happy home)*
Happy home *(happy home)*
Happy home *(happy home)*
That's where I'm gonna make my happy home

Words and music by Jesse Fuller

you Don't Have to Ask

If you wanna know what time it is, you
   don't have to ask
If you wanna know what hers and his is, you
   don't have to ask
If you wanna know what's real or not, you don't
   have to ask

Chorus:
If you wanna know where to find your spot,
   you don't have to ask
You don't have to ask
You don't have to ask
You already know
You already know

If you wanna leave your troubles behind, you
   don't have to ask
If you wanna go away and lose your mind,
   you don't have to ask
If it's peace that you're looking for
1 You got the key to every door, you already know

If there's a way out you'll find out and see all
   and be all
You'll never wonder what spell you been under
To make you forget all this time

If you're looking for the way, you don't have
   to ask
You can see it plain as day, you don't have to ask

(Chorus)

    Words and music by the Grateful Dead

1 key to every door
Presages the line in "Unbroken Chain": "They're
telling me forgiveness is the key to every door."

Notes:
First known performance: March 25, 1966, at
Trouper's Club in Los Angeles. The song was
played a few times during 1966, then dropped.
The version on *The Golden Road* box set is from
July 16, 1966, at the Fillmore in San Francisco.

1 cream puff
John Kessler, food critic of the *Denver Post,* writes eloquently of the cream puff:

Cream-puff dough is a near-magical melange of flour, butter, water, and eggs combined in just the right way so that it stretches, bubbles, puffs, and eventually hollows out in the oven. Steam is the only leavening. Once your puffs cool, they turn dry and brittle and can be kept at room temperature until they're ready to use. You can fill them with pastry cream and sprinkle the tops with powdered sugar for the classic preparation. Or you can get creative and throw in some fresh fruit, chocolate mousse, or sweetened cream cheese.

Here is his recipe for the basic cream puff, which he characterizes as one of the "classic recipes on which our traditions are based."

1 cup water
1/2 cup unsalted butter
1 cup all-purpose flour
pinch salt
4 eggs
  Preheat oven to 375 degrees.
  Place water and butter in saucepan. Heat over medium flame until water boils and butter is completely melted. Mix the flour and

No, no, she can't take your mind and leave
I know it's just another trick she's got up
  her sleeve
I can't believe that she really wants you to die
After all, it's more than enough to pay for
  your lie

Wait a minute, watch what you're doing with
  your time
All the endless ruins of the past must stay
  behind, yeah

Well, can't you see that you're killing each
  other's soul
You're both out in the streets and you got no
  place to go
Your constant battles are getting to be a bore
So go somewhere else and continue your cream
  puff war

Wait a minute, watch what you're doing with
  your time
All the endless ruins of the past must stay
  behind, yeah

Words and music by Jerry Garcia

salt and add dry ingredients all at once. Stir until the dough forms a ball in the center of the pan. Remove from heat. Let stand 5 minutes.

Add one egg and beat with electric beaters set on medium speed until smooth and glossy, about 1 minute. Add the other eggs, one at a time, beating until just blended. Avoid overbeating the dough.

If desired, place in a pastry bag fitted with a large, plain tip. Drop by heaping tablespoonfuls or pipe onto ungreased baking sheet, about 2 inches apart. Bake 40 minutes or until there are no beads of moisture on puffs. Cool. Cut off tops, fill as desired. 97

Notes:

Studio recording: *Grateful Dead* (March 17, 1967).

First documented performance: May 19, 1966, at the Avalon Ballroom in San Francisco. It was dropped from the repertoire after March 1967.

tastebud

Compare the
1937 Robert
Johnson song,
"Hellhound on
My Trail":

> Mmm, blues
> falling down
> like hail,
> blues
> falling down like hail
> And the day keeps on remindin' me, there's a
> hellhound on my trail

**2 Whoa it was but a while after midnight /
When the rooster crowed for day**
Compare line from "The Music Never Stopped":
"Crazy rooster crowin' midnight."

American weather folklore has a couple of sayings
along these lines:

> When the rooster crows at night,
> He tells you that a rain's in sight.

> Cockcrow before two in the morning
> Of two days wet it is a warning.

Notes:
Studio recording: June 1966 recording included
on *The Birth of the Dead* in *The Golden Road* box
set, 1967 studio version included as bonus track
for remastered *Grateful Dead,* also included on *The
Golden Road.*

First documented performance: May 19, 1966, at
the Avalon Ballroom in San Francisco. One other
performance exists on tape.

Well it was early in the morning
When my blues come falling down
I want to tell you, it was early in the morning now
When my blues come falling down   1
Well you know, you know, it felt so, so bad
When my baby, yeah, she's been around

Whoa it was but a while after midnight
When the rooster crowed for day
Whoa it was but a while after midnight
When that rooster began to crow for day   2
Well I been mistreating my baby
That's about a crime that I need to pay

Come back baby
Whoa, please don't go
I said come back baby
Come on darling, please don't go
Well you know the way I love you rider
More than you ever know

Yes Lord, please stop her
I won't get drunk no more
Whoa Lord, please stop her now
I want to tell you that I won't get drunk no more
Well you know she put me out in the morning
She drive this poor boy from her door

[*The 1967 studio version differed substantively:*]

Woke up way after midnight, people
Just a little while, a little while before day
I could find no satisfaction

Turned on my pillow to where my baby lay
I remembered I was in a strange old town then
My sweet little angel she's so far away

Now I ain't got no friends here
Ain't got no, no good place to go
All my friends are back home
And I can't, I can't go there no more
You know I done just a little bit wrong
And I can't go back no more

Take me back baby
I can't help it if I need you so
Well I've been a bad man darling
But I won't, I won't get drunk no more
But if you did not did like you do
Baby I wouldn't have had to go

I'm coming back baby, baby I'm coming home
I'm coming back baby, baby I'm coming home
The way I love you darling
You've got to, got to know

Words and music by Ron McKernan

NEW, NEW MINGLEWOOD BLUES

1 minglewood
"New Minglewood Blues" was originally written about a company mill village, Menglewood, Tennessee (built by the Menglewood Box Company). As a company town, it was wild and wide open with whiskey, women, and gambling. Menglewood is located about seventy-eight miles north of Memphis, Tennessee, alongside the Obion River, which is in the Mississippi River floodplain.

2 Timbuktu
An ancient city in the African country of Mali. Historically important as a stop on the trans-Saharan caravan route, it was founded about 1100 A.D. It was an intellectual and spiritual center for Islam through the fifteenth and sixteenth centuries.

It serves as a stand-in name for any far-off place in the middle of nowhere.

3 T for
Weir would insert the name of the city in which the band was playing at any given concert, whether or not it actually started with *T*.

Notes:

Studio recording: as "New New Minglewood Blues"

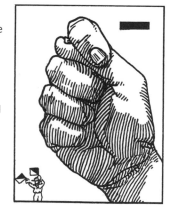

I was born in a desert, raised in a lion's den
I was born in a desert, raised in a lion's den
And my number one occupation is stealing
women from their men

Well I'm a wanted man in Texas, busted jail and
I'm gone for good
Well I'm a wanted man in Texas, busted jail and
I'm gone for good
Well the sheriff couldn't catch me
But his little girl sure wished she would

Yes and the doctor call me crazy, some says I
am some says I ain't
Yes and the doctor call me crazy, some says I
am some says I ain't
The preacher man call me a sinner, but his little
girl call me a saint

Well a couple of shots of whiskey, women
'round here start lookin' good
Well a couple of shots of whiskey, women
'round here start lookin' good
Couple more shots of whiskey, I'm goin' back to
Minglewood   1

It's T for Texas, yes and it's T for Timbuktu   2
It's T for Texas, yes and it's T for Timbuktu   3
Yes and it's T for _____
Where the little girls know what to do

Words and music by Noah Lewis
Arranged by the Grateful Dead

on *Grateful Dead* (March 17, 1967); as "All New Minglewood Blues" on *Shakedown Street* (November 15, 1978).

First documented performance: May 19, 1966, at the Avalon Ballroom in San Francisco. It was in the repertoire thereafter.

Here's a great example of a song that has been passed from player to player through the years and changed so much that it bears almost no relation to its original antecedent, a song called "Minglewood Blues" that was recorded in January 1928 by a black group called Cannon's Jug Stompers. Consisting of banjo and jug player Gus Cannon, guitarist Ashley Thompson, and harmonica player Noah Lewis, the Jug Stompers was one of a number of popular black jug bands that sprang up in the mid-South (particularly Memphis) between approximately 1915 and the beginning of the Depression. "Minglewood Blues" was written primarily by Lewis, who is also credited as the primary writer of "Viola Lee Blues," which was recorded about nine months after the session that yielded both "Minglewood Blues" and another staple of the Dead's, "Big Railroad Blues."

Strangely enough, though, "Minglewood Blues" is not at all similar to the Dead's "Minglewood." For the germ of the Dead's song, we have to jump forward two years to 1930 and a song by the Noah Lewis Jug Band (yes, Noah went solo!) called "New Minglewood Blues" (which can be found on a Origin Jazz LP called *The Great Jug Bands*). The first verse is virtually identical to the one Weir sings, but after that the song is largely dissimilar lyrically. Clearly the doubling of the word *new* in the Dead's version is a clever joke on Lewis's own update of his tune. Weir, who rearranged it (twice) for the Dead, has taken substantial liberties with the song, which, though seldom recorded, was popular among jug bands during an early-sixties revival.

And what exactly is Minglewood? Well, according to noted Memphis blues authority Bengt Olson, who interviewed old-timers from the early Memphis jug and blues scene, Minglewood was a sawmill/box factory in Ashport, Tennessee, north of Memphis; it was torn down in the early fifties. Noah Lewis and Eddie Green (who played guitar with Lewis for a brief period) were both employees at the Minglewood factory; Minglewood also became the name for the small region near the factory. (Jackson: *Goin' Down the Road*) 94

DON'T EASE ME IN

Notes:
Studio recording: *Go to Heaven* (April 28, 1980).

First documented performance: July 16, 1966, at the Fillmore Auditorium in San Francisco. A steady number in the repertoire thereafter.

Yet another popular folk and jug band number in the late fifties and early sixties, "Don't Ease Me In" was originally recorded in the late twenties by Henry Thomas, who generally traveled under his hobo moniker, Ragtime Texas. The child of slaves, Thomas lived in East Texas and worked on the Texas-Pacific Railroad. He was middle-aged when he made his only recordings, which have been compiled on several anthologies.

The Dead's version is fairly similar to Thomas's, though Thomas's vocal is more plaintive, almost sounding like Hank Williams (whom he predated, of course). One lyric difference that's worth noting arose, no doubt, from the song being passed down through the years by players who either didn't understand the original lyrics or chose to make them less specific. On Thomas's original recording of the song's chorus, for instance, he sings: "Don't ease, don't you ease / Ah, don't ease me in / It's a long night, Cunningham, don't ease me in." The Cunningham in the song was a well-known Texas businessman of the era who would lease convicts to work his sugarcane fields along the Brazos River. According to Mac McCormick's biography of Thomas on the liner notes of a Herwin Records album by Thomas, "Don't Ease Me In" was often heard along the Brazos in various local prison farms. I confess to mild bafflement on what the actual phrase "Don't ease me in" means in the context of the song, but a 1929 song called "Easin' In" by Texas blues singer Bobby Cadillac clearly has some sort of sexual implication. (Jackson: *Goin' Down the Road*) 94

Don't ease, don't ease
Don't ease me in
I've been all night long coming home
Don't ease me in

I was standing at the corner
Talking to Miss Brown
Well I turned around, sweet mama
She was way 'cross town

So I'm walking down the street
With a dollar in my hand
I've been looking for a woman, sweet mama
Ain't got no man

Don't ease, don't ease
Don't ease me in
I've been all night long coming home
Don't ease me in

The girl I love
She's sweet and true
You know the dress she wears, sweet mama
It's pink and blue

She brings me coffee
You know she brings me tea
She brings 'bout every damn thing
But the jailhouse key

Don't ease, don't ease
Don't ease me in
I've been all night long coming home
Don't ease me in

Words and music: traditional

cardboard cowboy

When the cardboard cowboy dreams and his
    cornucopia
Opens up the sky and blows my mind to the
    corners of
[Far in bar rent shine] running beneath high
    trembling dove
Leaving me transfixed and raving in the wake of
    the hammer blow

On my way out of town I stumbled on the shards
    of a hungry [scream]
And further up into the backdoor circle, where the
    [power and crystal sea]
[Could this go rise by all allow ———] on the
    strength of an anguished sigh
And a paranoid reentry blanket flies sleeping on
    a slingshot ride

As my patchwork [world/quilt] unravels, I ramble
    yes too high
1 [From the looping antrobus with his magic meant
    so high]
Shining out a masquerade from dawn to alpha
    plus
Watching mashed potatoes dribble in the heat of
    reality's earth

[For the intro doom from] running to him
It wasn't ever so
Turns the wall into the sky above me, there is
    no place to run

Words and music by Phil Lesh

1 **Antrobus**
A township in Cheshire County, England. See note under "Can't Come Down" for more discussion of Cheshire and its cat.

Notes:

No official recordings. Studio recording released as part of a bonus CD with Phil Lesh's autobiography, *Seaching for the Sound* (2005).

First of only two documented performances: July 17, 1966, at the Fillmore Auditorium in San Francisco.

This song is usually known as "Cardboard Cowboy" or "No Left Turn Unstoned" (named after a sign in front of Ken Kesey's old house in La Honda, California, which featured the phrase that was coined by Prankster Paul Foster). Weir introduced it as "No Left Turn Unstoned" in the show on July 29, 1966. Lesh, in a spoken introduction to the release on the bonus CD noted above, stated that they actually called the song "The Monster" because it was "big and ugly and hard to play." The cover for the bonus CD lists the song as "Cardboard Cowboy." Hence its title above.

  In an interview, Lesh was asked whether he had written any lyrics before writing "Childhood's End":

    Only once, but this [Childhood's End] came out a lot better than that one [which was] "No Left Turn Unstoned." [*Laughs*] It was a truly awful song I wrote for the Grateful Dead during the Matrix era—I think it was '67, maybe '68. It's on a couple of tapes, I think. It's so God-awful I can't even listen to it to find out what it was like. [*Laughs*] 2

The David Nelson Band song "Fable of a Chosen One" contains the phrase "no left turn unstoned."

Perhaps worth noting is the huge preponderance of NO LEFT TURN signs throughout San Francisco. Sometimes you just have to turn right three times in a row in order to effect a left turn.

standing on the corner

1   I was standing on the corner, wondering what's
      become of me (2x)
   Well things don't seem to be the way they used
      to seem to be

I think I'll go up on a mountain, I'll fling
      myself off into space (2x)
I'm not doing it because I'm desperate, I'm just
      trying to save some space

If you ask me what my name is, I'll just stop
      and scratch my head (2x)
Well they took away my name and gave me a
2   number instead

Well all the things I used to know seem so
      far behind
There's a lot of new things that are running
      around my mind

[*On July 27 1966, the Dead sang a different final verse:*]

If you ask me what I'm doing, I can't answer right
If you ask me what I'm doing, I can't answer right
Seems like nothin' ever changes, and nothing's
gonna turn out right

Words and music by the Grateful Dead

---

1 standing on the corner
Title of a 1956 hit for the Four Lads, written by
Frank Loesser.

Also the title of a Jimmie Rodgers song: "Standin'
on the Corner (Blue Yodel No. 9)," recorded in
1939 with Louis Armstrong (and also by the Jerry
Garcia Acoustic Band, much later).

**2 Well they took away my name and gave
me a number instead**
Compare the line from the 1966 Johnny Rivers
hit, "Secret Agent Man" (P .F. Sloan and Steve
Barri).

> They've given you a number
> And taken away your name.

Also worth noting is a British television series that
debuted in 1968, *The Prisoner,* in which a man is
kidnapped from his London home and wakes up
in a strange village where he is known only by
the name Number Six. Various village officers-in-
charge, always referred to as Number Two, set
about trying to find out why Number Six
resigned his job as a secret agent. Number Six is
interrogated, brainwashed, and manipulated by
the strange powers behind the mysterious village. Number Six's constant refrain was "I am
not a number. I am a free man!" The series was
the brainchild of Patrick McGoohan, who not
only starred as Number Six but was also instrumental in bringing the series to fruition.

Notes:
Released on *Rare Cuts and Oddities, 1966* (2005).

First documented performance, of four total,
believed to have been on February 23, 1966,
location unknown. The date is also questionable.

Oh my darling tell me where I'm bound
(Yesterday was your day of rest)
Now I see too much racing around
(Yesterday you had to beat up your [miss])
I've been here too many times before
(I don't know, I would resist)
I've got to see the other side of your door
(I don't know, no, I've got a call for you)

Whoa-oh, can't you see I got a lot to learn
(I've got to know, no, no, now what's going on)
Oh I don't even have a torch to burn
(I've got to go, have I done you wrong)
Now I can't be found by the wailing wall
(You better stop girl, and take a look around)
Sometimes you have got to be ten feet tall
(You better stop girl, and see what's going down)

   Sunday, Monday, Tuesday, Wednesday,
   Thursday, Friday, Saturday . . .
   Summer, winter, spring and fall
   Tick, tick, tick, tick . . .
   Tick, tick, tick, tick . . .

Well I been in your neighborhood for a
   long long time
(You say to me now that you know it all)

You breed confusion in that [you forge] my life
(You say to me that [you've done it all])
Years go by while I'm standing in the cold
(Well you tell me girl, everything's all right)
Well it's all I get to sing [and all men's soul]
(I find out now, well, late at night)
Well old man on the bus wants to [play one]
(Yesterday was your day of rest)
As he takes my dime and tells me how to die
(Yesterday now, now, now)
Here's my life, my love, set it up to [ ]
(I don't know if you what you say is true)
[ ] to say we're gonna really move
(I don't know, I got to, got to talk to you)

Chorus:

Time goes by, just a little bit, now
You gotta wait, you gotta wait until the time
   goes by, now
It doesn't matter what you do now
It's gonna keep on going on by
Going by
Going by now
Going by
Going by
Going by
Going by

Notes:
Live recording: June 1966 recording included on *The Birth of the Dead* in the *The Golden Road* box set.

Well you better
You may find you gotta wait awhile
But you can't wait because the time is
    right now
If you're going to lose it now, you're gonna
    lose it forever
'Cause time keeps rolling or going[?] on by
Na, na, na

Whoa-oh it goes on by
Keep on rolling
Keep on rolling
Keep on rolling
Keep on rolling by
Keep on rolling by

Go show your [fingers]
Out your hands
Out your pockets
Out your [bed]
It's going on
Keep on going
Keep on going, babe
Now, now, now, now

Keep on going now
Keep on going by

Well you may want to stop it babe
And you can't turn it around
Well you may want to turn it up babe
But you sure can't turn it down
You gotta slow down a little bit girl
Keep on rolling by
Keep on rolling by
Keep on rolling by
Time keep on going by
Ain't a thing you can do now
Just keep on going with it
And just stay on top of it for a little while
For a little while
Just for a little while
Just for a little while

(Chorus)

Keep on going by

Words and music by the Grateful Dead

ALice D MiLLionaire

1 wheel of fortune
In tarot, card number ten:

> The wheel of fortune revolves on its axis of
> two straight branches springing from the
> edge of a cliff of barren rock and dirt. Near
> the wheel of fortune grows a bed of red roses
> signifying hope. The blindfolded woman of
> fortune, with an expression of blissful
> unawareness, turns the wheel depicting the
> uncertainty of change. She is the dispenser of
> sorrow and joy. At the top of the wheel sits a
> man with his legs crossed in the form of an X
> while his right hand grasps the hand of a
> woman. The man holds a hat in his left hand,
> rejoicing in his deliverance and success. On
> the descending side of the wheel, a man falls
> off the edge of the cliff. Love and death are
> thus equally dispensed. The wheel of fortune
> has eight spokes signifying that each state of
> life is across the wheel from its opposite. The
> wheel of fortune is the perpetual motion of a
> continuously changing universe and the flow-
> ing of human life. (Kaplan) 3

Notes:
First verified performance: October 6, 1966, at
the Love Pageant Rally in Golden Gate Park, San
Francisco—on the occasion of the outlawing of
LSD. The first issue of the Haight-Ashbury period-
ical *The Oracle* was subtitled *The Love Pageant
Rally Issue.* Also present at the rally, usually seen
as a warmup for the milestone event the Human
Be-In, were Janis Joplin and Ken Kesey with the
Merry Pranksters. "Alice D. Millionaire" was
dropped from the repertoire later that same year,
after a limited number of performances.
Sometimes referred to as "No Time to Cry."

You say you're living in a world of trouble
All your schemes have popped like a bubble
Your mother told your sister
And your brother told your friend
Now your secret's out, and you don't have
    to pretend
You can see for yourself, it's really not the end

Chorus:
You're standing there with tears in your eyes
There's too much going on now, there's no time
    to cry

You say the walls are closing in on you child
All your friends have put you in exile
Bad luck seems to follow you all around
    the world
You can't seem to find no peace of mind girl
You will take a chance to seem so bad

(Chorus)

Every minute is a brand-new day
And there are some games that I'd just love to play
Even bad scenes are for real, there's no time to cry

Since you left your old scene behind you
Go ahead and let the green light find you
It's warm and friendly girl and it won't blind you
Come out in the street and the weeds won't
    grind you
See the love is in the air, you feel it all around you

(Chorus)

Your yesterdays are all left behind
There's a brand-new light in your mind
You don't need a key to define
What's written on the magic sign
There's no time to cry

When the season of the magic lantern
Is transformed into a funny pattern
1   And the wheel of fortune has a flat tire
You can't seem to get any higher
When you go above the [ ] machine, you
     find a horseshoe

(Chorus)

Words and music by the Grateful Dead

From *Living with the Dead:*

I have to get back to San Francisco State. . . .
I get out there in time for the last song,
"Alice D Millionaire," based on that wonder-
ful headline in *The San Francisco Chronicle*
when Owsley got busted for the first time.
The headline read LSD MILLIONAIRE *Arrested.*
(Scully) 4

This would place the first performance a few
days earlier than October 6, since the San
Francisco State College gig was on October
2, at the SF State Trips Festival.

From Tom Wolfe's *The Electric Kool-Aid Acid Test:*

Little by little, Owsley's history seeped out. He
was thirty years old, although he looked
younger, and he had a huge sonorous name:
Augustus Owsley Stanley III. His grandfather
was a United States Senator from Kentucky.
Owsley apparently had had a somewhat hun-
gup time as a boy, going from prep school to
prep school and then to a public high school,
dropping out of that, but getting into the
University of Virginia School of Engineering,
apparently because of his flair for sciences,
then dropping out of that. He finally wound
up enrolling in the University of California, in
Berkeley, where he hooked up with a hip,
good-looking chemistry major named Melissa.
They dropped out of the University and
Owsley set up his first acid factory at 1647
Virginia Street, Berkeley. 5

Wolfe goes on to tell of the quality of Owsley's
LSD, renowned worldwide, and of its influence
on the Beatles:

It was in this head world that the . . . Beatles
first took LSD. Now, just to get ahead of the
story a bit—after Owsley hooked up with
Kesey and the Pranksters, he began [working
with] a musical group called the Grateful
Dead. Through the Dead's experience with the
Pranksters was born the sound known as "acid
rock." And it was that sound that the Beatles
picked up on, after they started taking acid, to
do a famous series of acid-rock record albums,
Revolver, Rubber Soul, and *Sgt. Pepper's Lonely
Hearts' Club Band.* Early in 1967 the Beatles
got a fabulous idea. They got hold of a huge
school bus and piled into it with thirty-nine
friends and drove and wove across the British
countryside, zonked out of their gourds. They
were going to . . . make a movie. 6

Me and My Uncle

Notes:

Recording: *Grateful Dead* (Skull & Roses)
(October 1971)

First documented performance: November 29,
1966, at the Matrix in San Francisco. Played
throughout the band's career, capturing the
place as the most-performed song, cover or
original, in their repertoire.

From the liner notes to John Phillips's *Phillips 66*
album:

> John often used to tell the story behind "Me
> and My Uncle." Years ago he began receiving
> publishing royalties from a song on a Judy
> Collins record with which he was unfamiliar. It

Me and my uncle went riding down
South Colorado, West Texas bound
We stopped over in Santa Fe
That being the point just about halfway
And you know it was the hottest part of the day

I took the horses up to the stall
Went to the barroom, ordered drinks for all
Three days in the saddle, you know my body hurt
It being summer, I took off my shirt
And I tried to wash off some of that dusty dirt

West Texas cowboys, they's all around
With liquor and money, they're loaded down
So soon after payday, you know it seemed
   a shame
You know my uncle, he starts a friendly game
High-low-jacks and the winner take the hand

My uncle starts winning, cowboys got sore
One of them called him, and then two more
Accused him of cheating, well no it couldn't be
I know my uncle, he's as honest as me
And I'm as honest as a Denver man can be

One of them cowboys, he starts to draw
Well I shot him down, Lord, he never saw
Shot me another, hot damn he won't grow old
In the confusion my uncle grabbed the gold
And we hightailed it down to Mexico

Now I love those cowboys, I love their gold
I love my uncle, God rest his soul
Taught me good, Lord, taught me all I know
Taught me so well, I grabbed that gold
And I left his dead ass there by the side of
   the road

   Words and music by John Phillips

was titled "Me and My Uncle." He called Judy to let her know of the mistake because he hadn't written any such song. She laughed and told him that about a year before, in Arizona after one of her concerts, they had a "Tequila" night back at the hotel with Stephen Stills, Neil Young, and a few others. They were running a blank cassette and John proceeded to write "Me and My Uncle" on the spot. The next day, John woke up to the tequila sunrise with no recollection of the songwriting incident. Judy kept the cassette from that evening and then, without informing John, recorded the song for her own record. Over the years the song was recorded by several people, and eventually became a standard of the Grateful Dead. John used to joke that, little by little, with each royalty check, the memory of writing the song would come back to him.

According to Bob Weir, he learned this John Phillips–penned tune from "a hippie named Curly Jim," who I can only assume is Curly Jim Cook, onetime member of the Bar Area band A.B. Skhy. Phillips is best known as the leader and chief songwriter for the L.A.-based The Mamas and Papas. Judy Collins recorded a slower version of the song on a mid-sixties live album *The Judy Collins Concert,* and that may well be where Weir got it from. (Jackson: *Goin' Down the Road*) 94

morning dew

Notes:

Studio recording: *Grateful Dead* (March 17, 1967).

First documented performance: at the Human Be-In, January 14, 1967, in the Polo Field at Golden Gate Park, San Francisco. In the repertoire steadily thereafter.

Long before Weir and Barlow wrote their powerful condemnation of the arms race, "Throwing Stones," the Dead were regularly performing one of the most moving songs ever written about nuclear madness, "Morning Dew." There is an interesting story behind this song, which was written by Canadian singer-songwriter Bonnie Dobson in the very early sixties. On the Dead CDs where it appears, the song is credited to Dobson and Tim Rose, but in fact, Rose had no hand in writing the song. After months of searching, I finally tracked Dobson down at an address in London. What follows are comments about "Morning Dew" that she put down in a thoughtful, handwritten seven-page letter she penned in reply to a query I sent to her.

"I wrote 'Morning Dew' during my second or third engagement at the Ash Grove [the famous L.A. folk club] in 1961. When I'd go to Los Angeles I'd usually stay with my friend Joyce Naftulin, and it was in her apartment that I wrote 'Morning Dew.' I can't give you specific dates, but I do remember the circumstances. There had been a gathering of friends, and toward the end of the evening a discussion had ensued about the possibilities and the outcome of a nuclear war. It was all very depressing and upsetting. The following day I sat down and started putting together the song. I had never written or even attempted to write a song before.

Walk me out in the morning dew, my honey
Walk me out in the morning dew today
Can't walk you out in the morning dew, my honey
I can't walk you out in the morning dew today

I thought I heard a baby cry this morning
I thought I heard a baby cry today
You didn't hear no baby cry this morning
You didn't hear no baby cry today

Where have all the people gone, my honey?
Where have all the people gone today?
There's no need for you to be worrying about all
   those people
You never see those people anyway

I thought I heard a young man mourn this
   morning
I thought I heard a young man mourn today
I thought I heard a young man mourn this
   morning
I can't walk you out in the morning dew today

Walk me out in the morning dew, my honey
Walk me out in the morning dew today
Can't walk you out in the morning dew, my honey
I guess it doesn't matter anyway
Well I guess it doesn't matter anyway

Words and music by Bonnie Dobson and Tim Rose

"It took the form of a conversation between the last man and woman—postapocalypse—one trying to comfort the other while knowing there's absolutely nothing left. When I'd finished, I recall phoning another friend and singing it to her over the phone. She said it was good, but maybe that's just ancient fancy at work. I think I sang it in public for the first time at the first Mariposa Folk Festival in Ontario. Anyway, I recall that the critic from the Toronto *Globe and Mail* described it as a 'mournful dirge.' I have that clipping, amongst others, stored away in a large trunk in Toronto.

"In February of 1962 I recorded an album at Gerde's Folk City in New York [*Bonnie Dobson at Folk City* on Prestige International] and 'Morning Dew' was the last track on side B. [The two songs that preceded it on the record were also anti-nuke tunes, grouped together as "Two Carols for a Nuclear Age."]

"In 1964 I was contacted by Jac Holzman of Elektra Records, who told me that Fred Neil wanted to record 'Morning Dew' and that as I had not published it, would I like to do so with his company, Nina music. I signed a contract and Neil recorded the song. His is the original cover, on *Tear Down the Walls* by Vince Martin and Fred Neil. His singing of it differed from mine in that he altered the lyric slightly, changing 'Take me for a walk in the morning dew' to 'Walk me out in the morning dew.' He was also the first person to rock it. [Dobson's versions are definitely folk.]

"Among others who have recorded it are Jeff Beck, Lee Hazelwood, Lulu, Tim Rose, Nova, the Highwaymen, and, most recently, Nazareth. I'm probably leaving out a good many. I recorded it again on an album [*Bonnie Dobson*] for RCA in 1969.

"Now I must tell you about my involvement with Tim Rose. In 1967 while I was living in Toronto (from 1960 to 1965 I lived in the States), I had a call from Manny Greenhill, my agent, saying that Tim Rose wanted to record 'Morning Dew,' but that he wanted to change the lyric. I duly signed a new contract and Rose was written in as colyricist on the basis of his new lyric. Unfortunately, it wasn't till after the signing that I heard his 'changed' version. You can imagine that I was somewhat dismayed to discover that his new lyric was precisely the one that Fred Neil had recorded in 1964. So if anyone is entitled to be the colyricist, it is Neil and not Rose. You may be wondering why I signed the contract in the first place—some mistakes are only made once, and I guess I was pretty naive.

"In 1968, when Lulu released her single of 'Morning Dew,' a full-page ad was placed in *Billboard* referring to it as 'Tim Roses' Great Hit'—no mention of Ms. Dobson at all. From that time till now—particularly here in England—people have never believed that I had anything to do with the writing of 'Morning dew.' Rose never gave me any credit. Even Nazareth's single from 1981 has only him listed as composer. It has caused me a lot of aggravation and unhappiness. Even though I have and still do receive substantial royalties (75 percent as opposed to his 25 percent), it doesn't make up for the man's behavior."

She closed her letter with this:

"I always like the Dead's version of 'Morning Dew.' My one regret is that when they first appeared in Toronto—was it 1967 or 1968 at the O'Keefe Centre?—they didn't sing 'Morning Dew' in the concert I attended. I also regret that I was too shy to go backstage and meet them." (Jackson: *Goin' Down the Road*) 94

NEW POTATO CABOOSE

1 New Potato
"The New Potatoes" is the title of a traditional Irish jig.

2 Black Madonna
The Black Madonna has been documented as a worldwide manifestation of the feminine divine.

Scholars trace her back through European spiritual traditions to Ephesus, center of the worship of the Greek goddess Artemis (Roman goddess Diana).

Black Madonnas exist in Catholic churches throughout Europe and in Mexico as well. Scholars link this Black Madonna tradition, via archetypes, to the Indian Hindu goddess Tara, interchangeable with Kali.

From the 1965 Bob Dylan song "Gates of Eden":

Motocycle Black Madonna
Two-wheeled Gypsy queen. 7

3 All graceful instruments
"All Graceful Instruments" is the title of a song by the band Sandoz, on their 1994 album, *Unfamiliar Territory*.

Notes:
Studio recording: *Anthem of the Sun* (July 18, 1968).

First documented performance: January 1967 at one of the three shows at the Avalon Ballroom in San Francisco.

From Phil Lesh's autobiography:

It's interesting to consider the evolution of this

Last leaf fallen;
Bare earth where green was born
Black Madonna, two eagles hang against a cloud   2

Sun comes up blood red;
Wind yells among the stone
All graceful instruments are known   3

When the windows all are broken
and your love's become a toothless crone
when the voices of the storm sound like a crowd
winter morning breaks;
you're all alone

The eyes are blind
blue visions are all a seer can own
And touching makes the flesh to cry out loud
This ground on which the seed of love is sown
All graceful instruments are known

Words by Robert M. Petersen
Music by Phil Lesh

particular song: It didn't spring into being all at once, but rather amalgamated itself over time, with small but crucial contributions from the whole band. Pig added a celesta part to the intro, Jerry a melodic phrase for the verse, and Mickey a glockenspiel riff and a very important gong roll. Bob sang lead on the song, since I wasn't ready to try singing leads yet. 95

The Golden Road (to Unlimited Devotion)

See that girl, barefootin' along,
Whistlin' and singin', she's a-carryin' on
There's laughing in her eyes
Dancing in her feet
She's a neon-light diamond
She can live on the street

Chorus:
Hey hey, hey, come right away
Come and join the party every day

1 Well everybody's dancin' in a ring around the sun
Nobody's finished, we ain't even begun
So take off your shoes, child,
And take off your hat
Try on your wings
And find out where it's at

(Chorus)

Take a vacation, fall out for a while,
2 Summer's comin' in, and it's goin' outa style
Well, lie down smokin', honey
Have yourself a ball,
'Cause your mother's down in Memphis,
Won't be back till the fall

(Chorus)

Words and music by the Grateful Dead

1 **everybody's dancin' in a ring around the sun**
Compare the opening line from the song "Stealin'": "Put your arms around me like a ring around the sun." "Stealin'" (recorded on the Garcia-Grisman CD *Shady Grove*) was an early jug band tune recorded by the Memphis Jug Band. The Grateful Dead also recorded the tune as an early single.

Ice crystals in the atmosphere can cause the phenomenon known as a solar halo.

2 **Summer's comin' in . . .**
Compare the first line of the earliest recorded song in the history of the English language, "Cuckoo Song" (Anonymous, ca. 1250):

Summer is y-comen in,
Loude sing, cuckoo!
Groweth seed and bloweth meed
And spring'th the woode now—
Sing cuckoo!

Notes:
Studio recording: *Grateful Dead* (March 17,1967).

First documented performance: March 18, 1967, at the Winterland Arena in San Francisco.

Because it's the first song on the first album recorded by the Dead, this song has particular significance, deserved or not. Perhaps most notably, Blair Jackson and Regan McMahon's magazine, which ran from 1983 to 1993, for a total of twenty-seven issues, was named for this song.

ALLigator

1 **alligator**
When the Spaniards first saw this reptile in the New World, they called it *el lagarto* ("the lizard"). In American slang *alligator* has several figurative meanings, among them "a Mississippi River keel-boat sailor," derived from the real or supposed battles of early boatmen with alligators; hence it is a symbol of manliness. *(Brewer's)*

Alligator n. (1920s–1930s) a usually though not necessarily pejorative term probably coined by Louis Armstrong to describe white musicians who stole ("followed") the ideas of black players. It's a term used by black jazzmen, particularly in New Orleans, referring to white jazzmen and white jazz fans, jive black people, or jitterbugs. (Major)

2 **Call for his whiskey / He can call for his tea**
A reference to the nursery rhyme "Old King Cole":

Old King Cole
Was a merry old soul
And a merry old soul was he;
He called for his pipe
And he called for his bowl,
And he called for his fiddlers three.

Every fiddler, he had a fiddle,
And a very fine fiddle had he;
Twee tweedle-dee, tweedle-dee, went the
    fiddlers.
Oh there's none so rare
As can compare
With King Cole and his fiddlers three.

Sleepy alligator in the noonday sun   1
Sleepin' by the river just like he usually done
Call for his whiskey
He can call for his tea   2
Call all he wanta but he
can't call me

Oh no
I been there before
and I'm not comin back around
there no more

Creepy alligator comin' all around the bend
Talkin' bout the times when we was mutual
    friends
I check my mem'ry
I check it quick yes I will
I check it runnin'
some old kind of trick

Oh no
Well I been there before
and I ain't a comin' back around
there no more
no I'm not

Hung up waitin' for a windy day
Hung up waitin' for a windy day   3
Tear down the Fillmore,   4
Gas the Avalon

Ridin' down the river in an old canoe
a bunch of bugs and an old tennis shoe   5
out of the river all ugly and green

The biggest old alligator that I've ever seen
Teeth big and pointed and his eyes were buggin out
Contact the union, put the beggars to rout
Screamin' and yellin' and lickin' his chops
He never runs he just stumbles and hops
Just out of prison on six dollars bail
Mumblin' at bitches and waggin' his tail

Alligator runnin' round my door (4x)

Alligator creepin' 'round the corner of my
    cabin door
He's comin' 'round to bother me some more

Words by Robert Hunter and Ron McKernan
Music by Ron McKernan and Phil Lesh

The rhyme first appeared in print in 1708, according to *The Annotated Mother Goose*. The annotation for the rhyme also states that the King Cole being referred to in the rhyme is most likely to have been a third-century British ruler.

From this, Hunter's first lyric for the band, to Barlow's "Throwing Stones," the ancient form of the nursery rhyme has provided both text and rhythm and seems to fit particularly well into the playful sound of the Dead.

Those age-old lines "Rain, rain, go away" and "Ashes, ashes, all fall down" come easily to Barlow. And Hunter: "Heigh, ho, the carrion crow, folderolderiddle" from "Mountains of the Moon"; "Is it all fall down, is it all go under?" from "Doin' That Rag." "Saint Stephen" and "Ramble on Rose" are good examples of nursery rhyme format.

Nursery rhymes have contributed to the lyrics of popular song since long before the Grateful Dead. "Mairzy Doats" is an example from the 1930s; "Good Golly, Miss Molly" is another example. Doubtless there are hundreds more such examples. The Beatles quite often used nursery rhymes, noticeably in the *Abbey Road* chant "One two three four five six seven / All good children go to heaven."

For an excellent study of the use of nursery rhymes in popular music, see *Popular Music Perspectives* by B. Lee Cooper.

There are quite a large number of collections of nursery rhymes, and the best are Iona and Peter Opie's *The Oxford Dictionary of Nursery Rhymes* and *The Annotated Mother Goose*. So if these sketchy notes intrigue you at all, go find these books—they make surprisingly fun reading. Two things become clear as you read books about these rhymes. First, they cannot be dated. They are ancient and may have been collected as recently as a hundred years ago. Second, they are difficult to interpret. Scholars have over the years written lengthy conjectural articles on the possible meanings of just about every rhyme and can never seem to agree on any single interpretation.

Aside from the songs already noted, here are some more examples of lyrics showing evidence of nursery rhyme influence:

> When I was a little boy,
> My mammy kept me in,
> But now I am a great big boy
> Fit to serve the king

To which compare:

> When I was a young man,
> I needed good luck.
> But I'm a little bit older now
> And I know my stuff.
> —"Let Me Sing Your Blues Away"

> Ride a cock horse to Banbury Cross
> To see a fine lady upon a white horse
> Rings on her fingers and bells on her toes
> And she shall have music wherever she goes

To which compare:

> Rings on her fingers and bells on her shoes
> And I knew without asking she was into the blues. —
> "Scarlet Begonias"

As an interesting footnote to this last rhyme, its source is apparently a children's version of the May Ridings, a customary celebration of spring where two or three ride a horse simultaneously and which has been identified by folklorists as an outgrowth of fertility rites connected with the Teutonic goddess Hertha. So that lady in the rhyme is actually of divine descent, and her bells and attendant music are part of her worship.

"Blues for Allah," "Althea," "Throwing Stones," and "The Eleven" all have nursery rhyme elements. See the notes for those songs for particular references.

3 hung up waitin' for a windy day
This verse, according to Hunter, was written by the band as a whole. Hunter used this particular line in "Cosmic Charlie."

4 Tear down the Fillmore / Gas the Avalon
Also part of the verse written by the band, according to Hunter. The Carousel was a performance venue owned and operated by a few San Francisco bands, the Dead and the Airplane among them. The Dead opened the ballroom on February 14, 1968. The Avalon (located at 1268 Sutter, at Van Ness, and operated by Chet Helms and his Family Dog) and the Fillmore (southwest corner of Fillmore and Geary, owned and operated by Bill Graham) were relegated to competitor status, hence this dig at the Carousel's competition. Later in 1968, the Carousel was taken over by Graham, who renamed it the Fillmore West. It opened on August 5, with a show by Ornette Coleman.

5 Ridin' down the river . . .
This verse, according to Hunter, was by McKernan.

Notes:
Studio recording: *Anthem of the Sun* (July 18, 1968).

Hunter says this was the first of his lyrics recorded by the band. Additional lyrics were added by Pigpen, and Hunter includes those in the published version in *A Box of Rain*.

"Alligator" was played sixty times between its debut, possibly on January 27, 1967, and April 29, 1971.

Duane Allman first played "Mountain Jam" one night while sitting in with the Grateful Dead. The melodic strains of Donovan's "There Is a Mountain" can clearly be heard right at the 09:00-minute mark on the *Anthem of the Sun* version of "Alligator."

turn on your Love Light

Without a warning, you broke my heart
Taken it baby, tore it apart
And you left me standing, in a dark clime
Said your love for me was dyin'
So come on baby, baby please
I'm begging you baby, I'm on my knees

Chorus:

1 Turn on your light, let it shine on me
Turn on your love light, let it shine on me
Let it shine, let it shine, let it . . .

Well I get a little lonely in the middle of
 the night
And I need you darling to make things all right
So come on baby, baby please
And I'm begging you baby, 'cause I'm on
 my knees

(Chorus)

Without a warning, you broke my heart
Taken it baby, torn it apart
And you left me standing, in a dark clime
Said your love for me was dyin'
So come on baby, baby please
I'm begging you baby, I'm on my knees

(Chorus)

Well I get a little lonely in the middle of
 the night

1 She's got box-back nitties . . .
Pigpen's ad-lib rap at the end of "Love Light"
drew on old blues sources. Texas songster Mance
Lipscomb's tune "Shake Shake, Mama" contains
the following verse:

> Oh I like my babe but I don't like her teddy
> bear
> Oh, like my woman but I don't like her teddy
> bear
> I'm gon' buy her a box-back nittie to wear

Mack McCormick's 1960 liner notes to
Lipscomb's original Arhoolie LP discusses "one
verse lauding the 'box-back nittie' which
replaced the 'teddy bear' garment which men
found unappealing." Thus "nittie" could refer to
a knitted garment, or to a nightie. One theory
has it that box-back nitties are long flannel
underwear with a flap in the back.

Garcia:

> But, like, I have no idea where [Pigpen] got
> that thing he used to sing: "She got box-back
> nitties and great big noble thighs, working
> undercover with a boar hog's eye." Don't ask
> me—I don't know what the fuck that's all
> about! It's some weird mojo shit or something.
> But he could always pull that stuff out. He
> could do that as long as I knew him. When he
> was on, he was amazing. (Jackson, *Golden
> Road*) 8

2 boar hog's eye
Compare Texas Alexander's "Bo' Hog Blues":

> She got little bitty legs, gee, but below her
> thighs
> She got little bitty legs, gee, but below her
> thighs
> She got something on-a-yonder works like a
> bo' hog's eye

Notes:

Recording: *Live/Dead* (November 10, 1969).

First documented performance: August 5, 1967, at the O'Keefe Centre in Toronto, Canada. Performed regularly through mid-1972, then dropped from the repertoire after Pigpen's death. Brought back, sung by Weir, beginning in late 1981, after which it remained in the repertoire.

> One of the most popular of the Dead's late-sixties R&B rave-ups, "Love Light" was originally recorded by blues singer Bobby "Blue" Bland, who certainly must be considered among the most popular and influential singers of the fifties and early sixties. Bland first came to prominence as part of the Memphis blues scene of the early fifties. He recorded a few sides for Sam Phillips's Sun label, and appeared on Howlin' Wolf's radio program before the latter went on to greater fame in Chicago. His biggest successes, though, were in the early-sixties, when he recorded for the Texas-based Duke label. With that company, he had a number of R&B hits, including "Cry, Cry, Cry," "I Pity the Fool," "Stormy Monday Blues," "That's the Way Love Is," and "Turn On Your Love Light," which hit number two on the *Billboard* R&B charts in 1961. Besides influencing Pigpen, Bland was a definite influence on other rock singers, too, such as Van Morrison, who cut "Love Light" with his group Them. (Jackson: *Goin' Down the Road*.) 94

From Phil Lesh's biography:

> Pig brought in a whole bunch of songs to work on, and "Turn On Your Lovelight" was a showstopper that we all jumped on when we heard James Cotton do it when he opened one of our shows at the Fillmore. 95

And I need you baby to make things all right
So come on baby, baby please
And I'm begging you baby, 'cause I'm on
   my knees
Turn on your light, let it shine on me
Turn on your love light, let it shine on me

[Pigpen ad-lib]

Let it shine on me, let it shine on me
Let it shine on me, let it shine on me
Why don't you let it shine on me
Why don't you let it baby shine on me
Early in the morning let it shine on me
Late in the evening let it shine on me too
Well that's all I need, I just got to get some
That's all I need, I just got to get some
I just got to, I just got to
Get a little more, yes I do
And I don't want it all, I just want a little bit
I don't want it all, no no no no, I just want a
   little bit
A little of your lovin', a little of your kissin'
A little of your rollin', that's all I want
Baby please, baby please
Baby please, baby please
Just like a stingray, on a four-day ride

Now wait a minute, I wanna to tell you about my baby
I wanna tell you how come she make me feel so good
Yes she do, yes she do
I know she make me feel all right, yes she do

She's got box-back nitties
And great big noble thighs
2   Working undercover with a boar hog's eye

Words and music by Joseph Scott
and Deadric Malone

1 rose
One of the most pervasive symbols in Grateful Dead lyrics and iconography, the rose is a symbol

laden with meaning. This is its first appearance in a Dead lyric.

According to J. E. Cirlot's *A Dictionary of Symbols*, the

> single rose is, in essence, a symbol of completion, of consummate achievement and perfection. Hence, accruing to it are all those ideas associated with these qualities: the mystic Centre, the heart, the garden of Eros, the paradise of Dante, the Beloved, the emblem of Venus, and so on. 9

An extensive entry on the rose in *Funk & Wagnalls Standard Dictionary of Folklore, Mythology, and Legend* (Funk & Wagnalls, 1972) includes the following information:

> Originally from Persia, the rose is said to have been brought to the West by Alexander. To the Arabs the rose was a masculine flower. It was anciently a symbol of joy, later of secrecy and silence, but is now usually associated with love.

The entry continues for several hundred words and is worth tracking down.

Gabriele Tergit's *Flowers Through the Ages* contains many pages on the history and folklore of the rose. Some passages:

CRYPTICAL ENVELOPMENT

The other day they waited, the sky was dark
    and faded,
Solemnly they stated, "He has to die, you know
    he has to die."
All the children learnin', from books that they
    were burnin',
Every leaf was turnin', to watch him die, you
    know he had to die.

The summer sun looked down on him,
His mother could but frown on him,
And all the other sound on him,
He had to die, you know he had to die.

Words and music by Jerry Garcia

THE FASTER WE GO, THE ROUNDER WE GET

Spanish lady come to me, she lays on me this rose.   1
It rainbow spirals round and round,   2
It trembles and explodes.
It left a smoking crater of my mind,
I like to blow away.
But the heat came round and busted me   3
For smilin' on a cloudy day.

Chorus:
Comin', comin', comin' around, comin' around,
    comin' around in a circle,

Comin', comin', comin' around, comin' around
    in a circle,
Comin', comin', comin' around, comin' around
    in a circle.

4   Escapin' through the lily fields
    I came across an empty space
    It trembled and exploded
    Left a bus stop in its place
5, 6 The bus came by and I got on
    That's when it all began
7   There was cowboy Neal
    At the wheel
8   Of a bus to never-ever land

Comin', comin', comin' around, comin' around,
    comin' around in a circle,
Comin', comin', comin' around, comin' around
    in a circle,
Comin', comin', comin' around, comin' around
    in a circle.

Words by Bob Weir
Music by Bob Weir and Bill Kreutzmann

CRYPTICAL ENVELOPMENT REPRISE

And when the day had ended, with rainbow colors
    blended,
9   Their minds remained unbended,
    He had to die, oh, you know he had to die.

Words and music by Jerry Garcia

Soon the mysterious rose, sacred to Venus in earlier times, became the flower of the Virgin Mary, who herself became the *Rosa mystica*. The temple of Jupiter Capitolinus became St. Peter's, the temple of Juno Lucina the church of S. Maria Maggiore, and the processions honouring the Mother of God walked on rose petals, just as the processions carrying the images of the pagan gods had done.

and

The scholastics derived the origin of the rose from the drops of Christ's blood falling upon a thornbush.

and

The rose was dedicated to the goddess of love, that is, to the eternal mystery of the continuity of life. As such it was the symbol of mystery and secrecy. "Mystery glows in the rose bed, the secret is hidden in the rose," sang the Persian poet and perfumer Farid ud-din Attar in the twelfth century. A more prosaic explanation is that the folded structure of the rose, by its nature, conceals a secret inner core . . . in Germany, we read in Sebastian Brant's *Narrenschiff* [*Ship of Fools*], in the late fifteenth century: "What here we do say, shall under roses stay."

and

We do not know where the rose comes from. Rose fossils 32,000,000 years old have been found in Colorado and Oregon; they resemble the East Asian roses more than the American ones of today.

    The first record of an authentic European rose is a highly stylized one in a fresco at Knossos in Greece; it dates from the sixteenth century B.C.

It is possible that Central Asia is the home of the rose. The most beautiful woman of India, the goddess Lakshmi, is supposed to have been born from a rose composed of 108 large and 1,008 small petals.

Every country between twenty and seventy degrees north has its indigenous roses.

The Dictionary of Christian Art defines the rose as:

A floral symbol sacred to Venus and signifying love, the quality and nature of which was characterized by the color of the rose. A symbol of purity, a white rose represented innocence and or innocent (nonsexual) love, while a pink rose represented first love, and a red rose true love. When held by a martyr (such as Saint Stephen), the red rose signified "red martyrdom," or the loss of life, and the white rose "white martyrdom," or celibacy. According to Ambrose, the thorns of the rose were a reminder of human finitude and guilt as the roses in the Paradise Garden had no thorns. A thornless rose was an attribute of Mary as the Second Eve. (Apostolos-Cappadona)

The literature is voluminous, and the point is easily taken: Roses have had tremendous significance for as long as history has been recorded, and likely for long before that. The rose is a metaphor waiting to happen, and people have always ascribed to it some aspect of the mystery of life. In the words of Robert Hunter:

I've got this one spirit that's laying roses on me. Roses, roses, can't get enough of those bloody roses. The rose is *the* most prominent image in the human brain, as to delicacy, beauty, short-livedness, thorniness. It's a whole. There is no better allegory for, dare I say it, life than roses. (Jackson, *Grateful Dead*) 11

2 rainbow
According to *The Larousse Dictionary of World Folklore*:

In several mythologies the rainbow is a bridge connecting earth to a supernatural otherworld; for example, the Norse Bifrost, which connects heaven and earth and is guarded by Heimdall, is identified in the Prose Edda with the rainbow.

and later in the same entry:

a more general and enduring belief in Europe is that the end of the rainbow marks valuable buried treasure, generally a crock of gold.

Other references to rainbows are found in "The Eleven," "Crazy Fingers," "What's Become of the Baby?" "The Music Never Stopped," "Estimated Prophet," and "Saint of Circumstance."

3 heat came round and busted me
From an interview by David Gans with Bob Weir and Phil Lesh:

Weir: Interesting story with "The Other One." It was one of the first tunes I ever wrote. Actually, we came up with the "map," basically, for the song in a rehearsal somewhere, just kickin' stuff around. And then I took it and started shaping it up, and things like that. We went on a tour, in the Pacific Northwest, and I was, you know, I was not *done* with it, I was wondering what the song was about, and then one night it sort of *came* to me. Basically, it's a little fantastic episode about my meeting Neal Cassady. I wrote the two verses—that's all there is to it, really, is two vees—and then we played the gig that night and came home the next day, and when we came home we learned the news that Neal had *died* that night.

Gans: Wow.

Weir: The night that I wrote that. As legend has it, he died counting the railroad ties on the tracks.

Lesh: From Dallas to Denver.

Weir: Something like that. San Miguel de Allende [Mexico], I think, is where he was. So I guess that was a little visitation, that's—not unlike Neal.

Lesh: But if I remember correctly, as soon as you had the words, then we did the song.

Weir: Yeah.

Lesh: I mean, we did it that night. It didn't require *any* rehearsal.

Weir: Right.

Gans: Now, I remember a version from a little bit earlier, maybe late in '67, you had a different set of lyrics; the first verse is "the heat come 'round and busted me". . . and then there was a *second* verse that was about "the heat in the jail weren't very smart," or somethin' like that . . .

Weir: Yeah, that was after my little . . .

Lesh: Water balloon episode?

Weir: I got him good. I was on the third floor of our place in the Haight-Ashbury. And there was this cop who was illegally searching a car belonging to a friend of ours, down on the street—the cops used to harass us every chance they got. They didn't care for the hippies back then. And so I had a water balloon, and what was I gonna do with this water balloon? Come on.

Lesh: Just *happened* to have a water balloon, *in his hand*. . . . Ladies and gentlemen. . . .

Weir: And so I got him right square on the head, and . . .

Lesh: A prettier shot you never saw.

Weir: . . . and he couldn't tell where it was comin' from, but then I had to go and go downstairs and walk across the street and just grin at him . . . and sorta rub it in a little bit.

Gans: Smilin' on a cloudy day. I understand now.

Weir: And at that point, he decided to hell with due process of law, this kid's goin' to jail. He didn't have a thing on me. It never got to court, but on the other hand, I did get thrown in jail and beat up a little bit. I guess—what, what does a water balloon amount to, is that assault with a . . .

Gans: Friendly weapon. 12

4 Escapin'
Often written as "Skippin' through the lily fields."

5 The bus
Chapter Six of Tom Wolfe's *The Electric Kool-Aid Acid Test* is titled "The Bus." He says:

I couldn't tell you for sure which of the Merry Pranksters got the idea for the bus, but it had the Babbs touch. . . . Then somebody—Babbs?—saw a classified ad for a 1939 International Harvester school bus. The bus belonged to a man in Menlo Park. . . . Kesey bought it for $1,500—in the name of Intrepid Trips, Inc. Kesey gave the word and the Pranksters set upon it one afternoon. They started painting it and wiring it for sound and cutting a hole in the roof and fixing up the top of the bus so you could sit up there in the open air and play music, even a set of drums and electric guitars and electric bass and so forth, or just ride. Sandy went to work on the wiring and rigged up a system with which they could broadcast from inside the bus, with tapes or over microphones, and it would blast outside over powerful speakers on top of the bus. There were also microphones outside that would pick up sounds along the road and broadcast them inside the bus. There was also a sound system inside the bus so you could broadcast to one another over the roar of the engine and the road. You could also broadcast over a tape mechanism so that you said something, then heard your own voice a second later in variable lag and could rap off of that if you wanted to. Or you could put on earphones and rap simultaneously off sounds from outside, coming in one ear, and sounds from inside, your own sounds, coming in the other ear. There was going to be no goddamn sound on that whole trip, outside the bus, inside the bus, or inside your own freaking larynx, that you couldn't tune in on and rap off of.

The painting job, meanwhile, with everybody pitching in in a frenzy of primary colors, yellows, oranges, blues, reds, was sloppy as hell, except for the parts Roy Seburn did, which were nice manic mandalas. Well, it was sloppy, but one thing you had to say for it; it was freaking lurid. The manifest, the destination sign in the front, read: FURTHUR, with two *u's*. 13

Other buses in rock-music lyrics include the Who's "Magic Bus" and the Beatles' "Magical Mystery Tour."

6 I got on
Being "on the bus" means, well, let's hear Kesey explain it [via Tom Wolfe]:

> "There are going to be times," says Kesey, "when we can't wait for somebody. Now you're either on the bus or off the bus. If you're on the bus, and you get left behind, then you'll find it again. If you're off the bus in the first place—then it won't make a damn." And nobody had to have it spelled out for them. Everything was becoming allegorical, understood by the group mind, and especially this: "You're either on the bus . . . or off the bus." (Wolfe) 14

7 Neal
A reference to Neal Cassady:

> He didn't like his other verses, and now in Oregon, he thought of the Pranksters, and of course

of Neal Cassady. Neal had spent some ten days that January sleeping in the attic of 710 [Ashbury Street, in

San Francisco, the Grateful Dead's house], generally hanging out with Weir, who slept on a couch on the second floor, most of his belongings in a paper bag. The room with the couch also had the stereo, and Weir would lie there, still silenced by the effects of his past use of LSD, as Neal gobbled speed, juggled his sledgehammer, and raved. John Barlow later speculated that Weir was somehow "dreaming" Cassady. In their polarities, there was a powerful bond. In Portland, Weir reviewed what he had written about meeting Neal: *Escapin' through the lily field. . . .* That works, he thought to himself as he finally went off to sleep. A couple of thousand miles south, Neal Cassady lay dying of exposure on railroad tracks near San Migeul de Allende, Mexico. Found and brought to the hospital, he died later that day, February 4, 1968. The band learned of his death when they got home to 710 from the tour. (McNally) 15

8 never-ever land
A more-or-less direct reference to Never-Never- Land, from Sir James Matthew Barrie's 1902 play, *Peter Pan, or the Boy Who Wouldn't Grow Up*. Peter Pan, who says he ran away on the day he was born, and who never ages, takes visitors to Never-Never-Land (also called Neverland).

9 Their minds remained unbended
A letter from Willy Legate to the editors of *DeadBase* states that this line more or less alludes back to "Mindbender" (performed in early 1966; on the November 3, 1965, *Emergency Crew* demo):

> If only I could (be less fine)
> If only I knew what to find,
> Everywhere and all of the time—
> It's bending my mind

Phil and Jerry gave the title "Mindbender." (Each accuses the other of writing it.)

Notes:
Studio recording: *Anthem of the Sun* (July 18, 1968).

First documented performance: October 22, 1967, at Winterland Arena in San Francisco. It remained in the repertoire thereafter, though the Cryptical Envelopment portion was dropped after 1972 (it was brought back for eight performances in 1985). Therefore, the part of the lyric titled "The Faster We Go, the Rounder We Get" came to be known simply as "The Other One." "Cryptical Envelopment" was later revived by Phil and Friends, and by The Dead. Over the years, various inconsistencies in titling and crediting of the various portions of the suite have resulted in almost no one knowing anymore exactly who wrote what and what it was called, or why.

Some variant lyrics, from early performances:

1st verse:

When I woke up this morning my head was
  not attached
I asked my friends about it, try to find out
  where it's at
[inaudible] . . . came up inside of me, blew the
  dust clouds all away
The heat came 'round and busted me for
  smiling on a cloudy day

2nd verse:

Well the heat down in jail they weren't very
  smart
They taught me how to read and write, they
  taught me the precious arts
When I was breaking out of jail I learned that
  right away
That they didn't need me telling them about
  smiling first and running [ ]

1st verse:

When I woke up this morning with the sky in
  sight
I would ask the walls about it, but they
  vanished overnight
I could not think or spell my name or _?_ the
  words away
The heat came 'round and busted me for
  smiling on a cloudy day.

When I woke up this morning my head was
  not in sight

The band frequently dedicated this song to Owsley.

Garcia was asked about his portion of the lyric:

Seriously, I think that's an extension of my own personal symbology for "The Man of Constant Sorrow"—the old folk song—which I always thought of as being a sort of Christ parable. 16

MAN OF CONSTANT SORROW

I am a man of constant sorrow
I've seen trouble all of my days
I bid farewell to old Kentucky
Place where I was born and raised

All through this earth I'm bound to ramble
Through storm and wind, through sleet and
  rain
I'm bound to ride that northern railroad
Perhaps I'll take the very next train

For six long years I've been in trouble
No pleasure here on earth I've found
For in this world I'm bound to ramble
I have no friends to help me now

It's fare you well, my own true lover
I never expect to see you again
For I'm bound to ride that northern railroad
Perhaps I'll take the very next train

Your friends they say that I'm a stranger
You'll never see my face no more
There's just one promise that is given
We'll meet upon God's golden shore

I am a man of constant sorrow
I've seen trouble all of my days
I'm going back to California
Place where I was partly raised

born cross-eyed

1 in the sweet bye-and-bye
A reference to the 1902 song "In the Sweet Bye-and-Bye," words by Vincent P. Bryan, music by Harry von Tilzer. Also compare the song "Bye and Bye," a traditional tune recorded by Weir with Kingfish. For more information on that song, see the notes to "And We Bid You Goodnight."

2 about the time the sun rises west
A synonym for *never*, or for a lie, used repeatedly in the folk-song tradition. See, for example, "Bird in a Cage," "Blackwaterside," "False True Love," and "False Young Man."

3 Feeling groovy
Compare Paul Simon's "59th Street Bridge Song," aka "Feelin' Groovy" (1967).

Notes:
Studio recording: *Anthem of the Sun* (July 18, 1968).

First documented performance: January 17, 1968, at the Carousel Ballroom in San Francisco.

A song titled "Cross-eyed Blues" was recorded by Helen Humes in November 1927.

> Folks who's got
>   them cross eyes,
>   things they see in vain
> Folks who's got them cross eyes, things they see
>   is always wrong
> That's why me and cross eyes never gonna get
>   along

Seems like I've been here before
Fuzzy then and still so obscure
And I don't want to see anybody cry
Meet me some morning in the sweet bye and bye   1
Bye and bye

Song coming on
So pleasing to see come and gone
And you don't have to tell me why
Meet me some morning in the sweet bye and bye
Bye and bye

Think that I'm the only one left darling
About the time the sun rises west   2
Feeling groovy   3
Looking fine
Think I'll come back here again
Every now and then
From time to time

My, how lovely you are, my dear
The ball game has gone much too far, my dear
Sing to me
Do your thing to me
(Hop along honey, come along)
I'll meet you some morning
Meet you some morning in the sweet bye and bye
Bye and bye
Bye and bye

Words and music by Bob Weir

dark star

1 Dark star crashes
pouring its light
into ashes

Reason tatters
the forces tear loose
from the axis

Searchlight casting
for faults in the
clouds of delusion

Shall we go,
you and I
while we can
Through
the transitive nightfall
of diamonds

Mirror shatters
in formless reflections
of matter

Glass hand dissolving
to ice-petal flowers
revolving

Lady in velvet
recedes
in the nights of good-bye

Shall we go,
you and I
while we can?
Through

1 Dark star
An oxymoron: the brightest of objects, seen as the absence of brightness.

The phrase seems to have come to the English language by way of the astronomers who spoke Middle High German, who in turn borrowed it from Latin, translating the phrase *stella obscura*, used by Roman astronomers to describe a faint star. This was translated into the German of the Minnesingers and of the medieval German astronomers as *dunkler Stern*. The astronomers, according to an article by Arthur Groos, used it in a comparable manner to that of the Romans, while the Minnesingers adopted it as a literary metaphor.

He cites a song by Kurenberg, a mid-twelfth-century poet:

> Der tunkel Sterne, der birget sich.
> Als tuo Du, Frouwe schoene, so Du sehest mich.
> So la du diniu Ougen gen an einen andern Man.
> Son weiz doch luetzel iemen, wiez under uns
>   zwein ist getan.

> [The "dark star" hides itself.
> Do likewise, beautiful lady, when you see me:
> Let your eyes glance at another man,
> And no one will know how things are between
>   us.]

For many years, the phrase as used by the Minnesingers was taken to mean "Venus," the "star" obscured by cloudy vapors and representing Love in the age of chivalry. Groos's article contradicts this interpretation, arguing for a much more complex metaphor. His article ("Kurenberg's 'Dark Star,' in *Speculum: A Journal of Medieval Studies*, vol. 54 [1979], pp. 469–78) is worth reading.

John Michel, a British natural philosopher, first theorized the concept of a black hole in 1784, and *dark star* was the term by which the concept was referred to at the time. Incredibly, Michel reasoned that there were dark stars that had a "critical circumference" beyond which light did not escape. (Another John Michel is a contemporary English author who brought the subject of sacred geometry and earth mysteries forward. In 1972, during the Europe '72 tour, some of the Grateful Dead's entourage, including Garcia and Lesh, who were interested in the subject even then, long before the Dead's pyramid adventures in Egypt, met with Michel).

Astronomers today still use the phrase *dark star* to refer to the phenomenon of a faint star and in reference to dwarf stars. I'll cite one article: "Dark star throws light on missing mass," *New Scientist*, vol. 116 (November 19, 1987), p. 33. The subject tracings for the article indicate it is about dark matter (astronomy) and dwarf stars. In essence (and in one sense of dwarf), stars go through dwarf stages as they die. Our sun, for example, "will become a white dwarf, then a black dwarf—a cold corpse in space."

On the atomic level, the nucleus of an atom is surrounded with a cloud of electrons. At high stellar temperatures, atoms are ionized and the electrons run around free of the nuclei. As a star is crushed to higher densities in its evolution, the electrons form a degenerate electron gas.

In 1935, Subrahmanyan Chandrasekhar applied the physics of a degenerate electron gas to the model of a star. He found that the pressure exerted by the electrons could resist the force of gravity only for stars of less than 1.4 solar masses and that such stars would have a particular density. Such stars are known as white dwarfs. He also found the crucial point at which the star has the highest density and smallest radius possible. Any more mass at all added to this point and the star collapses. This point is known as the Chandrasekhar limit.

the transitive nightfall
of diamonds

spinning a set the stars through which the
   tattered tales of axis roll
about the waxen wind of never set to motion
   in the unbecoming
round about the reason hardly matters nor
   the wise through which
the stars were set in spin

Words by Robert Hunter
Music by Jerry Garcia, Bill Kreutzmann, Phil Lesh,
Ron McKernan, Bob Weir and Mickey Hart

So, a white dwarf is a star at the end point of its thermonuclear history, where no heavy elements are fused and no energy is produced—the end of the line of energy production. Slowly, the stored integral heat of a white dwarf then radiates into space (pouring its light into ashes, as it were). Eventually, it becomes a black dwarf, cold, without energy, and nonproductive.

Any number of books and songs have used the phrase, and it is now impossible to tell who influenced whom, and is it important, anyway? I find it interesting to see how often the phrase has been used, so I offer the following, doubtless far from complete, list of books, films, and songs using *dark star* in their titles:

BOOKS:

Fiction and drama:

Caldecott, Moyra. *Child of the Dark Star.* 1984.

Chambers, Robert William. *The Dark Star.* 1929.

Cost, March. *The Dark Star.* 1940.

Dowding, Hugh Caswell Tremenheere. *The Dark Star.* 1951.

Furst, Alan. *Dark Star.* 1991.

Gater, Dilys. *The Dark Star.* 1981.

Hill, Pamela. *A Dark Star Passing.* 1990.

Hilliard, Nerina. *Dark Star.* 1968. (A Harlequin romance)

Kahn, Florence Ring. *Dark Star, a Drama in One Act.* 1950.

Knight, Brigid. *Dark Star.* 1965.

Lloyd, Hugh. *The Mystery at the Dark Star Ranch.* 1934.

Maybury, Anne. *Dark Star.* 1977.

Moon, Lorna. *Dark Star.* 1929.

Muller, Marcia. *Dark Star.* 1989.

Silverberg, Robert. "To the Dark Star." Short story, anthologized in *The Cube Root of Uncertainty.* 1970.

Biographies (this seems to be a popular subtitle for biographies):

Amburn, Ellis. *Dark Star: The Roy Orbison Story.* 1990.

Bates, Robin. *The Dinosaurs and the Dark Star.* 1986.

Fountain, Leatrice. *Dark Star.* 1985 (A biography of the actor John Gilbert.).

Greenfield, Robert. *Dark Star: An Oral Biography of Jerry Garcia.* 1996.

Jones, Dylan. *Jim Morrison, Dark Star.* 1992.

Nonfiction:

Dugger, Ronnie. *Dark Star: Hiroshima Reconsidered in the Life of Claude Eatherly.* 1967.

MacLeod, Fiona. *The Dominion of Dreams: Under the Dark Star.* 1910.

Wolfe, Robert. *Dark Star.* 1984.

FILMS:

Dark Star. 1974. (A sci-fi feature film).

Holt, Nancy. *Art in the Public Eye: The Making of Dark Star Park.* 1988.

RECORDINGS:

Oldfield, Mike. "Dark Star." Track on *Tubular Bells 2.* 1992.

Stills, Stephen. "Dark Star." Track on *CSN.*

Note relationship to the title "Stella Blue." *Stella* is Latin for "star," so, a blue star.

A line in J. R. R. Tolkien's poem "Cat" refers to:

The pard dark-starred,
fleet upon feet . . .

(*Pard* is short for "leopard," so the dark stars being referred to are the leopard's spots.)

Dark Star was also the 1953 Kentucky Derby winner.

2 Shall we go, you and I

David Womack, in his *The Aesthetics of the Dead,* points up a parallel to T. S. Eliot's opening lines for "The Love Song of J. Alfred Prufrock":

Let us go then, you and I,
When the evening is spread out against the sky
Like a patient etherised upon a table.

"Prufrock" is also echoed in "Stella Blue."

Notes:

Recordings: Generally, the version from *Live/Dead* (November 10, 1969) is the acknowledged standard. However, a studio version (noted above) was released as a single, backed with "Born Cross-eyed" in April 1968.

First documented performance: December 13, 1967, at the Shrine Exhibition Hall in Los Angeles.

The verse at the end of the lyric was included on the studio recording of "Dark Star," released on the compilation *What a Long Strange Trip It's Been*, recited by Hunter himself. It was not sung in performance.

Hunter states in a note in *A Box of Rain* that "Dark Star" was the first song lyric he wrote *with* the band, though they had earlier arranged "Alligator," "Saint Stephen," and "China Cat Sunflower."

 "Dark Star" was included by Jim Henke, chief curator for the Rock and Roll Hall of Fame, on the list of the 500 most influential songs in rock and roll.

In *Garcia*, Charles Reich questions Garcia about "Dark Star":

> Reich: Well, then, if we wanted to talk about "Dark Star," uh, could you say anything about where it comes from?

> Garcia: You gotta remember that you and I are talking about two different "Dark Stars." You're talking about the "Dark Star" which you have heard formalized on a record, and I'm talking about the "Dark Star" which I have heard in each performance as a completely improvised piece over a long period of time. So I have a long continuum of "Dark Stars" which range in character from each other to real different extremes. "Dark Star" has meant, while I'm playing it, almost as many things as I can sit here and imagine, so all I can do is talk about "Dark Star" as a playing experience.

> Reich: Well, yeah, talk about it a little.

> Garcia: I can't. It talks about itself.

Tom Constanten said:

> "Dark Star" is going on all the time. It's going on right now. You don't begin it so much as enter it. You don't end it so much as leave it.

cLementine

1, 2   Chopped olive sandwiches, roses, and wine

3   Red ripe persimmons, my sweet Clementine

4   I go on, I go on, I can't fill my cup

5   There's a hole in the bottom, the well has dried up

    I run through the forest, I cut past the vine

    Head through the thickets, many a time
    Octave of voices, sweet voices belie
    I left for the comfort of cold Clementine

Words by Robert Hunter
Music by Phil Lesh

1 Chopped olive sandwiches
A recipe yielding 12 servings:

Ingredients:

1 (6 ounce) can ripe black pitted olives, drained,
  finely chopped
1/4 cup light mayonnaise
3 tablespoons drained sun-dried tomatoes packed
  in oil, chopped
3 tablespoons green onion, chopped
3 tablespoons fresh basil, chopped
3 tablespoons pine nuts
1/8 teaspoon salt
1/8 teaspoon freshly ground black pepper
12 slices firm white sandwich bread
6 tablespoons light cream cheese

Directions:

In a medium bowl, combine all ingredients except
bread and cream cheese; mix well. Cover; chill at
least 1 hour or up to 24 hours before assembling
sandwiches. Cut crusts from bread, forming 4-
inch squares; reserve crusts for another use.
Spread cream cheese over bread. Spread olive
mixture over 6 slices bread; close sandwiches with
remaining bread, pressing lightly. Cut diagonally
in half or lengthwise into rectangles.

2 roses
See note under "That's It for the Other One."

3 Clementine
The fruit by this name is a
seedless mandarin orange.

The title of a well-known folk
song, with the refrain:

Oh my darling, oh my darling
Oh my darling Clementine
Thou art lost and gone forever
Dreadful sorry, Clementine.

4 I can't fill my cup
Compare "Ripple":

Reach out your hand if your cup be empty

and, "Comes a Time":

You've got an empty cup
only love can fill

5 There's a hole in the bottom
Compare the folk song "There's a Hole in the Bucket":

There's a hole in the bucket, dear Liza, dear Liza
There's a hole in the bucket, dear Liza, there's
 a hole.
Then fix it, dear Henry, dear Henry, dear Henry
Then fix it, dear Henry, dear Henry, fix it.
With what shall I fix it, dear Liza, dear Liza
With what shall I fix it, dear Liza, with what?
With a straw, dear Henry, dear Henry, dear Henry
With a straw, dear Henry, dear Henry, with
 a straw.
But the straw is too long etc.
Then cut it, etc.
With what shall I cut it?
With an ax
The ax is too dull
Then sharpen it
With what shall I sharpen it?
With a stone
The stone is too dry
Then wet it
With what shall I wet it?
With water
How shall I get it?
In the bucket
There's a hole in the bucket. . . .

Notes:
The February 2, 1968, performance was released on the box set *So Many Roads.*

First performance: January 20, 1968, at the Eureka Municipal Auditorium in Eureka, California. It only appeared twice more in live performance.

Hunter's original lyrics as given to Lesh:

CLEMENTINE
Chopped olive sandwiches
roses, and wine,
cold ripe persimmons
my sweet Clementine

There's a chill in the meadow
of bottomless time
I go on I go on
I cannot fill my cup
theres a hole in the bottom
the spring has dried up

I run through the forests
of linear time,
chop through the branches
and cut through the vines

I'll be back in a moment
though it may take me years

in the lava rock canyons
corroded with fears
of corruptible bodies
and grief beyond tears

I'll go on till I hear
the sweet sweet voices behind
that I've left for the comfort
of cold Clementine

Hunter notes in an email to Alan Trist, 2005:

These are the lyrics I originally gave Phil for Clementine. I'm astounded that I remember this song intact after four decades!

china cat sunflower

1 Look for a while at the China Cat Sunflower
2, 3 proud-walking jingle in the midnight sun
4 Copper-dome Bodhi drip a silver kimono
    like a crazy-quilt star gown
    through a dream night wind

5 Krazy Kat peeking through a lace bandana
6 like a one-eyed Cheshire
    like a diamond-eye Jack
    A leaf of all colors plays
    a golden string fiddle
7 to a double-*e* waterfall over my back

    Comic book colors on a violin river
8 crying Leonardo words
    from out a silk trombone
    I rang a silent bell
9 beneath a shower of pearls
10 in the eagle wing palace
11 of the Queen Chinee

Words by Robert Hunter
Music by Jerry Garcia

1 China Cat
Porcelain cats in sleeping or beckoning postures are works of art in Japan and, to a lesser extent, China. A subset of the art form *kutani,* dating to the seventeenth century, the cats are painted with delicate patterns and very fine brushwork. *Satsuma* porcelain cats, also Japanese in origin, are decorated more whimsically, with an amazing array of colors and patterns.

2 proud-walking jingle
Compare the line in "The Eleven": "Six proud walkers on the jingle-bell rainbow."

3 midnight sun
An oxymoron, though one that is actually applied to arctic regions such as Alaska and Scandinavia (the land of the midnight sun). "So Many Roads" has these lines: "From the land of the midnight sun / where ice blue roses grow. . . ."

4 Bodhi
Sanskrit and Pali: "awakening," "enlightenment"; in Buddhism, the final Enlightenment, which puts an end to the cycle of transmigration and leads to Nirvana, or spiritual release; the experience is comparable to the Satori of Zen Buddhism in Japan. The accomplishment of this "awakening" transformed Siddhartha Gautama into a Buddha (an Awakened One).

The final Enlightenment remains the ultimate ideal of all Buddhists, to be attained by ridding oneself of false beliefs and the hindrance of passions. (*Encyclopedia Britannica*)

5 Krazy Kat

The supreme creation of George Herriman (1880–1944), the *Krazy Kat* comic strip appeared daily from 1913 to the time of its creator's death.

There are many ways to view *Krazy Kat,* and it has been analyzed exhaustively. It has been portrayed as a variation on the eternal triangle of tragic romances; as a grand statement on freedom versus authority; as an allegory on innocence meeting reality; and, of course, as a comic cacophony of obsessions. The strip had a Joycean affinity, especially in its high/low wealth of language. Herriman is supposed to have once responded to these analyses with the astonished reply that he merely drew a comic about a cat and mouse. (Marschall)

6 Cheshire

See note under "Can't Come Down."

7 double-*e*

This is a mystery phrase. I'm coming to think that it actually *originated* with Bob Dylan's 1965 song "It Takes a Lot to Laugh, It Takes a Train to Cry," which includes the line "Don't the brakeman look good, Ma, flaggin' down the double-e" 17 though I previously thought that it really was a type of train, probably standing for the Double Express—therefore, a fast train. Might also be a shortened version of the Double-Ender, defined in *Rail Talk* as "a steam locomotive built to run equally well in either direction. It had two boilers and a central cab and firebox." Double-Ender also exists in hobo slang as "a train with two engines and two cabooses." (Alpert)

See also Warren Zevon's "Poor Pitiful Me," which contains the line "Laid my head on the railroad track, waitin' on the Double E."

Perhaps no other phrase has engendered as much discussion and speculation in the many email messages I've received over the years since first posting *The Annotated Grateful Dead Lyrics* on the web. Ideas run a wide gamut: E. E. Cummings is mentioned (there's even a Cummings painting titled

"Waterfall"!); a guitar chord by the name, played high on the neck of the guitar, are two examples among many.

8 Leonardo words

Leonardo da Vinci wrote in mirror script.

9 pearls

Both pearls and the moon are "symbols of the Buddha-nature inherent in all beings." (Snyder)

According to Pao-chih (418–514),

Why should you look for treasure abroad? Within yourself you have a bright pearl!

(Quoted in Burton Watson's translations of the Cold Mountain poems.)

10 eagle wing palace

Compare Hunter's lyric "Invocation" from the Eagle Mall Suite: "To the Eagle Palace with walls of water we came. . . ."

11 palace of the Queen Chinee

A quote from the Dame Edith Sitwell poem "Trio for Two Cats and a Trombone":

When the phoca has the pica In the palace of the Queen Chinee!

In an interview in *Golden Road,* Hunter said:

"China Cat" took a long time to write. I wrote it in different settings and added this and that to it. It was originally inspired by Dame Edith Sitwell, who had a way with words—I like the idea of quick, clicky assonance and alliteration like "See me dance the polka, said Mr. Wag like a bear, with my top hat and my whiskers, that tra-la-la trapped affair." I just like the way she put things together. I'd have to admit that before you could trace it back that there was some influence. [18]

Notes:

Studio recording: *Aoxomoxoa* (June 20, 1969).

First documented performance: January 17, 1968, at the Carousel Ballroom in San Francisco. An enduring song in the band's repertoire, usually paired with "I Know You Rider" in concert, leading to the designation "China/Rider." Bruce Hornsby sampled the tune's signature lick for his 1998 song "Sunflower Cat (Some Dour Cat) (Down with That)."
In an interview in *Relix*, Hunter said: "I can sit right here and write you a "China Cat" or one of those things in ten minutes. . . . How many of those things do you need . . . ?"

In his *A Box of Rain*, Hunter wrote:

> Nobody ever asked me the meaning of this song. People seem to know exactly what I'm talking about. It's good that a few things in this world are clear to all of us.

Hunter says:

> I think the germ of "China Cat Sunflower" came in Mexico, on Lake Chapala. I don't think any of the words came, exactly—the rhythms came.
>
> I had a cat sitting on my belly, and was in a rather hypersensitive state, and I followed this cat out to—I believe it was Neptune—and there were rainbows across Neptune, and cats marching across the rainbow. This cat took me in all these cat places; there's some essence of that in the song. (Gans: *Conversations*) [19]

The Eleven

1 hat-rack
Rural slang for a bony cow whose hip-bones would protrude sufficiently to hang a hat on.

2 Six proud walkers

See "Green Grow the Rushes, Ho!" (either written by Robert Burns or collected by him—there's a debate going on) for the line "Six for the six proud walkers," echoed as well in "China Cat Sunflower."

I'll sing you one, O
Green grow the rushes, O
What is your one, O?
One is one and all alone and evermore shall
    be so.

I'll sing you two, O
Green grow the rushes, O
Two, two, lily-white boys, clothed all in
    green, O
One is one and all alone and evermore shall
    be so.

Three, three, the rivals . . .
Four for the gospel makers . . .
Five for the symbols at your door . . .
Six for the six proud walkers . . .
Seven for the seven stars in the sky . . .
Eight for the April rainers . . .
Nine for the nine bright shiners . . .
Ten for the Ten Commandments . . .
Eleven for the eleven who went to
    heaven .
Twelve for the twelve Apostles . . .

3 great white sperm whale
Perhaps an allusion to that greatest of all symbols

No more time to tell how
This is the season of what
Now is the time of returning
With thought jewels polished and gleaming

Now is the time past believing
The child has relinquished the reign
Now is the test of the boomerang
Tossed in the night of redeeming

Eight-sided whispering hallelujah hat-rack   1
Seven-faced marble eye transitory dream doll
Six proud walkers on the jingle-bell rainbow   2
Five men writing in fingers of gold
Four men tracking the great white sperm whale   3
Three girls wait in a foreign dominion
Ride in the whale belly   4
Fade away in moonlight
Sink beneath the waters
to the coral sand below
Now is the time of returning

Words by Robert Hunter
Music by Phil Lesh

in American literature, Moby-Dick. Benet has this to say:

> The whale, a symbol too complex for any one defini-
> tion, but perhaps representing knowledge of reality,
> is hunted by Ahab at the cost of his own dehuman-
> ization and the sacrifice of his crew. [20]

4 Ride in the whale belly

Neatly tying the already mentioned symbol of the great white whale to the story of Jonah in the Bible. Chapter 2 of the Book of Jonah "sees Jonah saved from drowning by a 'great fish' and praying to God from its belly. God responds and the fish vomits him out." (*Anchor Bible Dictionary*). [21]

Notes:
Recording: *Live/Dead* (November 10, 1969).

First documented performance: January 17, 1968, at the Carousel Ballroom in San Francisco. After steady inclusion in the live repertoire from 1968 to 1970, "The Eleven" was dropped, to be revived once, at a concert in Golden Gate Park, San Francisco, on September 28, 1975.

The piece is famous among Deadheads as a vehicle for furious jamming in an odd meter, eleven beats to the bar, presenting a unity of title and musical content, though not particularly of lyric content, since Hunter's countdown begins not with eleven, but eight.

Counting songs are a long-standing tradition. Everyone knows "The Twelve Days of Christmas." But how about "Children, Go Where I Send Thee"?

> Children, go where I send thee
> How shall I send thee?
> I'm gonna send thee one by one

> One for the little bitty baby
> That was born, born
> Born in Bethlehem.
> I'm gonna send thee two by two
> Two for Paul and Silas
> Three for the Hebrew children . . .
> Four for the four that stood at the door . . .

And, of course, counting rhymes are a major part of the heritage of nursery rhymes carried on by both Hunter and Barlow. One of the best known is "A Gaping Wide-mouthed Waddling Frog" (a cumulative verse, ending up with the following):

> Twelve huntsmen with horn and hounds,
> Hunting over other men's ground;
> Eleven ships sailing o'er the main,
> Some bound for France and some for Spain;
> Ten comets in the sky,
> Some low and some high;
> Nine peacocks in the air,
> I wonder how they all came there,
> I don't know, nor I don't care;
> Eight joiners in joiner's hall,
> Working with their tools and all;
> Seven lobsters in a dish,
> As fresh as any heart could wish;
> Six beetles against a wall,
> Close by an old woman's apple stall;
> Five puppies by our dog Ball,
> Who daily for their breakfast call;
> Four horses stuck in a bog,
> Three monkeys tied to a clog,
> Two pudding ends would choke a dog,
> With a gaping wide-mouthed waddling frog.

The counting portion of "The Eleven" was originally included by Hunter as part of "China Cat Sunflower."

and we bid you goodnight

Lay down my dear brothers, lay down and take
    your rest
Oh won't you lay your head upon your savior's
    breast
I love you, oh but Jesus loves you the best

Chorus:
And I bid you goodnight, goodnight, good-night
    (3x)
Lay down, my dear brothers, lay down and take
    your rest

Notes:

I first heard this song on the Incredible String
Band's wonderful LP, *The Hangman's Beautiful
Daughter.* (It was tucked into their epic composition, "A Very Cellular Song.") Simultaneously, the
Dead were using the song, sung a capella, to
close many of their late-sixties shows. According
to the String Band's Robin Williamson, who has
been a successful solo performer since his ISB
days, the song likely has its roots in English religious music. He and Heron, though, became
interested in the song after hearing it performed
by the Pindar family on a 1965 Nonesuch album
called *The Real Bahamas,* which was popular in
folk circles. Jenny Pindar was the sister of the
Bahama's greatest arranger and interpreter of
religious songs, guitarist Joseph Spence. This
might explain the slightly Caribbean lilt to the
longer Dead versions of the song (the *Live/Dead*
version contains only a fraction of it), with its
arching vocals and internal rhythms. (Jackson:
Goin' Down the Road) 94

Oh won't you lay your head upon your savior's
    breast
I love you, oh but Jesus loves you the best

(Chorus)

Walking in Jerusalem just like John *(bid you
    goodnight, goodnight)*
I remember right well, I remember right well
    (bid you goodnight, goodnight)
His rod and his staff shall comfort me
    (bid you goodnight, goodnight)
Tell *"A"* for the ark, that wonderful boat
    (bid you goodnight, goodnight)
Tell *"B"* for the beast at the ending of the wood
    (bid you goodnight, goodnight)
Well it eat all the children that would not be good
    (bid you goodnight, goodnight)
I'm walking in Jerusalem just like John
    (bid you goodnight, goodnight)
Walking in the valley of the shadow of death
    (bid you goodnight, goodnight, goodnight)

Lay down, my dear brothers, lay down and take
    your rest
Oh won't you lay your head upon your savior's
    breast
I love you, oh but Jesus love you the best

(Chorus)

    Words and music: traditional
    Arranged by the Grateful Dead

saint stephen

1, 2   Saint Stephen with a rose
In and out of the garden he goes
Country garland in the wind and the rain
Wherever he goes the people all complain

Stephen prosper in his time
Well he may and he may decline
Did it matter? Does it now?
Stephen would answer if he only knew how

Wishing well with a golden bell
3   Bucket hanging clear to Hell
Hell halfway 'twixt now and then

1 Saint Stephen

In an interview published in *Relix,* the following exchange took place:

> Relix: Was St. Stephen anyone specific?
> Hunter: No, it was just St. Stephen.
> Relix: You weren't writing about someone, you were writing about something?
> Hunter: Yea. That was a great song to write.

From the *New Catholic Encyclopedia:* "First deacon and apologist for the Christian faith . . . Stephen (from the Greek for 'crown') was a Hellenist, one of the Greek-speaking Jews of the Diaspora." He was the first ordained by the apostles as one of seven deacons. His story may be found in Acts 6–8. He was stoned to death for preaching that Israel had become more progressively opposed to God's word. He died ca. 34 A.D. and his feast day is December 26.

According to *The Dictionary of Christian Art,* "When held by a martyr, the red rose signified 'red martyrdom,' or the loss of life." However, paintings of St. Stephen usually depict him holding a palm, a censer, or a stone.

There are quite a number of other Saint Stephens. Most notable is Stephen I, King of Hungary (997–August 15, 1038). This Stephen is generally considered the real founder of the state of Hungary. Again, according to the *New Catholic Encyclopedia:* "Stephen was aware that his seminomadic people could survive only if they embraced Christianity. He eliminated all the pagan representatives of the old order with grim determination and quite ruthless methods to achieve this integration into the Christian commonwealth." His feast day is September 2.

Other Saint Stephens:
Stephen I, Pope (ca. 250)
Stephen of Die (1150–1208)
Stephen Harding (died 1134)
Stephen of Muret (ca. 1045–1124)
Stephen of Narbonne (died 1242)

Saint Stephen's Episcopal Church on Belvedere Island, Marin County, California was the site of the memorial service for Jerry Garcia, which was conducted by Matthew Fox. The Grateful Dead also played there in the late 1960s, according to the the Reverand Kathleen Patton, who served at Saint Stephens in the early 1990s. The performance is not documented in *DeadBase.*

2 rose
See note under "That's It for the Other One." The rose, as noted in that entry, takes on special

Stephen fill it up and lower down
   and lower down again

Ladyfinger dipped in moonlight   4
Writing "What for?" across the morning sky
Sunlight splatters dawn with answers
Darkness shrugs and bids the day good-bye

Speeding arrow, sharp and narrow
What a lot of fleeting matters you have spurned
Several seasons with their treasons
Wrap the babe in scarlet covers, call it your own   5

Did he doubt or did he try?
Answers aplenty in the bye and bye
Talk about your plenty, talk about your ills
One man gathers what another man spills   6

Saint Stephen will remain
All he's lost he shall regain
Seashore washed by the suds and the foam
Been here so long he's got to calling it home

Fortune comes a-crawling, Calliope woman   7
Spinning that curious sense of your own
Can you answer? Yes I can
But what would be the answer to the answer man?   8

High green chilly winds and windy vines in
loops around the
twining shafts of lavender,
   they're crawling to the sun

Underfoot the ground is patched with climbing
   arms of ivy

9 *wrapped around the manzanita, stark and shiny in*
         the breeze

   Wonder who will water all the children of the
         garden when they
   sigh about the barren lack of rain and droop
         so hungry 'neath the sky . . .

10 *William Tell has stretched his bow till it won't*
         stretch no
   furthermore and/or it may require a
         change that hasn't come
   before

                    Words by Robert Hunter
                    Music by Jerry Garcia; coda music by Phil Lesh

significance when held by a martyr such as Saint Stephen.

3 Bucket hanging clear to Hell . . .
A version of the ballad "The False Knight upon the Road" (Sharp, #2) contains the line: "I think I hear a bell. Yes, and it's ringing you to hell."

Compare also "Hell in a Bucket."

4 Ladyfinger
This has two associations (at least):
1. Simply a woman's finger.
2. A pastry called a ladyfinger. Here's a recipe:

LADY FINGERS
About 30 small cakes
Preheat oven to 375 degrees.
Have ingredients at about 75 degrees. Sift before measuring:
1/3 cup cake flour
Resift it 3 times. Sift:
1/3 cup confectioners' sugar
Beat until thick and lemon colored:
1 whole egg
2 egg yolks
Whip until stiff, but not dry:
2 egg whites
Fold the sugar gradually into the egg whites. Beat the mixture until it thickens again. Fold in the egg yolk mixture and:
1/4 teaspoon vanilla
Fold in the flour. Shape the dough into oblongs with a paper tube, on ungreased paper placed in a pan; or pour it into greased ladyfinger or small muffin tins. Bake

for about 12 minutes. *(The Joy of Cooking)*

Also the British word for okra, the vegetable *(Abelmoschus esculentus).* Hmm.

5 Wrap the babe in scarlet covers
A version of the ballad "The Cruel Mother" (Sharp, #10, version D) contains the line "O baby, O baby, if you were mine, . . . I would dress you in the scarlet so fine."

6 what another man spills
The line was used as the title of a 1998 CD by Lambchop.

7 Calliope woman
Calliope is "the Muse of epic poetry, and chief of the Muses. She was the mother of Orpheus by Apollo or King Oeagrus." (Benet) 22 She was also the muse of playing on stringed instruments.

A calliope is also a keyboard instrument, usually associated with the sound of circuses and carousels. The calliope is an American invention, attributed to Joshua C. Stoddard of Worcester, Massachusetts, who filed a patent to produce the instrument in 1855. Calliopes were also extensively mounted on showboats. The number of whistles on a calliope ranges from as few as 13 to as many as 588, and can be heard as far away as eight miles. The musical instrument is also mentioned in "Cosmic Charlie" and "The Music Never Stopped."

8 the answer man
The name of a radio show that went on the air in 1937. Listeners wrote in with their questions, and the "Answer Man," played by Albert Mitchell, with help from up to forty researchers, answered their questions on the air f or over fifteen years. The show's headquarters was right across the street from the New York Public Library, a perfect location for finding the answer to virtually any question.

9 manzanita
Aractostaphylos, shrub native to California with about forty-three species. Its bark is just as described in the song, with a deep reddish hue. Its berry fruit was prized by indigenous Californians and used for a variety of purposes ranging from cider and lotion (to treat poison oak) to a drink for headache.

10 William Tell
The story of the Swiss peasant who defied authority by refusing to remove his hat in the presence of the Austrian king supposedly dates from the early fourteenth century. He was forced, as punishment for his insubordination, to shoot an apple from his son's head. His subsequent escape from prison and assassination of the governor incited the Swiss people to rise up against Austrian rule.

Notes:
Studio recording: *Aoxomoxoa* (June 20, 1969).

First documented performance: May 24, 1968, at the National Guard Armory in St. Louis. In the repertoire steadily through 1971; reappeared from 1976 to 1979, then dropped again and brought back for three performances in 1983.

NOT Fade Away

I wanna tell you how it's gonna be
You're gonna give your love to me
I wanna love you night and day
You know our lovin' not fade away
You know our lovin' not fade away
Not fade away

My love is bigger than a Cadillac
I try to show you but you drive me back
Your love for me has gotta be real
You're gonna know just how I feel
A love that's real not fade away
Not fade away

Words and music by Norman Petty
and Buddy Holly

Notes:

Recording: *Grateful Dead* (Skull & Roses) (October 1971).

First documented performance: June 19, 1968, at the Carousel Ballroom in San Francisco. A steady song in the repertoire thereafter.

A true rock classic, this was cowritten by Buddy Holly and his producer-manager Norman Petty in 1957 as the flip side of "Oh, Boy!" for the Coral label. Holly died in a plane crash less than two years later, but his songs continue to be covered by countless rock artists. "Not Fade Away" was the Stones' first American chart hit, in 1964, and it appeared on two Stones albums during that era. (Jackson: *Goin' Down the Road*.) 94

cosmic charLie

1 Truckin'

A popular dance step of the 1920s and '30s. *Step It Down* has a section on the Zudie-O, a dance which incorporated *trucking*:

> You better say "strutting" instead of "trucking." They're about the same, but the old folks just didn't like you to say it so raw.

and later, describing the step:

> The step used in this dance also takes the same count and is a "strutting" two-step: Step forward with the right foot, bring the left foot up to a close, step in place with the right foot, and rest. Repeat with the opposite feet. (Jones, Bessie)

The Oxford English Dictionary cites many different meanings for *truck* and *trucking.* One shade has *truck* as rhyming slang for sexual intercourse, which may explain the statement above about *trucking* being too raw a word for the "old folks." And regarding the dance:

> 5. To dance the truck. *U.S. slang.* 1937 *Amer. Speech* XII. 183/1 Only Negroes can really truck.

and

> trucking 2. The action of dancing the truck. *slang.* 1944 C. CALLOWAY *Hepster's Dictionary* in *Of Minnie the Moocher* (1976) 260 *Trucking,* a dance introduced at the Cotton Club in 1933.

The *OED* also recognizes the phrase "Keep on trucking":

> to persevere: a phrase of encouragement. 1972. Sat. Rev. (U.S.) 28 Oct. 12 One poster . . . shows the famous R. Crumb cartoon characters and bears the caption: "Let's Keep on Truckin."

Cosmic Charlie, how do you do?
Truckin' in style along the avenue   1
Dumdeedumdee doodley doo
Go on home, your mama's calling you

Calico Kahlia, come tell me the news   2
Calamity's waiting for a way to get to her
Rosy red and electric blue
I bought you a paddle for your paper canoe

Say you'll come back when you can
Whenever your airplane happens to land
Maybe I'll be back here, too
It all depends on what's with you

Hung up waiting for a windy day
Kite on ice since the first of February

Mama Bee saying
     that the wind
     might blow
But standin' here I say
     I just don't know

New ones comin' as
     the old ones go

Everything's movin' here
     but much too slowly
Little bit quicker and we might have time to say,
     "How do you do?" before we're left behind
Calliope wail like a seaside zoo   3, 4
The very last lately inquired about you
It's really very one or two
The first you wanted, the last I knew

I just wonder if you shouldn't feel
less concern about the deep unreal
The very first word is: How do you do?
The last: Go home, your mama's calling you

Go on home
Your mama's calling you
Calling you . . .

Words by Robert Hunter
Music by Jerry Garcia

The New Grove Dictionary of American Music describes "Truckin'" as a dance step that was incorporated into the "lively and strenuous circle dance" the Big Apple. It describes the truckin' step, "with its shuffle step and waving index finger."

2 Calico
Calico is one of the oldest textiles known. Originally, calico came from Calcutta, a seaport in southwest Madras, India, from whence

it derives its name. It is known that Vasco da Gama brought calico, then called *pintadores,* to Europe from India about 1497.

> Calico was executed in a plain weave of carded cotton, printed by the resist method. . . . Naturalistic motifs were a favorite, and were done with polychrome effects. The designs were usually very small. (Jerde)

The calico referred to by Hunter in this line, however, is much more likely to be a reference to a type of cat. Generally, *calico,* in relation to animals, refers to a pattern of colorization similar to that of printed calico cloth.

Calico, one of the original Hog Farmers (along with Wavy Gravy), has been with Grateful Dead Ticket Sales "forever."

3 Calliope
See note under "Saint Stephen."

4 seaside zoo
There is a "seaside zoo" in San Francisco, the San Francisco Zoo on Sloat Boulevard at 45th Avenue. The zoo has a carousel. There's also an old carousel in Golden Gate Park, just north of Kezar Stadium; a very loud calliope plays while the carousel runs. The carousel in Golden Gate Park is big, old, and ornate, with many mirrors.

Notes:
Studio recording: *Aoxomoxoa* (June 20, 1969).

First verified performance: October 19, 1968, at the Matrix in San Francisco. The Dead revived the song in the post-Garcia era. Hunter titles this song "Cosmic Charley" in *A Box of Rain.*

1 Rosemary *Rosmarinus officinalis.* Alice Coats, in *Flowers and Their Histories,* calls rosemary the "herb of herbs: beloved above all, associated with innumberable legends and traditions, and put to a hundred uses." Among these innumerable legends and traditions is that of "rosemary for remembrance" and "therefore to friendship," according to Sir Thomas More. Other traditions include use in burials (in England, sprigs of rosemary were thrown into graves into the 1800s) and weddings (brides and grooms both carried it). *Ros marinus* means "dew of the sea" because it is supposed to grow best when the sound of the ocean is near.

Gabriele Tergit, in her *Flowers Through the Ages,* also has quite a bit to say about rosemary:

> To wake the Sleeping Beauty, she had to be touched by rosemary, a plant of many legends and ancient beliefs, and of many uses—curative, ornamental, culinary, as a love potion and a symbol of mourning.

and

> During the seventeenth and eighteenth centuries rosemary became also the flower of mourning. "I dreamed this night a dismal dream / Rosemary grew in my garden . . . " says a German folk song.
>
> "There's rosemary, that's for remembrance," said Ophelia in Shakespeare's

Boots were of leather
A breath of cologne 2
Her mirror was a window
She sat quite alone

All around her
the garden grew
scarlet and purple
and crimson and blue

She came and she went
and at last went away
The garden was sealed 3
when the flowers decayed

On the wall of the garden
a legend did say:
No one may come here
since no one may stay

Words by Robert Hunter
Music by Jerry Garcia

Hamlet, and it may be surmised that rosemary was placed on her grave. [23]

P. S. Also the name of my wonderful daughter.

2 cologne

Again, to cite Gabriele Tergit:

> Eau de cologne is probably the most popular toilet water of the world. It seems likely that it was invented at Cologne in 1709 by Johann Maria Farina, an Italian immigrant. Others say that it was invented by a Paul de Feminis, who imported the process of its manufacture from Milan in 1690. Many people named Farina have since come to Cologne, bringing with them the right to use the authentic name. . . . The ingredients were strictly secret. [24]

3 garden was sealed

Compare *The Secret Garden* (by Francis Hodgson Burnett, 1849–1924), in which the garden in the book is sealed because children no longer play in it and it therefore falls into decay.

Notes:
Studio recording: *Aoxomoxoa* (June 20, 1969).

Never played live, as far as we know. But the song listed in *DeadBase* as "unknown: Garcia singing" at the December 7, 1968, performance at Bellarmine College, Louisville, Kentucky, may have been "Rosemary," according to some sources.

DUPREE'S DIAMOND BLUES

Jelly roll is African American slang for the female genitals.

"Jelly Roll Blues" was written by Ferdinand "Jelly Roll" Morton, the great jazz composer-pianist of the 1920s, and recorded by an all-star roster of jazz musicians over the years, from Louis Armstrong to Sidney Bechet and Bunny Berrigan.

Notes:
Studio recording: *Aoxomoxoa* (June 20, 1969).

First documented performance: February 11, 1969, at the Fillmore East in New York. After 1969, dropped from the repertoire until the late seventies, when it made a brief reappearance; then brought back in 1982 for the duration of the decade.

The text of the song is a reworking of the song "Betty and Dupree," with many incarnations in American folk tradition. It was based on a true incident:

> The biography of the man and his crimes may be summarized as follows: Frank Dupree grew up in Abbeville, South Carolina. He came on the scene in December 1921 in Atlanta, Georgia, where he had a gal Betty. In trying to appropriate a diamond for her in a jewelry store, he shot a policeman down. Fleeing to Memphis and later to Chicago, where he was cornered, he killed a policeman and wounded several more. He was caught while getting his mail and sent to Atlanta for trial. He was executed for murder on September 1, 1922. (Roberts)

Here are two versions of the song:

> BETTY AND DUPREE
> Dupree was settin' in a hotel,

When I was just a little young boy,
Papa said "Son, you'll never get far,
I'll tell you the reason if you want to know,
'cause, child of mine, there isn't really very
    far to go"

Well, baby, baby wants a gold diamond ring
Wants it more than most any old thing
Well when I get those jelly roll blues   1
Why, I'd go and get anything in this world
    for you.

Down to the jewelry store packing a gun,
says, "Wrap it up. I think I'll take this one."
"A thousand dollars, please," the jewelry man said
Dupree, he said, "I'll pay this one off to you
    in lead"

Chorus:
Well, you know, son, you just can't figure,
First thing you know you're gonna pull that
    trigger
    and it's no wonder your reason goes
    bad—
    jelly roll will drive you stone mad
Judge said, "Son, this gonna cost you some time"
Dupree said, "Judge, you know that crossed
    my mind"
Judge said, "Fact, it's gonna cost you your life"
Dupree said, "Judge, you know that seems to
    me to be about right"

Well, baby, baby's gonna lose her sweet man

Dupree come out with a losing hand
Baby's gonna weep it up for a while
then go on out
and find another sweet man's
    gonna treat her with style

Judge said, "Son, I know your baby well
but that's a secret I can't never tell"
Dupree said, "Judge, well it's well understood,
and you got to admit that that sweet, sweet jelly's
    so good"

(Chorus)

Same old story and I know it's been told,
some like jelly-jelly—some like gold
Many a man's done a terrible thing
just to get baby that shiny diamond ring

Words by Robert Hunter
Music by Jerry Garcia

Wasn't thinkin' 'bout a doggone thing,
Settin' in a hotel,
Wasn't thinkin' 'bout a doggone thing.
Betty said to Dupree,
I want a diamond ring.

Dupree went to town
With a .45 in his hand.
He went to town with a .45 in
    his hand.
He went after jewelry—
But he got the jewelry man.

Dupree went to Betty cryin',
Betty, here is your diamond ring.
He went to Betty cryin'
Here is your diamond ring.
Take it and wear it, Betty,
'Cause I'm bound for cold old cold
    Sing Sing.

Then he called a taxi
Cryin', drive me to Tennessee.
Taxi, taxi, taxi,
Drive me to Tennessee.
He said, drive me, bubber,
'Cause the dicks is after me.

He went to the post office
To get his evenin' mail.

Went to the general
    delivery
To get his evenin' mail.
They caught poor
Dupree, lordy,
Put him in Nashville
    Jail.

Dupree said to the judge,
Lord,
I ain't been here
    before.
Lord, Lord, Lord,
    Judge,

I ain't been here before.
Judge said, I'm gonna break your neck, Dupree,
So you can't come here no more.

Betty weeped, Betty moaned
Till she broke out with sweat.
Betty weeped and she moaned
Till she broke out with sweat.
Said she moaned and she weeped
Till her clothes got soppin' wet.

Betty brought him coffee,
Betty brought him tea.
Betty brought him coffee,
Also brought him tea.
She brought him all he needed
'Cept that big old jailhouse key.

[Note relationship to "Don't Ease Me In"]

Dupree said, it's whiskey I crave,
Bring me flowers to my grave.
It's whiskey I crave.
Bring flowers to my grave.
That little ole Betty's
Done made me her doggone slave.

It was early one mornin'
Just about the break o' day,
Early, early one morning'
Just about break o' day,
They had him testifyin'
And this is what folks heard him say:

Give my pappy my clothes,
Oh, give poor Betty my shoes.
Give pappy my clothes,
And give poor Betty my shoes.
And if anybody asks you,
Tell 'em I died with the heartbreakin' blues.

They lead him to the scaffold
With a black cap over his face.
Lead him up to the scaffold,
Black cap over his face.
Some ole lonesome graveyard's

Poor Dupree's restin' place.

The choir followed him
Singin' "Nearer My God to Thee."
The choir followed him,
"Nearer My God to Thee."
Poor Betty, she was cryin'
Have mercy on Dupree!

[Note relationship to "Stagger Lee"]

Sail on! Sail on!
Sail on, Dupree, sail on!
Sail on! Sail on!
Sail on, sail on, sail on!
I don't mind you sailin'
But you'll be gone so doggone long!
(Courlander)

DUPREE

Dupree was a bandit,
He was so brave and bol',
He stoled a diamond ring
For some of Betty's jelly roll.

Betty tol' Dupree,
"I want a diamond ring."
Dupree tol' Betty,
"I'll give you anything."

"Michigan water
Taste like cherry wine,
The reason I know:
Betty drink it all the time.

"I'm going away
To the end of the railroad track.
Nothing but sweet Betty
Can bring me back."

Dupree tol' the lawyer,
"Clear me if you can,
For I have money to back me,
Sure as I'm a man."

The lawyer tol' Dupree,

"You are a very brave man,
But I think you will
Go to jail and hang."

Dupree tol' the judge,
"I am not so brave and bol',
But all I wanted
Was Betty's jelly roll."

The judge tol' Dupree,
"Jelly roll's gonna be your ruin."
"No, no judge, for that is
What I've done quit doin'."

The judge tol' Dupree,

"I believe you quit too late,
Because it is
Already your fate."
(Odum)

Jazz Anecdotes by Bill Crow mentions a swing-band era jazz musician named Reese Dupree who penned a tune called "Dupree's Blues" (he also wrote the song "Shortnin' Bread"). As an added bonus, the anecdote in Crow's book also mentions Dupree in connection with Jelly Roll Morton, the great jazz composer-pianist of the 1920s. Morton, of course, penned the classic jazz instrumental "Jelly Roll Blues."

mountains of the moon

1 Cold mountain

Gary Snyder, in *The Evergreen Review,* no. 6, 1958, published his translations of seventh-century Chinese poet Han-Shan. According to Snyder,

> Kanzan, or Han-shan, "Cold Mountain" takes his name from where he lived. He is a mountain madman in an old Chinese line of ragged hermits. When he talks about Cold Mountain he means himself, his home, his state of mind. He lived in the Tang dynasty—traditionally A.D. 627–650.

Snyder's translations reveal a mind speaking to us from the dim past with words that ring remarkably fresh today. Here's one that seems particularly pertinent:

> Spring-water in the green creek is clear
> Moonlight on Cold Mountain is white
> Silent knowledge—the spirit is enlightened
>   of itself
> Contemplate the void: this world exceeds
>   stillness.

2 jade merchant's daughter

Compare the title of Sharp, #64: "The Silk Merchant's Daughter," one of those ballads, like "Jack-a-Roe," (aka "Jack the Sailor"), in which a woman disguises herself as a man in order to go find her true love.

3 Mountains of the Moon

The popular name deriving from Ptolemy (second century A.D.), who thought them the source of the Nile River, for an actual region of Central Africa, the Ruwenzori mountains, bordering Uganda and the Democratic Republic of Congo.

Additionally, it is interesting to note that one of the most celebrated expeditions to the Mountains of the Moon was undertaken by none other than Sir Richard Francis Burton (1821–90),

Cold mountain water	1
the jade merchant's daughter	2
Mountains of the Moon, Electra,	3, 4
Bow and bend to me	5
Hi-ho the Carrion Crow	6
Folderolderiddle	
Hi-ho the Carrion Crow	
Bow and bend to me	
Hey, Tom Banjo	7
Hey, a laurel	8
More than laurel	
You may sow	
More than laurel	
You may sow	
Hey, the laurel	
Hey, the city	
In the rain	
Hey, hey,	
Hey, the white wheat	
Wavin' in the wind	
Twenty degrees of solitude	
Twenty degrees in all	
All the dancing kings and wives	
Assembled in the hall	
Lost is a long and lonely time	
Fairy Sybil flying	9
All along the	
All along the	
Mountains of the Moon	

Hey, Tom Banjo
It's time to matter
The Earth will see you
on through this time
The Earth will see you
on through this time
Down by the water

10, 11 The Marsh King's Daughter
Did you know?
Clothed in tatters
Always will be
Tom, where did you go?

Mountains of the Moon, Electra
Mountains of the Moon
All along the
All along the
Mountains of the Moon

Hi-ho the Carrion Crow
Folderolderiddle
Hi-ho the Carrion Crow
Bow and bend to me
Bend to me

Words by Robert Hunter
Music by Jerry Garcia

in 1858, in search of the source of the Nile.
(Cold Mountain water?) Burton also translated
the *Arabian Nights* collection, which is indirectly
mentioned in "What's Become of the Baby" and
in "Blues for Allah."

Edgar Allan Poe also mentions the "Mountains of
the Moon" in his poem "Eldorado" (1849):

Gaily bedight,
A gallant knight,
In sunshine and in shadow,
Had journeyed long,
Singing a song,
In search of Eldorado.
But he grew old—
This knight so bold—
And o'er his heart a shadow
Fell as he found
No spot of ground
That looked like Eldorado.
And, as his strength
Failed him at length,
He met a pilgrim shadow—
"Shadow," said he,
"Where can it be—
This land of Eldorado?"
"Over the Mountains
Of the Moon,
Down the Valley of the Shadow,
Ride, boldly ride,"
The shade replied,—
"If you seek for Eldorado."

The mountains also appear in Hunter's "Lay of
the Ring" from the "Eagle Mall Suite":

From the gates of Numinor
to the walls of Valentine
It's seven cold dimensions
past the Mountains of the Moon

4 Electra

It's unclear whether Hunter is naming the jade merchant's daughter or simply invoking the spirit of Electra. The name could refer to either (1) the daughter, in Greek mythology, of Agamemnon and Clytemnestra, who kills her mother with the aid of her brother, Orestes, to avenge the murder of her father; or (2) one of the Pleiades, daughters of Atlas, and the mother of Dardanus.

5 Bow and bend to me

This line, in a number of variations, is used as a refrain in the ballad "The Two Sisters" (Child #10; Sharp, #5). Bronson writes:

> This ballad is still in active traditional life, especially in those regions of the USA where the "play-party" dancing custom has persisted. In many variants the words of the refrain affirm the association.

Some of the variants found in Bronson and Sharp:

> Bow it's been to me
> The bough has bent to me
> Bow and balance to me
> The bough has been to me
> The boughs they bent to me
> The boughs were given to me
> The boys are bound for me
> The vows she made to me
> And thou hast bent to me

Of these variants, one is of particular note: "Bow and balance to me," because it is a dance step, and the Hunter lyric seems to be speaking of "kings and wives" assembling for a dance.

The balance is described as follows in the *Country Dance Book:*

> Balance Partners: Partners face each other, then each step to the side with right foot, point toe of left foot in front, step back to place with left and point toe of right foot in front of left foot.

You may see this step executed at the start of almost every dance at any contra dance in the United States today, and it is a very courtly step, lending the dance an air of chivalry.

6 Hi-ho the Carrion Crow / Folderoldriddle

This line is directly from an old nursery rhyme/ballad:

> As early as 1796 it ["The Carrion Crow"] was published as a ballad with the refrain: "With a heigh ho! the carrion crow! / Sing tol de rol, de riddle row!" *(The Annotated Mother Goose)*

Sharp lists the ballad as #222, "The Carrion Crow." It's a nonsense tune, with lines like: "Carrion crow sitting on an oak, with a ling dong dilly dol kiro me."

The crow appears in two other Hunter lyrics, "Uncle John's Band" and "Corrina." The "bird of paradise" mentioned in "Blues for Allah" is also known as a "paradise crow."

The carrion crow *(Corvus corone corone)* is found in Western Europe and eastern Asia.

7 Tom Banjo

If Uncle John is John Cohen, mightn't Tom Banjo be a reference to Tom Paley, who played banjo with the New Lost City Ramblers? Like "Uncle John's Band," "Mountains of the Moon" contains references to folk songs that the NLCR played or would have known about.

Or, possibly, a reference to Tom "Tom Banjo" Azarian, who now lives and sometimes performs around Burlington, Vermont. Azarian grew up in West Springfield,

Massachusetts, and was one of the best-known banjo players in that part of New England during the late 1950s through the 1970s. He's used the performing moniker Tom Banjo for a long time.

8 laurel
A wreath of laurel is a symbol of victory in battle.

9 Fairy Sybil
Benet says: "A prophetess of classical legend, who was supposed to prophesy under the inspiration of a particular deity. The name is now applied to any prophetess or woman fortune teller." 25

10 Marsh King
Nickname for Alfred the Great (849–899), King of England, 871–899. So named for his act of raising an army to defeat the invading Danes from the stronghold of the impenetrable British marshes, or Fens (Fennario?—see note under "Dire Wolf"). He is the only British monarch to have earned the designation "the Great." His name means, literally, "adviser to the elves." He had at least three daughters, all of whom hold significant places in English history:

> Ethelflaed, his eldest daughter, who married her father's friend Ethelred. After Ethelred died, she ruled Mercia, a province of Britain, and is known to history as the Lady of the Mercians.
> Aelfthryth, married to Baldwin, Count of Flanders.
> Ethelgifu, who became a nun and then abbess of a convent at Shaftesbury in Dorsetshire.

11 Marsh King's Daughter
This note (via email) from Hunter:

> "The Marsh King's Daughter" is a character in a fairy tale of the same name by Hans Christian Andersen. I just wanted to say that." 26

Notes:
Studio recording: *Aoxomoxoa* (June 20, 1969).

First documented performance: December 20, 1968, at the Shrine Exhibition Hall in Los Angeles. Revived by the Other Ones, Phil and Friends, and performed regularly by The Dead.

doin' that rag

1 Mangrove
The mangrove is a species of tree (families *Rhizophoraceae, Verbenaceae, Sonneratiaceae,* and *Arecaceae*) growing in marshes or along tidal estuaries in dense clumps, with roots that are exposed.

2 Hipsters
African American slang dating from the 1930s and '40s, denoting a person who is in the know, or hip. The word found its way into white American slang in the 1950s and '60s.

3 wade in the water
"Wade in the Water" is an American gospel tune:

> Wade in the water
> Wade in the water
> Children wade in the water
> God's gonna trouble the water
>
> Who's that young girl dressed in red?
> Wade in the water
> Must be the children that Moses led
> God's gonna trouble the water
>
> Wade in the water, wade in the water, children
> Wade in the water,
> God's gonna trouble the water
>
> Who's that young girl dressed in white?
> Wade in the water
> Must be the children of the Israelite
> Oh, God's gonna trouble the water
>
> Who's that young girl dressed in blue?
> Wade in the water
> Must be the children that's coming through
> God's gonna trouble the water, yeah
>
> You don't believe I've been redeemed
> Wade in the water
> Just so the whole lake goes looking for me
> God's gonna trouble the water

Sitting in Mangrove Valley chasing light beams   1
Everything wanders from baby to Z
Baby, baby, pretty, young on Tuesday
Old like a rum drinking demon at tea

Baby, baby, tell me what's the matter
Why, why tell me, what's your why now?
Tell me why will you never come home?
Tell me what's your reason if you got a good one

Everywhere I go
The people all know
Everyone's doin' that rag

Take my line go fishing for a Tuesday
Maybe take my supper, eat it down by the sea
Gave my baby twenty, forty good reasons
Couldn't find any better ones in the morning
   at three

Rain gonna come but the rain gonna go, you know
Stepping off sharply from the rank and file
Awful cold and dark like a dungeon
Maybe get a little bit darker 'fore the day

Hipsters, tripsters,   2
real cool chicks, sir,
everyone's doin' that rag

You needn't gild the lily, offer jewels to the sunset
No one is watching or standing in your shoes
Wash your lonely feet in the river in the morning
Everything promised is delivered to you

Don't neglect to pick up what your share is
All the winter birds are winging home now
Hey Love, go and look around you
Nothing out there you haven't seen before now

3   But you can wade in the water
    and never get wet
    if you keep on doin' that rag

4   One-eyed jacks and the deuces are wild
    The aces are crawling up and down your sleeve
    Come back here, Baby Louise,
    and tell me the name
    of the game that you play

    Is it all fall down?
    Is it all go under?
    Is it all fall down, down, down

5   Is it all go under?

    Everywhere I go
    the people all know
    everybody's doin' that rag

                Words by Robert Hunter
                Music by Jerry Garcia

According to a study of the meaning of African American spirituals, *Wade in the Water:*

> An example of a song composed for one purpose but used secretly for other, masked purposes is the familiar spiritual "Wade in the Water." This song was created to accompany the rite of baptism, but Harriet Tubman used it to communicate to fugitives escaping to the North that they should be sure to "wade in the water" in order to throw bloodhounds off their scent.

and later in the same book:

> In commenting on different versions of this song ["Wade in the Water"], observers have noted that it was sung in encouragement and celebration of the spirit of Africans in bondage as they participated in the Christian rite of baptism by immersion. However, these "Christian" baptismal ceremonies frequently served as a mask for a more traditional West African religious ceremony in which a tall cross, driven by a deacon into the river bottom, served as a bridge facilitating communication between the worlds of the living and the dead. In addition, the cross placed in the water in this manner also symbolized the four corners of the earth and the four winds of heaven. When the cross was utilized in this way by enslaved African worshipers, it was as if the sun in its orbit was mirrored, revealing the fullness of the Bakongo religion. And since those who lived a good life might experience rebirth in generations of grandchildren, the cycle of death and rebirth could hardly have been more suggestive than through the staff-cross—a symbol of communal renewal. (Jones) 27

Also the title of a folk song, with the lines:

> She waded in the water
> And she got her feet all wet.
> But she didn't get her (clap, clap) wet, yet

4 One-eyed jacks
The jacks of hearts
and spades are
one-eyed; the jack
of diamonds and
clubs each have
two eyes.

**5 Is it all fall
down? / Is it all
go under?**
From a children's rhyme, which, according to *The
Annotated Mother Goose,* is not really all that old, dating
back to Kate Greenaway's 1881 *Mother Goose.* So much
for all the theories claiming that the song refers to the
Black Death. It's basically a ring dance, where all the kids
get to "dance and shake their bones" and fall down at
the end. No heavy subtext.

There are many variations on the rhyme
(interesting or unbelievable that they all should have
developed since the 1880s.) Here are a few:

> Ring-a-ring-r-roses,
> A pocket full of posies;
> Hush! Hush! Hush! Hush!
> We've all tumbled down.
> *(The Annotated Mother Goose)*

> Ring-a-ring o' roses,
> A pocket full of posies
> A-tishoo! A-tishoo!
> We all fall down.
> The cows are in the meadow
> Lying fast asleep,
> A-tishoo! A-tishoo!

> We all get up again.
> *(The Oxford Nursery Rhyme Book)*

> A ring, a ring o' roses,
> A pocket full of posies,
> Ash-a! Ash-a!
> All stand still.
> The king has sent his daughter
> To fetch a pail of water,
> Ash-a! Ash-a!
> All bow down.
> The bird upon the steeple
> Sits high above the people,
> Ash-a! Ash-a!
> All kneel down.
> The wedding bells are ringing,
> The boys and girls are singing,
> Ash-a! Ash-a!
> All fall down.
> *(The Oxford Nursery Rhyme Book)*

And the way I remember from childhood:

> Ring a ring a rosies,
> Pocket full of posies,
> Ashes! Ashes!
> All fall down!

Played as a game in a swimming pool, the final line
"All go under" takes the place of "All fall down."

Notes:
Studio recording: *Aoxomoxoa* (June 20, 1969).

First documented performance: January 24, 1969.
Dropped from the repertoire after 1969.

Quite a few songs in American popular music have
had titles similar to this one:

> "Doin' the Ducky Wuck" (1935); words and
> music by Joe Penner and Hal Raynor.
> "Doin' the New Low-Down" (1928); words by
> Dorothy Fields, music by Jimmy McHugh.

"Doin' the Raccoon" (1928); words by Raymond Klages, music by J. Fred Coots.
"Doin' the Uptown Lowdown" (1933); words by Mack Gordon, music by Harry Revel.
"Doin' What Comes Naturally" (1946); words and music by Irving Berlin.

And the most closely allied lyric is Irving Berlin's 1911 hit, "Everybody's Doing It Now":

Ev'rybody's doin' it, doin' it, doin' it;
Ev'rybody's doin' it, doin, it, doin' it.
See that ragtime couple over there,
Watch them throw their shoulder in the air,
Snap their finger, honey, I declare,
It's a bear, it's a bear, it's a bear, there!

- COOK -

dire wolf

1 Fennario

Mentioned in the folk song "The Bonnie Lass of Fenario" (variously titled "Peggy-O," "Fennario," "The Bonnie Lass of Fyvie-O," "Pretty Peggy-O," "Pretty Peggy of Derby," etc.). The relevant line is "As we marched down to Fenario," which in turn is spelled variously as "Fernario," "Finario," "Fennario," "Finerio," etc.

The question becomes, is this really a place? I've seen the question posed and debated, usually

In the timbers of Fennario   1
the wolves are running 'round
The winter was so hard and cold
froze ten feet 'neath the ground

Chorus:
Don't murder me   2
I beg of you, don't murder me
Please
don't murder me

I sat down to my supper
'Twas a bottle of red whiskey   3

I said my prayers and went to bed
That's the last they saw of me

(*Chorus*)

4 When I awoke the Dire Wolf
Six hundred pounds of sin
Was grinning at my window
All I said was "Come on in"

(*Chorus*)

5 The wolf came in, I got my cards
We sat down for a game

6 I cut my deck to the queen of spades
but the cards were all the same

(*Chorus*)

In the backwash of Fennario
The black and bloody mire
The Dire Wolf collects his due
while the boys sing round the fire

(*Chorus*)

Words by Robert Hunter
Music by Jerry Garcia

facetiously, on many a Grateful Dead conference and email exchange, but no one has yet come up with anything approaching a definitive answer. So, in the absence of the definitive, I'm going to go out on a limb and propose a theoretical answer. This answer lies within the realm of "folk etymology," since I am not a trained etymologist. "Fennario" seems related to the word *fen,* defined by the *Oxford English Dictionary* as

Low land covered wholly or partially with shallow water, or subject to frequent inundations; a tract of such land, a marsh . . . esp. *the fens:* certain low-lying districts in Cambridgeshire, Lincolnshire, and some adjoining counties.

Combining this root with the suffix *-ario* could indicate "in the general vicinity," i.e., area of the Fens.

Hunter uses the word *fens* in another lyric, which seems to lend support to the identification of "Fennario" as a district of marshy lands; namely in the "Ivory Wheels/Rosewood Track" lyric of the *Terrapin* suite as performed by Hunter himself:

The demon's daughter used to lay for
  gin
In a shack way back on the skirts of the fens
Of Terrapin.

And marshes appear elsewhere in Hunter's lyrics as well: the Mangrove Valley and Marsh King's Daughter of "Mountains of the Moon."

So Hunter's "Fennario" is a rural, wooded, marshy region of the imagination, which bears no particular relation to the actual geographic "Fenario" referred to in the "Peggy-O" folk song lyric and its variants. (Child, in his *English and Scottish Popular Ballads,* places the "Peggy" ballads within the tradition of ballads gathered under #299: "Trooper and Maid." Sharp, in his *English Folk Songs from the Southern Appalachians,* names the collection of tunes gathered under #95: "Pretty Peggy-O.")

David Gans interviewed Alan Trist on KPFA in June 1990, and the following exchange took place:

Gans: Maybe you can tell us if there's a place called Fennario—and if so, where and what?

Trist: Well, David, I was able to find the answer to that question. If you're a songwriter and you need a word, you might refer to Alan Lomax's *Song Archivist,* and there he suggests that *Fennario* is a perfect place-name, if you need a generic name for an indeterminate place, because it has four syllables: fen-na-ri-o. If you a need a three-syllable place-name, you might use "Fyvie-O." So Fennario is a place in the imagination. The syllabic imagination, perhaps.

Gans: I was hoping there was some history to it.

Trist: [*Laughs*] You were hoping it was a real place that had a lot attached to it. Well, I think you can attach those things to it yourself. It's a very evocative name. 28

2 Don't murder me
Compare the folk song "I'm All Out an' Down":

> Doncha murder me,
> Please, baby,
> Don' murder me.

Garcia:

> I wrote that song when the Zodiac Killer was out murdering in San Francisco. Every night I was coming home from the studio, and I'd stop at an intersection and look around, and if a car pulled up, it was like, 'This is it, I'm gonna die now.' It became a game. Every night I was conscious of that thing, and the refrain got to be so real to me. 'Please don't murder me, please don't murder me.' It was a coincidence in a way, but it was also the truth at the moment.' (Krassner)

The band Stiff Dead Cat, in their version of "Dire Wolf," sings this line as "Don't kill me," on their 2003 recording *Snake Oil,* to great and hilarious effect.

3 red whiskey
From *The Book of Bourbon:*

There is solid evidence, however, that by the mid-1800s, some whiskeys were being aged long enough to give them a decent amount of color. In *The Lincoln Reader,* 1947, editor Paul M. Angle, included a personal recollection of one James S. Ewing, who was an eyewitness to an 1854 meeting between Abraham Lincoln and his formidable debating rival, Stephen A. Douglas. In Ewing's account of the event, he referred to a decanter of "red liquor"—a term for bourbon that would become widely used by the end of that century. When whiskey is first distilled, it is clear—it looks exactly like vodka. Only time in wood gives it color, and only time in charred wood results in the crimson-hued tint that is peculiar to bourbon. So we can draw from Ewing's reference to red liquor that in the mid-nineteenth century some whiskey was being aged in charred casks, and it was aged long enough for it to gain bourbon's characteristic crimson hue.

4 Dire Wolf
Dire Wolf, *Canis dirus* . . . One of the most common mammalian species in the Rancholabrean, the dire wolf has been found at more than 80 sites in North America ranging from late Illinoian and Sangamonian to late Wisconsinan. . . . The range covers most of the United States and Mexico and extends to Peru in the south.

Equaling a large gray wolf in size, *Canis dirus* was markedly heavier of build, with a very large and broad head and sturdy limbs with relatively short lower segments. The dentition was more powerful than that of any other species of *Canis,* the carnassial teeth being, on the average, much larger than those of *Canis lupus.* The braincase is relatively smaller than that of the gray wolf. The dire wolf may be referred to the subgenus *Aenocyon,* of which it is the sole known species. (Kurten)

5 The wolf

Wolf: Symbolic of valour among the Romans and the Egyptians. It also appears as a guardian in a great many monuments. In Nordic mythology we are told of a monstrous wolf, Fenris, that would destroy iron chains and shackles and was eventually shut up in the bowels of the earth. It was also said that, with the twilight of the gods—the end of the world—the monster would break out of this prison, too, and would devour the sun. Here, then, the wolf appears as a symbol of the principle of evil, within a pattern of ideas which is unquestionably related to the Gnostic cosmogony. . . . The myth is also connected with all other concepts of the final annihilation of the world, whether by water or fire. (Cirlot) 29

This summary presents an interesting link back to "Uncle John's Band," with its lines about knowing the fire from the ice, which similarly summon apocalyptic associations.

6 queen of spades

The queen of spades corresponds to the queen of the tarot suit Swords, and is characterized as follows:

> She stands with upraised sword. Her left hand is raised as if to signify recognition or generosity. She is one who has suffered a great loss.
> Divinatory meaning: This card means a sharp, quick-witted, keen person. Possibly the bearer of evil or slanderous words. . . . Mourning. Privation. Loneliness. Separation. (Kaplan) 30

There is a short story by Alexander Pushkin, a Russian writer of the early nineteenth century, titled "The Queen of Spades." In the story, a young Russian engineer kills an old woman to learn a gambling secret. The secret is for a card game in which the player selects a card and bets that the card the dealer draws will match it. The old woman's ghost appears to the engineer and tells him to bet on three, seven, ace. He goes to the gambling house and wins the first two bets. He selects an ace for his third card, and when an ace is dealt, he tries to collect his winnings. The dealer kindly asks him to show his card. He looks at it, and it is a queen of spades, with the old woman's face on it.

Notes:

Studio recording: *Workingman's Dead* (May 1970).

First documented performance: June 7, 1969, at the California Hall in San Francisco. Performed usually several times each year since, peaking in 1978 with twenty-seven performances.

Hunter's electronic journal entry from July 29, 1996:

> There's a large house visible across the fields which is reputed to be haunted by the ghost of a dog, probable inspiration for the Hound of the Baskervilles (an old local family). Funny tie in there. The song "Dire Wolf" was inspired, at least in name, by watching *The Hound of the Baskervilles* on TV with Garcia. We were speculating on what the ghostly hound might turn out to be, and somehow the idea that maybe it was a dire wolf came up. Maybe it was even suggested in the story, I don't remember. We thought dire wolves were great big beasts. Extinct now, it turns out they were quite small and ran in packs. But the idea of a great big wolf named Dire was enough to trigger a lyric. As I remember, I wrote the words quickly the next morning upon waking, in that hypnogogic state where deep-rooted associations meld together with no effort. Garcia set it later that afternoon. 31

casey jones

1 Casey Jones
"The Ballad of
Casey Jones" was
briefly part of the
band's repertoire,
appearing twice in
shows in 1970.

B. A. Botkin, in his
*A Treasury of
American Folklore,*
wrote:

The facts behind
the story of John Luther "Casey" Jones have
been well known since at least the early 1920s.
The incident to which the original song refers
took place on April 30, 1900. His nickname was
from the town of Cayce, Kentucky, near his
birthplace. He was an engineer on the Illinois
Central line, with a trademark way of blowing
the train's whistle, giving rise to the phrase
"Casey Moan."

"You see," said Mrs. Jones [his widow, in a 1928
interview published in the *Erie Railroad
Magazine,* vol. 24, no. 2 (April 1928), pp.
13–14], "he established a sort of trademark for
himself by his inimitable method of blowing a
whistle. It was a kind of long-drawn-out note
that he created, beginning softly, then rising,
then dying away almost to a whisper. People
living along the Illinois Central right of way
between Jackson and Water Valley would turn
over in their beds late at night and say: 'There
goes Casey Jones' as he roared by."

And A. J. "Fatty" Thomas, often a conductor on
trains driven by Jones, said:

"The 'whistle's moan' in the song is right.
Casey could just about play a tune on the
whistle. He could make the cold chills run up

This old engine
makes it on time
Leaves Central Station
at a quarter to nine
Hits River Junction
at seventeen to
at a quarter to ten
you know it's trav'lin' again

Drivin' that train
High on Cocaine
Casey Jones, you better   1
watch your speed
Trouble ahead
Trouble behind
and you know that notion
just crossed my mind

Trouble ahead
The Lady in Red   2
Take my advice
you be better off dead
Switchman sleepin'
Train hundred and two
is on the wrong track and
headed for you

Drivin' that train
High on cocaine
Casey Jones you better
watch your speed
Trouble ahead

Trouble behind
and you know that notion
just crossed my mind

Trouble with you is
The trouble with me
Got two good eyes
but we still don't see
Come 'round the bend
You know it's the end
The fireman screams and
The engine just gleams

Drivin' that train
High on cocaine
Casey Jones you better
watch your speed
Trouble ahead
Trouble behind
and you know that notion
just crossed my mind

Words by Robert Hunter
Music by Jerry Garcia

your back with it, and grin all the time.
Everybody along the line knew Casey Jones's
whistle."

Botkin, quoting the *Erie Railroad Magazine,*
continues:

> The common story of the wreck in which Jones
> was killed is that Casey had to meet two freight
> trains which were too long to clear the siding.
> For some reason, never clearly explained, Casey
> failed to stop and he piled them up when he
> struck the caboose and cars protruding out on
> the main line.
>
> Casey, according to the accounts, was very
> unlikely to have been high on anything,
> however, being a teetotaler "in the days when
> abstinence was rare."

The original song memorializing Casey Jones was
written a few days after the accident by Jones's
friend Wallace Saunders, an African American
engine wiper.

According to Fuld:

> John Luther "Casey" Jones was an engineer on
> Illinois Central Railroad's best railroad train, the
> 'Cannon Ball Express,' from Chicago to New
> Orleans. . . . Jones's friend Wallace Saunders . . .
> is said to have adapted or written a ballad
> regarding the heroic tale, which was sung by
> Negro railroad men and then allegedly adapted
> by two white vaudevillians, Eddie Newton and T.
> Lawrence Seibert.

John Lomax picks up the story in *Folk Song
U.S.A.:*

> The Casey Jones ballad familiar to most
> Americans, sprang from Wallace Saunders' song
> by way, curiously, of the vaudeville stage.
> Tallifero Lawrence Seibert (born June 4, 1877, in
> Bloomington, Indiana; died February 20, 1917,
> in Los Angeles) toured the vaudeville circuit in a
> five-character act. According to Elliot Shapiro

(one of the pundits of popular song), Seibert "undoubtedly heard" 'Been on the Cholly So Long.' He wrote a sketch about the brave engineer and incorporated it into his act." Out on the pier in Venice, California, he bumped into a ragtime piano player, Eddie Walter Newton (born September 25, 1869, in Trenton, Missouri; died September 1, 1915, and his ashes were scattered under the pier cafe in Venice). Together they turned out a ragtime ballad about Casey, set him up as the main "hogger" on a Western railroad line, and published the song themselves in the Southern California Music Company. By 1909 the song had swept the country as a popular hit, retaining so many folk song touches that folk singers have since then created scores of variants and parodies based on the Newton-Seibert ballad.

Their version of the song has these words:

Come all you rounders if you want to hear
The story of a brave engineer
Casey Jones was the rounder's name
On the "six-eight" wheeler, boys, he won
    his fame
The caller called Casey at half past four
He kissed his wife at the station door
He mounted to the cabin with the orders in
    his hand
And he took his farewell trip to that
    promis'd land

Chorus:
Casey Jones—mounted to his cabin
Casey Jones—with his orders in his hand
Casey Jones—mounted to his cabin
And he took his . . . land (last line of each
    verse)

He looked at his water and his water
    was low
He looked at his watch and his watch
    was slow
He turned to his fireman and this is what
    he said

"Boy, we're going to reach Frisco, but we'll
    all be dead"
He turned to the fireman, said, "Shovel on
    your coal
Stick your head out the window, see the
    drivers roll
I'm gonna drive her 'til she leaves the rail
For I'm eight hours late by that Western
    Mail"

Chorus:
Casey Jones—I'm gonna drive her
Casey Jones—'til she leaves the rail
Casey Jones—I'm gonna drive her
For I'm eight . . .

When he pulled up that Reno hill
He whistled for the crossing with an awful shrill
The switchman knew by the engine's moan
That the man at the throttle was Casey Jones
When he was within six miles of the place
There No. 4 stared him straight in the face
He turned to his fireman, said "Jim, you'd
    better jump
For there're two locomotives that are going
    to bump.

Chorus:
Casey Jones—two locomotives
Casey Jones—going to bump
etc.

Casey said just before he died,
"There're two more roads I would like to ride"
The fireman said, "Which ones can they be?"
"O the Northern Pacific and the Santa Fe"
Mrs. Jones sat at her bed a sighing
Just to hear the news that her Casey was dying
"Hush up, children, and quite your cryin'
For you've got another poppa on the Salt
    Lake Line"

(Chorus)

2 Lady in Red

Anna Sage, who betrayed John Dillinger to the FBI, was wearing red on the night Dillinger was shot—actually, she was wearing an orange skirt, which appeared red in the lights of the movie theater marquee. She was referred to in contemporary reports as "the Lady in Red." The song "Lady in Red" was written in 1935 by Mort Dixon and Allie Wrubel.

> 'Twas a cold winter's evening, the guests were all leaving, O'Leary was closing the bar,
> When he turned and he said to the lady in red,
> "Get out, you can't stay where you are."
> She shed a sad tear in her bucket of beer as she thought of the cold night ahead,
> Then a gentleman dapper stepped out of the (phone booth) and these are the words that he said:
> "Her mother never told her the things a young girl should know.
> About the ways of college men, and how they come and go (mostly . . . go).
> Now age has taken her beauty, and sin has left its sad scar;
> So remember your mothers and sisters, boys, and let her sleep under the bar.

Red and *lady* also have drug slang connotations: one for downers, the other for cocaine itself, leading to a reinforcement of the antidrug message of this lyric: Uppers lead to downers, and a vicious cycle ensues.

Notes:

Studio recording: *Workingman's Dead* (May 1970).

First performance: June 20, 1969, at the Fillmore East in New York. It remained in the repertoire fairly consistently through 1984, then was dropped until June 1992, when it reappeared for four more performances.

The Mississippi John Hurt version (recorded by him on his *Folk Songs and Blues:* Gryphon, 1963) is included on the Garcia-Grisman CD *Shady Grove.*

Garcia, interviewed on the song by Reich and Wenner:

> Reich: Does "Casey Jones" grate on you when you hear it sometimes?
>
> Garcia: Sometimes, but that's what it's supposed to do. [*Laughs*]
>
> Reich: It's such a singsongy thing.
>
> Garcia: Right. And it's got a split-second little delay, which sounds very mechanical, like a typewriter almost, on the vocal, which is like a little bit jangly, and the whole thing is, well . . . I always thought it's a pretty good musical picture of what cocaine is like. A little bit evil. And hard-edged. And also that singsongy thing, because that's what it *is*, a singsongy thing, a little melody that gets in your head. (*Garcia*)

And Hunter:

> The other one that comes to mind is "Drivin' that train / High on cocaine / Casey Jones, you better / watch your speed." I said the bad word—*cocaine*—and put it in a somewhat romanticized context, and people look at that as being an advertisement for cocaine rather than what a close inspection of the words will tell you. (Jackson: Excerpt from *Goin' Down the Road*). 94

what's become of the baby?

1 What's become of the baby
Compare Sharp, #228: "What'll We Do with the Baby?":

What'll
we do with the
 baby?
What'll we do with the baby?
What'll we do with the baby?
Oh, we'll wrap it up in calico
Oh, we'll wrap it up in calico
And send it to its pappy, O.

Also compare the line in Lewis Carroll's *Alice in Wonderland*, in which the Cheshire cat asks Alice, "What became of the baby?" She replies that the baby turned into a pig and ran away. For the full conversation, see the note on the Cheshire cat in "Can't Come Down."

2 ice caverns of Khan
A reference to Samuel Taylor Coleridge's *Kubla Khan: A Vision in a Dream* (1816):

Xanadu: a kingdom on the coast of Asia where Kubla Khan ordered a stately pleasure dome to be constructed, described as "a miracle of rare device." The caves of ice beneath the sunny dome are particularly enchanting. . . . It was in the nearby, ancient forests, in a savage, holy, and enchanted places where women can be heard wailing for their demon lovers, that a mighty fountain of water, flung up violently from a deep chasm, was revealed to be the source of the sacred river Alph. (*Dictionary of Imaginary Places*)

Waves of violet go crashing and laughing
Rainbow-winged singing birds fly 'round the sun
Sunbells rain down in a liquid profusion
Mermaids on porpoises draw up the dawn

What's become of the baby   1
This cold December morning?

Songbirds
frozen in their flight
drifting to the earth
remnants of forgotten dreaming
Calling . . .
answer comes there none
Go to sleep, you child
Dream of never-ending always

Panes of crystal
Eyes sparkle like waterfalls
lighting the polished ice caverns of Khan   2
But where in the looking-glass fields of illusion   3
wandered the child who was perfect as dawn?

What's become of the baby
this cold December morning?

Racing
rhythms of the sun
all the world revolves
captured in the eye of Odin   4
Allah   5
Pray, where are you now?
All Mohammed's men
blinded by the sparkling water

6 Sheherazade gathering stories to tell
from primal gold fantasy petals that fall

7 But where is the child
who played with the sun chimes
and chased the cloud sheep
to the regions of rhyme?

Stranded
cries the south wind
Lost in the regions of lead
Shackled by chains of illusion
Delusions of living and dead

Words by Robert Hunter
Music by Jerry Garcia

Coleridge received the vision of Xanadu, he said, while in an opium-induced trance. He awoke from the trance having been given the poem, which he wrote down, but he was interrupted and was only able to commit a small portion of the poem to the page. The introduction that Coleridge wrote for the publication of "Kubla Khan" included part of another poem, which is mentioned in the annotation to "Ripple."

The poem:

  In Xanadu did Kubla Khan
  A stately pleasure-dome decree:
  Where Alph, the sacred river, ran
  Through caverns measureless to man

Down to a sunless sea.

So twice five miles of fertile ground
With walls and towers were girdled round:
And there were gardens bright with sinuous
  rills,
Where blossomed many an incense-bearing
  tree;
And here were forests ancient as the hills,
Enfolding sunny spots of greenery.

But oh! that deep romantic chasm which
  slanted
Down the green hill athwart a cedarn cover!
A savage place! as holy and enchanted
As e'er beneath a waning moon was
  haunted
By woman wailing for her demon-lover!
And from this chasm, with ceaseless turmoil
  seething,
As if this earth in fast thick pants were
  breathing,
A mighty fountain momently was forced:
Amid whose swift half-intermitted burst
Huge fragments vaulted like rebounding
  hail,
Or chaffy grain beneath the thresher's flail:
And 'mid these dancing rocks at once
  and ever
It flung up momently the sacred river.
Five miles meandering with a mazy motion
Through wood and dale the sacred river
  ran,
Then reached the caverns measureless
  to man,
And sank in tumult to a lifeless ocean:
And 'mid this tumult Kubla heard from far
Ancestral voices prophesying war!

The shadow of the dome of pleasure
Floated midway on the waves;
Where was heard the mingled measure

From the fountain and the caves.
It was a miracle of rare device,
A sunny pleasure-dome with caves of ice!

A damsel with a dulcimer
In a vision once I saw:
It was an Abyssinian maid,
And on her dulcimer she played,
Singing of Mount Abora.
Could I revive within me
Her symphony and song,
To such a deep delight 'twould win me
That with music loud and long
I would build that dome in air,
That sunny dome! those caves of ice!
And all who heard should see them there,
And all should cry, Beware! Beware!
His flashing eyes, his floating hair!
Weave a circle round him thrice,
And close your eyes with holy dread,
For he on honey-dew hath fed
And drunk the milk of Paradise.

Kubla Khan (usually Kublai Khan) (1216–94): Grandson of
Ghengis Khan, ruled from Beijing, which he founded.
Marco Polo visited his court.

3 looking-glass

The mirror makes two appearances in the *Aoxomoxoa* song cycle, showing itself in "Rosemary" as well, though if you count the "Leonardo words" from "China Cat Sunflower," there are three mirrors. (And the palindromic album title itself may be taken as a mirror.) The evocations are many: among them, *Alice Through the Looking-Glass;* the album cover's own palin-dromic nature; and the film *Orphée* (1949) by Jean Cocteau. In Cocteau's vision, Orpheus, who is a candidate for the identity of the "baby," disappears into a looking-glass world.

4 Odin

According to *Bulfinch's Mythology:*

Odin. The Scandinavian name of the god called by the Anglo-Saxons Woden; the god of wisdom, poetry, war, and agriculture. He became the *All-wise* by drinking from Mimir's fountain at the cost of one eye. His remaining eye is the Sun. [!] . . . His two black ravens are Hugin (thought) and Munin (memory).

Mimir seems worth a look as well:

Mimir. In Norse mythology, a giant water demon. He dwells at "Mimir's Well," the source of all wisdom.

5 Allah

"The word presented in Islam as the proper name of God." (*Encyclopedia of Religion*) Appears to be etymologically derived from the ancient Semitic root *el,* meaning God. Used in this song, it seems to refer back to the Khan character, who is of nonspecific Asiatic derivation. The other reference to Allah in the Grateful Dead universe is the "Blues for Allah" lyric by Hunter.

6 Scheherazade

The storyteller of *The Arabian Nights.* According to *Benét's Reader's Encyclopedia:*

The Arabian Nights' Entertainments: A collection of ancient Persian-Indian-Arabian tales, orginally in Arabic, arranged in its present form about 1450, probably in Cairo. . . . Although the stories are discrete in plot, they are unified by Scheherazade, the supposed teller; she postpones her execution by telling her husband, Schahriah, a story night after night, without revealing the climax until the following session. 32

Hunter also refers to *The Arabian Nights* in "Blues for Allah," with the line "The thousand stories have come 'round to one again."

7 where is the child

Could it be that the baby who is lost is the same child who was wrapped in scarlet covers in "Saint Stephen"? If so, then this child could be Orpheus, the child of Calliope and Apollo. The tale of Orpheus appears a few times in the course of Hunter's career, most notably in "Reuben and Cerise."

Notes:

Studio recording: *Aoxomoxoa* (June 20, 1969). Due to an experiment in recording technology, this song is practically unlistenable, yet it has always been intriguing to those who follow the Dead's lyrics.

Only performance known: April 26, 1969, at the Electric Theater in Chicago.

- Baby -

High Time

You told me good-bye
How was I to know
You didn't mean good-bye
You meant *please*
don't let me go
I was having a high time
Living the good life
Well, I know

The wheels are muddy
Got a ton of hay
Now listen here baby
'cause I mean what I say
I'm having a hard time
Living the good life
Well, I know

I was losing time
I had nothing to do
No one to fight
I came to you
Wheels broke down
The leader won't draw
The line is busted
the last one I saw

Tomorrow come trouble
Tomorrow come pain
Now don't think too hard, baby
'cause you know what I'm saying
I could show you a high time
living the good life
Don't be that way

Nothing's for certain
It could always go wrong
Come in when it's raining
Go on out when it's gone
We could have us a high time
living the good life
Well, I know

Words by Robert Hunter
Music by Jerry Garcia

Notes:

Studio recording: *Workingman's Dead* (May 1970).

First documented performance: June 21, 1969, at
the Fillmore East in New York. Over the years,
the song dropped in and out of the repertoire,
never for more than six years, however.

Easy wind

I been ballin' a shiny black steel jackhammer

1 Been chippin' up rocks for the great highway
Live five years if I take my time

2 Ballin' that jack and a drinkin' my wine.

I been chippin' them rocks from dawn till doom

3 While my rider hide my bottle in the other
   room
Doctor say I better stop ballin' that jack
If I live five years gonna bust my back, yes I will

Easy wind 'cross the bayou today
There's a whole lotta women, Mama,

4 Out in red on the streets today
And the river keep a talkin'
But you never hear a word it say

Gotta find a woman be good to me
Won't hide my liquor try to
   serve me tea
'Cause I'm a stone jack baller
   and my heart is true
And I'll give everything that I
   got to you, yes I will

Easy wind blowing 'cross
   the bayou today
There's a whole lotta women,
   Mama,
Out in red on the streets today
And the river keep a talkin'
But you never hear a word it say

Words and music by Robert Hunter

1 great highway
Reminiscent of the rock-and-roll venue The Family Dog at the Great Highway, in San Francisco, a frequent venue for the Grateful Dead in 1969 and 1970. It was named for Highway 1, which runs through San Francisco. However, this "Great Highway" seems unlikely to be the one referred to by the protagonist of this song, as other geographical clues ("cross the bayou") seem to indicate a Louisiana setting.

2 Ballin' that jack
A 1913 Dixieland dance-craze song, words by Jim Burris; music by Chris Smith:

BALLIN' THE JACK
Folks in Georgia's 'bout to go insane
Since that new dance down in Georgia came
I'm the only person who's to blame
I'm the party introduced it there

So, give me credit to know a thing or two
Give me credit for springing something new
I will show this little dance to you
When I do you'll say that it's a bear.

First you put your two knees close up tight
Then you sway 'em to the left
Then you sway 'em to the right
Step around the floor kind of nice and light
Then you twis(t) around and twis(t) around
   with all your might
Stretch your lovin' arms straight out in
   space
Then you do the eagle rock with style and
   grace [compare "Let Me Sing Your Blues
   Away"]
Swing your foot way 'round then bring it
   back
Now that's what I call Ballin' the Jack.

It's being done in all the cabarets
All society now has got the craze

It's the best dance done in modern days
That is why I rave about it so

Play some good rag that will make you prance
Old folks, young folks all try to do the dance
Join right in now while you got the chance
Once again the steps to you I'll show. 33

3 my rider
Slang usage for an actively amorous partner.

Compare also Gregg Allman's "Midnight Rider" and the classic Grateful Dead repertoire number "C. C. Rider."

4 in red on the streets today
Another reference to women wearing red is to be found in "Casey Jones."

Notes:

Studio recording: *Workingman's Dead* (May 1970).

First known performance: September 1, 1969, at the Baton Rouge International Speedway in Prairieville, Louisiana. It was played steadily through April 1971.

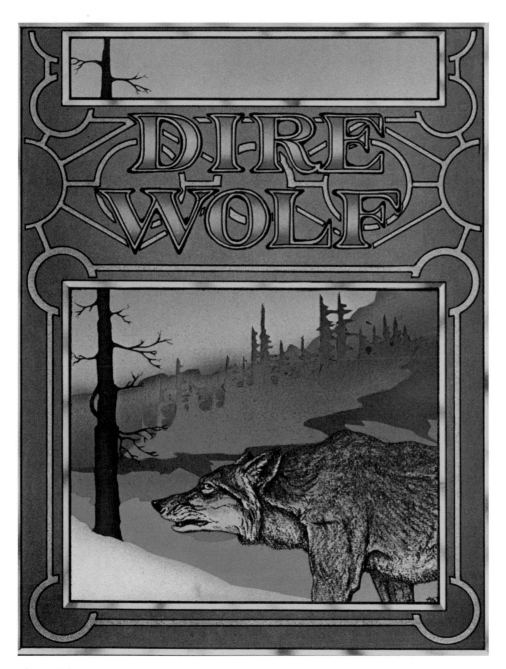

DIRE WOLF

Words by Robert Hunter, music by Jerry Garcia.

Illustration by Alton Kelley and Stanley Mouse for the *Grateful Dead* songbook (Ice Nine / WB Publications, 1972).

New Speedway Boogie
Words by Robert Hunter, music by Jerry Garcia.

Illustration by Alton Kelley and Stanley Mouse for the *Grateful Dead* songbook (Ice Nine / WB Publications, 1972).

Easy Wind
Words and music by Robert Hunter.

Illustration by Alton Kelley and Stanley Mouse for the *Grateful Dead* songbook
(Ice Nine / WB Publications, 1972).

sugar magnolia

Words by Robert Hunter, music by Jerry Garcia.

Illustration by Alton Kelley and Stanley Mouse for the
Grateful Dead Songbook (Ice Nine / WB Publications,
1972).

cumberLand blues

1 I can't stay much longer, Melinda
The sun is getting high
I can't help you with your troubles
If you won't help with mine

I gotta get down
I gotta get down
Got to get down to the mine

You keep me up just one more night
I can't sleep here no more

2 Little Ben clock says quarter to eight
You kept me up till four

I gotta get down
I gotta get down
Or I can't work there no more

Lotta poor man make a five-dollar bill
Keep him happy all the time
Some other fellow making nothing at all
And you can hear him cryin' . . .

"Can I go buddy
Can I go down
Take your shift at the mine?"

3 Got to get down to the Cumberland Mine
That's where I mainly spend my time
Make good money/five dollars a day
Made any more I might move away—

4 Lotta poor man got the Cumberland Blues
He can't win for losin'
Lotta poor man got to walk the line

1 Melinda
According to an email exchange with Hunter, the name Melinda comes from someone he knew in high school. He said he always loved the name and thought it was one of the most euphonious names he had ever heard.

2 Little Ben clock
Close to an actual brand name of an alarm clock, the Westclox Baby Ben, used as a facetious take-off on Big Ben, in London. Big Ben, according to *Brewer's Dictionary of Phrase and Fable*, is

> The name given to the large bell in the Clock Tower (or St. Stephen's [!] Tower) at the Houses of Parliament. It weighs thirteen and a half tons, and is named after Sir Benjamin Hall, chief commissioner of works in 1856, when it was cast.

3 Cumberland Mine
An infamous coal mine in Nova Scotia. *Sing Out!* magazine makes this note about the song by Peggy Seeger, "The Springhill Mine Disaster":

> Peggy Seeger wrote this song after reading about the terrible mine disaster in Spring Hill, Nova Scotia, in the latter part of 1958. This was the world-famous tragedy in which a number of trapped miners were miraculously rescued after eight days of entombment.

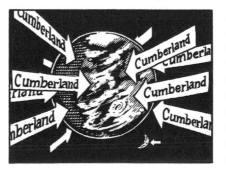

4 Cumberland
A geographical name with a rich history. The Cumberland being referred to in the song is probably the Cumberland Mountains or, possibly, the county or town (located in Harlan County) of Cumberland, Kentucky. All

place-names in the region stem from the name of the Cumberland River, which "flows through southern Kentucky and northern Tennessee, 687 miles long," according to the *American Places Dictionary*. (Also according to this source, the river was in turn named "for the county of Cumberland, England. Name made popular by Prince William Augustus (1721–65), Duke of Cumberland, victor over Highlander Scots at Culloden in 1746." Interestingly, Cumberland County, England, is an important mining region, principally for iron ore but also for coal.)

Another candidate is Cumberland, Maryland— the home of the first national road, the "Cumberland Road." The city was originally Fort Cumberland, and George Washington was stationed there in his younger days. Approximately nine miles from the city are several hundred coal mines, some of which continue to be mined today.

Also in Appalachia is the Cumberland Gap, a mountain pass, which is the title of a folk song:

Me and my wife and my wife's pap.
We all live down in the Cumberland Gap.

Chorus:
Cumberland Gap, Cumberland Gap.
We all live in the Cumberland Gap.

Cumberland Gap is a noted place
Three kinds of water to wash your face.

The first white man in the Cumberland Gap
Was doctor Walker, an English chap.

Daniel Boone on Pinnacle Rock,
Killed many Injuns with his old flintlock.

Cumberland Gap is a noted place,
Three kinds of water to wash your face.

Daniel Boone on Pinnacle Rock,
He killed Injuns with his old flintlock.

Just to pay his union dues

I don't know now
I just don't know
If I'm goin' back again
I don't know now
I just don't know
If I'm goin' back again

Words by Robert Hunter
Music by Jerry Garcia and Phil Lesh

Lay down, boys, and take a little nap.
Fo'teen miles to the Cumberland Gap

There are eight Cumberland counties in the United States: in Illinois, Kentucky, Maine, New Jersey, North Carolina, Pennsylvania, Tennessee, and Virginia.

Another song worth a look is "Those Old Cumberland Mountain Farm Blues":

It is hard to be bound down in prison,
But it's worse on these Cumberland
    Mountain farms.
Rather be in some old penitentiary,
Or up in old iron Tennessee.

How weary I've climbed them old
  mountains,
Through the rain and the sleet and the
  snow.
Tip yo' hat when you meet Mister Ridges,
Bow yo' head when you meet Captain Ross.

Young ____ ____, he run a commissary
Mister, you bet he was a thief,
He sold apples at fifty a dozen
And potatoes at fifty cents apiece.

When the Coffee County boys came to the
  mounting,
They expected to get a lot to eat,
But when they called them in to dinner,
They got salmon, corn dodgers, and meat.

It is seventy miles to Chattanooga,
It's a hundred and twenty to Bassell,
It's a thousand miles from here to
  civilization,
But it's only a few steps from here to hell.

Young people, you've all heard my story
And I hope you don't think it all wrong.

If you doubt the words I have told you
See Red Campbell, for he composed this
  song.

Notes:
Studio recording: *Workingman's Dead* (May 1970).

First performance: November 8, 1969, at the Fillmore
Auditorium in San Francisco. A fairly steady number in
the repertoire between 1969 and 1974, it was absent for
quite a while, reappearing in 1981 and played a few
times a year subsequently.

The title of a musical by Michael Norman Mann, built
around twenty classic Garcia-Hunter songs, and about a
family coal mine in the Appalachian Mountains in the
1940s. Briefly staged in San Jose and San Francisco in
1998, it is headed to Off Broadway as of this writing.

1 Black Peter
Black Peter is the traditional counterpart to Saint Nicholas. In the Netherlands, Saint Nick "is accompanied by Spanish blackamoor servants in medieval costumes. They are called Black Peters and carry bundles of switches to beat naughty children." (*Folklore of World Holidays*)

Compare the Arthur Conan Doyle story "The Adventure of Black Peter," from *The Return of Sherlock Holmes*.

Compare also a character "the keeper of the moat") in *The Once and Future King* by T. H. White.

And finally, there's a 1963 movie by Czech director Milos Forman.

2 Saint Angel
This seems to be a mythical place, perhaps near Fennario. The closest geographical name is San Angelo, Texas.

3 and it's just like / any other day / that's ever been
Seneca: "*Nihil interesse inter diem et saeculum.*" "A day differs not a whit from eternity," from *Epistulae ad Lucilium*.

and Thomas Carlyle:

All of my friends come to see me last night
I was laying in my bed and dying
Annie Beauneu from Saint Angel   2
say, "The weather down here so fine"

Just then the wind
came squalling through the door
but who can
the weather command?
Just want to have
a little peace to die
and a friend or two
I love at hand

Fever roll up to a hundred and five
Roll on up
gonna roll back down
One more day
I find myself alive
tomorrow
maybe go
beneath the ground

See here how everything
lead up to this day
and it's just like
any other day
that's ever been   3
Sun goin' up
and then the
sun it goin' down
Shine through my window and
my friends they come around

come around
come around

People may know but
the people don't care
that a man could be
as poor as me
"Take a look at poor Peter
he's lyin' in pain
now let's go run
and see"

Run and see
hey, hey,
run and see

Words by Robert Hunter
Music by Jerry Garcia

The poorest day that passes over us is the conflux of two eternities; it is made up of currents that issue from the remotest Past, and flow onwards to the remotest Future.
—*Signs of the Times*

The character Hamm in Samuel Beckett's *Endgame* at one point refers to the day of his death as "a day like any other day."

Notes:
Studio recording: *Workingman's Dead* (May 1970).

First documented performance: December 4, 1969, at the Fillmore West in San Francisco. It remained in the repertoire thereafter.

Patti Smith performed the song live in the days immediately following Garcia's death.

UNCLE JOHN'S BAND

1 Easy Street
Slang, dating roughly from the late 1800s, for a state in which everything is going well and one is comfortable; usually meant monetarily.

The title of a 1917 film by Charlie Chaplin.

"Easy Street," a 1941 tune by Alan Rankin Jones, became a jazz standard, performed by Nat "King" Cole and Thelonius Monk, among others.

2 Buck Dancer's Choice
A buck dancer is one who dances the buck-and-wing. From *The Dictionary of American Regional English*:

> buck-and-wing, n. . . . Also *buck (dance)* . . . A lively dance

usually performed by one person.

The word *wing* was used to describe a combination known as Buck and Wing—the general designation for tap dance (and almost anything else) at the turn of the century. Introduced on the New York stage in 1880 by James McIntyre, the Buck and Wing began to swing . . . and launched a new style of Negro-derived dancing.

Appalachian buck-dancing is the simplest and yet the most enigmatic kind of Southern mountain dancing. Essentially, buck-dancing is a

Well, the first days are the hardest days,
don't you worry anymore
When life looks like Easy Street   1
there is danger at your door
Think this through with me
Let me know your mind
Whoa-oh, what I want to know,
is are you kind?

It's a Buck Dancer's Choice, my friend,   2
better take my advice
You know all the rules by now
and the fire from the ice   3
Will you come with me?
Won't you come with me?
Whoa-oh, what I want to know,
will you come with me?

Goddamn, well, I declare
Have you seen the like?
Their walls are built of cannonballs,
their motto is "Don't tread on me"   4
Come hear Uncle John's Band
by the riverside   5
Got some things to talk about
here beside the rising tide

It's the same story the crow told me   6
It's the only one he know—
like the morning sun you come
and like the wind you go   7
Ain't no time to hate,   8

barely time to wait
Whoa-oh, what I want to know,
where does the time go?

I live in a silver mine
and I call it Beggar's Tomb
I got me a violin
and I beg you call the tune
Anybody's choice
I can hear your voice
Whoa-oh, what I want to know,
how does the song go?

Come hear Uncle John's Band
by the riverside
Come with me or go alone
He's come to take his children home
Come hear Uncle John's Band
playing to the tide
Come on along or go alone
he's come to take his children home

Words by Robert Hunter
Music by Jerry Garcia

dance for one but can be for more than one; the dance itself involves nothing more than moving your feet in time to the music. The origins of buck-dancing are unclear. The name probably came from the Indians who may have had a ceremonial dance danced by a brave costumed as a buck deer.

A note from the record jacket of Taj Mahal's 1973 album *Oooh So Good 'n' Blues,* which includes a song titled "Buck Dancer's Choice":

"Buck Dancer's Choice" is a tune that goes back to Saturday-night dances, when the Buck, or male dancer, got to choose who his partner would be. Sort of the opposite to "Ladies' Choice." While mostly used as a string-band tune, anyone calling this tune out would be sure to get a positive reaction from all the Does and Bucks.

In *The Anthropology of Dance,* Anya Royce says:

There existed also a genre that has been labeled "water dances." These, including such named dances as Set the Floor, Buck Dance, and Juba [compare line in "Mister Charlie"], all involved a test of skill in balancing a glass of water on the head while dancing. Juba and Buck dances appeared as well without the water balancing. . . . Emery also claims a long past for the Pigeon Wing and Buck Dance: "The Pigeon Wing and the Buck Dance appear as authentic dances of the Negro on the plantation, much before they were picked up for the minstrel shows and billed as the Buck and Wing.

Buck Dancer's Choice (1966) is the title of a volume of poetry by James Dickey.

Also the title of an old mountain fiddle tune. It was definitely in Garcia's repertoire in 1962, when he was a member of the Sleepy Hollow

Hog Stompers (Jerry Garcia, guitar and banjo; Marshall Leicester, banjo and guitar; Dick Arnold, fiddle. Leicester was Garcia's early music guru and banjo teacher.) Here's a set list of theirs from June 11, 1962:

Boar's Head Coffee House, Jewish Community Center, San Carlos, California

—Set I—
Run Mountain
Billy Grimes the Rover
Cannonball Blues
Devilish Mary
Buck Dancer's Choice
Little Birdie
Sally Goodin'
Hold the Woodpile Down

—Set II—
Crow Black Chicken
The Johnson Boys
Shady Grove
Hop High Ladies
Sweet Sunny South
All Go Hungry Hash House
Man of Constant Sorrow
Rabbit Chase
Three Men Went A-Hunting

3 fire from the ice
Compare Robert Frost's 1920 poem "Fire and Ice":

Some say the world will end in fire,
Some say in ice.
From what I've tasted of desire
I hold with those who favor fire.
But if it had to perish twice,
I think I know enough of hate
To say that for destruction ice
Is also great
And would suffice.

4 "Don't tread on me"
From *Twelve Flags of the American Revolution*, issued to accompany the exhibition on the bicentennial of American independence by the Library of Congress, 1976:

The Gadsden Flag: In January 1776 Col. Christopher Gadsden left Philadelphia, where he had served as a delegate to the Continental Congress and a member of the Marine Committee, to return to South Carolina. He brought with him to Charleston the flag he had designed for use by the commander in chief of the American Navy, whose vessels were assembled in the frozen Delaware River. His presentation of this flag to the Provincial Congress of South Carolina on February 9, 1776, is recorded in the congressional journals:

Col. Gadsden presented to the Congress an elegant standard, such as is to be used by the commander in chief of the American navy; being a yellow field, with a lively representation of a rattlesnake in the middle, in the attitude of going to strike, and these words underneath, "Don't Tread on Me!"

This flag was that day ordered preserved in the hall of the South Carolina Provincial Congress.

5 by the riverside
Evokes the folk song "Study War No More" aka "Down by the Riverside":

Gonna lay down my sword and shield
Down by the riverside
And study war
    no more

6 same story the crow told me

Compare "The Story the Crow Told Me":

> Caw, caw, one little story that the crow told me:
> Caw, caw, in a hickory tree.

In 1960 Johnny Horton, a popular singer, did a song called "Sink the Bismark" that rose to number three on the pop charts. The flip side (B side of the single) of the 45 rpm was a song called "The Same Old Tale the Crow Told Me."

> It's the same old tale that the crow told me
> Way down yonder by the sycamore tree
> It's the same old tale that the crow told me
> Way down yonder by the sycamore tree

7 like the morning sun you come / and like the wind you go

Compare *The Rubaiyat of Omar Khayyam*:

> Myself when young did eagerly frequent
> Doctor and Saint, and heard great Argument
> About it and about: but evermore
> Came out by the same Door as in I went.

> With them the Seed of Wisdom did I sow,
> And with my own hand labour'd it to grow:
> And this was all the Harvest that I reap'd—
> I came like Water, and like Wind I go.

8 Ain't no time to hate

Compare Emily Dickinson's poem number 478:

> I had no time to Hate—
> Because The Grave Would Hinder Me—

> And Life was not so
>   Ample I
> Could finish—enmity
>
> Nor had I time to Love—
> But since
> Some Industry must be—
> The little Toil of Love
> I thought
> Be large enough for Me

Notes:

Studio recording: *Workingman's Dead* (May 1970).

First documented performance: December 4, 1969, at the Fillmore West in San Francisco.

Garcia and Hunter discuss the origins of the song:

> Hunter: That [lyric] came from a tape that the band made of a tune of Jerry's. They had the whole tune together, drums and everything—in fact I still have that tape—and I played it over and over and tried writing to it. I kept hearing the words "Goddamn, Uncle John's mad," and it took a while for that to turn into "Come hear Uncle John's Band," and that's one of those little things where the sparkles start coming out of your eyes.

> Garcia: And for me, at that time I was listening to records of the Bulgarian Women's Choir and also this Greek-Macedonian music—these penny-whistlers*— and on one of those records there was a song that featured this little turn of melody that was so lovely that I thought, "Gee, if I could get this into a song, it would be so great." So I stole it. (Jackson: *Going Down the Road*) 34

> *This is probably a reference to the Pennywhistlers, an American women's singing group that performed Eastern European and American folk music, and recorded on the Folkways and Nonesuch labels. Members of the group were Francine Brown, Shelley Cook, Joyce*

Gluck, Alice Kogan, Deborah Lesser, Ethel Raim, and Dina Silberman. They produced at least three albums prior to the release of Workingman's Dead.

Included by Jim Henke, chief curator for the Rock and Roll Hall of Fame and Museum, on his list of the 500 most influential songs in rock-and-roll history.

An interesting and pertinent email thread, started by Jeff Place of Smithsonian/Folkways Records in an email to me in 1996:

> Mike Seeger of the New Lost City Ramblers was just here and we were showing him the web. For jollies I did a search on "New Lost City Ramblers" and turned up your Uncle John's Band page. The original NLCR was Seeger, John Cohen, and Tom Paley. It reminded me that once when John Cohen was visiting the office, he wondered aloud if Uncle John's Band might not be a song about the NLCR. Apparently, Uncle John was a nickname for Cohen. He noticed that lyrics of Uncle John's Band mention a number of their songs. He also remembered Garcia coming to a number of shows by them and the Kentucky Colonels in California in the early days. He wasn't sure, but it was something he has wondered about. Certainly could be true.

[Note: Mike Seeger was the recipient of the Rex Foundation's 1995 Ralph J. Gleason Award.]

Which in turn brought this response, a few days later, from Hunter:

> David,
> I like the direction of the discussion on UJB. It's right on the money. I thought I'd give you a piece to the puzzle which is not so obvious; a less direct allusion. Compare:
>
> > like the morning sun you come
> > and like the wind you go
>
> with:
>
> > Come all ye fair and tender ladies
> > Be careful how you court young men
> > They're like the stars on a summer's morning
> > First appear and then they're gone

(NLCR did that one, too.)

> and while we're at it, they're both what is known as "come all ye" tunes which is a rich tradition. Tom Paley was a math teacher at the University of Connecticut the year I was there. (I was president of the folk music club.) His replacement in the Ramblers, Tracy Schwartz, came to a party at Ellen Cavanaugh's house, along with Garcia, Nelson, and me, after one of the NLCR shows in 1964, and we played until way early in the morning. 35

The manuscript version of the song includes these lines:

> Why wait in the dark for dawn
> (while) when the sun's still going down?
> Maybe I'll dust off your chair
> if you say you're comin' 'round
> Keep your place in line
> all things come in time
> Whoa-oh, all I need to know,
> (will) do these coals glow?
>
> Would you carry me uphill
> back the way I carried you?
> Take me further, if you can,
> (You know) I'd do the same for you.
> Think this through with me,
> let me know your mind,
> Whoa-oh, all I want to know is
> Will you be kind?
>
> Well, now—I can hear
> The flutter of their wings,
> Standin' still on our little (not sure about that
>   word) hill
> can you hear the sirens sing?
>
> Come hear UJB
> playing to the tide etc.

mason's children

1, 2 Mason died on Monday
   3 We bricked him in the wall
      All his children grew and grew
      They never grew so tall before
      They may never grow so tall again

      We dug him up on Tuesday
      He'd hardly aged a day
      Taught us all we ever knew
      We never knew so much before
      We may never know so much again

      Mason was a mighty man
   4 A mighty man was he
      All he said: when I'm dead and gone
      don't you weep for me

   5 The wall collapsed on Wednesday
      We chalked it up to fate
      All his children ran and hid
      We never hid so well before
      Swore we'd never show our face again

      Thursday came and Friday
      with fires tall and bright
      Mason's children cooked the stew
      and cleaned up when the feast was through
      Swore we'd never had such times before

      Take me to the Reaper Man
      to pay back what was loaned
      If he's in some other land
      write it off as stoned

1 Mason

The Masons are a secret fraternal organization that has been the object of a great deal of speculation about intrigue and conspiracy over its approximately three-hundred-year history. Its full name is Free and Accepted Masons, also referred to as Freemasons. Included among its membership has been an impressive number of influential and famous men, ranging from George Washington to the composer George Antheil; from George Wallace to George M. Cohan. (Not all Masons are named George.)

2 Monday, etc.

In format, this is a days-of-the-week song, similar in some ways in its inherent structure to a counting song. The most familiar days-of-the-week rhyme is probably the one alluded to in "Althea,"(q.v.) in the line "You may be Saturday's child."

3 bricked him in the wall

Reminiscent of Edgar Allan Poe's story, "The Cask of Amontillado," in which the narrator, Montresor, describes a chilling and ruthless murder by means of bricking up the victim, Fortunado, in a wine cellar. The events take place during Carnival, and the victim is wearing fool's motley, with cap and bells. The story also contains a Masonic reference:

> I broke and reached him a flagon of De Grave. He emptied it at a breath. His eyes flashed with a fierce light. He laughed and threw the bottle

upwards with a gesticulation I did not understand.

I looked at him in surprise. He repeated the movement—a grotesque one.

"You do not comprehend?" he said.

"Not I," I replied.

"Then you are not of the brotherhood."

"How?"

"You are not of the masons."

"Yes, yes," I said; "yes, yes."

"You? Impossible! A mason?"

"A mason," I replied.

"A sign," he said.

"It is this," I answered, producing a trowel from beneath the folds of my *roquelaire.*

"You jest," he exclaimed, recoiling a few paces. "But let us proceed to the Amontillado."

4 mighy man was he
The 1940s folk song takeoff on "Casey Jones," "Steamboat Bill" has these lines:

Oh, Steamboat Bill, steamin' down the
    Mississippi
Steamboat Bill, a mighty man was he

5 wall collapsed on Wednesday
Compare lines from "Greatest Story Ever Told": *"You can't close the door when the wall's caved in";* and from "Brown-Eyed Women": *"1930 when the Wall caved in."*

6 don't you weep for me
A common folk song sentiment, notably in "Bruton Town":

Don't weep for me, my dearest jewel,
Don't weep for me nor care nor pine,
For your two brothers killed me so cruel—
In such a place you may me find.

Mason was a mighty man
A mighty man was he
All he said: When I'm dead and gone
don't you weep for me   6

Words by Robert Hunter
Music by Jerry Garcia

Notes:
Studio recording: 1970 recording included on the box set *So Many Roads.*

First known performance: December 19, 1969, at the Fillmore Auditorium in San Francisco. There are fifteen known live performances, all in 1969 and 1970, after which it was dropped from the repertoire.

Hunter's note for *A Box of Rain* says: "An unrecorded GD song dealing obliquely with Altamont."

New speedway Boogie

Please don't dominate the rap, Jack
if you got nothing new to say
If you please, don't back up the track
This train got to run today

Spent a little time on the mountain
Spent a little time on the hill
Heard some say: *Better run away*
Others say: *You better stand still*

Now I don't know but I been told
it's hard to run with the weight of gold
Other hand I heard it said
it's just as hard with the weight of lead

Who can deny? Who can deny?
It's not just a change in style
One step done and another begun
in I wonder how many miles?

Spent a little time on the mountain
Spent a little time on the hill
Things went down we don't understand
but I think in time we will

Now I don't know but I been told
in the heat of the sun a man died of cold
Do we keep on coming or stand and wait
with the sun so dark and the hour so late?

1 **New Speedway**
The site of the Altamont concert (December 6, 1969) was a racetrack in the hills east of Livermore, California (my hometown), called the Altamont Speedway. The "new" in the title may refer to the "old" speedway, Speedway Meadows in Golden Gate Park, site of numerous free, unscheduled concerts by the Grateful Dead in spring and summer 1967.

2 **I don't know but I been told**
Compare the line from "Swing Low, Sweet Chariot":

> I ain't never been to heaben but Ah been told
> Dat de streets in heaben am paved with gold.

3 **in the heat of the sun a man died of cold**
The man who was killed at the Altamont concert was Meredith Hunter, age eighteen.

The line is evocative of the line from Stephen Foster's "Oh, Susanna" (also echoed in "Black Muddy River"):

> The sun so hot I froze to death
> Susanna, don't you cry.

Compare also Geoffrey Chaucer's *Troilus and Criseyde*, which was finished in 1385. This particular bit is a direct translation of a sonnet by Boccaccio and a favorite formulation of the troubador poets in which the heat of passion is contrasted with the chill of the Lady's indifference. Troilus is madly in love with Criseyde, and he says this (Book I, Stanza 60):

> Alas! what is this wonder maladye?
> For heat of cold, for cold of heat, I dye.

Notes:
Studio recording: *Workingman's Dead* (May 1970).

First known performance: December 20, 1969, at the Fillmore Auditorium in San Francisco. It was played through September 1970, then dropped from the repertoire for more than twenty years, reappearing in February 1991. It appeared occasionally thereafter.

Hunter's footnote in *A Box of Rain* says:

> Written as a reply to an indictment of the Altamont affair by pioneer rock critic Ralph J. Gleason.

The title is reminiscent of song titles of the type: "New Minglewood Blues."

You can't overlook the lack, Jack
of any other highway to ride
It's got no signs or dividing lines
and very few rules to guide

Spent a little time on the mountain
Spent a little time on the hill
I saw things getting out of hand
I guess they always will

I don't know but I been told
if the horse don't pull you got to carry the load
I don't know whose back's that strong
Maybe find out before too long

One way or another
One way or another
One way or another
this darkness got to give
One way or another
One way or another
One way or another
this darkness got to give

Words by Robert Hunter
Music by Jerry Garcia

friend of the Devil

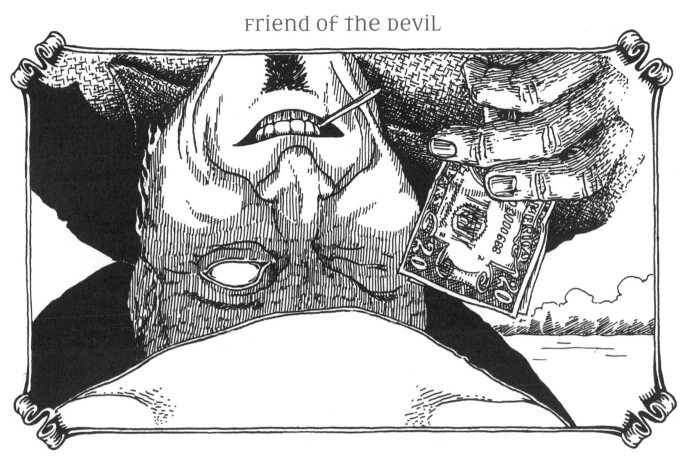

1   I lit out from Reno

2   I was trailed by twenty hounds
      Didn't get to sleep that night
      Till the morning came around

Chorus:

      I set out running but I take my time

3   A friend of the Devil is a friend of mine
      If I get home before daylight
      I just might get some sleep tonight

      I ran into the Devil, babe
      He loaned me twenty bills

1 Reno

A city in Nevada, county seat of Washoe County, founded in 1860. According to *The Illustrated Dictionary of Place Names*, Reno was named for Jesse Lee Reno (1823–62), Virginia-born Union general killed at the Battle of South Mountain, during the Antietam campaign of the Civil War. He had previously served as an ordinance officer during various western surveys, including those in the Territory of Utah.

It's interesting to note that Reno, for the space of one year, from its founding to the split of the Nevada from the larger Utah territory (of which it was originally a part) in 1861 was actually *in* Utah. This makes the character's one-day run from Reno to a cave in the hills of Utah seem a little more believable. Nevada became its own territory in 1861, then a state in 1864.

2 trailed by twenty hounds
Compare Robert Johnson's "Hellhound on My Trail":

> And the days keeps on
>   worryin' me
>   there's a hellhound on
>   my trail

3 the Devil
Here's an interesting comment from Eliade:

> Devils: The definition and derivation of the term *devil* need to be carefully delineated. This need for care in defining *devil* arises from the fact that the very class of creatures being designated as malign may have been originally benign or may be capable of acting in either a benign or malign way.

4 Utah
Forty-fifth state of the Union, admitted 1896.

> Utah. From the Indian name *Ute* . . . variously defined as "in the tops of the mountains" "high up," "the land of the sun," and "the land of plenty." *(Illustrated Dictionary of Place Names)*

5 Got a wife in . . .
This being set in Utah, perhaps the character is a Mormon practicing polygamy.

6 Chino

> Chino, California (San Bernardino County) From a land grant called Santa Ana del Chino. *Chino* is Spanish for a person with mixed blood; probably the landowner was a chino. *(Illustrated Dictionary of Place Names)*

I spent that night in Utah   4
In a cave up in the hills

(Chorus)

I ran down to the levee
But the Devil caught me there
He took my twenty-dollar bill
And he vanished in the air

(Chorus)

Got two reasons why I cry
away each lonely night
First one's named sweet Anne Marie
    and she's my heart's delight
Second one is prison, baby
the sheriff's on my trail
If he catches up with me
I'll spend my life in jail

Got a wife in Chino, babe   5, 6
And one in Cherokee
First one says she's got my child
But it don't look like me

(Chorus)

> *Words by Robert Hunter*
> *Music by Jerry Garcia and John Dawson*

Also the location of a prison in the California system.

The idea has been proposed that the geographical location might more logically be the Chino Valley in Arizona, given the proximity of another place, called Cherry Creek—easily pronounced Cher-o-kee.

7 Cherokee

There are several Cherokees in California, located in Butte County, Nevada County, San Joaquin County, and Tuolumne County. There are also towns named Cherokee in Alabama, Iowa, Kansas, North Carolina, Oklahoma, and Texas. All are named for the Native American Cherokee Nation, and there is an American Cherokee Confederacy of Utah.

Notes:

Studio recording: *American Beauty* (November 1970).

First performance: February 28, 1970, at the Family Dog at the Great Highway in San Francisco. It remained in the repertoire thereafter.

The version played by the band in later years was a slow, stately one, inspired, according to Garcia, by a Kenny Loggins version of the song.

Hunter, in an interview in *Relix,* said:

> I like "Friend of the Devil"; I thought that
> was the closest we've come to what may be a classic
> song.

candyman

1 Come all you
A typical folk song opening, and in fact, a genre of folk songs is called "Come-all-ye's."

2 Candyman
American slang for a drug dealer. Also for a man who has a way with women.

The Mississippi John Hurt version of the "Candy Man Blues" has these words:

He likes a stick of candy just nine inch long
He sells as fast as a hog can chew his corn
It's the candyman

3 roll those laughing bones
Early dice, discovered in archaeological digs, were made of a variety of materials, including bone, ivory, jet, and, most commonly, antler.

4 seven come eleven
In the dice game of craps, a "come" bet is identical to a "pass line" bet, with one exception: A come bet may be made on every throw of the dice once the shooter has established a point. A come bet is made by placing the amount of chips you wish to wager in the designated come area of the craps layout. After you have placed a come bet, the very next roll of the dice becomes the come-out roll for that wager. Thus, if the shooter rolls a seven, you will win even though pass line betters will lose. If an eleven is rolled, you will win while the line bets will not be affected. (www.crapshangout.com)

Also the title of a 1939 Charlie Christian tune.

Come all you pretty women   1
with your hair a-hanging down
Open up your windows 'cause
the Candyman's in town   2
Come on, boys, and gamble
Roll those laughing bones   3
Seven come eleven, boys   4
I'll take your money home

Chorus:

Look out
Look out
The Candyman
Here he come
and he's gone again
Pretty lady ain't
got no friend
till the Candyman
come 'round again

I come in from Memphis
where I learned to talk the jive   5
When I get back to Memphis
be one less man alive
Good mornin,' Mr. Benson   6
I see you're doin' well
If I had me a shotgun
I'd blow you straight to hell   7

(Chorus)

Come on, boys, and wager
if you have got the mind
If you got a dollar, boys

lay it on the line
8   Hand me my old guitar
Pass the whiskey 'round
Want you to tell everybody you meet
the Candyman's in town

(Chorus)

Words by Robert Hunter
Music by Jerry Garcia

5 jive

The Oxford English Dictionary defines *jive* as

> talk or conversation; *spec.* talk that is misleading, untrue, empty, or pretentious; hence, anything false, worthless, or unpleasant.

Partridge says

> n. and v. (A form of) dance: orig. devotees of the form, late 1940s, then ge.; ob. With change of fashion, by late 1950s. . . . probably of Negro origin (perhaps synon with *jazz*). . . . To talk: a talk: jazz fanatics': since ca. 1948.

And in his appendix, in an entry titled "Jive and Swing":

> This slang reached Britain from the U.S. in 1945; still in July 1947 was it very little known except among the *hepcats* or addicts of jive and swing. . . . All of it is American, most of it ephemeral. . . . ["Jive"] may mean "tricks," whence *jive* as a "tricky" form of playing.

Slang dictionaries agree that the origin of the word is unknown.

6 Mr. Benson

This is a character from the song "Midnight Special": "Sheriff Benson will arrest you" if you go to Houston, the song warns. The sheriff in the song may have a historical basis in an actual sheriff, T. A. Binford, county sheriff of Harris County, Texas, from December 1918 to January 1, 1937. Indeed, Leadbelly sang "Binford," not "Benson," in his version of "Midnight Special." Binford was involved in the infamous 1917 "mutiny" in Houston, as a colleague of Lee Sparks, who was city detective at the time of the incident.

In James Lee Burke's excellent novel *Lost Get-Back Boogie*, a character retorts: "Well, thanks, Mr. Benson," which is an indication that the word is a synonym for "the man." In this sense, it is a similar appellation to Mr. Charlie, referred to in the song of the same title.

7 I'd blow you straight to hell

Robert Hunter, on this line:

> Then there's the line in "Candyman" that always gets the big cheers: "If I had a shotgun, I'd blow you straight to hell." The first time I ran into that phenomenon was when I went to the movie *Rollerball* and saw the people were cheering the violence that was happening. I couldn't believe it. I hope that people realize that the character in "Candyman" is a character, and not me. (Jackson: *Goin' Down the Road*) 97

8 Hand me my old guitar

The opening line of the folk song "F.D.R.'s Back Again": "Just hand me my old Martin"—referring to a Martin guitar.

Notes:

Studio recording: *American Beauty* (November 1970).

"Candyman" debuted on April 3, 1970, at the Field House, University of Cincinnati, in Cincinnati. It remained in the repertoire.

Attics of My Life

1 tastes . . . lights . . . hear
Hunter uses the senses repeatedly in this lyric, evoking how it is we know "reality," and then counterposing the sensual world to the spiritual realm: the attics—"upstairs"—which contain the inner world of dreams. Hunter seems to be addressing the source of his inspiration, and in this the lyric has similarities to "Ripple" and "Terrapin Station."

2 And closed my eyes to see
"You fill to the full with most beautiful splendor those souls who close their eyes that they may see."—St. Denis's Prayer, a fourteenth-century poem from Saint Denis's *The Cloud of Unknowing.*

3 You flew to me
Asked about the meaning of the song, Robert Hunter wrote on www.rec.music.gdead:

> I guess I have to give the stock answer: If I could say it in prose, I wouldn't need to write the song. Poetry is evocative—it's meant to communicate to deeper levels and approach the levels of nonverbal experience. I guess the best I could say is that "You flew to me" is an affirmation of the concept of grace—No, this is not a song about being stoned. It's a song about the soul. 37

4 You dreamed of me
In Lewis Carroll's *Through the Looking-Glass,* Alice,

along with Tweedledee and Tweedledum, comes upon the sleeping Red King in the forest. They discuss what he may be

In the attics of my life
Full of cloudy dreams unreal
Full of tastes no tongue can know
And lights no eye can see
    When there was no ear to hear   1
    You sang to me

I have spent my life
Seeking all that's still unsung
Bent my ear to hear the tune
And closed my eyes to see   2
    When there were no strings to play
    You played to me

In the book of love's own dream
Where all the print is blood
Where all the pages are my days
And all my lights grow old
    When I had no wings to fly
    You flew to me   3

You
flew
to me

In the secret space of dreams
Where I dreaming lay amazed
When the secrets all are told
And the petals all unfold
    When there was no dream of mine
    You dreamed of me   4

Words by Robert Hunter
Music by Jerry Garcia

dreaming about, and Tweedledee says he's dreaming about Alice:

"Why, [he's dreaming] about you!" Tweedledee exclaimed, clapping his hands
triumphantly. "And if he left off dreaming about you, where do you suppose you'd be? . . . You'd be nowhere. Why, you're only a sort of thing in his dream!"

"If that there king was to wake," added Tweedledum, "you'd go out—bang!—just like a candle!"

Note:

Studio recording: *American Beauty* (November 1970).

First performance: May 14, 1970, at Meramec Community College in Kirkwood, Missouri. Never a frequent song in concert but revived in later years in a splendid, soaring arrangement.

-juggler-

sugar Magnolia / sunshine Daydream

1 Sugar Magnolia
Magnolias are a family of trees and shrubs, native to Asia and North and Central America. The species is notable for its showy blooms, and the most famous is that of *Magnolia grandiflora*, the Southern magnolia, which produces fragrant, creamy white flowers over eight inches in diameter. The tree itself can grow more than one hundred feet tall.

2 rushes
Etymology: Middle English, from Old English *rysc;* akin to Middle High German *rusch* rush, Lithuanian *regzti* to knit.
Date: before twelfth century
Any of various monocotyledonous, often tufted marsh plants (as of the genera *Juncus* and *Scirpus* of the family Juncaceae, the rush family) with cylindrical, often hollow stems that are used in bottoming chairs and plaiting mats.

Compare J.R.R Tolkien's Fellowship of the Ring, and the character Goldberry in the novel. She is described in the following verses.

I had an errand there: gathering water lilies
green leaves and lilies white to please my
    pretty lady
the last ere the year's end to keep them from
    the winter
to flower by her pretty feet til the snows are
    melted
Each year at summer's end I go to find them
    for her
in a wide pool, deep and clear, far down
    Withywindle
there they open first in spring and there they
    linger latest
By that pool long ago I found the River-
    daughter

Sugar Magnolia blossom's blooming   1
Head's all empty and I don't care
Saw my baby down by the river
Knew she'd have to come up soon for air

Sweet blossom come on under the willow
We can have high times if you'll abide
We can discover the wonders of nature
Rolling in the rushes down by the riverside   2, 3

She's got everything delightful
She's got everything I need
Takes the wheel when I'm seeing double
Pays my ticket when I speed

She come skimming through rays of violet   4
She can wade in a drop of dew
She don't come and I don't follow   5
Waits backstage while I sing to you

She can dance a Cajun rhythm
Jump like a Willys in four-wheel drive   6
She's a summer love in the spring, fall, and winter
She can make happy any man alive

Sugar Magnolia
Ringin' that blue bell
Caught up in sunlight
Come on out singing
I'll walk you in the sunshine

Come on, honey, come along with me

She's got everything delightful
She's got everything I need
A breeze in the pines in the summer night
   moonlight
Crazy in the sunlight yes indeed

7   Sometimes when the cuckoo's crying
When the moon is halfway down
Sometimes when the night is dying
I take me out and I wander round
I wander round

SUNSHINE DAYDREAM

Sunshine daydream
Walk you in the tall trees
Going where the wind goes
8   Blooming like a red rose
Breathing more freely
Light out singing
I'll walk you in the morning sunshine
Sunshine daydream
Walk you in the sunshine

Words by Robert Hunter and Bob Weir
Music by Bob Weir

fair young Goldberry, sitting in the rushes
Sweet was her singing then, and her heart was
   beating. 38

3 down by the riverside
See note under "Uncle John's Band."

4 rays of violet
Compare the line in "What's Become of the Baby":
"Waves of violet go crashing and laughing."

5 She don't come and I don't follow
Compare the lines from the folk song "Sourwood
Mountain":

   I got a girl in the head of the hollow,
   She won't come and I won't call 'er.

**6 Jump like a Willys in
four-wheel drive**
From Lesh's autobiography:

The tension between Weir
and Hunter finally came to a
head backstage at the
Capitol Theater when, after
an argument, probably
about Bob's addition of a line
to "Sugar Magnolia"—"[She]
jumps like a Willys in four-
wheel drive"—Hunter turned
all responsibility for Bob's lyrics over to Barlow,
with the words, "Take him, he's yours." 95

The Willys was made by the Overland Automotive
Company. This jeep-type vehicle, ubiquitous in
World War II, is no longer in production. When the
Willys first came out, there was some type of maneuver, or trick, that an experienced driver could do to
make the vehicle actually leap, jump, or catch air
somehow. Details are sketchy, but there was an arti-

cle in *Smithsonian* magazine (November 1992) that refers to the idea and has a great picture of an airborne jeep to boot.

7 cuckoo
A worldwide family of birds, the North American versions are the Black-billed cuckoo *(Coccyzus erythrophthalmus),* which attracts attention by its series of three-, four- or five-syllable stanzas, and the Yellow-billed cuckoo *(Coccyzus americanus),* which is known by its sequence of "kow-kow" calls that become slower toward the end. (Grzimek)

Greil Marcus's *Invisible Republic,* which documents the influence of American folk music on *The Basement Tapes* by Bob Dylan and the Band, has a significant amount of information on the cuckoo and its role in American folk tradition. Here's a passage from Marcus, taking off from a discussion of Clarence Ashley's recording of the fragmentary folk song "Coo Coo Bird":

> "We Americans are all cuckoos," Oliver Wendell Holmes said in 1872. "We make our homes in the nests of other birds." This is the starting point.

As long as seven hundred years ago, the English were singing that the cuckoo heralded the coming of summer [see "The Golden Road (to Unlimited Devotion)"], and yet the bird was hated. Its cry was reviled through the centuries as oppressive, repetitious, maniacally boring, a cry to drive you crazy, a cry that was already crazy, befitting a bird that was insane.

8 roses
See note under "That's It for the Other One."

Notes:
Studio recording: *American Beauty* (November 1970).

First performance: June 7, 1970, at the Fillmore West in San Francisco.

A note on performance practice: The band often divided the song into two distinct entities: "Sugar Magnolia" and "Sunshine Daydream." The space between these parts could be as brief as the space of several beats; could frame a set, as in the closing of Winterland; or could be as long as a week, as the case of the performance occurring in the week of Bill Graham's death, on October 25, 1991, when "Sunshine Daydream" came during the Polo Field concert in Golden Gate Park a week after the band opened a show with "Sugar Magnolia" (Graham's favorite Grateful Dead song) at the Oakland Coliseum Arena.

TO LAY ME DOWN

To lay me down
once more
To lay me down
with my head
1   in sparkling clover
Let the world go by
all lost in dreaming
To lay me down
one last time
To lay me down

To be with you
once more
To be with you
with our bodies
close together
Let the world go by
like clouds a-streaming
To lay me down
one last time
To lay me down

To lay me down
To lay me down

To lay me down
One last time
To lay me down

To lie with you
once more
to lie with you
with our dreams
entwined together
To lie beside you
my love still sleeping
to tell sweet lies
one last time
and say goodnight
to lay me down
to lay me down
to lay me down
one last time
to lay me down
to lay me down
one last time
to lay me down

Words by Robert Hunter
Music by Jerry Garcia

1 clover
Trifolium, with many
species. Usually three-
leaved (as implied by
the Latin name)—
rarely four-leaved. Its
flowers can be red,
purple, pink, yellow,
or white.

Notes:
Lyric written in
London, 1970.
Studio recording:
Garcia (January 1972).

First performance: July 30, 1970, at the Matrix in
San Francisco. The song's subsequent performance history is fairly unusual among Dead tunes,
dropping from the repertoire for the space of
two hundred to three hundred shows at a time,
several times.

Hunter's liner notes for the Garcia box set *All Good
Things*:

"To Lay Me Down" was written a while before
the others [on the *Garcia* album], on the same
day as the lyrics to "Brokedown Palace" and
"Ripple"—the second day of my first visit to
England. I found myself left alone in Alan Trist's
flat on Devonshire Terrace in West Kensington,
with a supply of very nice thick linen paper,
sun shining brightly through the window, a
bottle of Greek Retsina wine at my elbow. The
songs flowed like molten gold onto the page
and stand as written. The images for "To Lay
Me Down" were inspired at Hampstead Heath
(the original title to the song) the day before—
lying on the grass and clover on a day of
swallowtailed clouds, across from Jack Straw's
Castle [a pub], reunited with the girlfriend of
my youth, after a long separation.

Brokedown Palace

1 Brokedown Palace
The title of a 1986 science-fiction novel by Steven Brust, published by Ace and dedicated to the band ("and especially Billy and Mickey").

Also the title of a 1999 film starring Claire Danes and Kate Beckinsale.

2 weeping willow
Willow *(Salix babylonica)*—The willow is another water-loving tree. Willow bark contains Salicin, which is used in the treatment of rheumatic fever and various damp diseases; also the source of aspirin. Her catkins, which appear in early spring before her leaves, attract bees to start the cycle of pollination. In Western tradition, it is a symbol of mourning and unlucky love. The Latin name for the weeping willow refers to the psalm in which the Hebrews mourn their captivity in Babylon, by the willows. Willow indicates cycles, rhythms, and the ebb and flux. (Smith) 38a

Also worth noting is the comparison to the line in "Crazy Fingers": "Hang your heart on laughing willow."

3 Fare you well
There is an old sailor song called "Fare Thee Well Marianne":

Fare thee well, my own true love
Fare thee well, my dear
The ship is sailin' and the wind blows free
And I am bound away to the sea, Marianne

Ten thousand miles away from home
Ten thousand miles or more
The sea may freeze or the earth may burn
If I never more return to you, Marianne

The lobster boiling in the pot
The bluefish on the hook
Their suffering's long but it's nothing like

Fare you well, my honey
Fare you well, my only true one
All the birds that were singing
Have flown except you alone

Goin' to leave this brokedown palace   1
On my hands and my knees I will roll, roll, roll
Make myself a bed by the waterside
In my time—in my time—I will roll, roll, roll

In a bed, in a bed
by the waterside I will lay my head
Listen to the river sing sweet songs
to rock my soul

River gonna take me
Sing me sweet and sleepy
Sing me sweet and sleepy
all the way back back home
It's a far-gone lullaby
sung many years ago
Mama, Mama, many worlds I've come
since I first left home

Going home, going home
by the waterside I will rest my bones
Listen to the river sing sweet songs
to rock my soul

Going to plant a weeping willow   2
On the bank's green edge it will grow,
    grow, grow
Sing a lullaby beside the water
Lovers come and go—the river roll, roll, roll

3   Fare you well, fare you well
    I love you more than words can tell
    Listen to the river sing sweet song
    to rock my soul

Words by Robert Hunter
Music by Jerry Garcia

The ache I bear for you, Marianne

And if I had a flask of gin
Sugar here for two
And a great big bowl to mix them in
I'd pour a drink for you, Marianne

So fare thee well, my own true love
Fare thee well, my dear
The ship is sailing and the wind blows free
And I am bound away to the sea, Marianne

Also see "Dink's Song":

If I had wings like Noah's dove
I'd fly up the river to the one I love
Fare thee well, oh, honey, fare thee well

Notes:
Lyric written in London, 1970.

Studio recording: *American Beauty* (November 1970).

First performance: August 18, 1970, at the Fillmore West in San Francisco.

The title as given by Hunter in *A Box of Rain* was "Broke-down Palace." However, on albums and in most song lists, it is given without the hyphen: "Brokedown Palace."

The following email note reached me in 2002:

David,
   I've got a little story about "Brokedown Palace" that you might appreciate.

When I was a student at the University of Virginia, I had the fortune of hearing Ken Kesey give a talk and reading (this was about five years ago). Though his discussion was  somewhat confused and disjointed, he had many moments of genius. One which I remember in particular was when he was discussing the death of his son. His son had died when the high school wrestling team's van drove off a cliff during a snow storm. Kesey went to great lengths to discuss his struggle with grief following this tragedy. He commented that not long after his son's death, he was invited to see the Dead play a gig somewhere on the West Coast. Kesey said that sometime during the second set, the whole band turned to him (he was sitting in a balcony seat, or was close to the stage . . .) and began playing "Brokedown Palace." Kesey recounted with tears in his eyes that it wasn't until that moment that he really understood what art was. He said that "all my life I thought art was this [he stuck a fist in the air]. But at that moment I realized that art was really this [he made a hugging motion]."

It really was a moving story. Kesey went on to shock the English faculty by placing a purple-velvet top hat on his head and reading, not a portion of one of his works, but rather a children's story about a lovable, mischievious bear—which he acted out by romping around the stage.

May he rest in peace.

—*Tom McKnight*
Oxford, Mississippi

operator

1 Operator, can you help me? An entire genre of American popular song might be called Telephone Songs. Lee Cooper, in his book *Popular Music Perspectives* devotes an entire chapter to telephones in popular music and includes a huge list of songs. There are many songs; here's a list that's far from complete:

"Call Me"; words and music, Tony Hatch, 1967

"Call Me (Come Back Home)"; words and music, Al Green, Al Jackson Jr., 1973

"Call Me Up Some Rainy Afternoon"; words and music, Irving Berlin, 1910

"Hello, Central"; words and music, R. Ellen, recorded by Lightnin' Hopkins on a single, ca. 1959

"Hello, Central, Give Me Heaven"; words, and music, Charles K. Harris, 1901

"Hello, Central, Give Me No-Man's Land"; words, Sam M. Lewis, Joe Young, music, Jean Schwartz, 1918

"Hello, Frisco Hello"; words, Gene Buck, music, Louis A. Hirsch, 1915

"Memphis, Tennessee"; words and music, Chuck Berry; performed by Johnny Rivers, Sandy Denny, etc.

"Operator"; trad.? performed by Alexis Korner on *Bootleg him!*, ca. 1970

"Operator"; words and music, Len Bland, performed by him on a single, no date

Operator, can you help me?   1
Help me if you please.
Give me the right area code
and the number that I need.
My rider left upon the Midnight Flyer
singing like a summer breeze.

I think she's somewhere down south,
down about Baton Rouge.
But I just can't remember no number,
a number I can use.
Directory don't have it, Central done forgot it;   2
got to find a number to use.

Trying to check out her number,
trying to run down her line.
Operator said that's privileged information
and it ain't no business of mine.
It's flooding down in Texas, the poles are down   3
    in Utah;
got to find a private line.

She could be hanging round a steel mill,
working in a house of blue lights,
riding a getaway bus out of Portland,
talking to the night
I don't know where she's going, I don't care where
    she's been,
long as she's been doing it right,
long as she's been doing it right

Words and music by Ron McKernan

"Operator"; words and music, J. Burks, rhythm-and-blues tune performed by Jewton Burks on a single, no date

"Operator"; words and music, Dupree-Smith, a blues tune performed by Bob Gaddy on a single, 1956

"Operator"; words and music, B. Elgin, K. Rogers, and R. Jones, performed by Gladys Knight on a single released in 1962

"Operator (That's Not the Way It Feels)"; words and music, Jim Croce, 1972

"Operator"; words and music, William Spivey, performed by the Manhattan Transfer on the B side of a single, ca. 1975)

"Operator"; performed by DeDanann on *1/2 Set in Harlem*

"Operator"; performed by Ken Nordine on *Upper Limbo*, 1994

2 Central

From *The Oxford English Dictionary:*
> central, *sb. U.S.* A central telephone exchange; hence, any telephone exchange.
> 1889 Mark Twain *Conn. Yankee* xv. 184, I used to wake . . . and say 'Hello, Central!' just to hear her dear voice."

3 It's flooding down in Texas

Compare Larry Davis and Joseph Scott's "Texas Flood" (recorded by Stevie Ray Vaughn in 1983):

> Well, there's floodin' down in Texas
> All of the telephone lines are down
> Well, there's floodin' down in Texas
> All of the telephone lines are down
> And I've been tryin' to call my baby
> Lord, and I can't get a single sound [39]

4 house of blue lights

One particular establishment, the House of Blue Lights, was a Chicago after-hours club. It was connected to El Grotto (owned by Earl Hines) at the Pershing Hotel, in the mid-1940s.

The song "House of Blue Lights," words and music by Freddie Slack and Don Raye (1947), gives some idea of what, generically, a house of blue lights is:

> There's fryers and broilers and Detroit barbecue ribs
> But the treat of the treats is when they serve you all those fine eight beats

Notes:
Studio recording: *American Beauty* (November 1970).

The Grateful Dead performed this song live four times. The first performance was August 18, 1970, in a show at the Fillmore West in San Francisco.

Ripple

1 **On the harp unstrung**
The line also recalls William Butler Yeats's "The Madness of King Goll," in which the king speaks of a "harp all songless" that he has found:

> When my hand
> passed from wire
>   to wire
> It quenched, with a sound like falling dew
> The whirling and the wandering fire
> But lift a mournful ulalu
> For the kind wires are torn and still
> And I must wander wood and hill
> Through summer's heat and winter's cold
> They will not hush

King Goll was an Irish king of legend, having lived in the third century. Oddly, this is also the time when King Cole (close assonance) of Britain was supposed to have reigned. See the note under "Alligator" regarding Old King Cole.

Edward Gorey wrote a novel titled *The Unstrung Harp: Or, Mr. Earbrass Writes a Novel* (1953). A description by the publisher:

> "On November 18th of alternate years Mr. Earbrass begins writing 'his new novel.' Weeks ago he chose its title at random from a list of them he keeps in a little green notebook. It being teatime of the 17th, he is alarmed not to have thought of a plot to which *The Unstrung Harp* might apply, but his mind will keep reverting to the last biscuit on the plate."
>   So begins what the *Times Literary Supplement* called "a small masterpiece." *The Unstrung Harp* is a look at the literary life and

If my words did glow
with the gold of sunshine
And my tunes were played
on the harp unstrung   1
Would you hear my voice
come through the music
would you hold it near
as it were your own?

It's a hand-me-down
The thoughts are broken
Perhaps they're better
left unsung
I don't know
Don't really care
Let there be songs
to fill the air

Chorus:
Ripple in still water
when there is no pebble tossed
nor wind to blow

Reach out your hand
if your cup be empty   2
If your cup is full
may it be again
Let it be known
there is a fountain   3
that was not made
by the hands of men   4

There is a road
no simple highway
between the dawn
and the dark of night
And if you go
no one may follow
That path is for
5 your steps alone

Ripple in still water
when there is no pebble tossed
nor wind to blow

You who choose
6 to lead must follow
but if you fall
you fall alone
If you should stand
then who's to guide you?
If I knew the way
7 I would take you home

Words by Robert Hunter
Music by Jerry Garcia

its "attendant woes: isolation, writer's block, professional jealousy, and plain boredom." But as with all of Edward Gorey's books, *The Unstrung Harp* is also about life in general, with its anguish, turnips, conjunctions, illness, defeat, string, parties, no parties, urns, desuetude, disaffection, claws, loss, Trebizond, napkins, shame, stones, distance, fever, antipodes, mush, glaciers, incoherence, labels, miasma, amputation, tides, deceit, mourning, elsewards. You get the point. Finally, *The Unstrung Harp* is about Edward Gorey the writer, about Edward Gorey writing *The Unstrung Harp*. It's a cracked mirror of a book, and it's dedicated to RDP, or Real Dear Person.

Additionally, I have always wondered about an episode in Chris Van Allsburg's wonderful *The Mysteries of Harris Burdick*, titled "The Harp." (This book is a collection of drawings, with a title and first line for each, presented as a source of inspiration for children to write their own stories to go with the drawings.) The first line given is "So it's true, he thought, it's really true." And the drawing shows a boy peering at a stream-fed pond, beside which sits a harp; and there is an expanding set of ripples beside the harp.

2 Still Water and If Your Cup be Empty
Several lines in this lyric conjure up the Twenty-third Psalm, which for many listeners will be an evocation of peace and reassurance. In particular, the lines referring to "still water," the filling of an empty cup, and the walking on a path in the shadow of the dark of night are strong references.

Hunter invokes the psalm's associations in the first verse, with his mention of the traditional psalmist's accompaniment, the harp.

TWENTY-THIRD PSALM:

> The Lord is my shepherd, I shall not want
> He maketh me to lie down in green pastures
> He leadeth me beside the still waters
> He restoreth my soul
> He leadeth me in the paths of righteousness
> for his name's sake
> Yea, though I walk through the valley of the
> shadow of death
> I will fear no evil, for thou art with me
> Thy rod and thy staff they comfort me
> Thou preparest a table before me in the
> presence of mine enemies
> Thou annointest my head with oil, my cup
> runneth over
> Surely goodness and mercy shall follow me all
> the days of my life
> And I will dwell in the house of the Lord
> forever

In some ways, the song could be viewed as an updating, or a humanizing, of the psalm. *The Interpreter's Bible* states that:

> psalms are also notable as being the literary record of
> a reproducible religious experience. . . . Later genera-
> tions can . . . stand, as it were, on their shoulders; they
> can think their thoughts after them and catch some of
> their faith and vision.

This is a remarkable passage in that it can be seen to shed direct light on Hunter's line "It's a hand-me-down, the thoughts are broken." The poet has a psalmist's duty to hand down his version of the religious experience through his poetry. In this case, the psalmist admits, and even celebrates, his humanity: "If I knew the way, I would take you home." *If I knew.*

The Twenty-third Psalm plays a role in two other Hunter lyrics: "Alabama Getaway" and the unrecorded song from the *Eagle Mall Suite,* "John Silver," both of which mention "the valley of the shadow."

Hunter's choice of a pool of water being momentarily disturbed by a ripple is in accordance with Samuel Taylor Coleridge's imagery in describing the fleetingness of the altered state in "Kubla Khan":

> Then all the charm
> Is broken—all that phantom-world so fair
> Vanishes, and a thousand circlets spread,
> And each mis-shape the other. Stay awhile,
> Poor youth! who scarcely dar'st lift up thine
> eyes—
> The stream will soon renew its smoothness,
> soon
> The visions will return! And lo, he stays,
> And soon the fragments dim of lovely forms
> Come trembling back, unite, and now once
> more
> The pool becomes a mirror.

For more on Taylor and "Kubla Khan," see the annotations for "What's Become of the Baby?"

3 fountain

Cirlot, in *A Dictionary of Symbols:*

> Fountain (or Source). In the image of the terrestrial
> Paradise, four rivers are shown emerging from the
> centre, that is, from the foot of the Tree of Life itself, to
> branch out in the four directions of the Cardinal Points.
> They well up, in other words, from a common source,
> which therefore becomes symbolic of the "Centre" and
> of the "Origin" in action. Tradition has it that this fount
> is the *fons juventutis* whose waters can be equated
> with the "draught of immortality"— *amrita* in Hindu
> mythology. Hence it is said that water gushing forth is a
> symbol of the life-force of Man and of all things. For this

reason, artistic iconography very frequently uses the motif of the mystic fount. 40

4 That was not made by the hands of men
The Merle Travis song "I Am a Pilgrim" has these lines:

There is a home in that yonder city
That was not made by hand.

5 That path is for your steps alone
Walt Whitman's "Song of Myself":

Not I—not anyone else, can travel that road for you,
You must travel it for yourself.

Friedrich Nietzsche's 1881 preface to *Daybreak:*

For he who proceeds on his own path in this fashion encounters no one: This is inherent in "proceeding on one's own path." No one comes along to help him; all the perils, accidents, malice, and bad weather which assail him he has to tackle by himself. For his path is his alone.

The folk song "Lonesome Valley":

You got to walk that lonesome valley
You got to walk it by yourself;
There's no one here can walk it for you
You got to walk it for yourself.

6 You who choose to lead must follow
From the *Tao te Ching:*

Therefore, desiring to rule over
    the people,
One must in one's words humble
    oneself before them
And, desiring to lead the people,
One must, in one's person, follow
    behind them.

Mark 10:444:

"and whosoever would be first among you must be slave of all."

7 I would take you home
This line presages the Barlow-Mydland song "I Will Take You Home."

Notes:
Lyric written in London, 1970.

Studio recording: *American Beauty* (November 1970).

First performed on August 18, 1970, at the Fillmore West in San Francisco. It never found a permanent place in the Dead's live repertoire, but was played on special occasions such as the 1980s fifteenth-anniversary shows in San Francisco and New York, both of which included acoustic sets.

See Keith Abbott's *Downstream from Trout Fishing in America* (Santa Barbara: Capra Press, 1989). In this memoir, Abbott recalls a dinner party at Richard Brautigan's Bolinas, California, residence in the early 1970s, at which the poet Robert Creeley was a guest.

Just before dinner was served, Richard made a big show of putting on a Grateful Dead record. He said that he had been saving the record as a surprise for Creeley. Bob nodded his thanks. When the first cut started Creeley brought his head up abruptly. "This is my favorite cut on that record," he announced. Richard beamed happily. As Creeley listened to the song Richard told a story of all the obstacles that he had encountered during the day in his attempt to find this particular record for Bob. Content that he had made Creeley happy, Richard went back to the kitchen to attend to dinner. When the song was over, Creeley got up, went over to the stereo, and, trying to play the cut again, raked the needle across the record, ruining it. "Uh-oh," he said. Then he went back to the couch and resumed his discussion. At the sound of the record's being ruined, Richard came rushing out of the kitchen and stood there, watching the whole 'uh-oh' performance by Creeley. Going over to the stereo he brought out a second copy of the album from the stack alongside it. In his own funny, precise way, Richard congratulated himself. "I'm ready for Bob this time," he boasted. Then he went on to relate how Creeley had wrecked the very same album on a previous visit. [41]

Asked via email in 2002 about which song was the "favorite cut" on that record, Creeley replied:

That was one drunken evening, like they say—of probably all too many. Richard knew my failings, call them, and so had backed up the record he expected me witlessly to scratch with another, which I seem then to have x'd as well. Ah eagerness—and drink. We were neighbors at that time in Bolinas, with him just down the road from us headed into town.

Anyhow the terrific song, as I remember at least, is Robert Hunter's "Ripple" and one of my prized possessions is Robert Hunter's collected lyrics, *A Box of Rain,* which he generously sent me some years after. Anyhow I love that echoing "Ripple in still water. . . ."

Best to you,
Robert Creeley

TRUCKIN'

1 Truckin'—got my chips cashed in

2 Keep Truckin'—like the doodah man
Together—more or less in line
Just keep Truckin' on

Arrows of neon and flashing marquees out
   on Main Street
Chicago, New York, Detroit, it's all on the
   same street
Your typical city involved in a typical daydream
Hang it up and see what tomorrow brings

3 Dallas—got a soft machine
Houston—too close to New Orleans
New York—got the ways and means
but just won't let you be

Most of the cats you meet on the street speak of
   True Love
Most of the time they're sittin' and cryin' at home
One of these days they know they gotta get goin'
out of the door and down to the street all alone

Truckin'—like the doodah man
once told me you got to play your hand
sometime—the cards ain't worth a dime
if you don't lay 'em down

4 Sometimes the light's all shining on me
Other times I can barely see
Lately it occurs to me

5 What a long strange trip it's been

1 Truckin'
See note under "Cosmic Charlie."

The Great Song Thesaurus lists one other song titled "Truckin'": words, Ted Koehler; music, Rube Bloom, 1935.

2 doodah man
Skeleton Key cites Hunter as saying that the doodah man was just lifted from the "doodah" chorus of "Camptown Races" by Stephen Foster (1850).

3 soft machine
Possibly an allusion to the William Burroughs novel *The Soft Machine*. According to *The Dictionary of Literary Biography*:

> The "soft machine" is both the "wounded galaxy," the Milky Way seen as a biological organism diseased by the viruslike Nova Mob, and the human body, riddled with parasites and addictions and programmed with the "ticket" (that is, obsolete myths and dreams) written on the "soft typewriter" of culture and civilization.

There was also a British rock band by the name Soft Machine, in the late sixties and early seventies. According to Martin C. Strong in *The Great Rock Discography*, the band "phoned up novelist William Burroughs to ask his permission on use of group name."

The Pop-o-Pies on their version of "Truckin'," sang, "Dallas, got a soft-drink machine."

4 Sometimes the light's all shining on me / Other times I can barely see
Dark and light are frequent motifs in Robert Hunter lyrics. See, for example, "Comes a Time," "Terrapin Station."

5 What a long strange trip it's been
One of the best-known lines in rock and roll and in the culture at large, this snippet has served as title and subtitle to a large number of books and articles invoking, as it does, the epoch from which it stems.

Among them are:

20 Years of Rolling Stone: What a Long, Strange Trip It's Been (1987)

Some Lessons About Libel Law and Communication Science from the Long, Strange Trip of Jeffrey Masson and the Case of the Fabricated Quotations by Clay Calvert (1994)

What a Long Strange Trip It's Been: A Hippie's History of the Sixties and Beyond by Lewis Sanders (1989)

"Illicit Drug Use Revisited: What a Long, Strange Trip It's Been" by P. A. Selwyn in *Annals of Internal Medicine*, November 15, 1993.

"Magellan Star Scanner Experiences: What a Long, Strange Trip It's Been," by Eric H. Seale in *Advances in Astronautical Sciences*, vol. 74, p. 513

A Long Strange Trip: The Inside History of the Grateful Dead by Dennis McNally (2002)

What in the world ever became of sweet Jane?   6
She lost her sparkle, you know she isn't
    the same
Living on reds, vitamin C, and cocaine
All a friend can say is "Ain't it a shame"

Truckin'—up to Buffalo   7
Been thinkin'—you got to mellow slow
Takes time—you pick a place to go
and just keep Truckin' on

Sitting and staring out of a hotel window
Got a tip they're gonna kick the door in again
I'd like to get some sleep before I travel
but if you got a warrant I guess you're gonna
    come in

Busted—down on Bourbon Street   8
Set up—like a bowling pin
Knocked down—it gets to wearing thin
They just won't let you be

You're sick of hanging around and you'd like
    to travel
Tired of travel, you want to settle down
I guess they can't revoke your soul for trying
Get out of the door—light out and look
    all around

Sometimes the light's all shining on me
Other times I can barely see
Lately it occurs to me
What a long strange trip it's been

Truckin'—I'm goin' home
Whoa-oh, baby, back where I belong
Back home—sit down and patch my bones
and get back Truckin' on

Words by Robert Hunter
Music by Jerry Garcia, Phil Lesh, and Bob Weir

6 sweet Jane
Robert Hunter provides an explanation for this
line:

> The intention was a parody of the forties warn-
> ing-style of singing commercial, specifically
> "Poor Millicent, poor Millicent / She never
> used Pepsodent/ Her smile grew dim / And
> she lost her vim / So, folks, don't be like
> Millicent / Use Pepsodent! " I'm sure that the
> allusiveness, not that entirely outré in the six-
> ties, is well lost here in the nineties. So, it's
> perhaps an in-joke, but not one meant for pri-
> vate consumption. Just a bit of black humor
> that fails to fire and emerges, instead, as an
> enigma. 41a

Listeners may well tend to think of the Velvet
Underground's 1970 song "Sweet Jane."

On a recording from May 28, 1982, Bob Weir
sings "What in the world ever became of Sweet
Jane / she lost her sparkle, you know, she isn't
the same / ever since she went and had a sex
change / All a friend can say is ain't it a shame."

7 Truckin'—up to Buffalo
Compare the song title "Shuffle Off to Buffalo"
(Al Dubin and Harry Warren, 1932):

> I'll go home and get my panties,
> You go home and get your scanties,
> And away we'll go;
> Mm, off we're gonna shuffle,
> Shuffle off to Buffalo.
> To Niag'ra in a sleeper,
> There's no honeymoon that's cheaper,
> And the train goes slow;
> Ooh, off we're gonna shuffle,
> Shuffle off to Buffalo. 42

8 Busted
The entire band was arrested for possession of marijuana in New Orleans in 1970. They vowed never to return. (However, they played concerts there four times in the 1980s.)

Notes:
Studio recording: *American Beauty* (November 1970).

First performance: August 18, 1970, at the Fillmore West in San Francisco. It remained in the repertoire thereafter.

Weir, Hunter, Lesh, and Hart were interviewed about the song in the 1997 film *Anthem to Beauty:*

> Weir: There was a romance about being a young man on the road in America, and you had to do it! It was a rite of passage. And at the same time, it was the material that you drew from to write about. We were starting to become real guys, and really enjoying the hell out of it. We toured more or less four to six months out of the year. It was our bread and butter—we weren't selling that many records. And we had a lot of fun out on the road, got into a lot of trouble. . . . We left some smoking craters in some Holiday Inns, I'll say that, and there were a lot of places that wouldn't have us back. All of this is absolutely autobiographical, all the stuff in "Truckin'."

> Hunter: This was written over a long period of time. . . .

> I had a verse: "Once in a while the music gets into the street / fifty old ladies bug every cop on the beat / they're putting the lock on Lindley Meadow and Kezar / beginning' to look like we can't play in the park." Yea, that kind of stuff had lots and lots of verses I thought, we had all thought, that we could keep adding to "Truckin'" over the years, but the funny thing is, once you get it down, it is down. You don't go back, you don't revisit it.

> Hart: It was autobiographical. We told our story in song. So I knew that the words were strong. They were powerful, they were depicting real events in real people's lives, and they became part of the fabric, part of the history of our day. People could sing it and know there were events directly connected with it.

> Lesh: In those days there wasn't any rock-and-roll bubble that would isolate us from the world as we went through it. So the walls of the hotels were all thin and we didn't charter planes, so we flew commercial when we flew, and a lot of times we took buses. And I see a group of much younger people doing things in a way that I envy now, looking back on it.

The song, translated into French, was published in the band's sixth newsletter (December 1972), and the lyrics were included in copies of *Europe '72,* distributed in francophone European nations.

Till the Morning Comes

1 Till the morning comes
It'll do you fine
Till the morning comes
like a highway sign
Showing you the way
leaving no doubt
Of the way on in
or the way back out

Chorus:
Tell you what I'll do
I'll watch out for you
You're my woman now
Make yourself easy
Make yourself easy
Make yourself easy

Till we all fall down
It'll do you fine
Don't think about
what you left behind—
the way you came
or the way you go
Let your tracks be lost in the dark
and snow

(Chorus)

When the shadows grow
It'll do you fine

When the cold winds blow
It'll ease your mind
The shape it takes
could be yours to choose—
what you may win
what you may lose

(Chorus)

Words by Robert Hunter
Music by Jerry Garcia

1 Till we all fall down
Echoing the nursery rhyme "Ring a Ring a Rosie,"
which is also quoted in two other Grateful Dead
songs: "Throwing Stones" and "Doin' That Rag."
See note under "Doin' That Rag" for more detail.

Notes:
Studio recording: *American Beauty* (November
1970).

First performance: September 18, 1970, at the
Fillmore East in New York. It remained in the
repertoire for only five performances.

GOIN' DOWN THE ROAD FEELIN' BAD

Notes:
Recording: *Grateful Dead* (Skull & Roses) (October 1971) is generally accepted as the standard recording. Never recorded in the studio.
First performance: October 10, 1970, at Colden Auditorium, Queens College, Queens, New York. It remained in the repertoire thereafter.

This is one of those songs that have been popular in both black and white musical traditions for many decades, and with a number of different titles. According to noted folk and blues authority Dave Evans of Memphis State, the tune is of Negro origin, but it surfaced as an Appalachian Mountain tune in the twenties. It became a popular song among Okies during the Dust Bowl era (for obvious reasons), and as impoverished farmers fled the Southwest, they took the song with them to California's blossoming fruit orchards, the beet farms of Michigan, Oregon's cherry orchards, and a hundred other points scattered around the land. As the song traveled, the verses changed frequently, so the Dead's version is most likely a hodgepodge of lyric ideas from all over. For instance, a couple of the verses in the first Okie versions contained such sentiments as "Ain't got but one old lousy dime / But I'll find me a new dollar some day," and "A two-dollar shoe won't fit my feet /Ain't gonna be treated this way." (Jackson: *Goin' Down the Road*) 94

Goin' down the road feeling bad
Goin' down the road feeling bad
Goin' down the road feeling bad
Don't wanna be treated this-a way

Going where the climate suits my clothes
Going where the climate suits my clothes
Going where the climate suits my clothes
Don't wanna be treated this-a way

Going where the water tastes like wine
Going where the water tastes like wine
Going where the water tastes like wine
Don't wanna be treated this-a way

Words and music: traditional

box of rain

1   Look out of any window
    any morning, any evening, any day
    Maybe the sun is shining
    birds are winging or
    rain is falling from a heavy sky—
    What do you want me to do,
    to do for you to see you through?
    this is all a dream we dreamed
2   one afternoon long ago

    Walk out of any doorway
    feel your way, feel your way
    like the day before
    Maybe you'll find direction
    around some corner
    where it's been waiting to meet you—
    What do you want me to do,
    to watch for you while you're sleeping?
    Well please don't be surprised
    when you find me dreaming, too

    Look into any eyes
    you find by you, you can see
    clear through to another day
    I know it's been seen before
    through other eyes on other days
3   while going home —
    What do you want me to do,
    to do for you to see you through?
    It's all a dream we dreamed
    one afternoon long ago

1 Look out of any window
Bruce Hornsby recorded a song called "Look Out
Any Window" on his 1988 *Scenes from the
Southside* album.

2 this is all a dream we dreamed / one
afternoon long ago
Compare to the line in "Stella Blue": "It seems
like all this life / was just a dream."

3 on other days / while going home
The title of a book by Michelle Carter (Morrow,
1987).

4 dead dreams
The title of a book by Lewis Sanders, *Dead
Dreams: Under Eternity with the Grateful Dead, A
Mythological History* (1998).

5 box of rain
This exchange appeared in Hunter's mailbag on
August 6, 1996:

> From: (Charles E. Bass)
> Dear Robert,
>   After reading through a number of mailbags
> posted at your website, I finally decided that
> it was time to contribute a thought and a
> question.
>   Between your evocative, thoughtful lyrics
> and Jerry's powerful melodies, I have apho-
> risms and meditations aplenty to help me
> through my days and in my life. For that,
> thank you, thank you, thank you.
>   I sat down the other day and figured out
> the chord changes to "Mission in the Rain."
> My wife (who is not a Deadhead) especially
> likes that song. Maybe it is because we live
> in San Francisco and there is a reference to
> the Mission. When I play it she always starts
> dancing.
>   Robert, if you would, please tell me what
> you were thinking when you penned the

phrase "box of rain." What, for you, does a box of rain represent? I am not asking for the meaning of the song, or for you to explain the song to me—I spent plenty of time on my own doing that. I am just terribly curious how you came to choose that image.

Well, I won't take any more bandwith. There is much I would like to say, but I've said it in my mind for so long now, it feels funny and self-conscious trying to put it onto "paper."

Regards,

Charlie Bass

Hunter replied:

Charlie,

Well, I don't like to do this, since it encourages others to ask about what I had in mind when I wrote a song, and mostly you'd need to have my mind to understand even approximately what I had in it. By "box of rain," I meant the world we live on, but "ball" of rain didn't have the right ring to my ear, so box it became, and I don't know who put it there.

[RH] 43

6 moth before a flame This line resonates with several proverbial and poetic snippets:

"The fate of the moth in the flame"—Aeschylus, *Fragments* (Fragment no. 288)

Another old Greek proverb is "Rejoicing with the moth's joy" as it flutters about the candle that will consume it.

Walk into splintered sunlight
Inch your way through dead dreams   4
to another land
Maybe you're tired and broken
Your tongue is twisted
with words half spoken
and thoughts unclear
What do you want me to do
to do for you to see you through?
A box of rain will ease the pain   5
and love will see you through

Just a box of rain
wind and water
believe it if you need it
if you don't just pass it on
Sun and shower, wind and rain
in and out the window
like a moth before the flame   6

It's just a box of rain
I don't know who put it there
Believe it if you need it
or leave it if you dare
But it's just a box of rain
or a ribbon for your hair
Such a long, long time to be gone
and a short time to be there   7

Words by Robert Hunter
Music by Phil Lesh

A Chinese proverb, as collected and translated by William Scarborough (1875) reads:

> The moth that dashes into the flame
> And burns has only itself to blame. (Proverb 864)

Stanza two of Percy Shelley's "To _____: One Word Is Too Often Profaned" reads:

> The desire of the moth for the star,
> Of the night for the morrow,
> The devotion to something afar
> From the sphere of our sorrow.

7 long, long time to be gone / and a short time to be there

"Little Birdie" ("an old Southern mountain banjo tune"), as performed by Pete Seeger, who learned it from a member of the Coon Creek Girls when they were visiting New York, in 1940, from Kentucky:

> Little birdie, little birdie,
> What makes you fly so high?
>
> It's because I am a true little bird
> and I do not fare to die.
>
> Little birdie, little birdie,
> What makes your wings so blue?
>
> It's because I been a-grievin',
> a-grievin' after you.
>
> Little birdie, little birdie,
> What makes your head so red?
>
> After all that I been through,
> its a wonder I ain't dead.
>
> Little birdie, little birdie,
> come sing to me your song.
>
> *I've a short while to be here,*
> *and a long time to be gone.*
>
> Little birdie, little birdie,
> What makes you fly so high?
>
> It's because I am a true little bird
> and I do not fare to die.

And, in the opening verses of this version, as performed by the Stanley Brothers at the Newport Folk Festival in 1964, it is clear that "Little Birdie" is related to the long-time Grateful Dead–performed traditional song "Dark Hollow":

> Little Birdie, Little Birdie,
> Won't you sing to me a song,
> But a long time to stay here,
> And a short time to be gone.
>
> Rather be in some dark holler,
> Where the sun don't never shine,
> Than you be another man's darlin'
> And to know that you'll never be mine.

Notes:

Studio recording: *American Beauty* (November 1970).

First performance: October 9, 1972, at the Winterland Arena in San Francisco. Disappeared from the repertoire less than a year later, brought back on March 20, 1986, at the Coliseum in Hampton, Virginia. It remained in the repertoire thereafter—often sung in response to the chant "We Want Phil," from Deadheads—and was the final song ever performed by the Grateful Dead, on July 9, 1995, at Soldier Field in Chicago, given as a second encore, following "Black Muddy River."

Hunter notes in his anthology of lyrics, named for this song:

> Phil Lesh wanted a song to sing to his dying father and had composed a piece complete with every vocal nuance but the words. If ever a lyric "wrote itself," this did—as fast as the pen would pull.

Lesh, from his autobiography:

> Hunter has said elsewhere that I had asked specifically for a song for my father; actually, I merely mentioned casually that I'd be working out the vocals as I drove to visit him. One way or another, that must have been a catalyst for his imagination—a day later, he presented me with some of the most moving and heartfelt lyrics I've ever had the good fortune to sing. The result was

"Box of Rain," probably my most well-known and best-loved song, and also the first song on which I sang lead vocal. To this day, I'm asked to sing and dedicate this song to those who are recovering, sick, dying, or who have already passed on. [95]

From *Classic Albums: American Beauty*, a film by Jeremy Marre:

Lesh: The lyrics came about in an unusual way. This was the first time I had written a song in a long time, and I had worked out the melody and the chords, and in fact the whole song, from beginning to end—introduction, coda, and everything—and I put it on a tape and gave it to Hunter.

Hunter: He'd just written these lovely changes and put 'em on a tape for me, and he sang along (scat singing of melody)—so the
phrasing was all there, I think I went through it two or three times, writing as fast as I could, and that song was written. I guess it was written for a young man whose father was dying.

Lesh: And at that time, my dad was dying of cancer, and I would drive out to visit with him, in the hospital, and also at the nursing home he spent his final days in, and after Bob gave me the lyrics, on the way out there I would practice singing the song. I sort of identified that song with my dad and his approaching death. The lyrics that he produced were so apt, so perfect. It was very moving, very moving for me to experience that during the period of my dad's passing. I felt like singing it in other situations similar to that since then.

Carl Hiaasen's book *Stormy Weather* (1995) has a wonderful passage in which the lead character, Skink, sings "Box of Rain" to a child in a shelter for people left homeless by a hurricane.

Bertha

I had a hard run
Running from your window
I was all night running, running, running
I wonder if you care?
I had a run-in
Run around and run down
Run around a corner
Run smack into a tree

Chorus:
I had to move
Really had to move
That's why, if you please
I am on my bended knees
Bertha, don't you come around here anymore

Dressed myself in green
I went down to the sea
Try to see what's going down
Try to read between the lines
Had a feeling I was falling, falling, falling
Turned around to see
Heard a voice a-calling, calling, calling
You was coming after me
Back to me

(Chorus)

Ran into a rainstorm
Ducked into a bar door
It was all night pouring, pouring rain
But not a drop on me
Test me, test me
Why don't you arrest me?
Throw me in the jailhouse
Until the sun goes down
Till it go down

(Chorus)

Words by Robert Hunter
Music by Jerry Garcia

1 Bertha
The name given to a
large fan (a machine,
not a Deadhead) in the
Grateful Dead's office.
Apparently, the fan
would walk itself across
the floor when activated.

Notes:
Recording: *Grateful Dead*
(Skull & Roses) (October
1971).

First performance: February 18, 1971, at the
Capitol Theater in Port Chester, New York. It
remained in the repertoire thereafter.

1 Greatest Story Ever Told
Also the title of a 1965 film, produced and directed by George Stevens, about the life of Jesus. Based on a 1949 book of the same title by Fulton Oursler.

2 guitar
Hunter notes in *A Box of Rain:* "Bob Weir . . . sings *quasar* rather than *guitar*."

However, when the song was first sung with the Dead, Weir actually did sing *guitar* rather than *quasar.*

3 left-handed monkey wrench
Richard McKenna, in his book *The Left-Handed Monkey*

Wrench, explains that the left-handed monkey wrench is an item every novice sailor is sent to fetch, as an initiation. This is what's known in the folklore trade as a "fool's errand." Here's a list of similar tools that a new apprentice or recruit may be sent to find:
  Carpenters: *crooked straightedge, round square, rubber hammer for glass nails* or *flannel hammer.*
  Storemen could often do with a *wall-stretcher.*
  Painters: *red, white, and blue paint.*
  Printers: *cubic type*
  Nautical: *galley down-haul, key of the starboard watch.*
  Miscellaneous: *left-handed spanner, horseladder, yard-wide pack thread.* (Partridge)

Moses come riding up on a guitar
2
His spurs were a-jingling, the door was ajar
His buckle was silver, his manner was bold
I asked him to come on in out of the cold
His brain was boiling, his reason was spent
He said: *If nothing was borrowed, then nothing was lent*
I asked him for mercy, he gave me a gun
Said: *Now 'n' again these things just got to be done*

Abraham and Isaac
sitting on a fence
You'd get right to work
if you had any sense
Y'know the one thing we need
is a left-hand monkey wrench
3

Gideon come in with his eyes on the floor
4
Says: *Y'ain't got a hinge, you can't close the door*
Moses stood up a full six-foot-ten
Says: *You can't close the door when the wall's caved in*
I asked him for water, he poured me some wine
5
We finished the bottle, then broke into mine
You get what you come for, you're ready to go
It's one in ten thousand just come for the show
6

Abraham and Isaac
Digging on a well
Mama come quick
with the water witch spell
7
Cool clear water
8
where you can't never tell

Words by Robert Hunter
Music by Bob Weir

There are many others, including a boar stretcher, a sky hook, and the forty-foot-of-water line (which is actually a line that is painted on the bottom of the ship to show where the average water height would be).

4 Gideon

Jewish tribal leader, ca. twelfth century B.C.E. His story is to be found in Judges 6–8. He is remembered for mobilizing a force that at last put an end to annual raids at harvest time and is "also remembered for having an exceptional penchant for oracle-seeking and divinatory inquiry" *(Anchor Bible Dictionary)*. 44

5 asked him for water

Compare the line in the "Cool Drink of Water Blues," recorded sometime between 1928 and 1930 by Tommy Johnson:

> Well, I asked for water and
> She gave me gasoline. (Oakley)

Howlin' Wolf also recorded this song as "I Asked for Water (She Gave Me Gasoline)" (ca. 1959). He is credited as the song's author.

John 2: 1–11 records Jesus's first miracle:

> And the third day there was a marriage in Cana of
>   Galilee; and the mother of Jesus was there:
> And both Jesus was called, and his disciples, to
>   the marriage.
> And when they wanted wine, the mother of Jesus saith
>   unto him, They have no wine.
> Jesus saith unto her, Woman, what have I to do with
>   thee? mine hour is not yet come.
> His mother saith unto the servants, Whatsoever
>   he saith unto you, do it.
> And there were set there six waterpots of stone,
>   after the manner of the purifying of the Jews,
>   containing two or three firkins apiece.
> Jesus saith unto them, Fill the waterpots with
>   water. And they filled them up to the brim.
> And he saith unto them, Draw out now, and bear unto
>   the governor of the feast. And they
>   bare it.
> When the ruler of the feast had tasted the
>   water that was made wine, and knew not
>   whence it was: (but the servants which drew
>   the water knew); the governor of the feast
>   called the bridegroom,
> And saith unto him, Every man at the begin-
>   ing doth set forth good wine; and when
>   men have well drunk, then that which is
>   worse: but thou hast kept the good wine
>   until now.
> This beginning of miracles did Jesus in Cana of
>   Galilee, and manifested forth his glory; and
>   his disciples believed on him.

See also John: 19: 28–30:

> After this, Jesus knowing that all things were
>   now accomplished, that the scripture might
>   be fulfilled, saith, I thirst.
> Now there was set a vessel full of vinegar: and
>   they filled a sponge with vinegar, and put
>   it upon hyssop, and put it to his mouth.
> When Jesus therefore had received the vingar,
>   he said, It is finished: and he bowed his
>   head, and gave up the ghost.

6 ten thousand

Is it worthwhile to note that two songs on *Ace* contain the number ten thousand? The other is in "Black-Throated Wind": ". . . ten thousand cafes and bars." Weir seeems to like this number: He also sings it in the Dead's version of the traditional song "Samson and Delilah": "And when he got to move, ten thousand were dead." "Ten thousand" is also the literal translation of the Chinese word for "a great number" and is a primary unit by which higher numbers are expressed.

7 water witch spell

Water-witching, or dowsing, is the art of finding water sources using a divining rod, or even one's hand. *The*

Beginner's Handbook of Dowsing by Joseph Baum cites Moses as the first dowser, based on the biblical passage "and Moses . . . smote the rock with his rod and water came forth abundantly" (*Numbers* 20:11).

8 Cool clear water
The Marty Robbins ("El Paso," "Big Iron") song "Cool Water" has the last line, "Cool clear water," repeated twice.

Notes:

Studio recording: *Ace* (May 1972).

First performed: February 18, 1971, at the Capitol Theater in Port Chester, New York.

According to Hunter's note in *A Box of Rain,*

> Also known as "Pumpman" and "Moses"—I wrote this to the rhythm of the pump in Mickey Hart's well.

It was titled "Pump Song" on the first Mickey Hart solo album, *Rolling Thunder*.

Loser

If I had a gun for every ace I've drawn

1   I could arm a town the size of Abilene

Don't you push me, baby, 'cause I'm
    moaning low

You know I'm only in it for the gold

2   All that I am asking for is ten gold dollars

I could pay you back with one good hand

You can look around about the wide
    world over

You'll never find another honest man

Last fair deal in the country, sweet Suzy

Last fair deal in the town

Put your gold money where your love is, baby

Before you let my deal go down

Don't you push me, baby

because I'm moaning low

I know a little something

you won't ever know

Don't you touch hard liquor

just a cup of cold coffee

Gonna get up

in the morning and go

Everybody's bragging and drinking that wine

I can tell the queen of diamonds by the

3   way she shine

4   Come to Daddy on an inside straight

I got no chance of losing this time

No, I got no chance of losing this time

Words by Robert Hunter
Music by Jerry Garcia

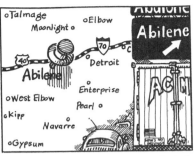

1 Abilene

Abilene, Kansas (present population 6,242), was settled in 1858.

. . . it became the first railhead of the Union Pacific Railroad at the N terminus of the Chisholm Trail from Texas (1867–71) at a leading distribution point on the Smoky Hill Trail to the West. One of the most famous of the wide-open cow towns, it was "cleaned up" by Wild Bill Hickok, who became its marshal in 1871. *(The Cambridge Gazetteer of the United States and Canada)*

Abilene, Texas, founded in 1881, was named for the Kansas town because it was also a railhead for cattle drives. When Hunter speaks of a "town the size of Abilene," we can assume he meant the Kansas town at the height of its "wide-open" period, ca. 1870. According to the *Encyclopedia Britannica*, the town was first known as Mud Creek, and was named Abilene around 1860, for the biblical Abilene, which means "grassy plain." The *Britannica* also gives a clue to the town's population at its height, noting that "the biggest year of cattle drives to Abilene over the Chisholm Trail was 1871, when more than 5,000 cowboys driving 700,000 cows arrived at the yards."

"Abilene," by Lester Brown and Bob Gibson was recorded by Gibson in 1957).

2 gold dollars
The gold dollar coin referred to in the song may have been of several possible designs: The 1849–54 Liberty Head; [1854-56] Small Indian Head; the 1856–89 or the 1856–89 Large Indian Head.

3 queen of diamonds by the way she shine
In divination with cards, this card indicates a flirtatious, sophisticated, witty, fair-haired woman.

In this reference, "the way she shine" may refer to a marked card needed to complete the following line's inside straight.

4 inside straight
An *inside straight* is a drawing hand in poker with a single missing rank to draw a straight. A hand with an ace, a king, a jack, and a ten would need a queen to fill an inside straight. This is how the player knows he will not lose, the card on the top of the deck has the shine of the queen of diamonds, so he knows he will make his hand, even though it is a statistical long shot. Good poker players will almost never draw to an inside straight.

Notes:
Studio recording: *Garcia* (January 1972).

First performance: February 18, 1971, at the Capitol Theater in Port Chester, New York. It remained in the repertoire thereafter.

Gambling
A function of Art is to preserve tradition and evoke strong associated affect. A picture may tell a thousand words, but a single word can also stand for a picture. The lyricist choosing the word or tersest phrase can evoke allusions plumbing deep-seated emotions.

Words connected with gambling have a long tradition and drag in their trail romantic associations tied to the Wild West frontier—a frontier now gone, in fact, but a concept that we try continually to re-create in film, music, painting, and some types of play. In lyrics, the Old West of drifters, free spirits, living by one's wits and fists, and traveling light, come alive. Truckin', gambler, ace, bluff, raise—place-names such as Abilene, Deadwood, Texas—each immediately conjures a past time in a newly opened country.

Ironically, a recent burst of interest in poker, now omnipresent on TV and the Internet, is a dark mirror image of what poker in song and the West represented. Song celebrated the desire to quit the safety of home, family ties, traditional job—the romance of being on the road with no specific direction and taking your chances in the next saloon with a poker game running. Ballads celebrated whisky and wild women and staking it all on a single hand, celebrating the illusion that one good hand will make your fortune forever—the universal fantasy of every gambler. ("Loser "—"I could pay you back with one good hand." "Ramble On Rose"—"Sittin' plush with a royal flush"). But winning can also be beside the point. It's the action that counts. "Stella Blue" evokes endless nights in every "blue-light cheap hotel"—unable to win but keep on bucking. There is the old classic joke about the cowboy who plays in a game he knows is fixed. When asked why he plays in a game he can't beat, his response is, "It's the only game in town."

That was then—play for the high, not the money. Compare that with playing on the Internet from the comfort and safety of your own easy chair—no road, no wild women, and in lieu of whiskey, a backup computer to figure the odds on each hand. Nerds fighting with computer programs—no six-guns. Or competing in casinos with thousands in a single tournament, many playing as partners. Not the image of the lone rider braving Dodge to take on the other passing strangers. Co-opted by large corporate interests, all is safe, sanitary, secure, even respectable—you might as well be at home. (Throwing Stones—"Commissars and pinstripe bosses / Roll the dice.")

Gambling and the potential for danger—violence—had always been part of the spice. "Mississippi Half-Step" takes it back to Cain and Abel, citing loaded dice and an ace behind the ear as motivation for the "first murder." The World Series of Poker, which started the current craze, was created by a man twice indicted for murder, Benny Binion, who fled Texas to the safety of Las Vegas and filled his game with "West Texas" gamers. Now a mere curse word in a casino will get you suspended from play.

Twenty years ago, when I started playing with the big boys, poker was still pretty wide open—cussin', fistfights, whisky, cigars, wild women, and all of it face-to-face. I got the moniker "Deadman" because of my association with the Grateful Dead, but also because when I won my World Series Championship bracelet, the loser held aces and eights, known as the "dead man's hand," as Wild Bill Hickok held when shot to death in Deadwood. Today, I doubt that many poker players know about Hickok, Deadwood, the frontier, or give a damn. They are chasing dreams of money on a new variety of the spinning wheel. Poker, with its huge number of participants, has reduced the value of skill, increased the factor of random luck, and come closer to roulette or the lottery.

So where is the outlaw mystique of the game now? In the songs, in the pages of this book. Balladeer sing on!

—Hal Kant, General Counsel to the
Grateful Dead, 1970–2000

Notes:
Studio recording: *Garcia* (January 1972).

First performance: February 18, 1971, at the Capitol Theater in Port Chester, New York. It remained in the repertoire thereafter.

Playing in the Band

1 Others trust to might
The principle of "might makes right" has its origins in the thought of Plato (*Republic* I.xii) and Seneca (*Hercules Furens*).

On *Rolling Thunder,* Weir sings this line as "others trust to sight."

2 Just look to see the sights
On *Ace,* Weir sings: "Just lookin' for their kites."

3 Let him cast a stone at me
A reference to the New Testament passage, John 8, in which Jesus, in his sermon on the Mount of Olives, explicates the principle "Judge not, and ye shall not be judged." Specifically, this is a reference to verse 7, in which Jesus says to a gathered crowd that has brought him a woman found in adultery: "He that is without sin among you, let him first cast a stone at her." The principle is also elaborated in the version of the Sermon on the Mount found in Matthew 7:1–5, a reference also echoed in "Throwing Stones."

4 Daybreak / Daybreak on the land
On *Ace,* Weir sings this line the final time as "Daybreak while I'm playing in the band." He also sings the line "Playing, like a wave upon the sand" on this album.

Some folks trust to reason
Others trust to might   1
I don't trust to nothing
But I know it come out right

Say it once again now
Oh, I hope you understand
When it's done and over
Lord, a man is just a man

Chorus:
Playing
Playing in the band
Daybreak
Daybreak on the land

Some folks look for answers
Others look for fights
Some folks up in treetops
Just look to see the sights   2

I can tell your
    future
Look what's in your
    hand
But I can't stop for
    nothing
I'm just playing in
    the band

(Chorus)

Standing on a tower
World at my command
You just keep a-turning
While I'm playing in the band

If a man among you
Got no sin upon his hand
3   Let him cast a stone at me
For playing in the band

Playing
Playing in the band
Daybreak
4   Daybreak on the land
Playing
Playing in the band
Daybreak
Daybreak on the land

Words by Robert Hunter
Music by Bob Weir and Mickey Hart

Notes:

Studio recording: *Ace* (May 1972).

First performance: February 18, 1971, at the Capitol Center in Port Chester, New York. The song remained in the repertoire thereafter.

The tune is also known as "The Main Ten," and is so listed on Hart's *Rolling Thunder* because of its ten-beat meter.

wharf Rat

1 Wharf Rat
From the *Dictionary of Americanisms:*

> 2. Wharf rat . . . one who is frequently found on or near wharves, esp. a vagrant or petty criminal who haunts wharves . . . 1836 *Franklin Repository* (Chambersburg, PA) 4 Oct 1/3 "I've an idea, my man, that you are one of the wharf rats; and, if so, the less lip you give me the better."

Additionally, Wharf Rats is the name of a group of sober Deadheads who patterned themselves roughly on the Alcoholics Anonymous model of a twelve-step program to maintain sobriety in the often slippery atmosphere of a Grateful Dead concert. Their motto is "One show at a time."

The lyrics bear a certain similarity in context to Samuel Taylor Coleridge's "Rime of the Ancient Mariner." Here are its final stanzas:

And ever and anon throughout his future life an agony constraineth him to travel from land to land;

> Since then, at an uncertain hour,
> That agony returns:
> And till my ghastly tale is told,
> This heart within me burns.
> I pass, like night, from land to land;
> I have strange power of speech;
> That moment that his face I see,
> I know the man that must hear me:
> To him my tale I teach.
> What loud uproar bursts from that door!
> The wedding-guests are there:
> But in the garden-bower the bride
> And bride-maids singing are:
> And hark the little vesper bell,
> Which biddeth me to prayer!

> O Wedding-Guest! this soul hath been
> Alone on a wide wide sea:

Old man down
way down
down, down by the docks of the city,
Blind and dirty
asked me for a dime—
a dime for a cup of coffee
I got no dime but
I got some time to hear his story:

My name is August West
and I love my Pearly Baker best
more than my wine
. . . more than my wine
more than my maker
though He's no friend of mine

Everyone said
I'd come to no good
I knew I would
Pearly believed *them*

Half of my life
I spent doing time for
some other fucker's crime
Other half found me stumbling around
drunk on burgundy wine

But I'll get back
on my feet someday
the good Lord willing
if He says I may
I know that the life I'm
living's no good

I'll get a new start
live the life I should

5 I'll get up and fly away
I'll get up and
fly away . . .
. . . fly away

Pearly's been true
true to me, true to my dying day he said
I said to him:
I'm sure she's been
I said to him:
I'm sure she's been true to you

I got up and wandered
Wandered downtown
nowhere to go
but just to hang around
I got a girl
named Bonny Lee
I know that girl's been true to me
I know she's been
I'm sure she's been
true to me

Words by Robert Hunter
Music by Jerry Garcia

So lonely 'twas, that God himself
Scarce seemed there to be.

O sweeter than the marriage-feast,
'Tis sweeter far to me,
To walk together to the kirk
With a goodly company!—

To walk together to the kirk,
And all together pray,
While each to his great Father bends,
Old men, and babes, and loving friends
And youths and maidens gay!

And to teach, by his own example, love and rev-
erence to all things that God made and loveth.

Farewell, farewell! but this I tell
To thee, thou Wedding-Guest!
He prayeth well, who loveth well
Both man and bird and beast.
He prayeth best, who loveth best
All things both great and small;
For the dear God who loveth us,
He made and loveth all.

The Mariner, whose eye is bright,
Whose beard with age is hoar,
Is gone: and now the Wedding-Guest
Turned from the bridegroom's door

He went like one that hath been stunned,
And is of sense forlorn:
A sadder and a wiser man,
He rose the morrow morn.

2 asked me for a dime— / a dime for a cup of coffee
In the 1954 film *On the Waterfront* (starring Marlon Brando, directed by Elia Kazan), there is a scene where Terry Malloy, played by Brando, is walking from the church with Edie, played by Eva Marie Saint, after the union has come to break up a meeting of potential "rats." An old bum in

the park stops the couple and asks, "Can you spare a dime? Just a dime for a cup of coffee?"

3 August West

Garcia's only known artwork titled after a Grateful Dead song lyric was *August West (Wharf Rat)* measuring 8.5" by 5.75." According to gallery owner Roberta Weir:

> Jerry preferred to keep his art separate from his music. When *August West* was first exhibited, it was immediately sold. A disappointed fan then asked if Jerry would draw Annie Bonneau for him. Jerry said, "No. Absolutely not. The art and the music are two separate things in my head. They don't connect at all."

4 Pearly Baker

Purley Baker headed the Anti-Saloon League, a temperance organization, from 1903 to the early 1920s. In the song, of course, Pearly Baker, with the different spelling, becomes a woman.

5 I'll get up and fly away

Compare the folk song "I'll Fly Away":

One bright morning, when this life is o'er
I'll fly away,
To that home on God's celestial shore
I'll fly away.

I'll fly away (O glory)
I'll fly away (in the morning)
When I die, Hallelujah bye and
bye,
I'll fly away, fly away.

When the shadows of
this life have gone
Like a bird from prison
bars has flown

Just a few more weary
days and then
To a land where joys shall
never end

Notes:

Recording: *Grateful Dead* (Skull & Roses) (October 1971).

First performance: February 18, 1971, at the Capitol Theater in Port Chester, New York. It remained in the repertoire thereafter.

bird song

All I know is something like a bird

1   within her sang

All I know, she sang a little while

and then flew on

Tell me all that you know

I'll show you

Snow and rain

If you hear that same sweet song again

will you know why?

Anyone who sings a tune so sweet

is passing by

Laugh in the sunshine

sing

cry in the dark

fly

through the night

Don't cry now

Don't you cry

Don't you cry

anymore

la-la-la-la

Sleep

in the stars

don't you cry

dry your eyes on the wind

la-la-la-la

la . . .

1 within her sang
Lesh began to sing "within him" in homage to Garcia, after his death in 1995.

Notes:
Studio recording: *Garcia* (January 1972).

First performance: February 19, 1971, at the Capitol Theater in Port Chester, New York. The song remained in the repertoire steadily through September 1973, then was dropped until September 1980, after which it remained in steady rotation.

Hunter includes the dedication *". . . for Janis"* with the lyric as it appears in *A Box of Rain*. He also lists the title as "Birdsong." In his notes for the *All Good Things* box set, he wrote:

> Don't remember where I wrote the words for "Bird Song." Probably when we were all living in Larkspur (where we wrote *Workingman's Dead* and *American Beauty*) because it's intended as a tribute to Janis [Joplin], after her death, and she lived down the block from us in Madrone Canyon. The birdsong image came from a beautiful collage someone had constructed and hung on the wall when I was a waiter at St. Michael's Alley on University Avenue in Palo Alto. . . . The collage had a picture of a bird and a quote: "All I know is something in me sang that in me sings no more." I don't know whose quote that is, but it stuck with me over the years and finally found its expression in "Bird Song." [45]

All I know is something like a bird
within her sang
All I know, she sang a little while
and then flew on

Tell me all that you know
I'll show you
Snow and rain

Words by Robert Hunter
Music by Jerry Garcia

- elder -

DEAL

Since it cost a lot to win
and even more to lose
You and me bound to spend some time
wondering what to choose

Chorus:

Goes to show you don't ever know
Watch each card you play
and play it slow
Wait until your deal come 'round
1 Don't you let that deal go down

I been gambling hereabouts
for ten good solid years
If I told you all that went down
it would burn off both your ears

(Chorus)

Since you poured the wine for me
and tightened up my shoes
I hate to leave you sitting there
composin' lonesome blues

It goes to show you don't ever know
Watch each card you play
and play it slow
Wait until your deal come 'round
Don't you let that deal go down [ad lib]

Words by Robert Hunter
Music by Jerry Garcia

1 **Don't you let that deal go down**
Reminiscent of the folk song "Don't Let Your Deal Go Down.":

> I've been all around this whole wide world,
> Way down in Memphis, Tennessee.
> Any old place I hang my hat
> Seems like home to me.
>
> Don't let your deal go down.
> Don't let your deal go down.
> Don't let your deal go down, sweet mama
> Till your last old dollar's gone.
>
> When I left my love behind,
> She's standin' in the door;
> She throwed her little arms around my neck
>   and said,
> "Sweet daddy please don't go!"
>
> Now it's who's gonna shoe your pretty little
>   feet?
> Who's gonna glove your hand?
> And who's gonna kiss your ruby lips?
> Honey, who's gonna be your man?
>
> She says, "Papa will shoe my pretty little feet,
> Mama will glove my hand.
> You can kiss my rosy lips
> When you get back again."
>
> Where did you get them high-heel shoes.
> And that dress you wear so fine?
> Got my shoes from a railroad man
> Dress from a driver in the mine.

Notes:
Studio recording: *Garcia* (January 1972).

First performance: February 19, 1971, at the Capitol Theater in Port Chester, New York. The song never left the repertoire thereafter.

mister charlie

1 Chuba-chuba
Possibly a variant spelling of *juba*, which is the
name of a type of dance in African American culture that flourished, along with the Buck Dance
(see "Uncle John's Band"), from the early nineteenth to the early twentieth century.

Step It Down, by Bessie Jones and Bess Lomax
Hawes, contains an entire section on "clapping
plays," to which category the *Juba* dance
belongs:

> That's one of the oldest plays I think I can
> remember our grandfather telling us about,
> because he was brought up in Virginia. He
> used to tell us about how they used to eat
> ends of food; that's what *juba* means. They
> said "jibba" when they meant "giblets"; we
> know that's ends of food. They had to eat left-
> overs.

> "Mrs. Jones is right; this is one of her oldest
> rhymes. George Washington Cable saw African
> slaves doing a dance called the Juba in New
> Orleans' Congo Square, long before emanci-
> pation; today it may be seen in some of the
> Caribbean Islands. In the United States, occa-
> sional mention of "juba" may be found in
> songs, generally associated with hand-clap-
> ping, but the dance itself appears to have
> been lost. . . .

> Juba, Juba
> Juba this and Juba that
> And Juba killed a yellow cat
> And get over double trouble, Juba.
> You sift-a the meal,
> You give me the husk;
> You cook-a the bread,
> You give me the crust;

I take a little powder
I take a little salt
I put it in my shotgun
and I go walking out

Chuba-chuba   1
Wooley-booley   2
Looking high
Looking low
Gonna scare you up and shoot you
'Cause Mister Charlie told me so   3

I won't take your life
Won't even take a limb
Just unload my shotgun
and take a little skin

Chuba-chuba
Wooley-booley
Looking high
Looking low
Gonna scare you up and shoot you
'Cause Mister Charlie told me so

Well, you take a silver dollar
Take a silver dime
Mix 'em both together
in some alligator wine

I can hear the drums
Voodoo all night long

Mister Charlie tellin' me
I can't do nothin' wrong

Chuba-chuba
Wooley-booley
Looking high
Looking low
Gonna scare you up and shoot you
'Cause Mister Charlie told me so

Now Mister Charlie told me
Thought you'd like to know
Give you a little warning
before I let you go

Chuba-chuba
Wooley-booley
Looking high
Looking low
Gonna scare you up and shoot you
'Cause Mister Charlie told me so

Words by Robert Hunter
Music by Ron McKernan

You fry the meat,
You give me the skin;
And that's where my mama's trouble begin.
And then you Juba,
You just Juba.

And there's the parallel to the Beatles' "I Am the Walrus," which has a nonsense "juba juba" chorus.

2 Wooley-booley
Partridge refers to the standard army-issue heavy jumper (pullover), worn as part of barracks dress since around 1960.

There is also the famous hit song "Wooly Bully," words and music by Domingo Samudio (1965).

3 Mister Charlie
From *The Random House Historical Dictionary of American Slang:*

Charlie: white men regarded as oppressors of blacks—used contemptuously. Also Mr. Charlie, Boss Charlie. [1923 in E. Wilson *Twenties:* Mista Charlie, I hear—I hear the niggers is free, is that right?] . . . 1928 McKay *Banjo:* We have words like ofay, pink, fade, spade, Mr. Charlie, cracker, peckawood, hoojah, and so on—nice words and bitter.

An article by John Cowley, "Shack Bullies and Levee Contractors: Bluesmen as Ethnographers," in *The Journal of Folklore Research,* vol. 28, nos. 2

and 3, pp. 135–162, recounts the story of the Lowrence family, a set of seven brothers—the oldest named Charley—who were notorious contractors of cheap labor, mostly African American, that built the levees alongside the Mississippi in the 1920s. A number of songs quoted in the article refer to "Mr. Charley" specifically in this context, giving rise to speculation on the part of Alan Lomax that he may have "discovered the identity of the elusive Mr. Charley." Cowley's article goes on, however, to quote a comment by Alan Dundes regarding Lomax's article, that "Mr. Charley would appear to date from antebellum times." But the repeated reference to a "Mr. Charley" by Southern bluesmen was undoubtedly in reference to Charley Lowrence.

A similar sense of the white man in authority as oppressor has been ascribed to Mr. Benson, familiar from "Candyman."

James Baldwin's 1964 play *Blues for Mr. Charlie,* based on the murder of Emmett Till, in 1955, also immortalized this characterization of the white oppressor.

Notes:
Recording: *Europe '72* (November 1972).

First performance: July 31, 1971, at the Yale Bowl, Yale University, New Haven, Connecticut.

sugaree

1

When they come to take you down
When they bring that wagon 'round
When they come to call on you
and drag your poor body down

Chorus:
Just one thing I ask of you
Just one thing for me
Please forget you knew my name
My darling Sugaree

2   Shake it, shake it, Sugaree
Just don't tell them that you know me

You thought you was the cool fool
Never could do no wrong
Had everything sewed up tight
How come you lay awake all night long?

(Chorus)

Shake it, shake it, Sugaree
Just don't tell them that you know me

You know in spite of all you gained
you still have to stand out in the pouring rain
One last voice is calling you
and I guess it's time you go

(Chorus)

Shake it, shake it, Sugaree
Just don't tell them that you know me

Shake it up now, Sugaree
3   I'll meet you at the Jubilee

1 Sugaree
The title is reminiscent of the Elizabeth Cotten song "I've Got a Secret (Shake Sugaree)." Fred Neil recorded the tune in a version in which he reworked the melody somewhat.

From Hunter's liner notes for the reissue of *Garcia* in the box set *All Good Things:*

> Sugaree was written soon after I moved from the Garcia household to China Camp. People assume the idea was cadged from Elizabeth Cotten's "Sugaree," but, in fact, the song was originally titled "Stingaree," which is a poisonous South Sea manta. The phrase "Just don't tell them that you know me" was prompted by something said by an associate in my pre-Dead days, when my destitute circumstances found me fraternizing with a gang of minor criminals. What he said when departing was: "Hold your mud and don't mention my name."
>
> Why change the title to "Sugaree"? Just thought it sounded better that way, made the addressee seem more hard-bitten to bear a sugarcoated name. The song, as I imagined it, is addressed to a pimp. And yes, I knew Libba's song and did indeed borrow the new name from her, suggested by the "Shake it" refrain.

It has further been suggested that the use of "Sugaree" by Cotten was derived ultimately from *shivaree:*

> *shivaree* n. Midwestern & Western U.S. A noisy mock serenade for newlyweds. Also called regionally charivari, belling, horning, serenade. [Alteration of charivari.]
> Regional Note: Shivaree is the most common American regional form of charivari, a French word meaning "a noisy mock serenade for

newlyweds" and probably deriving in turn from a Late Latin word meaning "headache." The term, most likely borrowed from French traders and settlers along the Mississippi River, was well established in the United States by 1805; an account dating from that year describes a shivaree in New Orleans: "The house is mobbed by thousands of the people of the town, vociferating and shouting with loud acclaim. . . . [M]any [are] in disguises and masks; and all have some kind of discordant and noisy music, such as old kettles, and shovels, and tongs. . . . All civil authority and rule seems laid aside" (John F. Watson). The word *shivaree* is especially common along and west of the Mississippi River. Its use thus forms a dialect boundary running north-south, dividing western usage from eastern. This is unusual in that most dialect boundaries run east-west, dividing the country into Northern and Southern dialect regions. Some regional equivalents are *belling,* used in Pennsylvania, West Virginia, Ohio, Indiana, and Michigan; *horning,* from upstate New York, northern Pennsylvania, and western New England; and *serenade,* a term used chiefly in the South Atlantic states. *(American Heritage Dictionary of the English Language)* 46

Sugaree was also the name of a town in Liberia. A map in *Mitchell's School Atlas: Comprising the Maps and Tables Designed to Accompany Mitchell's School and Family Geography* (Thomas, Cowperthwait & Co, 1853) shows Sugaree on the northern coast, in the region called Ohio.

2 Shake it

Shake it! interj. (1900s–1990s) a cry of encouragement to a dancer, usually a dancing woman. *Shake* n., v. (1900s–1930s) an Oriental dance

If that Jubilee don't come   4
Maybe I'll meet you on the run

(Chorus)

Shake it, shake it, Sugaree
just don't tell them that you know me
Shake it, shake it, Sugaree
Just don't tell 'em that you know me

Words by Robert Hunter
Music by Jerry Garcia

style done in sensuous jazz terms; to dance eroti-
cally; shaking added to Oriental dance motions.
(Major)

3 Jubilee
In ancient Jewish times, Jubilee held every forty-nine
years, was a ritualized way of giving everyone a
clean slate. The tradition is outlined in the Bible in
Leviticus 25:10:

> And ye shall hallow the fiftieth year, and proclaim
> liberty throughout all the land unto all the inhabi-
> tants thereof: it shall be a jubilee unto you; and ye
> shall return every man unto his possession, and ye
> shall return every man unto his family.

The basic tenet of Jubilee is that all debts should be forgiv-
en. This included indenture and mortgage of person and
property. Thus the concept was readily embraced by
America's slave population and entered our folklore.

4 If that
A formulation commonly known from "The Mocking Bird
Song" (Sharp, #234): "If that mocking bird don't sing. . . ."

Notes:
Studio recording: *Garcia* (January 1972).

First performance: July 31, 1971, at the Yale Bowl, Yale
University, New Haven, Connecticut. The song remained in
the repertoire thereafter.

brown-eyed women

1 1920 when he stepped to the bar
Prohibition lasted from the passage of the 18th Amendment in 1919 to the passage of the 21st Amendment, which repealed the 18th, in 1933.

2 1930 when the Wall caved in
Wall Street crashed in 1929, setting off the Great Depression.

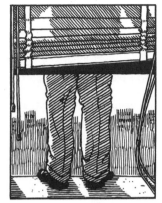

3 Red-eye
Redeye: n. 1. Whisky of very poor quality. In full redeye whisky. . . . 1819 QUITMAN in Claiborne *Life Quitman* I. 42 Whiting and I had a treat to 'red-eye,' or 'rot-gut,' as whiskey is here [Ky.] called. (*Dictionary of Americanisms*)

4 Bigfoot County
There is no Bigfoot County in the United States. The closest is a town named Bigfoot, in Texas, but given the line about snow, a Texas setting seems unlikely.

5 Cost two dollars
Compare the folk song "Moonshiner," which has the line "I'll make you one gallon for a two-dollar bill."

Gone are the days when the ox fall down
he'd take up the yoke and plow the fields
   around
Gone are the days when the ladies said: "Please,
gently, Jack Jones, won't you come to me?"

Chorus:
Brown-eyed women and red grenadine
the bottle was dusty but the liquor was clean
Sound of the thunder with the rain
   pouring down
and it looks like the old man's getting on

In 1920 when he stepped to the bar   1
he drank to the dregs of the whiskey jar
In 1930 when the Wall caved in   2
he paid his way selling red-eye gin   3

(Chorus)

Delilah Jones was the mother of twins
two times over and the rest was sins
Raised eight boys, only I turned bad
Didn't get the lickings that the other ones had

(Chorus)

Tumble down shack in Bigfoot County   4
Snowed so hard that the roof caved in
Delilah Jones went to meet her God
and the old man never was the same again

(Chorus)

Daddy made whiskey and he made it well
5   Cost two dollars and it burned like hell
I cut hick'ry just to fire the still
Drink down a bottle and you're ready to kill

Brown-eyed women and red grenadine
the bottle was dusty but the liquor was clean
Sound of the thunder with the rain
   pouring down
and it looks like the old man's getting on

Words by Robert Hunter
Music by Jerry Garcia

Notes:
Recording: *Europe '72* (November 1972).

First performance: August 23, 1971, at the
Auditorium Theater in Chicago. It remained in
the repertoire thereafter.

There has long been confusion over the song's
title. Hunter, in *A Box of Rain,* titles it "Brown-
Eyed Women," while the listing on the cover of
Europe '72 calls it "Brown-Eyed Woman."
According to *DeadBase VIII:*

> Willy Legate of the Grateful Dead Archives
> kindly informed us that although the title was
> copyrighted as "Brown-Eyed Woman" (that's
> how it appears on the album and/or song-
> book), Robert Hunter actually wrote and
> intended it to be "Brown-Eyed Women," the
> way Jerry Garcia really sings it. This is a classic
> case of a typographical error.

Empty Pages

Notes:
No official recording.

First performance: August 24, 1971, at the Auditorium Theater in Chicago. It was only played twice.

Empty pages before my eyes
Do not deny or criticize
Empty bedrooms where 1 paid my dues
Watching the ceiling instead of you
Can you tell me where you've gone?
Ain't no one around to hear my song

I've got some songs I'd like to sing
Always brings down some other thing
Where can I go? my [hands/gloves?] are
  broken
It seems like your love is just a token
So won't you stay with me?

Up in the morning and out the door
No one won't come in I gotta live alone
Back in the evening with the [   ]
I got a mind to push out

Words and music by Ron McKernan

tennessee jed

2 Cold iron shackles and a ball and chain
Listen to the whistle of the evening train
You know you bound to wind up dead
if you don't head back to Tennessee, Jed

Rich man step on my poor head
When you get up you better butter my bread
Well, you know it's like I said
You better head back to Tennessee, Jed

Chorus:
Tennessee, Tennessee
There ain't no place I'd rather be
Baby, won't you carry me
3 Back to Tennessee

Drink all day and rock all night
Law come to get you if you don't walk right
Got a letter this morning and all it read:
You better head back to Tennessee, Jed

I dropped four flights and cracked my spine
Honey, come quick with the iodine
Catch a few winks down under the bed
Then head back to Tennessee, Jed

(Chorus)

I ran into Charley Phogg
He blacked my eye and he kicked my dog
My dog he turned to me and he said:
Let's head back to Tennessee, Jed

1 Tennessee Jed
Tennessee Jed was the title character of a radio show that ran from 1945 to 1947. The show was carried on ABC and was sponsored by Tip-Top Bread (as in "when you get up you better butter my. . . .")

2 Cold iron shackles and a ball and chain
Uncle Dave Macon and, later, the New Lost City Ramblers recorded a song called "Old Plank Road," which refers to wearing a ball and chain and wanting to get back to Tennessee, or, to be more specific, to "Chattanoogie":

> Rather be in Richmond with all the hail and
> rain
> Than to be in Georgia, boys, wearin' that
> ball and chain
>
> Won't get drunk no more (3x)
> Way down the Old Plank Road
>
> I went down to Mobile, but I got on the
> gravel train
> Very next thing they heard of me, had on that
> ball and chain
>
> Doney, oh, dear Doney, what makes you treat
> me so
> Caused me to wear that ball and chain, now
> my ankle's sore
>
> Knoxville is a pretty place, Memphis is a
> beauty

Wanta see them pretty girls, hop to
  Chattanoogie
I'm going to build me a scaffold on some
  mountain high
So I can see my Doney girl as she goes
  riding by

My wife died on Friday night, Saturday she
  was buried
Sunday was my courtin' day, Monday I
  got married

Eighteen pounds of meat a week, whiskey here
  to sell
How can a young man stay at home, pretty
  girls look so well

3 won't you carry me / Back to Tennessee
This line recalls the A. P. Carter song "Clinch
Mountain Home," with its chorus:

Carry me back to old Virginia,
Back to my Clinch Mountain home
Carry me back to old Virginia,
Back to my old mountain home.

Notes:
Recording: *Europe '72* (November 1972).

First performance: October 19, 1971, at
Northrop Auditorium, University of Minnesota,
Minneapolis. The song remained in the repertoire
from then on.

Hunter, in *A Box of Rain,* says:

"Tennessee Jed" originated in Barcelona,
Spain. Topped up on *vino tinto,* I composed it
aloud to the sound of a jaw harp twanged
between echoing building faces by someone
strolling half a block ahead of me in the late
summer twilight. 47

I woke up a-feeling mean
Went down to play the slot machine
The wheels turned 'round and the letters read:
Better head back to Tennessee, Jed

(Chorus)

Words by Robert Hunter
Music by Jerry Garcia

jack straw

We can share the women
We can share the wine
We can share what we got of yours
'Cause we done shared all of mine

Keep a-rolling
Just a mile to go
Keep on rolling, my old buddy
You're moving much too slow

I just jumped the watchman
Right outside the fence
Took his ring, four bucks in change
Now ain't that heaven-sent?

Hurts my ears to listen, Shannon
Burns my eyes to see
Cut down a man in cold blood, Shannon
Might as well be me

We used to play for silver
Now we play for life
One's for sport and one's for blood
1 *At the point of a knife*
Now the die is shaken
Now the die must fall
There ain't a winner in this game
Who don't go home with all
Not with all . . .

Leaving Texas
Fourth day of July
Sun so hot, clouds so low
The eagles filled the sky

1 **blood / At the point of a knife**
A line from the Child ballad (#13) "Edward":

What makes that blood on the point of your
  knife?
My son, now tell to me
It is the blood of my old gray mare
Who plowed the fields for me, me, me
Who plowed the fields for me.

It is too red for your old gray mare
My son, now tell to me
It is the blood of my old coon dog
Who chased the fox for me, me, me
Who chased the fox for me.

It is too red for your old coon dog
My son, now tell to me
It is the blood of my brother John
Who hoed the corn for me, me, me
Who hoed the corn for me.
What did you fall out about?
My son, now tell to me
Because he cut yon holly bush
Which might have been a tree, tree, tree
Which might have been a tree.

What will you say when your father comes
  back
When he comes home from town?
I'll set my foot in yonder boat
And sail the ocean round, round, round
I'll sail the ocean round.

When will you come back, my own dear son?
My son, now tell to me
When the sun it sets in yonder sycamore tree
And that will never be, be, be
And that will never be.

The ballad is noteworthy in another respect as
well, namely that it is structured for two voices,
as is "Jack Straw."

2 Great Northern out of Cheyenne

The Great Northern (GN) was not a train but a large railroad, which ran from St. Paul to Portland, Oregon, Seattle, and Vancouver. The Burlington did go to Cheyenne, Wyoming, and the Great Northern and Burlington worked together. The Burlington ran GN trains from Chicago to St. Paul as well as the Northern Pacific (NP) trains. In 1970, GN, NP, and Burlington merged into Burlington Northern.

> The Great Northern Railroad Company originated as the St. Paul and Pacific in 1862, becoming the 'Great Northern' in 1889, eleven years after the Canadian James J. Hill, "the empire builder," took it over. (Flexner)

3 From sea to shining sea

A quote from "America the Beautiful," words by Katherine Lee Bates (1859–1929), first printed in the *Congregationalist,* July 4, 1895. Bates was a professor of English literature at Wellesley College and is said to have written the poem after visiting the summit of Pike's Peak.

The music to which the poem was set is the tune "Materna" by Samuel A. Ward, composed in 1882. He apparently never heard his music linked with Bates's words.

Catch the Detroit Lightning
Out of Santa Fe
Great Northern out of Cheyenne   2
From sea to shining sea   3

Gotta get to Tulsa
First train we can ride
Got to settle one old score
And one small point of pride . . .

Ain't no place a man can hide, Shannon
Keep him from the sun
Ain't no bed will give us rest, man,
You keep us on the run

Jack Straw from Wichita   4
Cut his buddy down
Dug for him a shallow grave
And laid his body down

Half a mile from Tucson
By the morning light
One man gone and another to go
My old buddy, you're moving much
   too slow

We can share the women
We can share the wine . . .

Words by Robert Hunter
Music by Bob Weir

4 Jack Straw
A mysterious figure dating from the Great Revolt in England of 1381, aka the Peasants' Revolt, or Wat Tyler's Rebellion, mentioned in Chaucer's *Nonnes Preestes Tale.* The revolt, a response  to heavy and frequent taxes, started in Essex at the end of May 1381, though most events were concentrated in June of that year. Jack Straw is a figure of some controversy:

> Even Jack Straw, the most notable of them, is a vague figure who flits across Essex no less than Kent, and though he is mentioned, we seldom or never detect him actually at work till the entry of the rebels into London. He is probably identical with the John Rackstraw mentioned in some of the chronicles and in the judicial proceedings which followed the insurrection. (Oman)

A footnote to the above passage states:
> An article, more ingenious than convincing, in the *Hist. Rev.* for January, 1906, by Doctor F. W. Brie, will have it that Jack Straw is no real person at all but a mere nickname of Wat Tyler. It is quite true that the Continuator of Knighton held this view, . . . and that two or three ballads and several fifteenth-century chroniclers . . . speak of Jakke Straw being killed by Walworth at Smithfield.

There is also a Jack Straw in Tennessee Williams's *Cat on a Hot Tin Roof,* Act One:
> Maggie: . . . when he was just overseer here on the old Jack Straw and Peter Ochello place.

The game "pick up sticks" is sometimes referred to as "playing jack straw(s)."

From the *American Heritage Dictionary:*
> jackstraw n. 1. Plural. A game played with a pile of straws or thin sticks, with the players attempting in turn to remove a single stick without disturbing the others. Used with a singular verb. Also called "spilikins." 2. One of the straws or sticks used in this game. Also called spilikin. 48

Webster's Dictionary (2nd ed.):
> 1. An effigy stuffed with straw; a man of straw; a man without property, worth, or influence. Milton.
> 2. One of a set of straws or of strips of ivory, bone, wood, etc., for playing a game, the jackstraws being thrown in a heap on a table, to be gathered up singly by a hooked instrument, without disturbing the rest of the pile; also pl., the game so played.
> 3. Any of several small European birds; esp., the whitethroat, the garden warbler, or the blackcap, which use bedstraw (Galium) in their nests. Local, Eng.
> 4. A flower spike of the common ribwort. Dial, Eng.

Notes:
Recording: *Europe '72* (November 1972).

First performance: October 19, 1971, at Northrop Auditorium, University of Minnesota, Minneapolis.

A note on performance practice: It is worth a mention that the lead vocal of "Jack Straw" was originally sung only by Weir. It seems that Garcia and Weir actually started trading lines in the middle of the 1972 Europe tour.

mexicali blues

Bakersfield, a city in Southern California, owes its name to one of its founders, Col. Thomas Baker (1810–1872), who was also a U.S. senator. The city is the county seat of Kern County. The Grateful Dead played there once, on January 14, 1978, but did not include "Mexicali Blues" in their show. They did play it the night before, a Friday the thirteenth show in Santa Barbara, California, as well as the night after, in Fresno. Go figure.

2 Mexicali

According to *Cities of the World:*

> The city of Mexicali, at the northern extremity of Baja California State [Mexico], is adjacent to Calexico, California. It is a duty-free port, with customs offices open 24 hours. . . . The city is accessible by highway, railroad, and air from the southwestern United States.

A 2005 population estimate puts Mexicali at 618,889, up from 348,500 in 1993.

3 And he made me trade the gallows for the Mexicali blues

Sometime between 1972 and 1973, Bob Weir changed this line to "Now I spend my lifetime running with the Mexicali blues."

Notes:

Written February 1971 in Middletown, Connecticut. Studio recording: *Ace* (May 1972).

First performance: October 19, 1971, at Northrop Auditorium, University of Minnesota, Minneapolis. "Mexicali Blues" made it into the permanent repertoire, often performed in quick succession following either "Mama Tried" or "Me and My Uncle."

Laid back in an old saloon, with a peso in my
    hand
Watching flies and children on the street
And I catch a glimpse of black-eyed girls who
    giggle when I smile
There's a little boy that wants to shine my feet
And it's three days ride from Bakersfield   1
And I don't know why I came
I guess I came to keep from payin' dues
So instead I've got a bottle and a girl who's
    just fourteen
And a damned good case of the Mexicali blues   2

Is there anything a man don't stand to lose
When the devil wants to take it all away
Cherish well your thoughts, keep a tight grip
    on your booze
'Cause thinking and drinking are all I have today

She said her name was Billie Jean and she was
    fresh in town
I didn't know a stage-line ran from hell
She had raven hair, a ruffled dress, a necklace
    made of gold
And all the French perfume you'd care to smell
She took me up into her room and whispered in
    my ear
Go on my friend, do anything you choose
Now I'm payin' for those happy hours I spent
    there in her arms
With a lifetime's worth of the Mexicali blues

Is there anything a man don't stand to lose
When the devil wants to take it all away
Cherish well your thoughts, keep a tight grip
    on your booze
'Cause thinking and drinking are all I have today

And then a man rode into town, some thought
    he was the law
Billie Jean was waiting when he came
She told me he would take her if I didn't use
    my gun
And I'd have no one but myself to blame
I went down to those dusty streets, blood was
    on my mind
I guess that stranger hadn't heard the news
'Cause I shot first and killed him, Lord he
    didn't even draw
3   And he made me trade the gallows for the
    Mexicali blues

Is there anything a man don't stand to lose
When he lets a woman hold him in her hands
You just might find yourself out there on
horseback in the dark
Just riding and running across those desert sands

Words by John Barlow
Music by Bob Weir

comes a time

1 when the blind man takes your hand / says: don't you see?
Compare Sophocles' *Oedipus*. Tiresias is the blind man as well as the prophet. "If my eyes of flesh are closed, it is so that I can see better with the eyes of the spirit."

Also compare the final line of the Dylan Thomas poem, "Was There a Time":

> Was there a time when dancers
>   with their fiddles
> In children's circuses
>   could stay their troubles?
> There was a time they could
>   cry over books,
> But time has set its maggot
>   on their track.
> Under the arc of the sky
>   they are unsafe.
> What's never known is safest in this life.
>   Under the skysigns they who have no arms
> Have cleanest hands, and, as the heartless
>   ghost
> Alone's unhurt, so the blind man sees best. 49

Comes a time
when the blind man
takes your hand
says: Don't you see?   1
got to make it somehow
on the dreams you still believe
Don't give it up
you've got an empty cup   2
only love can fill
only love can fill

Been walking all morning
Went walking all night
I can't see much difference
between the dark and the light   3
And I feel the wind
And I taste the rain
Never in my mind
to cause so much pain

Comes a time
when the blind man
takes your hand
says: Don't you see?
got to make it somehow
on the dreams you still believe
Don't give it up

you've got an empty cup
only love can fill
only love can fill

From day to day
just letting it ride
you get so far away
from how it feels inside
You can't let go
'cause you're afraid to fall
till the day may come
when you can't feel at all

Comes a time
when the blind man
takes your hand
says: Don't you see?
got to make it somehow
on the dreams you still believe
Don't give it up
you've got an empty cup
only love can fill
only love can fill

Words by Robert Hunter
Music by Jerry Garcia

ACE of CUPS

2 empty cup
Again, as in "Ripple," Hunter invokes the image of an empty cup. In tarot, the Cups represent the emotions, and indeed, "Comes a Time" addresses the malaise of feeling nothing—being so afraid to fall that you learn to turn off your feelings. "The day may come / when you can't feel at all."
   The line echoes a poem by W. B. Yeats, "The Empty Cup."

3 I can't see much difference / between the dark and the light
Between the Dark and the Light was used as the title for Jay Blakesberg's collection of Grateful Dead photographs (2002).

Notes:
Studio recording: *Reflections* (February 1976).

First performance: October 19, 1971, at Northrop Auditorium, University of Minnesota, Minneapolis. The song never became part of the permanent rotation but reappeared periodically over the years.

one more saturday night

1 One more Saturday night

Used as the title of a book by Sandy Troy: *One More Saturday Night: Reflections with the Grateful Dead, Dead Family, and Dead Heads* (1991).

2 local armory

The Grateful Dead rehearsed for a time at the Santa Venetia Armory in Marin County, California, and played gigs there on July 8 and 9, 1966; December 29, 1966; and February 10, 1967. Also, the first time they played in St. Louis (May 24 and 25, 1968), their venue was the National Guard Armory.

3 His wife says don't get crazy

During Ronald Reagan's presidency, Bob Weir sometimes sang, "*Nancy* says don't get crazy *Ron*, you know just what to do." Similarly, with The Dead on August 9, 2003 (and perhaps on other occasions), he sang, "His wife says don't get crazy, *George*, you know just what to do."

Notes:

From Dennis McNally's *A Long Strange Trip*:

> [Weir and Hunter] clashed again over "One More Saturday Night." Having gotten Hunter's lyrics, Weir rewrote them—badly in Hunter's opinion—and then asked to call the resulting song "U.S. Blues," which Hunter refused to permit. In the end, he declined any association with the song and it was credited to Weir alone. 50

I went down to the mountain, I was drinking
    some wine
I looked up into heaven, Lord, I saw a mighty sign
Writ in fire across the heaven, plain as black
    and white
Get prepared, there's gonna be a party tonight

Chorus:
Uh-huh, hey, Saturday night
One more Saturday night   **1**
Hey, Saturday night

Everybody's dancing down at the local armory   **2**
With a basement full of dynamite and live
    artillery
Temperature keeps rising, everybody getting high
Come the rocking stroke of midnight, the
    whole place is gonna fly

(Chorus)

I turn on Channel Six, the President comes
    on the news
Says I got no satisfaction, that's why I sing
    the blues
His wife says don't get crazy, Lord, you know   **3**
    what to do
Just crank up that old Victrola, put on your
    rocking shoes

(Chorus)

Then God way up in heaven, for whatever it
    was worth

Thought he'd have a big old party, thought
   he'd call it Planet Earth
Don't worry about tomorrow, Lord, you'll know
   it when it comes
When the rocking, rolling music meets the rising,
   shining sun

(Chorus)

    Words and music by Bob Weir

This throws an interesting light on the line "You can call *this* song the United States Blues," in "U.S. Blues."

First performance: Tuesday, October 19, 1971, at Northrop Auditorium, University of Minnesota, Minneapolis. The song remained in the repertoire from then on. Although it was usually played on Saturday nights, this was not always the case.

-Fore-

Ramble on Rose

1 Jack the Ripper
Opening the song is Jack number one, a notorious, mysterious, frightening, just plain *bad* individual whose identity remains unknown. Between August 31 and November 9, 1888, five prostitutes in London were murdered by an

assailant who identified himself in letters to the press as "Jack the Ripper." The killer used a knife to cut throats and mutilate bodies. Over the years, many suggestions have been made to solve the puzzle of the madman's identity. "Jack," of course, is the colloquial equivalent of "John Doe." The most famous theory is that the Ripper was Albert Edward—"Eddy"—Prince of Wales, Duke of Clarence. For a thorough exploration of this theory, see Michael Harrison's *Clarence: Was He Jack the Ripper?* (1972). The book concludes that a tutor of Eddy's, one J. K. Stephen, a poet, was the actual murderer. Part of the evidence given by Harrison is an alleged similarity between poems sent to the press by the Ripper and Stephen's own poetry.

Another theory, which enjoyed brief popularity, was that "Jack" was actually "Jill" the Ripper—based on the assumption that a woman would be less suspect and could escape undetected while everyone searched for a male killer.

2 Mojo Hand
See note under "Caution (Do Not Stop on Tracks)."

Just like Jack the Ripper   1
Just like Mojo Hand   2
Just like Billy Sunday   3
In a shotgun ragtime band   4, 5
Just like New York City
Just like Jericho   6
Pace the halls and climb the walls
Get out when they blow

Chorus:
Did you say your name was
Ramblin' Rose?   7
Ramble on, baby
Settle down easy
   Ramble on, Rose

Just like Jack and Jill   8
Mama told the sailor
One heat up and one cool down
Leave nothing for the tailor
Just like Jack and Jill
My papa told the jailer
One go up and one come down   9
Do yourself a favor

(Chorus)

I'm gonna sing you a hundred verses in ragtime
I know this song it ain't never gonna end
I'm gonna march you up and down the local
   county line

10 Take you to the leader of the band

11 Just like Crazy Otto

12 Just like Wolfman Jack

13 Sitting plush with a royal flush
Aces back to back

14 Just like Mary Shelley

15 Just like Frankenstein
Clank your chains and count your change

16 Try to walk the line

(Chorus)

Goodbye, Mama and Papa
Goodbye, Jack and Jill

17 The grass ain't greener, the wine ain't sweeter
either side of the hill

(Chorus)

Words by Robert Hunter
Music by Jerry Garcia

3 Billy Sunday

Billy Sunday, listed in the *Baseball Encyclopedia* as William Ashley (the evangelist). Sunday, was one of the founders of the American evangelistic movement—his heirs today being Billy Graham et al. He started out as a baseball player for major- league teams in Chicago, Pittsburgh, and Philadelphia, beginning his sports career in 1883, quitting the game in 1890. He then began his religious career, starting out as a desk clerk at the YMCA, working his way up as a helper to itinerant preachers, and finally becoming the most popular evangelist of the time, preaching to huge crowds.

Sunday's style was highly flamboyant and included colloquial baseball lingo, which won him a mass audience. One important aspect of his road show was the music that accompanied it, which consisted of a huge choir with piano and trombone accompaniment. The music is said to have been "far from unctuous; it approached the jazzy." (Weisberger)

4 shotgun

Shotgun: passing into *adj.* Made or done hastily or under pressure of necessity. *(Oxford English Dictionary).*

5 ragtime band

In popular music, this phrase conjures up the famous Irving Berlin song "Alexander's Ragtime Band." (See lyrics, below.) Evoking Irving Berlin is a way of evoking the entire Tin Pan Alley tradition of American popular music. The phrase "in a shotgun ragtime band" matches the rhythm of the Irving Berlin title perfectly.

"Alexander's Ragtime Band" was published in March 1911 and was first popularized by Emma Carus. According to James J. Fuld, in *The Book of World-Famous Music,* "The 'Alexander' in the title is reportedly Jack [!] Alexander, a cornet-playing bandleader who died in 1958. It has been frequently pointed out that the song is not in real ragtime. Berlin was born in Temun, Russia, in 1888."

Alec Wilder, in his book *American Popular Song: the Great Innovators, 1900–1950,* devotes thirty pages to the role of Irving Berlin and comments as follows on the subject of "Alexander's Ragtime Band":

> I have heard enough ragtime to wonder why "Alexander's Ragtime Band" was so titled. For I find no elements of ragtime in it, unless the word *ragtime* simply specified the most swinging and exciting of the new American music. It is a very strong, solid song, verse and chorus. More than that, it is not crowded with notes. There are constant open spots in it. At the outset, in the verse, the first three measures begin on the second beat. This "kicks" the song, and immediately. Incidentally, this is the earliest popular song I know of in which the verse and chorus are in different keys. . . . Could the slight, chromatic opening phrase of the song have caused all the furor, the grass fire that spread over the face of Europe? Or was the restatement of this phrase a fourth higher the device which did the trick? In any event, the song was a high point in the evolution of popular music. [51]

Hunter, if he is alluding to Berlin's song, manages to evoke two strains of American popular music simultaneously: ragtime and Tin Pan Alley. This becomes significant as the song progresses, evoking more and more tributaries to the mainstream of American music.

ALEXANDER'S RAGTIME BAND

Oh! ma honey, Oh! ma honey,
Better hurry, and let's meander;
Ain't you goin', ain't you goin'
To the leader man, ragged meter man?
Oh! ma honey, Oh! ma honey,
Let me take you to Alexander's grandstand,
  brass band,
Ain't you comin' along?

Come on and hear, come on and hear

Alexander's Ragtime Band;
Come on and hear, come on and hear,
It's the best band in the land.
They can play a bugle call
Like you never heard before,
So natural that you want to go to war;
That's just the bestest band what ma, honey
  lamb!
Let me take you by the hand
Up to the man, up to the man
Who's the leader of the band;
And if you care to hear the Swanee River
  played in ragtime,
Come on and hear, come on and hear
Alexander's Ragtime Band.

Oh! ma honey, Oh! ma honey,
There's a fiddle with notes that screeches
Like a chicken, like a chicken,
And the clarinet is a colored pet.
Come and listen, come and listen
To a classical band what's peaches, come now,
  somehow,
Better hurry along!

6 Jericho

The biblical account of the fall of Jericho is found in Joshua 6:1–20.

The reference to Jericho also calls to mind the spiritual "Joshua Fit the Battle of Jericho." Since so much of this song evokes various aspects of American popular music, this evocation gains significance.

In *Wade in the Water,* Arthur Jones titles one entire chapter "Joshua Fit the Battle of Jericho: Struggle and Resistance":

> A song like "Joshua Fit the Battle of Jericho," for example, could honor the actions of any number of "Joshuas" in the African community who led their people in battle in many different "Jerichos." It could also be used as biblical support for planned battles. For

example, in his meetings with coconspirators in Charleston, South Carolina, Denmark Vesey preached from the Bible, using verse from the book of Joshua to draw parallels between the biblical story of Joshua and the plans for the insurrection in Charleston.

7 Ramblin' Rose

See note under "That's It for the Other One" for roses, in general.

A rambling rose is an old-fashioned and now rarely cultivated type of rose that would spread low across the ground on long, whippy canes. Ramblers are now grown usually as climbers instead.

Three songs in American popular music have borne the name "Ramblin(g) Rose." The most famous of the three is the 1962 "Ramblin' Rose," words and music by Joe and Noel Sherman. It was introduced by Nat "King" Cole, who at first did not wish to record it. He was talked into it, however, by his twelve-year-old daughter, Natalie, and her instincts were good, because it was a hit, reaching the number two position on the charts in August 1962. It has since been recorded by Chuck Berry, Jerry Lee Lewis, and Willie Nelson, among others.

The second most popular tune of this title is the 1948 "Rambling Rose" by Joseph McCarthy (not the infamous Senator Joe McCarthy) and Joe Burke.

The third is of unknown date, titled "Ramblin' Rose," by Wilkin and Burch, recorded by Slim Whitman.

A fourth song, dating from 1931, is titled "Marta (Rambling Rose of the Wildwood)" by Gilbert and Simons.

It is also the title of a 1991 movie starring Laura Dern and Robert Duvall.

8 Jack and Jill

The well-known, perhaps the *best*-known, nursery rhyme has been ingrained in our memories from early childhood. Jack number two of the song is thus introduced, along with his feminine counterpart. References to this pair predate even the nursery rhyme, according to the *Oxford Dictionary of Nursery Rhymes*, which dates the rhyme from the first half of the seventeenth century. Shakespeare says, "Jack shall have Jill, Nought shall go ill" *(Midsummer Night's Dream),* using the names in the general sense of "lad and lass." (And in *Love's Labours Lost,* there is the line "Jack hath not Gill.")

Many theories have risen regarding the origin of the rhyme, but most agree that it can be traced to the Scandinavian *Edda* epic and that it may have pagan ritualistic significance. To most listeners, however, Jack and Jill conjure an image of childhood, just like Mama and Papa.

As with much of this song, there is music associated with the words, and it is likely that most of us have chanted this nursery rhyme, so that the inclusion of Jack and Jill adds still another component to the swirl of music conjured up by this song.

JACK AND JILL, AND OLD DAME DOB

Jack and Jill
Went up the hill
To fetch a pail of water;
Jack fell down
And broke his crown,
And Jill came tumbling after.
Then up Jack got
And home did trot,
As fast as he could caper,
To old Dame Dob,
Who patched his nob
With vinegar and brown paper.
When Jill came in,
How she did grin
To see Jack's paper plaster;
Her mother, vexed,
Did whip her next
For laughing at Jack's disaster.
Now Jack did laugh
And Jill did cry,

But her tears did soon abate;
Then Jill did say,
That they should play
At seesaw across the gate. (Opie)

9 One go up

The Annotated Mother Goose contains the following rhyme: "Gay go up and gay go down / To ring the bells of London Town."

Percy Green, in *A History of Nursey Rhymes,* explains the rhyme as a children's game:

> This almost forgotten nursery song and game of "The Bells of London Town" has a descriptive burden or ending to each line, giving an imitation of the sounds of the bell-peals of the principal churches in each locality of the City and the old London suburbs. The game is played by girls and boys holding hands and racing sideways, as they do in "Ring a Ring a Rosies," after each line has been sung as a solo by the children in turns. The
>
> *"Gay go up and gay go down*
> *To ring the bells of London Town"*
>
> is chorused by all the company, and then the rollicking dance begins, the feet stamping out a noisy but enjoyable accompaniment to the words "Gay go up, gay go down."

The line is also echoed in the folk song "Maid Freed from the Gallows, "and may therefore be a reference to hanging" (Sharp, #28, version H). The song is also registered as a Child Ballad, #95, "The Prickly Bush."

10 leader of the band

See the interview with Robert Hunter in *Relix,* vol. 5, no. 2:

> Relix: We're interested in the "Leader of the band" concept. . . . Do you feel that there is a leader?
>
> Hunter: [partial response] Well, it would be hard to imagine the Grateful Dead without Garcia, wouldn't it?
>
> Relix: Were you getting at anything like that in

"Ramblin' Rose?" [sic] Was talking about taking someone to the leader of the band talking about the Dead per se?

> Hunter: I suppose there's an element of the Dead in a lot of my songs. It's hard to scramble it out from what's pure fancy.

"Alexander's Ragtime Band" also highlights the "leader of the band" idea.

11 Crazy Otto

This reference is to one (or both?) of two pianists who were known by that name in the 1950s. The first was the German pianist Fritz Schulz-Reichel, whose career was comparable to that of Peter Schickele, who composes under the pseudonym of P. D. Q. Bach. Schulz-Reichel alternated between playing "serious" music and playing ragtime, for which he donned an absurd-looking fake goatee and Kaiser Willie mustache, along with the moniker Otto der Schrage (Crazy Otto).

Most reference works on ragtime mentioning a Crazy Otto, however, are referring to Johnny Maddox, another popular piano player. A phone call from Maddox to me on October 22, 1997, revealed the entire story of Maddox's association with the Crazy Otto name and music. Maddox says that a returning GI brought back a copy of the Otto der Schrage record from Germany, and brought it to the deejay Walt Henrich at WERE radio in Cleveland. Henrich in turn brought it to Bill Randall, also a deejay at that station, who played some tracks from the record on the air. Such was the reaction of the listening public that Randall got in touch with Randy Wood, who was a producer of "copy" records, and who in turn commissioned Maddox to record a copy of the ragtime pieces as a medley, which was released as "The Crazy Otto Medley—Played by Johnny Maddox."

At the time (1954), Maddox was rated the number one jukebox artist in America, independent of any association with Crazy Otto. According to Maddox, it was a common practice at the time for independent producers to commission "cover records"—virtual note-for-note copies of records that were not readily available. Maddox never wanted to be known as Crazy Otto, though, and he only released one other record that contained a reference to the character, *Crazy Otto Piano.* He released over forty albums of ragtime and other popular piano pieces under his own name. His biggest album, mentioned in most standard ragtime discographies, was *Authentic Ragtime.* (As an interesting side note, Maddox noted that many of today's reverential ragtime performers make the music sound like it belongs in a funeral home rather than a place for dancing.) Maddox hailed from Gallatin, Tennessee.

12 Wolfman Jack

An elusive character in more ways than one, Wolfman Jack's real name is Bob Smith. Born in Brooklyn in 1938, Wolfman says, "We all emulated the black culture. There wasn't any other." His major early influence was a black deejay named Dr. Jive, and while still a teenager he dropped out of school and hit the road, heading south, working for rhythm- and-blues radio stations. Finally, in 1957, he became the station manager and late- night deejay at XERF, in Ciudad Acuña (and later on, XERB out of Baja), Mexico, just over the border from Del Rio, Texas. On a good night, you could hear him north to Canada and west to California, as Mexican stations were allowed far higher wattage than American stations were. Throughout the late fifties and all through the sixties, Wolfman cultivated a vocal persona that led everyone to think he was actually a black deejay. With his first appearance in the flesh, in the movie *American Graffiti,* he shocked everyone

with the revelation that he was, indeed, white. "Nobody knew if I was white or black or whatever," he said in an interview with *Time* in 1973, "and I kept the mystique up. No pictures, no interviews."

The appellation *Wolfman* conjures up a wild and supernatural being, as introduced into American pop culture with the 1941 movie *The Wolf Man,* starring Lon Chaney Jr. (See "Werewolves of London" by Warren Zevon, for mention of Chaney in song.) Bela Lugosi as Frankenstein's monster met Chaney as the Wolf Man in a 1943 sequel, *Frankenstein Meets the Wolf Man.* They reunited in the 1944 film *House of Frankenstein.* And, of course, they meet again in this song.

The Dead are not the only ones to have included Wolfman Jack in a song. Leon Russell's "Living on the Highway" is about the deejay.

Wolfman Jack appears as Jack number three in the song.

13 royal flush, / Aces back to back

The phrase "back to back" describes the first two hole cards in seven-card stud poker, or the hole card and the first upcard when they are paired, or "wired." Thus, the hand being described in the song is a seven-card stud-poker hand just prior to being dealt the final down card, made up of a ten, a jack, a queen, a king, and an ace all of one suit (the highest hand in poker), with an extra ace in the hole.

Aces Back to Back: A Guide to the Grateful Dead, by Scott Allen, was published in 1992.

14 Mary [Godwin] Shelly

(1797–1851) Author of *Frankenstein* (1818). Her mother was the famous early feminist theorist Mary Wollstonecraft. Mary Godwin married Percy Shelley, the poet, at age sixteen and wrote *Frankenstein* at the suggestion of her husband and Lord Byron, after beginning the story as impromptu entertainment around the fire in Geneva in the summer of 1816.

15 Frankenstein

Victor Frankenstein, the doctor who created a monster in Mary Shelley's book. Usually, *Frankenstein* refers not to the doctor but to the monster. Castle Frankenstein still stands near Darmstadt, West Germany. Konrad Dippel (1673–1734) spent his youth there, later studied alchemy at Giessen University, under the name Frankensteina, and had particular interest in theories fashionable at the time concerning the life force.

16 walk the line

This saying seems to have its origin in an old sobriety test given to sailors: walking between two parallel lines chalked onto the deck—also known as "walking the chalk." The meaning of the saying in the present day is inclusive of sobriety, but much broader, having to do with good behavior, usually under some form of pressure or even duress.

The line also summons up echoes of Johnny Cash and his 1956 song "I Walk the Line," adding some country flavor to the stew that already includes everything from ragtime to "Dark Star."

17 the grass ain't greener

Ovid's *Ars Amatoria (The Art of Love),* Book 1, line 349: *"Fertilior seges est alienis semper in agris,"* or "The crop seems always more productive in our neighbor's field." Juvenal's *Satires,* in Satire XIV, line 142, says, *"Majorque videtur et melior vicina seges,"* or "And the crop of our neighbor's seems greater and better than our own."

The earliest notation of "The grass is greener" as an American phrase is found in an article by Helen Pearce in the *California Folklore Quarterly,* vol. 5 (July 1946), titled "Folk Sayings in a Pioneer Family of Western Oregon." She recorded the phrase as "The greener pasture's over yonder (or The grass is always greener on the other side of the fence)."

Two songs, "Green, Green" and "The Grass Is Greener," use this saying in their titles. The first dates from 1963, words and music by Barry McGuire and Randy Sparks and based on fragments of traditional material, according to its authors. (This "fragmentary material" has yet to come to light.) The song was a hit record for the New Christy Minstrels. The second tune, written by Barry Mann and Mike Anthony, was a best-selling record for Brenda Lee, also in 1963.

Notes:
Recording: *Europe '72* (November 1972).

First performance: October 19, 1971, at the Northrop Auditorium at the University of Minnesota, Minneapolis. It remained in the repertoire thereafter.

Robert Hunter stated in an interview in *Relix* that "Ramble on Rose" is a particular favorite—there's something funny about that song." He also said:

> I think "Ramble on Rose" is the closest to complete whimsy I've come up with. I just sat down and wrote numerous verses that tied around "Did you say. . . ." (Gans: *Conversations*) 52

chinatown shuffle

Take it, you can have it
What I got baby I can't hold
If you find the secret
Tell me how to build a mold

And I can't handle your problems
So don't try to handle mine
Get yourself a shotgun a pocketful of shells
And we can while away the time

Look up at the wall, do it right
If you make a mistake, you're gonna pay for
   it twice
But if you need it, got to have it
Get yourself a shotgun and bring it back home
Look up at the wall, you know you gotta crawl
Before you start crawling get ready to fall

Chorus:

And if you fall in my direction
Don't expect no help at all

Get it right, do it nice
But if you make a mistake you're gonna pay for
   it twice
But if you need it, gotta have it
Get yourself a shotgun and bring it back home
Look up the walls
You know you gotta crawl
But if you start calling you're ready to fall

(Chorus)

Words and music by Ron McKernan

1 Chinatown

Bernard P. Wong, in his book *Chinatown: Economic Adaptation and Ethnic Identity of the Chinese* (Holt, Rinehart and Winston, 1982), gives a good background for the development of Chinatowns throughout the United States. He says:

> Active prejudice and harassment stemming from mainstream American racism and fear of economic competition has resulted in the tightening of internal bonds within the minority group and the development of protective associations of one kind or another. The internal cohesiveness thus developed became the distinguishing characteristic of the Chinese American communities in cities like San Francisco and New York.

There are lively and vital Chinatown districts in many U.S. cities, including New York, Chicago, San Francisco, Oakland, San Jose, Boston, Philadelphia, Honolulu, and Los Angeles.

2 Shuffle

Shuffle (1) A dance step of indefinite Southern black-American origin, perhaps dating from the 18th century, in which the feet are moved rhythmically across the floor without being lifted. (2) A rhythm derived from the dance step. The term is onomatopoeic, "sh" describing its characteristic smoothness (and especially its sound when played on the snare drum). The alternation of long and short syllables (shuf-fle, shuf-fle . . .) evokes its distinguishing rhythm, a subdivision of the beat into uneven triplets which is more specific than the fundamental, swing or boogie-woogie rhythm only in that it is usually played legato and at a relaxed tempo. The shuffle rhythm is generally confined to earlier styles of jazz, up to and including swing. *(New Grove Dictionary of Jazz)*

Song titles that have contained the word *shuffle* include:

"Showboat Shuffle" by King Oliver
"Riverboat Shuffle" by Frankie Trumbauer
"Syncopated Shuffle" by Duke Ellington
"Futuristic Shuffle" by Jan Savitt
"Boogie Stop Shuffle" by Charles Mingus
"Boneyard Shuffle" by Hoagy Carmichael and
    Irving Mills

"Harlem Shuffle" by Bob Relf and Earl Nelson
"Shuffle Along" by Noble Sissle and Eubie
    Blake
"Shuffle Off to Buffalo" by Al Dubin and Harry
Warren (see note under "Truckin'")
"Shufflin' Sam" by P. G. Wodehouse and
    Jerome Kern
"Soft Shoe Shuffle" by Spencer Williams and
    Maurice Burman

Notes:
Recording: The May 11, 1972, performance was released as part of the *So Many Roads* box set.

First performance: December 31, 1971, at Winterland in San Francisco.

Black-Throated Wind

Bringing me down
I'm running aground
Blind in the light of the interstate cars
Passing me by
The buses and semis
Plunging like stones from a slingshot on Mars

But I'm here by the road
Bound to the load
That I picked up in ten thousand cafés and bars
Alone with the rush of the drivers who won't pick
  me up
The highway, the moon, the clouds, and the stars

1 The black-throated wind keeps on pouring in
   With its words of a life where nothing is new
2 Ah, Mother American Night, I'm lost from
     the light
   Ohh, I'm drowning in you

3 I left St. Louis, the City of Blues
   In the midst of a storm I'd rather forget
   I tried to pretend it came to an end
   'Cause you weren't the woman I thought
     I once met

But I can't deny that times have gone by
When I never had doubts or thoughts of regret
And I was a man when all this began
Who wouldn't think twice about being there yet

The black-throated wind keeps on pouring in
And it speaks of a life that passes like dew

1 Black-throated wind
Chapter twenty-five of *The Sutra of the Lotus Flower of the Wonderful Law* (Banno Kato's 1930 translation):

If there be hundreds, thousands of *kotis* of beings who in search of gold, silver, lapis lazuli, moonstones, agate, corals, amber, pearls, and other treasures, go out on the ocean and if a black gale blows their ships to drift upon the land of the *rakshasa*-demons, and if amongst them there be even a single person who calls upon the name of the Bodhisattva Regarder-of-the-Cries-of-the-World, all those people will be delivered from the woes of the rakshasas.

On the same page, as a footnote, Kato defines the black gale as "a black wind. There are six kinds of wind, viz. black, red, blue, of heaven, of earth, and of fire."

Or, this might just be a reference to vehicle exhaust, given that the protagonist is a hitchhiker.

2 Mother American Night
Reminiscent of the title of the Kurt Vonnegut novel, *Mother Night,* which, in turn, brings up the James Weldon Johnson (1871–1938) poem "Mother Night":

ETERNITIES before the first-born day,
  Or ere the first sun fledged his wings of
    flame,
  Calm Night, the everlasting and the same,
  A brooding mother over chaos lay.
And whirling suns shall blaze and then decay,
  Shall run their fiery courses and then claim
  The haven of the darkness whence they
    came;
  Back to Nirvanic peace shall grope their way.

So when my feeble sun of life burns out,
  And sounded is the hour for my long sleep,
  I shall, full weary of the feverish light,
  Welcome the darkness without fear or doubt,
  And heavy-lidded, I shall softly creep
  Into the quiet bosom of the Night.

3 St.Louis, the City of Blues
St. Louis was an early "major center of blues
activity" (Brown), along with ragtime. W. C.
Handy is known as the father of the blues, and
he wrote the classic "St. Louis Blues" (1914).

Notes:
Written in Cora, Wyoming and San Anselmo,
California. February 1972.

Studio recording: *Ace* (May 1972).

First performance: March 5, 1972, at Winterland
in San Francisco. It was played fairly regularly
until 1974, then dropped from the repertoire
until March 16, 1990. It remained something of
a concert rarity, as Weir and Barlow experiment-
ed with a new set of words for a while, eventually returning to the original lyrics.

Here are the alternate lyrics, used briefly in 1990:

[Verse 2]
*Well, it's me and the road, yeah, we're lacking the
  code
That will lead us to some as yet unforseen bar*

It's forced me to see that you've done better
  by me
Better by me than I've done by you

What's to be found, racing around
You carry your pain wherever you go
Full of the blues and trying to lose
You ain't gonna learn what you don't want
  to know

So I give you my eyes, and all of their lies
Please help them to learn as well as to see
Capture a glance and make it a dance
Of looking at you looking at me

The black-throated wind keeps on pouring in
With its words of a lie that could almost be true
Ah, Mother American Night, here comes
  the light
I'm turning around, that's what I'm gonna do

Goin back home that's what I'm gonna do
Turnin' around
That's what I'm gonna do

'Cause you've done better by me
Than I've done by you . . .

Words by John Barlow
Music by Bob Weir

Alone with the rush of the drivers who won't pick
  me up
The highway, the moon, the clouds, and the
  stars

But I'm here by the road, yea, unraveling the code
That will lead us to some as yet unforseen bar

The black-throated wind keeps on pouring in
Like a siren it promises everything new
Ah, Mother American Night, *invisible light*
Ohh, I'm *flying* in you

The black-throated wind keeps on pouring in
With its words of a life where *everything's* new

I left St Louis, the City of Blues
On a screaming blue bender I'd rather forget
With no scars that show, the keys to the road
A couple of tens and some stale cigarettes

But I can't deny that times have gone by
Nothing is left but thoughts of regret
When I was a man, with so much in hand
That a bird in the bush would be singing there yet

But I can't deny that times have gone by
When being with her was as good as it gets

The black-throated wind, *whispering sin*
And speaking of life that passes like dew
It's led me to see if you want to be free

Have your way with each day as its granted to you
What's to be found, racing around
You carry your *blues to the edge of the sky*
Think a coyote could care about birds in the air?
Think a raven thinks coyotes should learn how to
  fly?

We drew lines all around us when I was down
So now mine turns out to go right to the sky

So I give you my eyes, *they were just a disguise*
Anyway, where I'm going it's too dark to see
Yes, and toss me to Chance and watch me dance
Choreography certain as bats on the breeze

So I *leave* you my eyes . . .

The black-throated wind keeps on pouring in
With its words of a lie *I think just might* be true
Oh, Mother American Night, here comes the
  light
I'm *going right on ahead,* that's what I'm gonna
  do

The black-throated wind keeps on pouring in
The prophet that promises everything new
Ah, Mother American Night, *come wrong or come*
  right
I will always go onward in you

LOOKS Like Rain

1 **Written in the letters of your name**
I used to try to figure out what names might be spelled using only letters corresponding to notes in the musical scale, but I gave up. The available letters are *A* through *G*, or through *H*, if you use the German convention for naming B natural. And the Germans also use "es" (pronounced like the letter *S*) for E-flat. Or maybe this isn't what Barlow means at all!

Perhaps he is referring to simple love songs that take a name and than create a phrase for each letter of the name. For example, the name Trish could be parsed in the following way: *T* is for the tenderness of your soul, *R* is for the reflective way you look at me, *I* is for your insightful thoughts in troubled times . . . and so on until the full name is spelled out with corresponding lines.

During the 1980 simulcast of the Halloween show at Radio City Music Hall, Al Franken and Tom Davis engaged in some very funny skits. Weir was asked about songwriting, and he proceeded to demonstrate that he merely took events from his life and set them to music. Franken rolls out a chalkboard and gives Weir the chalk. "For instance, the song 'Looks Like Rain' has a line about 'written in the letters of your name.' That song starts in the key of G, goes to A, then goes to D, then goes to E, and ends on a C minor. GADEC Minor was the name of this beautiful girl I knew in Prague—the Soviet tanks rolled in in '68 and I had to leave town in a hurry." Franken, amazed, says, "So the song 'Looks Like Rain' is actually about the Soviet invasion of Czechoslovakia? Amazing." Of course, Weir delivered this whole spiel with an absolute straight face.

I woke today . . .
And felt your side of bed
The covers were still warm where you'd been
   laying
You were gone . . .
My heart was filled with dread
You might not be sleeping here again

It's alright, 'cause I love you
And that's not gonna change
Run me round, make me hurt again and again
But I'll still sing you love songs
Written in the letters of your name   1
And brave the storm to come,
For it surely looks like rain

Did you ever waken to the sound   2
Of street cats making love
And guess from their cries
You were listening to a fight?
Well, you know . . .
Hate's just the last thing they're thinking of
They're only trying to make it through the night

It's alright, 'cause I love you
And that's not gonna change
Run me round, make me hurt again and again
But I'll still sing you love songs
Written in the letters of your name
And brave the storm to come,
For it surely looks like rain

I only want to hold you
I don't want to tie you down
Or fence you in the lines
I might have drawn
It's just that I've gotten used to
Having you around
My landscape would be empty
If you were gone

3   Rain, rain, go away . . .

Words by John Barlow
Music by Bob Weir

Compare, also, two poems by
Edgar Allan Poe:

AN ENIGMA
"Seldom we find," says Solomon
    Don Dunce,
"Half an idea in the profoundest
    sonnet.
Through all the flimsy things we
    see at once
As easily as through a Naples
    bonnet—
Trash of all trash?—how can a
    lady don it?
Yet heavier far than your Petrarchan stuff—
Owl-downy nonsense that the faintest puff
Twirls into trunk-paper while you con it."
And, veritably, Sol is right enough.
The general tuckermanities are arrant
Bubbles—ephemeral and so transparent—
But this is, now,—you may depend on it—
Stable, opaque, immortal—all by dint
Of the dear names that lie concealed within't.

Take the first letter of the first line (*S*), the second
of the second (*a*), and so on, and you get the
name Sarah Anna Lewis, a writer Poe was in contact with. (He sent her the poem, asking her to
solve the riddle.)

A VALENTINE
For her these lines are penned, whose luminous
    eyes,
Brightly expressive as the twins of Leda,
Shall find her own sweet name, that nestling lies
Upon the page, enwrapped from every reader.
Search narrowly the lines! They hold a treasure
Divine—a talisman—an amulet
That must be worn at heart. Search well the
    measure—

The words—the syllables! Do not forget
The trivialest point, or you may lose your labor
And yet there is in this no Gordian knot
Which one might not undo without a sabre,
If one could merely comprehend the plot.
Enwritten upon the leaf where now are peering
Eyes scintillating, soul, there lies perdus "Three
eloquent works oft uttered in the hearing
Of poets, by poets, as the name is a poet's, too.
Its letters, although naturally lying—
Like the knight Pinto—Mendez Ferdinando—
Still form a synonym for truth—Cease trying!
You will not read the riddle, though you do the best
 you can do.

Poe used the same method here; the name is
Frances Sargent Osgood.

Assuming that John Barlow did the same, I get the
name of (this is exciting; I'm finding out as I type
this, who Barlow's valentine was in '72?) INE WAG-
ISN LHS . . .

2 Did you ever waken to the sound / Of street cats making love

Pigpen struck up an acquaintance with Janis
Joplin, Big Brother's new singer. . . . Their
friendship soon ripened into something more.
On many a night, they would kill off a couple
of bottles of Southern Comfort, play and sing
themselves into a romantic mood, and retire to
Pig's room, which was situated just above mine.
I could hear them grunting and screeching
ecstatically very clearly, and I often wonder if the
line "Did you ever waken to the sound / of
street cats making love," from Bob's song "Looks
like Rain," was inspired by the music Pig and
Janis made in the dead of night. (Lesh) 95

3 Rain, rain go away

While not included in Barlow's version of the lyrics,
Weir always sang these lines as a rave-up at the tail
end of the song. They're a good example of the
use of nursery rhyme in Grateful Dead lyrics. The
"Rain, rain, go away, come again another day"
rhyme was first recorded by John Aubrey in 1687.

Notes:
Written in Cora, Wyoming, January 1972.

Studio recording: *Ace* (May 1972).

First performance: Probably March 21, 1972, at the
Academy of Music in New York. It remained in the
repertoire from then on, often sung as a "weather
magic" invocation when rain threatened an open-
air concert.

the stranger (two souls in communion)

What are they seeing, when they look in each
   other's eyes?
What are they feeling, when they see each
   other smile?
Is it love, I don't know—or an emotion that
   I've outgrown?

Did I take a wrong turn on life's winding road?
Won't somebody help me find the right way
   to go?
My life needs some correction, alteration
   in direction
Won't somebody stand by [comfort?] me—yes,
I'm lost, yes, I'm lost
Yes, I'm lost

1   What is the secret of this tie that binds?
Two souls in communion, both body and mind
Is it special magic, or just the nature of things?
Conceived of [Come see the?] great spirit, not
   for beggars but for kings

You who have found it please help me along
I'm a man, I'm a man,—I'm not made out of
   stone
My needs they are simple, I don't want anything
But I surely want to fly on those wings, on
   the run, one more time

All I wanna do, fly up, fly home
Fly on those wings of love, fly up, fly home,
I'm a stranger [a staying?] in your town, fly up,
   fly home,

Help me somebody please, fly up, fly home
I wake up early in the morning, fly up,
   fly home,
You know I never saw you babe, fly up,
   fly home

I just can't seem to understand,
Can't seem to understand what's wrong, fly
   up, fly home
What I wanna do is take a little ride with you,
On the wings of love, woh-oh one more time,
   one more time

Words and music by Ron McKernan

1 **tie that binds**
An eighteenth-century English hymn, words by
John Fawcett, "Blest Be the Tie That Binds":

> Blest be the tie that binds
> Our hearts in Christian love;
> The fellowship of kindred minds
> Is like to that above.

Notes:
Recording: live performance included on the
vault release *Steppin' Out with the Grateful Dead:
England '72.*

First performance: March 21, 1972, at the
Academy of Music in New York. It was performed
a total of twelve times in concert.

HE'S GONE

1 Steal your face
This line was lifted out as the title of an ill-fated album issued under duress in order to fulfill a contractual obligation to United Artists. Since the album's cover featured the logo designed by Owsley Stanley and rendered by Bob Thomas (who also

designed the famous dancing bears), a grinning skull, and lightning bolt inside the circle, that logo has been identified primarily as the "steal your face," or "stealie" logo, perhaps incorrectly.

2 he's gone
"He's Gone," as originally written, referred to the disappearance of Mickey Hart's father, Lenny Hart, who was acting as the band's manager and carrying a good deal of money. Since then, the song has become riddled with meaning, and is played quite tenderly when someone close to the band dies. And since the death of Jerry Garcia, the song always evokes his passing.

3 Cat on a tin roof
An old English proverbial saying, first collected in 1670 by John Ray in his *English Proverbs*. Originally, it referred to being like a cat "on hot bricks" or "upon a hot bake stone."

American listeners will probably be reminded of the title of the Tennessee Williams (1911-83) play *Cat on a Hot Tin Roof* (1955), the final line of which, at least in some versions, is "Nothing's more determined than a cat on a tin roof—is

Rat in a drain ditch
Caught on a limb
You know better but
I know him
Like I told you
What I said
Steal your face   1
right off you head

Chorus:
Now he's gone   2
Lord, he's gone
Like a steam locomotive
rolling down the track
He's gone
He's gone
and nothing's gonna bring him back
He's gone

Nine-mile skid
on a ten-mile ride
Hot as a pistol
but cool inside
Cat on a tin roof   3
Dogs in a pile
Nothing left to do but
smile, smile, smile   4

(Chorus)

Going where the wind don't blow so strange
Maybe on some high cold mountain range
Lost one round but the price wasn't anything
Knife in a back and more of the same
Same old rat in a drain ditch
Out on a limb
You know better but I know him

(Chorus)

Words by Robert Hunter
Music by Jerry Garcia

there? Is there, baby?" The line is spoken by the character Maggie the Cat. (Not actually a cat.)

4 smile, smile, smile
A campaign slogan of William Howard Taft, the successful Republican candidate for President in 1908. Taft was known as the most jovial man in politics.

Notes:
Recording: *Europe '72* (November 1972).

First performance: April 17, 1972, at the Tivoli Gardens, Copenhagen, Denmark.

STELLA BLUE

1 Stella Blue
Stella is Latin for "star."

The Stella brand guitar was "particularly popular among blues players during the 1920s and 1930s." (Evans) Evans also notes that Leadbelly played a Stella 12-string, while Blind Blake and Blind Willie McTell also played Stellas. Great-sounding, cheap (about $15 new), and cheaply made guitars, Stellas were manufactured by the Oscar Schmidt Company of Jersey City, New Jersey.

Note the lines "A broken angel sings / from a guitar," and "Dust off those rusty strings just / one more time": The song has a strong connection to guitars and guitar players. Whether Stella manufactured a guitar with a blue finish is one for the guitar fanatics to figure out. It seems more likely that the color reference is to "the blues," rather than to the color of the guitar if, indeed, it is a reference to the guitar.

The guitar-woman double meaning in "Stella Blue" is historically interesting as well. Leadbelly affectionately referred to his 12-string as "Stella" (and where would B. B. King be without "Lucille"?).

Compare lines from the 1937 poem by Wallace Stevens called "The Man with the Blue Guitar":

> They said, "You have a blue guitar,
> You do not play things as they are."

> The man replied, "Things as they are
> Are changed upon the blue guitar." 53

Stevens's inspiration for the poem was one of the many paintings of guitars by Picasso (Stevens said he didn't have any one in particular in

All the years combine
they melt into a dream
A broken angel sings
from a guitar
In the end there's just a song
comes crying like the wind
through all the broken dreams
and vanished years

Stella Blue   1, 2

When all the cards are down
there's nothing left to see
There's just the pavement left
and broken dreams
In the end there's still that song
comes crying like the wind
down every lonely street
that's ever been

Stella Blue

I've stayed in every blue-light cheap hotel   3
Can't win for tryin'   4
Dust off those rusty strings just   5
one more time
Gonna make 'em shine

It all rolls into one
and nothing comes for free
There's nothing you can hold
for very long
And when you hear that song
come crying like the wind
it seems like all this life
6   was just a dream

Stella Blue

Words by Robert Hunter
Music by Jerry Garcia

mind). The most famous, of course, is his *Old Man with a Guitar,* which was painted during Picasso's "blue period"—which is interesting in itself: Picasso's blue period occurred historically before the term *the blues* took hold in the American lexicon—and Picasso was living between Paris and Spain at the time. His blue period was an artistic response to his depression over a friend's suicide.

On the surface, "Stella Blue" sounds like a name of a woman, or the nickname of a woman. The most famous Stella in American literature must be Tennessee Williams's character in the 1947 play *A Streetcar Named Desire.* Her name is shouted, in a famous and all-too-easily imitated scene, by Marlon Brando in the film (1951) version.

However, there is also a character named Stella Blue in Vladimir Nabokov's novel *Pale Fire* (1962). In the "Commentary" portion of the novel, in the note to line 627, which discusses the "great Starover Blue," an astronomer, Nabokov writes:

> The star over the blue eminently suits an astronomer though actually neither his first nor second name bears any relation to the celestial vault: the first was given him in memory of his grandfather, a Russian *starover* . . . , that is, Old Believer (member of a schismatic sect), named Sinyavin, from *siniy,* Russ. "Blue." This Sinyavin migrated from Saratov to Seattle and begot a son who eventually changed his name to Blue and married Stella Lazurchik, an Americanized Kashube.

Additionally, there are two very famous Stellas in English literature, both pseudonymous names for actual women in the lives of the poets who addressed them, Sir Philip Sidney and Jonathan Swift. Sidney's Stella was celebrated in his sonnet sequence "Astrophel and Stella," and the real-life Stella was Lady Penelope Devereux. Swift's Stella, in real life, was Esther Johnson.

2 Blue

Dr. Jill L. Morton, an expert on color, provided the following insight:

> I might suggest that there is a psycho/physiological link. Psychologically, blue relaxes the mind. However, after ten minutes of treatment with blue rays, most people tire and begin to feel depressed. Color is electromagnetic energy and affects the hypothalamus gland. Blood pressure, respiratory rate, pulse, appetite, and mood are altered by the presence of large quantities of specific colors or colored rays. (Morton) 54

3 Blue-light cheap hotel

Compare T. S. Eliot's line in "The Love Song of J. Alfred Prufrock": "Of restless nights in one-night cheap hotels. . . ."

Pigpen sang, "working in a house of blue lights," in "Operator," which in turn seems to take its cue from the 1947 song "House of Blue Lights" (words and music by Freddie Slack and Don Raye). The "house of blue lights" seems to be a dance hall in this context.

4 Can't win for tryin'

A saying signifying futility: "No matter how hard I try, I can't win." A relative of "Can't win for losing."

5 Dust off those rusty strings

As far as "Dust[ing] off those rusty strings" is concerned, history has pretty much forgotten how important the advent of the steel guitar string was to the development of popular music. Before the twentieth century, the guitar was a polite parlor instrument strung with gut. And even in the early decades of this century, the guitar was noth-

ing, as far as popularity, compared to the banjo and mandolin (which were steel-stringed instruments). It wasn't until the bluesmen came along and started experimenting with steel strings on guitars that a particular sound was born. Steel gave the guitar a brighter and louder sound. According to Wolfe and Lornel:

> the use of steel strings probably came into Texas and Louisiana from Mexico, and it is quite likely that blacks in the area had been experimenting with them long before the guitar makers began to switch over to them.

6 it seems like all this life / was just a dream

Compare to several quotations:

> Is all our Life, then, but a dream
> Seen faintly in the golden gleam
> Athwart Time's dark resistless stream?
> —Lewis Carroll, *Sylvie and Bruno*

"Row, row, row": The famous folk song round with the surreal "Life is but a dream" tag.

> His life was a sort of dream, as are most lives with the mainspring left out.
> —F. Scott Fitzgerald, *The Crack-Up*

> What is life? A madness. What is life? An illusion, a shadow, a story. And the greatest good is little enough: for all life is a dream, and dreams themselves are only dreams.
> —Pedro Calderon de la Barca
> (1600– 1681), *Life Is a Dream*

Notes:

Written, according to *A Box of Rain,* at the Chelsea Hotel in New York in 1970. This places "Stella Blue" in distinguished company. It's where Arthur C. Clarke wrote *2001: A Space Odyssey,* Bob Dylan wrote "Sad-Eyed Lady of the Lowlands," and Arthur Miller wrote *After the Fall.* It's been home, in its hundred-year-plus history (built in 1883), to Mark Twain, Sarah Bernhardt, O. Henry, Hart Crane, Nelson Algren, Willem de Kooning, Jasper Johns,

Vladimir Nabokov (see note under "Stella Blue," above, for more on Nabokov), Jane Fonda, Charles Jackson, Milos Forman, Edie Sedgwick, Yevgeny Yevtushenko, Brendan Behan, Dylan Thomas, Thomas Wolfe, Edgar Lee Masters, and a slew of others. The Grateful Dead played on the rooftop of the Chelsea on August 10, 1967. Lesh says:

[The Diggers'] chief honcho, Emmett Grogan, knew some people in New York and set up a sort of benefit on the roof of the Chelsea, attended by such luminaries as Shirley Clarke, the theatrical director, and artist Andy Warhol, who entered looking like an ambulatory black hole. . . . It was kind of cool, playing on a rooftop in New York, but whatever energy we could muster fell flat on the floor, oozing over to Warhol's feet where it disappeared into the singularity. Not a fun event. . . . (Lesh) 95

Studio recording: *Wake of the Flood* (November 15, 1973).

First performance: June 17, 1972, at the Hollywood Bowl in Los Angeles. (This was Pigpen's last show with the band. He was found dead of complications arising from liver failure on March 8, 1973.) It remained a staple of the live repertoire thereafter.

Mississippi Half-Step Uptown Toodleloo

1 Cain caught Abel / rolling loaded dice
Could this be the motive for the first murder in recorded Judaeo-Christian human history (that of Abel by Cain)? The biblical story of Cain and Abel is found in Genesis 4:8.

An old African American song, "Creation," contains the lines:

> Cain thought Abel played a trick
> (Dese bones gwine rise ergain)
> Hit 'em in the head wid a piece of brick
> (White)

2 Toodleloo
From the *Oxford English Dictionary:*

> toodle-oo *int. colloq.* [Origin unknown; perh. f. TOOT (An act of tooting...)] Goodbye. Cf. PIP-PIP. 1907 *Punch* 26 June 465 'Toodle-oo, old sport.' Mr. Punch turned 'round at the amazing words and gazed at his companion. Also toodle-, tootle-pip.

Partridge speculates:

> or maybe, as Mr. F. W. Thomas has most ingeniously suggested, a Cockney corruption of the French equivalent of '(I'll) see you soon': *à tout à l'heure.*

3 Hello, baby, I'm gone, good-bye
Compare "Hello, I Must Be Going," from the 1930s film *Animal Crackers,* sung by Groucho Marx.

Also compare the Beatles' "Hello Goodbye."

4 rock and rye
A sweet alcoholic beverage made from putting rock candy and fruit in rye whiskey.

On the day that I was born
Daddy sat down and cried
I had the mark just as plain as day
which could not be denied
They say that Cain caught Abel
rolling loaded dice,   1
ace of spades behind his ear
and him not thinking twice

Chorus:
Half-step
Mississippi Uptown Toodleloo   2
Hello baby I'm gone, good-bye   3
Half a cup of rock and rye   4
Farewell to you old Southern sky
I'm on my way—on my way

If all you got to live for
is what you left behind
get yourself a powder charge
and seal that silver mine
I lost my boots in transit, babe   5
A pile of smoking leather
Nailed a retread to my feet
   and prayed for better weather

(Chorus)

They say that when your ship comes in
the first man takes the sails
The second takes the afterdeck

The third the planks and rails
What's the point to calling shots?
This cue ain't straight in line
Cueball's made of Styrofoam
and no one's got the time

(Chorus)

Across the Rio Grand-eo
  Across the lazy river
  Across the Rio Grand-eo
  Across the lazy river

Words by Robert Hunter
Music by Jerry Garcia

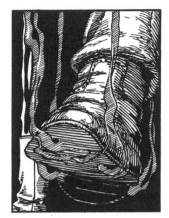

5 Lost my boots in transit, babe
[Garcia:] Events in my life suggested to me that maybe it was going to be my responsibility to keep upping the ante. I was in an automobile accident in 1960 with three other guys . . . ninety plus miles an hour on a back road. We hit these dividers and went flying, I guess. All I know is that I was sitting in the car and there was this . . . disturbance . . . and the next thing, I was in a field, far enough away from the car that I couldn't see it.

The car was crumpled like a cigarette pack . . . and inside it were my shoes. I'd been thrown completely out of my shoes and through the windshield. One guy [Paul Speegle] in the group did die. It was like losing the golden boy, the one who had the most to offer. For me, it was crushing, but I had the feeling that my life had been spared to do something . . . not to take any bullshit, to either go whole hog or not at all. . . . That was when my life began. Before that, I had been living at less than capacity. That event was the slingshot for the rest of my life. It was my second chance, and I got serious. (Gans, *Playing in the Band*) 55

Notes:
Studio recording: *Wake of the Flood* (November 15, 1973).

First performance: July 16, 1972, at Dillon Stadium in Hartford, Connecticut. It remained a staple of the repertoire thereafter.

Compare the title "East St. Louis Toodeloo" by Duke Ellington; also covered by Steely Dan.

Compare the lines from an African American folk song:

Farewell to Tom and Jerry
Farewell to rock and rye
It's a long way to old Kentucky
For Alabama done gone dry.
(White: Reported from Auburn, Alabama 1915–16; to the tune of "Tipperary")

china DOLL

1 bells of heaven ring
The African American "judgment day song" "Didn't
You Hear" contains the line "Didn't you hear the
heaven bells ring?"

Also compare the 1866 hymn title "Ring the Bells
of Heaven," words by William O. Cushing, music
by George F. Root:

> Ring the bells of Heaven! There is joy today,
> For a soul, returning from the wild!
> See, the Father meets him out upon the way,
> Welcoming his weary, wandering child.

Cirlot says of the bell as a symbol:

> Its sound is a symbol of creative power. Since it is in
> a hanging position, it partakes of the mystic signifi-
> cance of all objects which are suspended between
> heaven and earth. It is related, by its shape, to the
> vault and, consequently, to the heavens. 56

**2 Yesterday I begged you / before I hit the
ground**
William Camden, an antiquary and scholar who lived
between 1551 and 1623, wrote in his *Remains
Concerning Britain:* "Betwixt the stirrup and the
ground, Mercy I ask'd; mercy I found."

These lines express the Christian concept that,
even in the split second as you fall dying from
your horse, there is still time to repent, ask for
mercy, and be given absolution.

A pistol shot at five o'clock
The bells of heaven ring   1
Tell me what you done it for
"No I won't tell you a thing

"Yesterday I begged you
before I hit the ground—   2
all I leave behind me
is only what I found

"If you can abide it
let the hurdy-gurdy play—   3
Stranger ones have come by here
before they flew away

"I will not condemn you
nor yet would I deny . . ."
*I would ask the same of you
but failing will not die . . .*

*Take up your china doll
it's only fractured—
just a little nervous
from the fall*

*Words by Robert Hunter
Music by Jerry Garcia*

3 hurdy-gurdy

The hurdy-gurdy is a stringed instrument in which the strings are rubbed by a rosined wheel instead of a bow. The wheel is turned by the player's right hand, while the left hand plays the tune on the keys of the key box. Two of the strings (usually), called the chanters or the melody strings, run though the key box, and their vibrating length is shortened by the key pressing against it. Several drone strings are outside the key box, and so sound the same note all the time. For this reason, the hurdy-gurdy sounds similar to a bagpipe. A small movable bridge on one of the drones can be made to vibrate rhythmically by cranking the wheel harder, and this buzzing is used for a rhythmic accompaniment to the tune.

The line may bring up a resonance with the Donovan song "Hurdy Gurdy Man" (1968, words and music by Harold Levey).

Often depicted in late medieval/early Renaissance art as being played by a skeleton (ha!) at the side of a dying man. Most famously it can be seen in Pieter Brueghel's majestic *Triumph of Death* played by a skeleton watching the enormous rampant destruction of Life by Death passing before his eyes.

Notes:
Studio recording: *Grateful Dead from the Mars Hotel* (June 27, 1974).

First live performance: February 9, 1973, at Roscoe Maples Pavilion, Stanford University, Palo Alto, California.

Originally titled "The Suicide Song."

Erstwhile band member Bruce Hornsby included a song of his own composition titled "China Doll" on his *Harbor Lights* album.

eyes of the world

1 nuthatch
A bird:

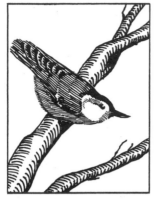

Nuthatches:
Family:
Sittidae.
Twenty-one
species in
four genera.
Distribution:
N. America,
Europe, N.
Africa, Asia,
New Guinea, and Australia.
Size: length 4 to 7.5"; weight .35 to 1.75 oz.
Plumage: upperparts blue-gray; two species
have a bright blue back; some species have a
black stripe through each eye; underparts
grayish white to brown.
Voice: repeated piping phrases, chattering
calls.

  The word *nuthatch* is derived from the
fondness of the Eurasian species for hazelnuts.
[Regarding the phrase: "wondering where the
nuthatch winters":] Only a few species are
known to undertake migrations. The Red-
breasted nuthatch migrates from the woods of
Canada as far as the southern montane wood-
lands of North America. In some winters, the
east Siberian subspecies of the Eurasian
nuthatch moves west as far as Finland.
[Regarding "wings a mile long":] They have
long wings and a short to medium tail.
(From *The World Atlas of Birds* and *The
Encyclopedia of Birds*)

Invariably mispronounced by Garcia as "nut
thatch."

Right outside this lazy summer home
you don't have time to call
your soul a critic, no
Right outside the lazy gate
of winter's summer home
wondering where the nuthatch winters   1
Wings a mile long
just carried
the bird
away

Chorus:
Wake up to find out
that you are the eyes of the world   2
but the heart has its beaches
its homeland and thoughts
of its own
Wake now, discover that
you are the song that
the morning brings
but the heart has its seasons   3
its evenings
and songs of its own

There comes a redeemer
and he slowly, too, fades away
There follows a wagon behind him
that's loaded with clay
and the seeds that were silent

all burst into bloom and decay
The night comes so quiet
and it's close on the heels of the day

(Chorus)

4   Sometimes we live no
particular way but our own
Sometimes we visit your country
and live in your home
Sometimes we ride on your horses
Sometimes we walk alone
Sometimes the songs that we hear
are just songs of our own

(Chorus)

Words by Robert Hunter
Music by Jerry Garcia

2 eyes of the world

At least two movies, one book, and more than eleven songs have used this phrase as a title, among them:

A 1914 novel by Harold Bell Wright
A 1917 silent film based on the book (above) by Wright
A 1930 remake of the 1917 film
A song by Richie Blackmore and Roger Glover for Rainbow's 1979 album, *Down to Earth.*
A song by Lindsey Buckingham for Fleetwood Mac's 1982 album, *Mirage.*

"You are the eyes of the world" is a translation of the noted Buddhist practitioner Longchenpa's practical guide to the tantra *(The Jewel Ship: A Guide to the Meaning of Pure and Total Presence, the Creative Energy of the Universe*, or *byang chub kyi sems kun byed rgyal po'i don khrid din chen sgru bo).* It was translated by Kennard Lipman and Merrill Peterson and published by Lotsawa of Novato, California. The song itself obviously held importance for the folks involved in its production, for part of Hunter's lyrics are printed opposite the title page.

3 the heart has its seasons

Compare the quote by Blaise Pascal (1623–62), from his *Pensées* (1670):

The heart has its reasons, which reason does not know. We feel it in a thousand things. I say that the heart naturally loves the Universal Being, and also itself naturally, according as it gives itself to them; and it hardens itself against one or the other at its will. You have rejected the one and kept the other. Is it by reason that you love yourself?

4 Sometimes we . . .

Compare the song "Goodnight Irene" (a song the band performed *once*) with its lines

Sometimes I live in the country
Sometimes I live in town
Sometimes I take a great notion
To jump in the river and drown.

Also, the four lines quoted from "Goodnight, Irene" are the same ones that inspired Ken Kesey's title *Sometimes a Great Notion.* In counterculture legend, Kesey, a great generator of the sixties, was a subject in the CIA's MK-ULTRA "acid tests" at the Menlo Park Veterans Hospital, under the direction of Dr. Leo Hollister, one of the company's prized psychiatrists. The early Warlocks, who were to become the Grateful Dead, were Kesey's house band for some of the Pranksters' Acid Tests.

Notes:

Studio recording: *Wake of the Flood* (November 15, 1973)

First performance: February 9, 1973, at Roscoe Maples Pavilion, Stanford University, Palo Alto, California. It remained in the repertoire thereafter.

here comes sunshine

Wake of the flood
laughing water
’49
Get out the pans
don’t just stand there dreaming
get out the way
get out the way

Here comes sunshine
. . . here comes sunshine!

Line up a long shot
Maybe try it two times
Maybe more
Good to know
you got shoes to wear
when you find the floor
Why hold out for more?

Here comes sunshine
. . . here comes sunshine!

Asking you nice now
keep the mother rolling
one more time
Been down before
but you just don’t have to
go no more
no more

Here comes sunshine
. . . here comes sunshine!

Words by Robert Hunter
Music by Jerry Garcia

Notes:
Studio recording: *Wake of the Flood* (November 15, 1973).

First performance: February 9, 1973, at Roscoe Maples Pavilion, Stanford University, Palo Alto, California. The song was played regularly through February 1974, after which it was dropped from the repertoire until December 6, 1992. It remained in the repertoire thereafter.

Hunter's note in *A Box of Rain:* "Remembering the great Vanport, Washington, flood of 1949, living in other people's homes, a family abandoned by father; second grade."

LOOSE LUCY

1 birds on the hot wire

In response to a query about what a bird on a hot wire might sense, I received  this answer from a long-time power company employee:

> With regard to birds on a wire, the wire ordinarily doesn't run at much higher temperature than the ambient air unless the cable is heated by the sun. They can get fried if they get between one of the three transmission lines or between one line and neutral or ground.

2 Bebop

Synonym for *bop:*

> A style of jazz developed in the early 1940s in New York, which came to full maturity by 1945 in the work of Dizzy Gillespie (trumpet), Charlie Parker (alto saxophone) [et al]. The word *bop* is a shortened form of the vocables (nonsense syllables) "bebop" or "rebop," which were commonly used in scat singing to accompany the distinctive two-note rhythm. . . . *(New Grove Dictionary of American Music)*

Notes:

Studio recording: *Grateful Dead from the Mars Hotel* (June 27, 1974).

First performance: February 9, 1973, at the Roscoe Maples Pavilion, Stanford University, Palo Alto, California. It remained in the repertoire

Loose Lucy is my delight
She comes running and we ball all night
Round and round and round and round
Don't take much to get me on the ground

She's my yo-yo, I'm her string
Listen to the birds on the hot wire sing   1

Chorus:
Singing: Yeah, yeah, yeah, yeah
Singing: Thank you
for a real good time

I got jumped coming home last night
Shadow in the alley turned out all my lights
Round and round and round and round
Don't take much to get me on the ground

Loose Lucy—she was sore!
Says I know you don't want my love no more

(Chorus)

Bebop baby, how can this be?   2
I know you've been out a-cheating on me
Round and round and round and round
Don't take much to get the word around

Cross my heart and hope to die
I was just hanging out with the other guys

(Chorus)

Went back home with two black eyes
You know I'll love her till the day I die
Round and round and round and round
Don't take much to get the word around

I like your smile but I ain't your type
Don't shake the tree when the fruit ain't ripe

(Chorus)

Words by Robert Hunter
Music by Jerry Garcia

through 1974, then disappeared until 1990, after which time it remained in fairly steady rotation. In post-Garcia formations, the song has been sung by guest artists, most notably Sammy Hagar in The Dead's first concert as The Dead, on February 14, 2003, at the Warfield in San Francisco.

They Love Each Other

Merry run around
sailing up and down
just looking for a shove
in some direction—
got it from the top
it's nothing you can stop
Lord, you know they
made a fine connection

Chorus:
They love each other
Lord, you can see it's true
Lord, you can see that it's true
Lord, you can see that it's true

He could pass his time
'round some other line
But you know he
chose this place beside her

Don't get in the way
there's nothing you can say
Nothing that you need
to add or do

They love each other
Lord, you can see it's true
Lord, you can see that it's true
Lord, you can see that it's true

It's nothing they explain
It's like a diesel train—
you better not be there
when it rolls over
And when that train rolls in
you don't know where it's been
You gotta try and see
a little further

They love each other
Lord, you can see it's true
Lord, you can see that it's true
Lord, you can see that it's true

Words by Robert Hunter
Music by Jerry Garcia

Notes:
Studio recording: *Reflections* (January 1976).

First performance: February 9, 1973, at Roscoe
Maples Pavilion, Stanford University, Palo Alto,
California.

ROW JIMMY

Julie catch a rabbit by his hair
Come back step, like to walk on air
Get back home where you belong
and don't you run off no more

Don't hang your head let the two-time roll
Grass shack nailed to a pine wood floor
Ask the time? Baby, I don't know
Come back later, gonna let it show

Chorus:

And I say row, Jimmy, row
Gonna get there?
I don't know
Seems a common way to go
Get down, row, row, row
row, row

1   Here's a half a dollar if you dare
    double-twist when you hit the air
    Look at Julie down below
2   the levee doin the do-pas-o

(Chorus)

Broken heart don't feel so bad
Ain't got half a what you thought you had
Rock your baby to and fro
Not too fast and not too slow

1 double-twist when you hit the air
Compare the lines in the folk song "Sad
Condition" (Sharp, #263):

> Turn my elbow to my wrist,
> I'll turn back in a double twist.

Hunter says:

> The main thrust of that is, do you dare jump
> in the air at all? And if you jump in the air, are
> you gonna have presence of mind enough to
> do a trick? (Gans: *Conversations*) 57

Compare Jelly Roll Morton's "Winin' Boy":

> Mama, Mama, Mama look at Sis'
> She's out on the levee doing the double twist
> I'm a Winin' Boy, don't deny my name

2 do-pas-o
A square-dance step:

DO PASO
Starting formation—circle
of two or more couples.
DEFINITION: Each dancer
faces partner or directed
dancer and does a left
arm turn half (180°) to
face in the opposite direction. Releasing arm-holds
and moving forward,
each dancer goes to the corner for a right arm
turn half (180°). Each returns to the starting
partner to courtesy turn to face the center of
the set or to follow the next call.
STYLING: All dancers' hands in position for
forearm turns, alternating left and right. When
the courtesy turn portion of the do paso is
replaced by a different logical basic, then the
styling reverts to that basic.
TIMING: SS from start to finish of courtesy

turn, sixteen steps; to the next call, twelve (CALLERLAB) 58

3 jukebox
juke — (via Gullah from Wolof *dzug,* to misbehave, lead a disorderly life . . .) 1936, a brothel, cheap tavern, or low dive. 1939—juke boxes. (Flexner)

Notes:
Studio recording: *Wake of the Flood* (November 15, 1973).

First performance: February 9, 1973, at Roscoe Maples Pavilion, Stanford University, Palo Alto, California. It remained in the repertoire thereafter.

In an interview in *Relix,* Hunter said: "I really feel that 'Row Jimmy' is happening in New Mexico."

Hunter says the title came from a line originally but no longer, in "Fair to Even Odds."

(Chorus)

That's the way it's been in town
ever since they tore the jukebox down   3
Two-bit piece don't buy no more
not so much as it done before

And I say row, Jimmy, row
Gonna get there?
I don't know
Seems a common way to go
Get down, row, row, row
row, row

> *Words by Robert Hunter*
> *Music by Jerry Garcia*

weather report suite, part 1

1 Winter rain, now tell me why
Summers fade and roses die
The answer came, the wind and rain

Golden hills now veiled in gray
Summer leaves have blown away
Now what remains, the wind and rain

And like a desert spring my lover comes and
spreads her wings
(Knowing)
Like a song that's born to soar the sky
(Flowing)
Till the waters all are dry
(Growing)
The loving in her eyes

Circle songs and sands of time
And seasons will end in tumbled rhyme
And little change, the wind and rain

And like a desert spring my lover comes and
spreads her wings
(Knowing)
Like a song that's born to soar the sky
(Flowing)
Till the rivers all are dry
(Growing)
The loving in her eyes

Winter gray and falling rain
We'll see summer come again
Darkness fall and seasons change
(Gonna happen every time)

Same old friends the wind and rain
(We'll see summer by and by)
Winter gray and falling rain
(Summers fade and roses die)
We'll see summer come again
(Like a song that's born to soar the sky)

Words by Eric Andersen and Bob Weir
Music by Bob Weir

1 roses
See note under "That's It for the Other One."

Notes:
Studio recording: *Wake of the Flood* (November 15, 1973).

First performance: September 7, 1973, at the Nassau Veterans Memorial Coliseum in Uniondale, New York. It was played throughout 1973 and 1974, then dropped from the repertoire, as was the suite's instrumental "Prelude."

Eric Andersen, born in Pittsburgh in 1943, is a singer-songwriter whose career spans decades. He began on the folk club circuit in San Francisco and New York, releasing his first recording, *Today Is the Highway,* in 1965. His best-known song "Thirsty Boots," while his 1971 album, *Blue River,* is regarded as his best work. Stylistically, Andersen moved through a range of music, from country to pop. He moved to Norway in the 1980s and formed a trio with Rick Danko and Jonas Fjeld, captured on *Danko/Fjeld/Andersen.* Andersen was along for the ride on the 1970 Festival Express Tour with the Grateful Dead and other West Coast musicians of the period (he was the only solo acoustic act on the tour), memorialized in "Might As Well."

weather report suite, part 2 (Let It grow)

1 Lightly sung . . .
Studio outtakes from *Wake of the Flood* sessions show this line being sung originally as "Stepping free, she places her feet where they fell before."

2 work of his day
Compare Hesiod's *Works and Days,* which extols the intrinsic virtue of a pastoral life.

3 What shall we say, shall we call it by a name?
Frederick Mathewson Denny, in his article on "Names and naming" in the *The Encyclopedia of Religion,* says:

> It is common to nearly all religious practices that in order to communicate with a deity, one must know its name. Knowledge of a divine name gives the knower both power and an avenue of communication with its source. This intimate relationship between knowing a name and participating in its power has both religious and magical aspects.

Denny then proceeds to examine the tradition of the naming of deities throughout world religious practices. See also the note under "I am," below.

4 As well to count the angels dancin' on a pin
From the article "Angel/Angelology" by E. Ann Matter, in the *Dictionary of the Middle Ages:*

> Aquinas devoted fourteen books of the *Summa theologiae* to the nature and powers of angels. He held that angels have form but not matter, and are therefore eternal and incorruptible. Angels are able to assume bod-

Morning comes, she follows the path to the
  river shore
Lightly sung, her song is the latch on the   1
  morning's door
See the sun sparkle in the reeds; silver beads pass
  into the sea

She comes from a town where they call her the
  woodcutter's daughter
She's brown as the bank where she kneels down to
  gather her water
And she bears it away with a love that the river has
  taught her
Let it flow, greatly flow, wide and clear

'Round and 'round, the cut of the plow in the
  furrowed field
Seasons round, the bushels of corn and the
  barley meal
Broken ground, open and beckoning to the spring;
  black dirt live again

The plowman is broad as the back of the land he
  is sowing
As he dances the circular track of the plow
  ever knowing
That the work of his day measures more than the   2
  planting and growing
Let it grow, let it grow, greatly yield

Chorus:
What shall we say, shall we call it by a name   3
As well to count the angels dancing on a pin   4

Water bright as the sky from which it came
And the name is on the earth that takes it in
We will not speak but stand inside the rain
5   And listen to the thunder shout
6   I am, I am, I am, I am

So it goes, we make what we made since the
    world began
Nothing more, the love of the women, work
    of men
7   Seasons round, creatures great and small, up and
    down, as we rise and fall

What shall we say, shall we call it by a name
As well to count the angels dancing on a pin
Water bright as the sky from which it came
And the name is on the earth that takes it in
We will not speak but stand inside the rain
And listen to the thunder shout
I am, I am, I am, I am

Words by John Barlow
Music by Bob Weir

ies; these bodies take up space, so only one
angel can be in a particular place at a certain
time. In contrast, Duns Scotus asserted that
angels consist of both form and a non
corporeal matter particular to them alone,
which makes it possible for more than one
angel to occupy the same place at the same
time (*De Anima, XV; De rerum principio,
VII–VIII*). The ensuing debates over these positions may have given rise to the early modern
legend that the Scholastics argued over such
questions as how many angels can dance on
the head of a pin.

5   thunder shout
Compare T. S. Eliot's *The Wasteland,* "What the
Thunder Said."

6   I am
Again quoting from
Denny's article on
"Names and naming":

Moses asked the voice
from the burning bush,
identified as "the god of
your father," what his
name was, and was
answered "I am" *(ehyeh),*
which, in a different
Hebrew grammatical
form, is rendered *Yahveh* (approximately, "He
causes to be"; Exodus, 3:13–14).

There is some debate within the academic
community surrounding this, with some scholars
asserting that the translation for *ehyeh* should be
"I will be."

Barlow's turn of phrase in associating the sound
of thunder with the name of the deity resonates
throughout world religion as the "sky-god,"

who has the power of thunder and is often the chief god in the pantheon of any given religious system.

In Australian Aboriginal culture, the name of the sky god is divulged in the sound of the bull-roarer, which Mickey Hart writes about in *Drumming at the Edge of Magic.*

7 creatures great and small
Compare the hymn "All Things Bright and Beautiful" (1848) by Cecil Frances Alexander (1818–95):

> All things bright and beautiful,
> All creatures great and small,
> All things wise and wonderful,
> The Lord God made them all.

Barlow exhibits a fondness for this hymn in his lyrics for "Just a Little Light" as well, with the line "Holding little but contempt for all things beautiful and bright."

Notes:
Written in Salt Lake City, February 1973.

Studio recording: *Wake of the Flood* (November 15, 1973).

First performance: September 7, 1973, at the Nassau Veterans Memorial Coliseum in Uniondale, New York. It remained in the repertoire thereafter.

Let me sing your blues away

Well hop in the hack
Turn on the key
Pop in the clutch
Let the wheels roll free

Not a cloud in the sky
Such a sunny day
Push in the button
Let the Top Ten play

C'mon honey, let me sing 'em away
C'mon honey, let me sing 'em away
Oh, honey, let me sing your blues away

Give me a little of that old-time love
'Cause I ain't never had near enough

Honey, walk that walk
with style and grace
This ain't no knock-down
drag-out race

It don't matter much
Pick any gear
1 Grind you a pound and
drop the rear
Baby, baby, what can I say?
I'm here to drive those blues away

Sent a letter to a man I know
2 Said one for the money and two for the show
Waited all summer for his reply

Three to get ready and four to fly

Only two things in the world I love

1 grind you a pound
From the old catcall uttered upon hearing the sounds of poor clutch operation from a passing car: "Grind me a pound!"

2 one for the money and two for the show
Echoes of the classic rock-and-roll song "Blue Suede Shoes":

> Well, it's one for the money
> Two for the show
> Three to get ready, now go, cat, go

See note under "U.S. Blues."

3 turtle dove
While the line probably refers to a sweetheart, the pigeon known as the turtle dove (*Streptopelia turtur*) resides throughout Northern Europe and into Asia and North Africa. There are about fifteen species of Old World turtle doves (genus *Streptopelia*) residing in Africa, Asia, and Europe. In America, three genera of medium-size pigeons, including *Zenaidura, Zenaida,* and *Ectopistes,* live in the tropics.

Notes:
Studio recording: *Wake of the Flood* (November 15, 1973).

First performance: September 8, 1973, at Nassau Veterans Memorial Coliseum in Uniondale, New York.

3   That's rock and roll and my turtle dove

When I was a young man
I needed good luck
But I'm a little bit older now
and I know my stuff

C'mon honey, let me sing 'em away

C'mon honey, let me sing 'em away
Oh, honey, let me
sing your
blues
away

Words by Robert Hunter
Music by Keith Godchaux

- wrench -

peggy-o

1   As we rode out to Fennario
As we rode out to Fennario
Our captain fell in love with a lady like a dove
And he called her by name pretty Peggy-O

Will you marry me, pretty Peggy-O?
Will you marry me, pretty Peggy-O?
If you will marry me, I will set your cities free.
And free all the ladies in the area-O

I would marry you, sweet William-O?
I would marry you, sweet William-O?
I would marry you, but your guineas are too few
And I feel my mother would be angry-O

What would your mother think, pretty Peggy-O?
What would your mother think, pretty Peggy-O?
What would your mother think when she hears
   the guineas clink?
And saw me marching at the head of my
   soldiers-O

If ever I return, pretty Peggy-O
If ever I return, pretty Peggy-O
If ever I return, all your cities I will burn
Destroy all the ladies in the area-O

Come stepping down the stairs, pretty Peggy-O
Come stepping down the stairs, pretty Peggy-O
Come stepping down the stairs, combing back
   your yellow hair
And bid a last farewell to young Willie-O

Sweet William he is dead, pretty Peggy-O
Sweet William he is dead, pretty Peggy-O
Sweet William he is dead, and he died for
   a maid
And he's buried in the Louisiana
   country-O

Words and music: traditional

1 Fennario
See note under "Dire Wolf" for more on this
place name.

Notes:
Recorded on *Dozin' at the Knick* (October 1996).

First performance: December 10, 1973, at the
Charlotte Coliseum in Charlotte, North Carolina.

Often called "Fennario," this song has a very
long lineage. According to the *Joan Baez
Songook*, Joan recorded it on her 1962 LP, *In
Concert Vol. 2*. "Cecil Sharp discovered several
versions of this ballad in the Southern
Appalachians on his collecting trips during the
first World War, though it seems to have disappeared from American tradition since that
time. It is still extremely popular in Scotland as
'The Bonnie Lass o' Fyvie-O' and was earlier
known in England as 'Pretty Peggy of Derby.'"
There *are* precedents for calling the tune
"Peggy-O," however: Simon and Garfunkel
recorded it under that title; Bob Dylan's first
album calls it "Pretty Peggy-O"; and one of
the most respected volumes of folk song lyrics,
The Folksinger's Wordbook by Irwin and Fred
Silber, lists the song as "Peggy–O." (Jackson:
Goin' Down the Road) 94

U.S. BLUES

1 blue suede shoes
An echo of the song of the same title by Carl Perkins (1956), one of the most famous rock and roll songs ever. Elvis Presley covered it, as have countless others.

2 Uncle Sam
A jocular name for the United States Government, coined during the War of 1812. Nowadays, we think of Army-recruiting posters of the man with the red, white, and blue top hat and the wispy goatee. The co-optation of this emblem by the Dead was inspired mockery.

The United States. A nickname.
Troy Post 7 Sep. 3/3 'Loss upon loss,' and 'no ill luck stirring but what lights upon Uncle Sam's shoulders,' exclaim the Government editors, in every part of the Country. . . . This cant name for our government has got almost as current as 'John Bull.' The letters U.S. on the government waggons, &c are supposed to have given rise to it. *(Dictionary of Americanisms)*

And Bob Weir had this to say:

And one of our figures is Uncle Sam. And he's up there with Marilyn Monroe and Paul Bunyan and people you may not know, James Dean, Otis Redding, the great ball players. We have our pantheon, and one of the figures in the pantheon is Uncle Sam. He's sort of like the godfather figure of American culture. So we actually have a fair bit of respect for him. And he comes around in different guises, you

Red and white/blue suede shoes   1
I'm Uncle Sam/how do you do?   2
Gimme five/I'm still alive
Ain't no luck/I learned to duck

Check my pulse/it don't change
Stay seventy-two/come shine or rain
Wave the flag/pop the bag
Rock the boat/skin the goat

Chorus:
Wave that flag   3
Wave it wide and high
Summertime
Done come and gone
My, oh, my

I'm Uncle Sam/that's who I am
Been hidin' out/in a rock-and-roll band
Shake the hand that shook the hand   4
Of P. T. Barnum/and Charlie Chan   5, 6

Shine your shoes/light your fuse
Can you use/them ol' U.S. Blues?
I'll drink your health/share your wealth   7
Run your life/steal your wife

(Chorus)

Back to back/chicken shack
Son of a gun/better change your act
We're all confused/what's to lose?
You can call this song/the United States Blues   8

(Chorus)

Words by Robert Hunter
Music by Jerry Garcia

know—in our little region, he comes around as a skeleton, but he's still wearing the same hat. (*Dupree's Diamond News*)

3 Wave that flag

An earlier version of the piece, titled "Wave That Flag," first appeared on February 9, 1973, and was dropped after June of that year:

Wave the flag, pop the bag
Skin the goat, [command?] the coat
Bell the cat, trap the rat
Ball the jack, chew the fat

Shoot the breeze, lose the keys
Pass the cheese, scratch the fleas
Make a sign, connect the lines
Pay your fines, save your dimes

Wave that flag, wave it wide and high
Summertime done come and gone, my oh my

[Bring the dead], read the rest
Hide in caves, walk on waves
Stretch the truth, pull the tooth
Feed the poor, start the war

Get your licks, catch the picks
Play your rags, pick up sticks
[   ]
Try your tricks, impress the chicks

Wash the fence, dig [a dent?]
Live in shame, die in vain
Burn the stew, catch the flu
Shine your shoes, sing the blues

4 Shake the hand that shook the hand

Compare the song "Let Me Shake the Hand That Shook the Hand of Sullivan" (1898), words by Monroe H. Rosenfeld, music by Alfred Williams:

The Bradys and O'Gradys, ye may talk about them all,
The Laceys and the Caseys from Bombay to Donegal;

I'd like to find another man that's fit to breathe the air
With Sullivan, the gentleman from good old County Clare,
It's him that's easy with the girls and solid with the men,
and when the whiskey jug goes 'round can drink enough for ten;
If anyone does know him here, I don't care who's the man,
Le me shake the hand that shook the hand of Sullivan.

(Chorus)

He's the pride of the ward, happy as a lord,
He's got the reputation of a man;
Arrah, good luck to yez all, let's have another ball,
Let me shake the hand that shook the hand of Sullivan.

On several occasions in 1979 and 1980, Garcia sang:

Shake the hand that shook the hand
Of P. T. Barnum and the Shah of Iran

5 P. T. Barnum

Barnum, P[hineas] T[aylor] (1810–91), showman, author. Born in Connecticut, Barnum began his career as showman in 1835 when he bought and exhibited a slave who claimed to be 161 years old and the nurse of George Washington. Seven years later he opened his American Museum, in New York City, exhibiting the Fiji Mermaid (half monkey, half fish), General Tom Thumb (a midget less than three feet tall), and the original Siamese Twins, Chang and Eng. He also arranged the

American tour of Jenny Lind, known as the Swedish Nightingale. After serving as mayor of Bridgeport and as a member of the Connecticut legislature, he organized "The Greatest Show on Earth," a circus that opened in Brooklyn, New York, in 1871. A merger in 1881 created Barnum and Bailey's. *(Benet's)* 59

6 Charlie Chan

The pudgy, wise, smiling Chinese detective living in Hawaii who appears in a number of stories by Earl Derr Diggers. Chan has a large and constantly growing family—a son in the latter tales begins to learn the sleuthing business from his father—and Charlie is given to philosophical reflections, many of them supposedly culled from Chinese sages. . . . Chan first appeared in *The House Without a Key* (1925), later in other novels, in the movies, and in many radio sketches. *(Benet's)* 60

7 share your wealth

Huey P. Long (1893–1935), nicknamed the Kingfish, was governor of Louisiana from 1928 to 1932 and a U.S. Senator for that state from 1932 to his death by assassination in September 1935. As a senator, he promoted a program called the Share-Our-Wealth Society, in which he proposed instituting restrictions on corporate power and a system of graduated income tax that heavily taxed the wealthiest citizens. Under the motto "Every Man a King," Long promulgated a platform on the floor of the Senate in opposition to Franklin Delano Roosevelt's New Deal:

To share our wealth by providing for every deserving family to have one-third of the average wealth would mean that, at the worst, such a family could have a fairly comfortable home, an automobile, and a radio, with other reasonable home conveniences, and a place to educate their children. Through sharing the work, that is, by limiting the hours of toil so that all would share in what is made and produced in the land, every family would have enough coming in every year to feed, clothe, and provide a fair share of the luxuries of life to its members. Such is the result to a family, at the worst. (*Congressional Record,* February 5, 1934)

8 You can call this song / the United States Blues
See note under "One More Saturday Night."

Notes:
Studio recording: *Grateful Dead from the Mars Hotel* (June 27, 1974).

First performance: February 22, 1974, at Winterland in San Francisco. The tune remained in the repertoire steadily, often occupying the encore position.

IT MUST Have Been the ROSeS

1   Annie laid her head down in the roses
She had ribbons, ribbons, ribbons
in her long brown hair
I don't know, maybe it was the roses
All I know, I could not leave her there

Chorus:
I don't know
it must have been the roses
The roses or the ribbons in her long brown hair
I don't know, maybe it was the roses
All I know, I could not leave her there

Ten years the waves rolled the ships home from
   the sea
Thinking well how it may blow in all good
   company
If I tell another what your own lips told to me
Let me lay 'neath the roses and my eyes no
   longer see

(Chorus)

One pane of glass in the window
No one is complaining, though, come in and shut
   the door
Faded is the crimson from the ribbons that
   she wore
And it's strange how no one comes 'round
   anymore

(Chorus)

Words and music by Robert Hunter

1 roses
See note under "That's It for the Other One."

Notes:
Studio recording: *Reflections* (January 1976).

First performance: February 22, 1974, at the Winterland Arena in San Francisco. A steady number in the repertoire thereafter.

ship of fools

1 Ship of Fools
From the *Dictionary of the Middle Ages'* article on Sebastian Brant (1457–1521):

Brant's fame stems from *Das Narrenschiff* (The ship of fools), published in 1494.

In concept and style *Das Narrenschiff* belongs to the satiric genre of the Middle Ages, and stands in an old tradition, to a degree biblical in origin. . . .

Brant sees follies as sins. This concept makes

Went to see the captain
strangest I could find
Laid my proposition down
Laid it on the line;
I won't slave for beggar's pay
likewise gold and jewels
but I would slave to learn the way
to sink your ship of fools

Chorus:
Ship of fools
on a cruel sea
Ship of fools
sail away from me

1

It was later than I thought
when I first believed you
now I cannot share your laughter
Ship of Fools

Saw your first ship sink and drown
from rocking of the boat
and all that could not sink or swim
was just left there to float
I won't leave you drifting down
but—whoa!—it makes me wild
with thirty years upon my head
to have you call me child

(Chorus)

The bottles stand as empty
as they were filled before
Time there was and plenty
but from that cup no more
Though I could not caution all
I still might warn a few:
Don't lend your hand to raise no flag
atop no ship of fools

(Chorus)

It was later than I thought
when I first believed you
now I cannot share your laughter
Ship of fools
No I cannot share your laughter
Ship of fools

Words by Robert Hunter
Music by Jerry Garcia

up the framework of his book: A ship—an entire fleet at first—sets off from Basel to the paradise of fools. . . .

Each chapter chastises a type of fool who is depicted graphically in the accompanying woodcut.

From Jose Barchilon's introduction to Michel Foucault's *Madness and Civilization:*

Renaissance men developed a delightful yet horrible way of dealing with their mad denizens: They were put on a ship and entrusted to mariners.

Katherine Anne Porter's novel *Ship of Fools* (1962) uses the metaphor of the ship *Vera* to represent the entire world as it drifts into World War II. Her note at the start of the novel states:

The title of this book is a translation from the German of *Das Narrenschiff,* a moral allegory by Sebastian Brant first published in Latin as *Stultifera Navis* in 1494. I read it in Basel in the summer of 1932 when I had still vividly in mind the impressions of my first voyage to Europe. When I began thinking about my novel, I took for my own this simple almost universal image of the ship of this world on its voyage to eternity. It is by no means new—it was very old and durable and dearly familiar when Brant used it; and it suits my purpose exactly. I am a passenger on that ship.
—K.A.P. 61

Porter's book was made into a memorable movie with an all-star cast including Vivian Leigh, Jose Ferrer, Lee Marvin, and many others in 1965.

Notes:
Studio recording: *Grateful Dead from the Mars Hotel* (June 27, 1974).

First performance: February 22, 1974, at the Winterland Arena in San Francisco.

cassidy

1 Cassidy
The following essay is by John Barlow:

   This is a song about necessary dualities: dying
& being born, men & women, speaking & being
silent, devastation & growth, desolation & hope.

   It is also about a Cassady and a Cassidy, Neal
Cassady and Cassidy Law. (The title could be
spelled either way as far as I'm concerned, but I
think it's officially stamped with the latter. Which
is appropriate since I believe the copyright was
registered by the latter's mother, Eileen Law.)

   The first of these was the ineffable, inimitable,
indefatigable Holy Goof Hisself, Neal Cassady,
aka Dean Moriarty, Hart Kennedy, Houlihan, and
The Best Mind of Allen Ginsberg's generation.

   Neal Cassady, for those whose education has
been so classical or so trivial or so timid as to
omit him, was the Avatar of American Hipness.
Born on the road and springing full-blown from a
fleabag on Denver's Larimer Street, he met the
hitchhiking Jack Kerouac there in the late forties
and set him and, through him, millions of others
permanently free.

   Neal came from the oral tradition. The writing
he left to others who had more time and attention span, but from his vast reserves flowed the
high-octane juice that gassed up the Beat
Generation for eight years of Eisenhower and a
thousand days of Camelot until it, like so many
other things, ground to a bewildered halt in
Dallas.

   Kerouac retreated to Long Island, where he
took up Budweiser, the *National Review,* and the
adipose cynicism of too many thwarted revolu-
tionaries. Neal just caught the next bus out.

   This turned out to be the psychedelic nose-
cone of the sixties, a rolling cornucopia of
Technicolor weirdness named Further. With Ken

I have seen where the wolf has slept by the
   silver stream
I can tell by the mark he left you were in his
   dream
Ah, child of countless trees
Ah, child of boundless seas
What you are, what you're meant to be
Speaks his name, though you were born to me,
Born to me,
Cassidy . . .   1

Lost now on the country miles in his Cadillac
I can tell by the way you smile he's rolling back
Come wash the nighttime clean
Come grow this scorched ground green
Blow the horn, tap the tambourine   2
Close the gap of the dark years in between
You and me
Cassidy . . .

Quick beats in an icy heart
catch-colt draws a coffin cart   3
There he goes now, here she starts:
Hear her cry
Flight of the seabirds, scattered like lost words
Wheel to the storm and fly

Faring thee well now
Let your life proceed by its own design
Nothing to tell now
Let the words be yours, I'm done with mine
   (repeat verse)

Words by John Barlow
Music by Bob Weir

Kesey raving from the roof and Neal at the wheel, Further roamed America from 1964 to 1966, infecting our national control delusion with a chronic and holy lunacy to which it may yet succumb.

From Further tumbled the Acid Tests, the Grateful Dead, Human Be-Ins, the Haight-Ashbury, and, as America tried to suppress the infection by populariz-ing it into cheap folly, the Summer of Love: and Woodstock.

I, meanwhile, had been initiated into the Mysteries within the sober ashrams of Timothy Leary's East Coast, from which distance the Pranksters' psychedelic psircuses seemed, well, a bit psacreligious. Bobby Weir, whom I'd known since prep school, kept me somewhat current on his riotous doings with the Pranksters et al, but I tended to dismiss on ideological grounds what little of this madness he could squeeze through a telephone.

So, purist that I was, I didn't actually meet Neal Cassady until 1967, by which time Further was already rusticating behind Kesey's barn in Oregon and the Grateful Dead had collectively beached itself in a magnificently broke-down Victorian palace at 710 Ashbury Street, two blocks up the hill from what was by then, according to *Time* magazine, the axis mundi of American popular culture. The real party was pretty much over by the time I arrived.

But Cassady, the Most Amazing Man I Ever Met, was still very much Happening. Holding court in 710's tiny kitchen, he would carry on five different conversa-tions at once and still devote one conversational chan-nel to discourse with absent persons and another to such sound effects as disintegrating ring gears or exploding crania. To log in to one of these conversa-tions, despite their multiplicity, was like trying to take a sip from a fire hose.

He filled his few and momentary lapses in flow with the most random numbers ever generated by man or computer or, more often, with his low signature laugh, a "heh, heh, heh, heh" which sounded like an engine being spun furiously by an overenthusiastic starter motor.

As far as I could tell, he never slept. He tossed back green hearts of Mexican Dexedrine by the shot-size bottle, grinned, cackled, and jammed on into the night. Despite such behavior, he seemed, at 41, a paragon of robust health. With a face out of a recruiting poster (leaving aside a certain glint in the eyes) and a torso, usually raw, by Michelangelo, he didn't even seem quite mortal. Though he would shortly demonstrate himself to be so.

Neal and Bobby were perfectly contrapuntal. As Cassady rattled incessantly, Bobby had fallen mostly mute, stilled perhaps by macrobiotics, perhaps a less than passing grade in the Acid Tests, or, more likely, some combination of every strange thing which had caused him to start thinking much faster than anyone could talk. I don't have many focused memories from the Summer of 1967, but in every mental image I retain of Neal, Bobby's pale, expressionless face hovers as well.

Their proximity owed partly to Weir's diet. Each meal required hours of methodical effort. First, a variety of semi-edibles had to be reduced over low heat to a brown, gelatinous consistency. Then, each bite of this preparation had to be chewed no less than forty times. I believe there was some ceremonial reason for this, though maybe he just needed time to get used to the taste before swallowing.

This all took place in the kitchen where, as I say, Cassady was also usually taking place. So there would be Neal, a fountain of language, issuing forth clouds of agitated, migratory words. And across the table, Bobby, his jaw working no less vigorously, producing instead a profound, unalterable silence. Neal talked. Bobby chewed. And listened.

So would pass the day. I remember a couple of nights when they set up another joint routine in the music room upstairs. The front room of the second floor had once been a library and was now the location of a stereo and a huge collection of communally abused records.

It was also, at this time, Bobby's home. He had set up camp on a pestilential brown couch in the middle of the room, at the end of which he kept a paper bag containing most of his worldly possessions.

Everyone had gone to bed or passed out or fled into the night. In the absence of other ears to perplex and dazzle, Neal went to the music room, covered his own with headphones, put on some bebop, and became it, dancing and doodley-ooooping a capella to a track I couldn't hear. While so engaged, he juggled the thirty-six-ounce machinist's hammer that had become his trademark. The articulated jerky of his upper body ran monsoons of sweat, and the hammer became a lethal blur floating in the air before him.

While the God's Amphetamine Cowboy spun, juggled, and yelped joyous "doo-WOPs," Weir lay on his couch in the foreground, perfectly still, open eyes staring at the ceiling. There was something about the fixity of Bobby's gaze that seemed to indicate a fury of cognitive processing to match Neal's performance. It was as though Bobby were imagining him and going rigid with the effort involved in projecting such a tangible and kinetic image.

I also have a vague recollection of driving someplace in San Francisco with Neal and an amazingly lascivious redhead, but the combination of drugs and the terror at his driving style has fuzzed this memory into a dreamish haze. I remember that the car was a large convertible, possibly a Cadillac, made in America at a time we still made cars of genuine steel, but that its bulk didn't seem like armor enough against a world coming at me so fast and close.

Nevertheless, I recall taking comfort in the notion that to have lived so long this way Cassady was probably invulnerable and that, if that were so, I was also within the aura of his mysterious protection.

Turned out I was wrong about that. About five months later, four days short of his forty-second birthday, he was found dead next to a railroad track outside San Miguel de'Allende, Mexico. He wandered out there in an altered state and died of exposure in the high desert night. Exposure seemed right. He had lived an exposed life. By then, it was beginning to feel like we all had.

In necessary dualities, there are only protagonists. The other protagonist of this song is Cassidy Law, who is now, in the summer of 1990, a beautiful and self-possessed young woman of twenty.

When I first met her, she was less than a month old. She had just entered the world on the Rucka Rucka Ranch, a dust pit of a one-horse ranch in the Nicasio Valley of West Marin, which Bobby inhabited along with a variable cast of real characters.

These included Cassidy's mother, Eileen, a good woman who was then and is still the patron saint of the Deadheads, the wolflike Rex Jackson, a Pendleton cowboy turned Grateful Dead roadie in whose memory the Grateful Dead's Rex Foundation is named, Frankie Weir, Bobby's ol' lady and the subject of the song "Sugar Magnolia," Sonny Heard, a Pendleton bad ol' boy who was also a GD roadie, and several others I can't recall.

There was also a hammer-headed Appaloosa stud, a vile goat, and miscellaneous barnyard fowl that included a peacock so psychotic and aggressive that they had to keep a two-by-four next to the front door to ward off his attacks on folks leaving the house. In a rural sort of way, it was a pretty tough neighborhood. The herd of horses across the road actually became rabid and had to be destroyed.

It was an appropriate place to enter the seventies, a time of bleak exile for most former flower children. The Grateful Dead had been part of a general Diaspora from the Haight as soon as the Summer of Love festered into the Winter of Our Bad Craziness. They had been strewn like jetsam across the further reaches of Marin County and were now digging in to see what would happen next.

The prognosis wasn't so great. Nineteen sixty-eight had given us, in addition to Cassady's death, the Chicago Riots and the election of Richard Nixon. Nineteen sixty-nine had been, as Ken Kesey called it, "the year of the downer," which described not only a new cultural preference for stupid pills but also the sort of year that could mete out Manson, Chappaquiddick, and Altamont in less than six weeks.

I was at loose ends myself. I'd written a novel, on the

strength of whose first half Farrar, Straus, and Giroux had given me a healthy advance with which I was to write the second half. Instead, I took the money and went to India, returning seven months later a completely different guy. I spent the first eight months of 1970 living in New York City and wrestling the damned thing to an ill-fitting conclusion before tossing the results over a transom at Farrar, Straus, buying a new motorcycle to replace the one I'd just run into a stationary car at 85 mph, and heading to California.

It was a journey straight out of *Easy Rider*. I had a no-necked barbarian in a Dodge Super Bee try to run me off the road in New Jersey (for about twenty high-speed miles) and was served, in my own Wyoming, a raw, skinned-out lamb's head with eyes still in it. I can still hear the dark laughter that chased me out of that restaurant.

Thus, by the time I got to the Rucka Rucka, I was in the right raw mood for the place. I remember two bright things glistening against this dreary backdrop. One was Eileen holding her beautiful baby girl, a catch colt (as we used to call foals born out of pedigree) of Rex Jackson's.

And there were the chords that Bobby had strung together the night she was born, music which he eventually joined with these words to make the song "Cassidy." He played them for me. Crouched on the bare boards of the kitchen floor in the late afternoon sun, he whanged out chords that rang like the bells of hell.

And rang in my head for the next two years, during which time I quit New York and, to my great surprise, became a rancher in Wyoming, thus beginning my own rural exile.

In 1972, Bobby decided he wanted to make the solo album that became *Ace*. When he entered the studio in early February, he brought an odd lot of material, most of it germinative. We had spent some of January in my isolated Wyoming cabin working on songs, but I don't believe we'd actually finished anything. I'd come up with some lyrics (for "Looks Like Rain" and most of "Black-Throated Wind"). He worked out the full musical structure for "Cassidy," but I still hadn't written any words for it.

Most of our time was passed drinking Wild Turkey, speculating grandly, and fighting both a series of magnificent blizzards and the house ghost (or whatever it was) that took particular delight in deviling both Weir and his malamute dog.

(I went in one morning to wake Bobby and was astonished when he reared out of bed wearing what appeared to be blackface. He looked ready to burst into "Swanee River." Turned out the ghost had been at him. Weir had placed a 3 A.M. call to the Shoshone shaman Rolling Thunder, who'd advised him that a quick and dirty ghost repellant was charcoal on the face. So he'd burned an entire box of Ohio Blue Tips and applied the results.)

I was still wrestling with the angel of "Cassidy" when Bobby went back to California to start recording basic tracks. I knew some of what it was about . . . the connection with Cassidy Law's birth was too direct to ignore . . . but the rest of it evaded me. I told him that I'd join him in the studio and write it there.

Then my father began to die. He went into the hospital in Salt Lake City and I stayed on the ranch, feeding cows and keeping the feed trails open with an ancient Allis-Chalmers bulldozer. The snow was three and a half feet deep on the level and blown into concrete castles around the haystacks.

Bobby was anxious for me to join him in California, but between the hardest winter in ten years and my father's diminishing future, I couldn't see how I was going to do it. I told him I'd try to complete the unfinished songs, "Cassidy" among them, at a distance.

On the eighteenth of February, I was told that my father's demise was imminent and that I would have to get to Salt Lake. Before I could get away, however, I would have to plow snow from enough stack yards to feed the herd for however long I might be gone. I fired up the bulldozer in a dawn so cold it seemed the air might break. I spent a long day in a cloud of whirling ice crystals, hypnotized by the steady 2,600 rpm howl of its engine, and, sometime in the afternoon, the repeating chords of "Cassidy."

I thought a lot about my father and what we were and had been to one another. I thought about the delicately balanced dance of necessary dualities. And for some reason, I started thinking about Neal, four years dead and still charging around America on the hot wheels of legend.

Somewhere in there, the words to "Cassidy" arrived, complete and intact. I just found myself singing the song as though I'd known it for years.

I clanked back to my cabin in the gathering dusk. Alan Trist, an old friend of Bob Hunter's and a new friend of mine, was visiting. He'd been waiting for me there all day. Anxious to depart, I sent him out to nail wind-chinking on the horse barn while I typed up these words and packed. By nightfall, another great storm had arrived. We set out in it for Salt Lake, hoping to arrive there in time to close, one last time, the dark years between me and my father.

Grateful Dead songs are alive. Like other living things, they grow and metamorphose over time. Their music changes a little every time they're played. The words, avidly interpreted and reinterpreted by generations of Deadheads, become accretions of meaning and cultural flavor rather than static assertions of intent. By now, the Deadheads have written this song to a greater extent than I ever did.

The context changes and, thus, everything in it. What "Cassidy" meant to an audience, many of whom had actually known Neal personally, is quite different from what it means to an audience that has largely never heard of the guy.

Some things don't change. People die. Others get born to take their place. Storms cover the land with trouble. And then, always, the sun breaks through again. 62

2 Blow the horn and tap the tambourine
Compare Psalm 81, with its lines about sounding the tambourine (aka timbour) and blowing the trumpet.

3 catch colt
According to *The Dictionary of American Regional English*:

catch colt n . . . chiefly West, Inland Nth See Maps
1 The offspring of a mare bred accidentally.
1940–41 Cassidy [!] *WI Atlas* csWI, *Catch*— Colt that was unintentionally bred. 1958 *AmSp* 33.271, *Ketch-colt*. An offspring obviously not from the herd sire. . . .
2 By ext: a child born out of wedlock.

Notes:
Written in Cora, Wyoming, February 1972.

Studio recording: *Ace* (May 1972).

First performance: March 23, 1974, at the Cow Palace in Daly City, California. A steady number in the repertoire thereafter.

Jackson: Can you talk about how your songs evolve with you onstage?

Weir: Well, after a few years of seasoning, a song will generally get better, and easier to deliver. Oftentimes when I'm writing a song there are lines in there I don't fully understand.

Jackson: What's an example of that?

Weir: Most of "Cassidy." I really couldn't have told you what it meant way back when, and I really don't know that I could tell you now, though I know for myself it's come to mean certain things. It hangs together better for me now, whereas when we first wrote it, it had an integrity I could recognize right away, but I didn't understand parts of it. As we've done it over the years, each of the lines has come to mean more to me. (Jackson: *Goin' Down the Road*) 63

scarlet begonias

1, 2 As I was walkin' 'round Grosvenor Square
not a chill to the winter
but a nip to the air
from the other direction
she was calling my eye
It could be an illusion
but I might as well try
Might as well try

She had rings on her fingers and
3 bells on her shoes
And I knew without asking she was
into the blues
She wore scarlet begonias
tucked into her curls
I knew right away
she was not like other girls—
other girls

In the thick of the evening
when the dealing got rough
she was too pat to open and
4 too cool to bluff
As I picked up my matches and
was closing the door
I had one of those flashes:
I'd been there before—
been there before

5 I ain't often right
but I've never been wrong
It seldom turns out the way
it does in the song

1 As I was walkin'
A standard opening line in the British tradition, used in ballads and nursery rhymes. Along with the reference to Grosvenor Square, this line sets the song squarely in Britain.

One nursery rhyme that the song clearly echoes is "Pippen Hill":

As I was going up Pippen Hill,
Pippen Hill was dirty;
There I met a pretty Miss,
And she dropped me a curtsy.

2 Grosvenor Square
A square in London, built in 1932 and named for Sir Richard Grosvenor. The American embassy is located there.

3 rings on her fingers and / bells on her shoes
This line echoes another nursery rhyme, "Banbury Cross":

Ride a cock-horse to Banbury Cross,
To see an old lady upon a white horse.
Rings on her fingers, and bells on her toes,
She shall have music wherever she goes.

Ray Stevens's 1962 song "Ahab the Arab" also contains similar lines.

"Sure, I've got rings on my fingers and bells on my toes" also comes from the chorus to a popular Irish song "I've Got Rings on My Fingers" composed by R. P. Watson and F. J. Barnes. It was one of the top twenty songs of 1910.

4 too pat to open and too / cool to bluff
In poker, "too pat to open" usually indicates that someone else opens, allowing the player who passed to raise the stakes from the onset. "Too cool to bluff" would seem like the hand is pat, or, all aces or the like, and therefore the player has no need to bluff.

5 ain't often right
The folk song "Number Twelve Train" contains the line "I may be wrong, but I'll be right someday"

6 love
Garcia sang, "the *look* that's in her eye."

7 wind in the willows
"Blueberry Hill," a song by Al Lewis, Larry Stock, and Vincent Rose, first appeared when sung by Gene Autry in the 1941 movie *The Singing Hills.* Glenn Miller made it a hit in the same year. Louis Armstrong recorded it in 1949, and Fats Domino in 1957. The line echoed:

The children's book by Kenneth Grahame (1859–1932), published in 1908, featuring a cast of animal characters. Frances Clarke Sayers, in a 1959 preface to the book, says:

"On the surface, it is an animal story concerned with the small creatures of field and wood and river bank. Aside from their ability to talk, and a brief interlude of mysticism in which the great god of nature makes his presence known, it is a world of reality like that of the fable. . . . It is a prose poem spoken in praise of the commonplace; a pastoral set in an English landscape which

Once in a while
you get shown the light
in the strangest of places
if you look at it right

Well there ain't nothing wrong
with the way she moves
Or scarlet begonias or a
touch of the blues
And there's nothing wrong with
the love that's in her eye   6
I had to learn the hard way
to let her pass by—
let her pass by

The wind in the willows played tea for two   7, 8
The sky was yellow and the sun was blue
Strangers stopping strangers
just to shake their hand
Everybody's playing
in the Heart of Gold Band
Heart of Gold Band

Words by Robert Hunter
Music by Jerry Garcia

sings the grace of English life and custom. But it is something more. The tragedy inherent in all life is here, the threat of 'evil' and the great mysteries are touched upon."

The title of the book comes from the beautiful chapter, dead in the book's center, titled "The Piper at the Gates of Dawn," in which Rat and Mole listen as the wind in the reeds and trees by the riverbank slowly transforms into pipe music:

Breathless and transfixed the Mole stopped rowing as the liquid run of that glad piping broke on him like a wave, caught him up, and possessed him utterly. He saw the tears on his comrade's cheeks, and bowed his head and understood. . . . And the light grew steadily stronger, but no birds sang as they were wont to do at the approach of dawn; and but for the heavenly music all was marvellously still. . . . In midmost of the stream, embraced in the weir's [!] shimmering armspread, a small island lay anchored, fringed close with willow and silver birch and alder.

A yellow sky and a blue sun would not be out of place in Grahame's evocative writing.

8 tea for two

The name of a song published in 1924; music by Vincent Youmans (1898–1946), words by Irving Caesar (1895–1996). From the musical comedy *No, No, Nanette,* which opened in Detroit in April 1924. This is one of the most familiar and catchiest melodies in the world, and has been extensively covered, especially by jazz performers.

Alec Wilder, in his *American Popular Song: The Great Innovators, 1900–1950,* says:

The phenomenal hit of *No, No, Nanette* was, of course, "Tea for Two." Because of the abrupt key shift in the second section from A-flat major to C major, it is very surprising to me that the song became such a success. And not only that, but after the key change and at the end of the C-major section, the song is virtually wrenched back into A-flat by means of a whole note, E-flat, and its supporting chord, E-flat-dominant seventh. Irving Caesar has said that the opening section of the lyric was never intended to be more than a "dummy" one by means of which the lyricist is able to recall later on, while writing the true lyric, how the notes and accents fall. He also says that, in order to use the words he wanted in the second section, the C-major section, he persuaded Youmans to add notes which resulted in its being similar to, but not an exact imitation of, the first section. . . . But for the rhythmic variance in the second section, the entire song is made of dotted quarter and eighth notes. This certainly ran the risk of monotony, yet the record stands: It was one of Youmans's biggest songs and it remains a standard forty-odd years later. [64]

Notes:

Studio recording: *Grateful Dead from the Mars Hotel* (June 27, 1974).

First performance: March 23, 1974, at the Cow Palace in Daly City, California. Two days later, the group began recording *From the Mars Hotel,* on which the song appears. "Scarlet Begonias" remained a steady number in the repertoire thereafter.

On June 1, 2002, when Hunter opened for Phil and Friends, he introduced his wife and said he had written the song for her. And on August 4, he added a verse after the final one, beginning with "As I was walking down Grosvenor Square":

She had two white vermilions in her snow-
    white hair
She must have been Mattie, but she looked
    like my wife
I gazed into the future, could be all right,
    gettin' old with her,
Gettin' old with her, my Scarlet Begonias

money, money

My baby gives me them finance blues
tax me to the limit of my revenues
Here she comes finger poppin', clickety-click
She say "Furs or diamonds, you can take your
    pick"

Chorus:

She wants money (what she wants) (4x)
Money, money, money, money, money (2x)

She say "Money, honey," I'd rob a bank
I just load my gun and mosey down to the bank
knockin' off my neighborhood savings and loan
1   to keep my sweet chiquita in eau de cologne

(Chorus)

Mama don't send me down to rob that bank
   again
I got a notion you're leadin' me to sin
Won't you relax, won't you lay way back
don't you bug your honey 'bout no Cadillac
It's only bucks, you don't need no jack
so won't you please relax, and lay 'way back

My baby's lovin' gives me such a thrill
give me inspiration makin' counterfeit bills
Now some folks say the best things in life are
   free
I sure don't get no lovin' livin' honestly

(Chorus)

Lord made a lady out of Adam's rib
next thing you know you got women's lib
Lovely to look upon, heaven to touch
it's a real shame they got to cost so much

(Chorus)

Words by John Barlow with Bob Weir
Music by Bob Weir

1 eau de cologne
See note under "Rosemary."

Notes:

Written in Cora, Wyoming, and Mill Valley, California, February 1974. Barlow's title for the song is "Finance Blues."

Studio recording: *Grateful Dead from the Mars Hotel* (June 27, 1974).

First performance: May 17, 1974, at the Pacific National Exhibition Coliseum in Vancouver, British Columbia. It was only played in concert three times, in three consecutive concerts, then dropped from the repertoire.

pride of cucamonga

Out on the edge of the empty highway
Howling at the blood on the moon
A diesel Mack come rolling down my way
Can't hit that border too soon

1 Running hard out of Muskrat Flats
It was sixty days or double life
Hail at my back like a shotgun blast
High wind chimes in the night

2 Oh, oh, pride of Cucamonga
3 Oh, oh, bitter olives in the sun
Oh, oh, I had me some loving
And I done some time

Since I came down from Oregon
There's a lesson or two I've learned
By standing in the road alone
Standing watching the fires burn

The northern sky it stinks with greed
You can smell it heavy for miles around
4 Good old boys in the Graystone Hotel
Sitting doing that git-on-down

Oh, oh, pride of Cucamonga
5 Oh, oh, silver apples in the sun
Oh, oh, I had me some loving
And I done some time

I see your silver shining town
But I know I can't go there
Your streets run deep with poisoned wine
Your doorways crawl with fear

1 Muskrat Flats
This doesn't seem to be an actual geographical location. There is a Muskrat Creek in Wyoming, and a Muskrat Falls in Newfoundland, but from the context of the song, this should be a place in Oregon or California. The Oregon place-name of Idanha, in Marion County, on the North Santiam River southeast of Salem, and about four miles upstream from Detroit, Oregon, may have originally been named Muskrat Camp.

The "Flats" designation is a common one in American slang, according to *The Dictionary of American Regional English,* which says that it is used "often in combinations; used as a jocular or derogatory nickname for a town or district." Some examples given are: Goose Flats, Oakie Flats, Poverty Flats, Pot Liquor Flats, Tar Hill Flats, Penrose Flats. A strong case has been made for the possibility that Muskrat Flats refers to Klamath Falls, Oregon, from clues within the song, and from Petersen's own history.

2 pride of Cucamonga
Cucamonga is a city in San Bernardino County, in the foothills of the San Gabriel Mountains. Population ca. 110,000; elevation

1,110 feet. The word *cucamonga* is from the Shoshone and means "sandy place." The city's corporate name is Rancho Cucamonga.

It was mentioned in the Jan and Dean song "The Anaheim Azuza and Cucamonga Sewing Circle, Book Review and Timing Association." There is a mention of this place in another song as well: Louis Jordan's "How Long Must I Wait for You" ("Track 99 for CoupeCaMonga").

Anne Lamott's novel *Rosie* (North Point Press, 1983) repeatedly refers to one of its characters as the "Pride of Cucamonga," in a joking way, but in explicit reference to "an old Grateful Dead song."

Unconfirmed but convincing correspondence over the years has held up Pride of Cucamonga as a brand of cheap jug wine sold in the 1970s and a fruit label from the 1930s.

3 bitter olives
Also the title of a poem by Petersen, in the collection *Alleys of the Heart:*

> those long fires of
> autumn
> pigpen & i saw along
> highway 99
> *bitter olives*
> *in the stare & blister of*
> *sun.* 65

4 Graystone Hotel
Graystone is the name applied by inmates to almost every jail building and is often formalized into the actual name of the jail, as was the infamous maximum-security Graystone at the Santa Rita Jail in Alameda County, California. Robert Petersen spent some time, indeed, in such hotels.

So I think I'll drift for old where it's at
Where the weed grows green and fine
And wrap myself around a bush
Of that bright whoa, oh, Oaxaca vine   6

Yes it's me, I'm the pride of Cucamonga
I can see golden forests in the sun
Oh, oh, I had me some loving
And I done some time
And I done some time
And I done some time

Words by Robert Petersen
Music by Phil Lesh

Graystone College *n. Und.* a prison. Also
Graystone Hotel, Gray-Rock Hotel. *Joc.* Cf. GRAY-
BAR HOTEL.
1933 Ersine *Pris. Slang* 41: *Graystone College,* any
prison. 1962 Crump *Killer* 198: I nodded to the
County Jail: "There's the Graystone Hotel," I said. .
. . *(Random House Historical Dictionary of American
Slang)*

5 silver apples in the sun

Compare "Silver Apples of the Moon," one of
Hunter's whimsical titles for the instrumental out-
takes captured on *Infrared Roses* (1991).
Morton Subotnick's 1967 work for synthesizer *Silver
Apples of the Moon,* commissioned by Nonesuch
Records, became a best-selling album in the classical-
music category. Subotnick's piece, in turn, was
named for a line from William Butler Yeats's "The
Song of Wandering Aengus":

> and walk among long dappled grass,
> and pluck till time and times are done
> the silver apples of the moon,
> the golden apples of the sun.

6 Oaxaca vine

A likely reference to marijuana grown in the southern Mexican
state of Oaxaca.

Notes:

Studio recording: *Grateful Dead from the Mars Hotel* (June
27, 1974)

Never performed live by the Grateful Dead. First performance by The Dead: June 15, 2004, at Red Rocks
Amphitheater in Morrison, Colorado.

unbroken chain

See note under "Operator."

2 unbroken chain
The concept of an "unbroken chain" usually applies to the theory of transmission of authority down across the generations, often used in the sense of *religious* authority, which fits in well with the song. Religious scholars speak of the "unbroken chain of Moses, Jesus, Paul, Augustine, etc. . . ." An essay on the concept of authority in *Dictionary of the History of Ideas: Studies of Selected Pivotal Ideas* states, "The idea of church authority . . . juxtaposed ideas of authorized power, . . . of *unbroken binding tradition.* . . ." [Italics added]

Petersen contrasts the unbroken chain of authority, of the preacher and his hounds, and of the hypocrisy of religion epitomized by "They say love your brother but you will catch it when you try," with the unbroken chain of natural existence, of individuals in the world whose conscience is the true authority: "Unbroken chain of you and me."

A personal note: One day while in college, I hopped on my bicycle, singing this very tune. As I got to the words *unbroken chain,* I stepped down on my pedals, and my bike chain broke. Really!

3 windowpane
Resonance with "Box of Rain": "Look out of any window. . . ."

Also an LSD-delivery method, "windowpane," in which a gelatin chip was saturated with liquid LSD.

4 searching for the sound
Used by Phil Lesh as the title for his autobiogra-

Blue light rain, whoa, unbroken chain   1, 2
Looking for familiar faces in an empty
    window pane   3
Listening for the secret, searching for the sound   4
But I could only hear the preacher and the
    baying of his hounds

Willow sky, whoa, I walk and wonder why
They say love your brother but you will catch
    it when you try
Roll you down the line boy, drop you for a loss   5
Ride out on a cold railroad and nail you to a cross

November and more as I wait for the score
They're telling me forgiveness is the key to   6
    every door
A slow winter day, a night like forever
Sink like a stone, float like a feather

Lilac rain, unbroken chain
Song of the Saw-Whet owl   7
Out on the mountain it'll drive you insane
Listening to the winds howl

Unbroken chain of sorrow and pearls
Unbroken chain of sky and sea
Unbroken chain of the western wind
Unbroken chain of you and me

Words by Robert M. Petersen
Music by Phil Lesh

phy, subtitled *My Life with the Grateful Dead.* (Little, Brown, 2005).

5 drop you for a loss

An American football idiom, in which the carrier of the ball is sacked behind the line of scrimmage, resulting in a net loss of yards.

6 forgiveness is the key

The "Key of Forgiveness" (six feet long) was wielded by "Queen of the Mardi Gras" Goldie Carolyn Rush, longtime member of the Grateful Dead extended family, on the Phil Zone float, Mardi Gras, February 12, 2005. Goldie died at age fifty-eight on March 28, 2005.

7 Song of the Saw-Whet owl

Saw-Whet Owl: *Aegolius acadicusAegolius arcadicus.* (Length: seven inches, Wingspan: seventeen inches") Commoner than generally believed, but nocturnal and seldom seen unless found roosting in dense young ever-greens or in thickets. . . . Common call is a long series of short whistles. (Robbins)

Its range covers the entire United States, with the exception of the far Southeast.

From a monograph on the saw-whet, on the topic of its song:

Vocal array. At least nine different vocalizations reported. . . . There is little consensus in the literature as to which is the "saw-whet" call after which the species is named.
(1) Advertising call, a monotonous series of whistled notes on a constant pitch of about 1,100 Hz. Given almost entirely by males, but females do produce a ver-

sion of it during courtship; female version softer and less consistent in pitch and amplitude than that of the male. Male's advertising song is audible to the human ear up to 300 meters away through forest and one kilometer over water.
(2) A short, rapid, and soft series of whistled notes, similar to the response version of the advertising song described above, given by the male when approaching the nest with food.
(3) A nasal whine or wail produced at about the same pitch as the advertising song, but lasting for two or three seconds; pitch changes throughout as harmonics are added with increasing volume. This is perhaps the "gasping and decidedly uncanny *ah-h-h*" mentioned by Brewster in Bent (1938).
(4) A short series (usually three) of loud, sharp, squeaking calls (e.g., *ksew-ksew-ksew*) given by both sexes, often mentioned as the "saw-whet" call.
(5) A high-pitched *tsst* call apparently given only by females, usually in response to the male's advertising song or the shorter version of it given before visiting the nest.
(6) Nestlings give chirruping begging calls.
(7) A short, insectlike buzz reported during a threat display.
(8) Twittering call similar to that of the American woodcock. . . .
(9) Captured birds sometimes give a single, short, relatively guttural "chuck" call immediately upon release. (Cannings) 96

Cannings goes on to talk about the circumstances surrounding the song of the saw-whet owl:

Song usually given from within a half hour of sunset to just before sunrise. . . . Advertising song usually given from high but concealed perches, e.g., from within the crown of a tree.

And, in an email correspondance, he adds: "Also, after reading the lyrics, I thought I'd mention that on several occasions I've had people call me to complain about a saw-whet owl calling in their backyard. The incessant tooting whistles were driving them crazy! Just like the song says . . . These birds start tooting as soon as it's dark and often keep going until dawn, two notes every second."

More on the song of the saw-whet owl:

As with many owls, especially the smaller species, the saw-whet owl is capable of producing remarkably ven-triloquistic effects. The authors have actually watched one of these interesting little owls calling from a branch about twenty feet in front of us and yet both of us were utterly convinced for a time that another owl was calling, first from behind us, then off to the left, and finally from far ahead of us past the owl we were watching. It was only through associating the sounds we were hearing with the movements of the bird's beak as it sang that we were able to convince ourselves that the bird we were watching was the one who was doing all the singing.

One of the more pleasant calls for which the saw-whet owl is noted is a very melodious, tinkling sound that just cannot be reproduced in print but which has the remarkable quality of *sounding almost exactly like a tricklet of water falling into a quiet little pool.* [Italics added] (Eckert) 66

Which means that the funny sound on the album may be in imitation of the owl itself!

Notes:

Studio recording: *Grateful Dead from the Mars Hotel* (June 27, 1974).

First live performance: March 19, 1995, at the Spectrum in Philadelphia.

Blues for Allah

Arabian wind
1 The Needle's Eye is thin
  The Ships of State sail on mirage
  and drown in sand
  out in No-man's Land
2 where Allah does command

  What good is spilling
  blood? It will not
  grow a thing

  "Taste eternity"
  the sword sings Blues for Allah

1 The Needle's Eye is thin
Three of the four writers of the New Testament gospels include nearly identical quotations of Jesus saying:

> And I say unto you, It is easier for a camel to go through the eye of a needle than for a rich man to enter into the kingdom of God."
> Matthew 19:24

The other passages are found in Mark 10:25 and Luke 18:25. This is usually pretty good evidence that the quotation may be truly ascribed to Jesus. The other piece of evidence is that this is one of those "unpopular" sayings, one of the difficult things that the teacher said. So we can be pretty certain that this is an accurate quote. Some biblical scholars have attempted to soften the message by ascribing its meaning to a narrow gate in Jerusalem through which a camel could actually pass, but most scholars seem united in the view that Jesus meant to say that it is impossible for a rich man to enter the "kingdom of God." Whatever that might be meant to be.

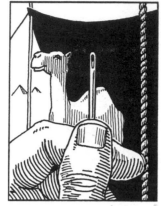

Hunter's use of this image for his second line reinforces the first line's geographical placement of the song in the landscape of the Holy Land, and adds the element of admonition.

Some maintain that the original Greek in the passage, *camelas* (rope), was mistakenly rendered as *camelos* (camel), thus altering the meaning of the passage.

2 Allah
This is the second use of the word *Allah* in a lyric by Hunter. For the first, and for a footnote on the word, see "What's Become of the Baby?"

3 In'sh'Allah
According to the *Oxford English Dictionary*: "Representing Arab. *in sa' Allah* if Allah wills (it), a very frequent pious ejaculation among Muslims."

4 The flower of Islam / the fruit of Abraham
A reference to the contestants in the Middle East conflict. Reminiscent of the nursery rhyme couplet:

In'sh'Allah   3

They lie where they fall
There's nothing more to say
The desert stars are bright tonight,
let's meet as friends
The flower of Islam
The fruit of Abraham   4

The thousand stories have
come 'round to one again   5
Arabian Night
our gods pursue their fight
What fatal flowers of
darkness spring from
seeds of light

Bird of Paradise—Fly   6
In white sky
Blues for Allah
In'sh'Allah

Let's see with our heart
these things our eyes have seen
and know the truth must still lie
somewhere in between

Under eternity
Under eternity
Under eternity
Blue
Bird of Paradise
Fly

In white sky
Under eternity
Blues
for Allah
In'sh'Allah

Words by Robert Hunter
Music by Jerry Garcia

Flour of England, fruit of Spain,
Met together in a shower of rain

5 The thousand stories have / come
'round to one again
A reference to *The Arabian Nights.* See the note
under "What's Become of the Baby?" for more
information.

6 Bird of
Paradise
The bird of paradise
is of the family
Paradisaeidae, with
forty-three species
occurring in the
Moluccas, New
Guinea, and
Australia. One of
their environments
of choice is the man-
grove (see "Doin'
That Rag") swamp. They are well known for their
extravagant plumage, especially those of the
male, which often has huge, iridescent feather
structures, though this varies widely from species
to species.

Notes:
Studio recording: *Blues for Allah* (September 1,
1975).

First performance: March 23, 1975 at the SNACK
benefit, Kezar Stadium, Golden Gate Park, San
Francisco. Performed live only five times, all in
1975.

Hunter's note in *A Box of Rain* says, "This lyric is a
requiem for King Faisal of Saudi Arabia, a progressive and democratically inclined ruler [and
incidentally, a fan of the Grateful Dead] whose
assassination in 1975 shocked us personally."

Garcia and Hunter, talking about the song in
Goin' Down the Road:

Hunter: But "Blues for Allah," specifically, I
remember them saying to me, "Dammit, we
need the line right now!"

Garcia: Oh, that song was a bitch to do! When
we got toward the end of the album, we had
some time restrictions and we started working
pretty fast. But up until then we'd been pretty
leisurely about it. That song was another total-
ly experimental thing I tried to do. In terms of
the melody and the phrasing and all, it was
not of this world. It's not in any key and it's
not in any time. And the line lengths are all
different.

Hunter: I remember trying to get a scan for
that, the first line I came up with [he sings it
to the song melody] was "Here comes that
awful funky bride of Frankenstein." [*Laughs*]
Sometimes you need nonsense just to get it
flowing.

Garcia: [*Laughs*] We should've used that!
(Jackson) 67

The song title "Blues for Allah" may be a nod to
the title of the Charlie Parker tune "Blues for
Alice."

crazy fingers

1 crazy fingers
"Crazy Fingers" was the nickname of jazz pianist Claude Hopkins (born in Alexandria, Virginia, August 29, 1903; died New York, February 19, 1984). Played with Sidney Bechet, was music director for Josephine Baker. From 1968 on was a member of the Jazz Giants. He made a recording titled *Crazy Fingers,* in 1972. His autobiography is *Crazy Fingers: Claude Hopkins' Life in Jazz,* Smithsonian Institution Press, 1992.

Crazy Otto, of "Ramble On Rose" fame, recorded a piece titled "Crazy Fingers" on his *Crazy Otto Plays Crazy Tunes* (1963).

2 Hang your heart on laughing willow
Compare the old song "There Is a Tavern in the Town," words and music Anonymous, ca. 1883:

> Fare-thee-well, for I must leave thee,
> Do not let the parting grieve thee,
> And remember that the best of friends must part, must part.
> Adieu, adieu, kind friends, adieu, adieu, adieu,
> I can no longer stay with you, stay with you,
> I'll hang my harp on a weeping willow tree,
> And may the world go well with thee.

Another resonance is to be found in Psalm 137: "We hanged our harps upon the willows." This is the psalm from which the song "By the Waters of Babylon" takes its words.

3 Reaching for the gold ring
To "reach for the brass ring" has been absorbed into idiomatic English:

Your rain falls like crazy fingers   1
Peals of fragile thunder keeping time

Recall the days that still are to come
Some sing blue

Hang your heart on laughing willow   2
Stray down to the water
Deep Sea of Love

Beneath the sweet calm face of the sea
Swift undertow

Life may be sweeter for this, I don't know
See how it feels in the end
May Lady Lullaby sing plainly for you
Soft, strong, sweet and true

Cloud hands reaching from a rainbow
Tapping at the window touch your hair

So swift and bright
Strange figures of light
Float in air

Who can stop what must arrive now?
Something new is waiting to be born

Dark as the night
You're still by my side
Shining side

Gone are the days we stopped to decide
Where we should go
We just ride

Gone are the broken eyes we saw through
    in dreams
Gone—both dream and lie

Life may be sweeter for this, I don't know
Feels like it might be alright
While Lady Lullaby sings plainly for you
Love still rings true

Midnight on a carousel ride
3   Reaching for the gold ring down inside

Never could reach
It just slips away but I try

Words by Robert Hunter
Music by Jerry Garcia

brass ring, *Informal*, 1. wealth, success, or a prestigious position considered as a goal or prize: *Few of those who reach for the brass ring of the presidency achieve it.* 2. the opportunity to try for such a prize. [from the practice of picking a ring from a box while riding a merry-go-round: whoever selected a brass ring received a free ride.] —*Random House Dictionary of the English Language,* second ed.

Notes:

Studio recording: *Blues for Allah* (September 1975).

First live performance: June 17, 1975, at Winterland in San Francisco. The song was in and out of the live repertoire thereafter.

Hunter:

"Crazy Fingers" was, in fact, all written beforehand. It was a page or two of haiku I'd been working on in a notebook. Jerry looked at them and said, "Hey, this might fit together as a song." (Jackson, *Goin' Down the Road*) 68

Paradise waits
on the crest of a wave
her angels in flame
She has no pain
Like a child, she is pure
She is not to blame

Poised for flight
Wings spread bright
Spring from night
into the sun
Don't stop to run
She can fly like a lie
She can't be outdone

Tell me the cost
I can pay
Let me go

Tell me love is not lost
Sell everything
Without love, day to day,
insanity is king

I will pay
day by day
anyway
Lock, bolt, and key   1
Crippled but free
I was blind
all the time
I was learning to see

Help on the way
I know only this
I've got you today
Don't fly away
'cause I love what I love
and I want it that way

I will stay
one more day
Like I say
Honey, it's you
Making it too
Without love in the dream
It'll never come true

Words by Robert Hunter
Music by Jerry Garcia

1 Lock, bolt, and key
Reminiscent of the
expression "lock, stock,
and barrel," which
describes the three
parts of a gun.

Notes:
Studio recording: *Blues
for Allah* (September 1,
1975).

First performance: June
17, 1975 at the Bob Fried Memorial Boogie,
Winterland, San Francisco. It was performed
without its lyrics. It remained in the repertoire
thereafter.

Franklin's Tower

1 In another time's forgotten space
   your eyes looked from your mother's face
   Wildflower seed on the sand and stone
   may the four winds blow you safely home

2 Roll away . . . the dew
   Roll away . . . the dew
   Roll away . . . the dew
   Roll away . . . the dew

3 I'll tell you where the four winds dwell
4 In Franklin's Tower there hangs a bell
   It can ring, turn night to day
   It can ring like fire when you lose your way

1 In another time's forgotten space
Compare Van Morrison's 1968 song "Astral Weeks":

> In another time
> In another place
> In another time
> In another place
> In another face 69

2 Roll away . . . the dew
Compare the folk song "Blow Away the Morning Dew" (Child, #112), with its refrain:

> Sing, blow away the morning dew,
> the dew and the dew

Compare also *A Midsummer Night's Dream* and some lines (117–118) from 4.1: Theseus is describing his hounds, which "are bred out of the Spartan kind," and he states, "Their heads are hung / With ears that sweep away the morning dew."

3 four winds

In Greek mythology, the winds were Boreas or Aquilo, the north wind; Zephyrus or Favonius, the west; Notus or Auster, the south; and Eurus, the east.

The Tower of Winds, in Athens, located on the Agora, is an eight-sided tower constructed ca. 100–35 B.C.E. A frieze depicting the eight winds (yes, eight) runs along the top of the tower, which was used as a giant hydraulic timepiece.

Pursuing that tidbit, I also stumbled across a Tower of the Winds in the Vatican, built by Gregory XIII, and known as the *Torre dei venti.* So the idea of the winds living in a tower seems to be ancient and pervasive.

There is also a biblical reference to the four winds in Zechariah 2:6: "I have spread you abroad as the four winds of heaven."

Fats Domino had a hit with a song titled "Let the Four Winds Blow."

4 Franklin's

A franklin was a medieval English landowner of free but not noble birth.

Roll away . . . the dew . . .

God save the child who rings that bell
It may have one good ring baby, you can't tell
One watch by night, one watch by day
If you get confused listen to the music play

Roll away . . . the dew . . .

Some come to laugh their past away
Some come to make it just one more day
Whichever way your pleasure tends
if you plant ice you're gonna harvest wind   5

Roll away . . . the dew . . .

In Franklin's Tower the four winds sleep
Like four lean hounds the lighthouse keep   6
Wildflower seed in the sand and wind
May the four winds blow you home again

Roll away . . . the dew
Roll away . . . the dew
Roll away . . . the dew
Roll away . . . the dew
You better roll away the dew

Words by Robert Hunter
Music by Jerry Garcia

5 if you plant ice you're gonna harvest wind

Compare the biblical quotation from Hosea 8:7:

> For they have sown the wind, and they shall reap the whirlwind.

Also compare the wonderful concept, invented by Kurt Vonnegut in *Cat's Cradle,* of Ice Nine (after which the Grateful Dead's publishing company was named, whose logo is the I Ching symbol for Gathering Together, Holding Together).

6 four lean hounds

Compare E. E. Cummings's "All in green went my love riding" (1923):

> All in green went my love riding
> on a great horse of gold
> into the silver dawn.
>
> four lean hounds crouched low and smiling
> the merry deer ran before.
>
> Fleeter be they than dappled dreams
> the swift sweet deer
> the red rare deer.
>
> Four red roebuck at a white water
> the cruel bugle sang before.
>
> Horn at hip went my love riding
> riding the echo down
> into the silver dawn.
>
> four lean hounds crouched low and smiling
> the level meadows ran before.
>
> Softer be they than slippered sleep
> the lean lithe deer
> the fleet flown deer.
>
> Four fleet does at a gold valley
> the famished arrows sang before.
>
> Bow at belt went my love riding
> riding the mountain down
> into the silver dawn.
>
> four lean hounds crouched low and smiling
> the sheer peaks ran before.
>
> Paler be they than daunting death
> the sleek slim deer
> the tall tense deer.
>
> Four tall stags at a green mountain
> the lucky hunter sang before.
>
> All in green went my love riding
> on a great horse of gold
> into the silver dawn.
>
> four lean hounds crouched low and smiling
> my heart fell dead before. 70

Notes:

Studio recording: *Blues for Allah* (September 1, 1975).

First performance: June 17, 1975, at Winterland in San Francisco. The tune remained in the repertoire thereafter.

showboat

Well look what's going down the river now
Big steam whistle gonna blow, man, blow
Look what's going down the river now
Let the wheel stop turning, let the anchors go

Showboat, pretty boat, stop a while
Make a little music for the baby to smile
Showboat, slow boat, you and me
gonna sail on down to the shiny sea

They go down the fields to the sandy shore
Lay down the plough, leave the milk in the cow
They go down from the fields to the
   sandy shore
just to look what's going down the river now

Master's in the cabin with his head hung low
The tide's been a-turning but the boat
   won't go

Hit rock bottom left high and dry
down in the delta where the river runs high

There's a church on the hill got a brand-new choir
Got a big bell tower and a burnin' hot fire
The graveyard's empty and the book's been closed
Don't pass the plate, just put down the rose   1

Down in the pasture there's a golden cow
She gives no milk 'cause she don't know how
Grab that heifer by the end of the tail
then get out the buckets and bail, bail, bail

The baby's in the cradle rockin' to and fro
Gonna get out the valley so the shadow don't grow
And if that brand-new choir don't sing
gonna get that baby a bell to ring

I got a feelin' deep down in my soul
the baby's awake and the bell's gonna toll
I got a love deep down in my soul
Move out of the way and let the riverboat roll

Words by Brian Godchaux
Music by Keith and Donna Godchaux

1 rose
See note under "That's It for the Other One."

Notes:
Studio recording: Keith and Donna Godchaux's
Keith and Donna (1975).

Studio rehearsal recording from August 12,
1975, released as a bonus track for the *Blues for
Allah* CD in the box set *Beyond Description*.

Never performed live by the Grateful Dead.

the music never stopped

There's mosquitoes on the river,
fish are rising up like birds
It's been hot for seven weeks now,
too hot to even speak now
Did you hear what I just heard?

Say, it might have been a fiddle,
or it could have been the wind
But there seems to be a beat, now,
I can feel it in my feet, now
Listen, here it comes again!

There's a band out on the highway,
they're high-steppin' into town
It's a rainbow full of sound
1   It's fireworks, calliopes, and clowns

Everybody's dancin'
C'mon, children, c'mon, children,
Come on clap your hands

Sun went down in honey,
and the moon came up in wine
Stars were spinnin' dizzy,
Lord, the band kept us so busy,
We forgot about the time

They're a band beyond description
like Jehovah's favorite choir
People joining hand in hand
while the music plays the band
Lord, they're settin' us on fire

Crazy rooster crowin' midnight,
balls of lightning roll along

1 calliopes
See note under "Doin' That Rag."

2 The music never stopped
The sentence "The music never stopped" appears in a science-fiction novel called *The Stars My Destination* (1956) by Alfred Bester, the story of the apotheosis of Gulliver Foyle, a brutish interstellar merchant seaman who, through a series of growth experiences sparked by a desire for revenge, inadvertently changes the course of human history. The sentence appears in a passage describing the "Four Mile Circus," an absurd traveling circus under the tutelage of "Fourmyle of Ceres" (Gulliver Foyle disguised as a nouveau riche fool).

There was a roar of laughter and cheering and the Four Mile Circus ripped into high gear. The kitchens sizzled and smoked. There was a perpetuity of eating and drinking. *The music never stopped.* [Italics mine] The vaudeville never ceased.

Notes:
Written in Cora, Wyoming, and Mill Valley, California, June 1975.

Studio recording: *Blues for Allah* (September 1, 1975).

First performance: August 13, 1975, at the Great American Music Hall in San Francisco. This is the performance captured on *One from the Vault*. It remained in the repertoire thereafter.

Old men sing about their dreams,
Women laugh and children scream
and the band keeps playin' on

Keep on dancin' through to daylight,
Greet the mornin' air with song
No one's noticed, but the band's all packed
  and gone
Was it ever here at all?

But they kept on dancing

C'mon, children, c'mon, children,
Come on clap your hands

Well, the cool breeze came on Tuesday
And the corn's a bumper crop
The fields are full of dancin',
full of singing and romancin'
The music never stopped   2

Words by John Barlow
Music by Bob Weir

- guitar -

Lazy Lightnin' / Supplication

1 Lazy lightnin'
Sleepy fire in your eyes
Is it desire in disguise?
I keep on tryin' but I—
I can't get through

Lazy lightnin'
I'd like to find the proper potion
To kinda capture your emotion
You're right beside me but I—
I can't get through

You're a loop of lazy lightnin'
Liquid loop of lazy lightnin'
Must admit you're kinda fright'nin'
But you really get me high

So exciting,
When I hear your velvet thunder
Seems so near I start to wonder,
Would you come closer if I—
I asked you to?

So inviting,
2 The way you're messin' with my reason
It's an obsession but it's pleasin'
Tell me a lie and I will swear
I'll swear it's true

You're a loop of lazy lightnin'
Liquid loop of lazy lightnin'
Must admit you're kinda fright'nin'
Liquid loop of lazy lightnin'
Rope of fire 'round my heart

1 lightnin'
A frequent motif in Grateful Dead lyrics. It's interesting that that other thunder and lightning song, "The Wheel," also appeared for the first time in a Grateful Dead show at the June 3, 1976, concert.

Lazy Lightnin' was the title of a 1926 silent Western, featuring Art Acord as Lance Lighton and Fay Wray as Lila Rogers. Directed by William Wyler, who also directed such classics as *Ben Hur* and *Funny Girl.*

2 reason
Always an interesting topic in Grateful Dead songs, from "Dark Star" to "Playing in the Band."

Notes:
Written in Mill Valley, California, October 1975.

Studio recording by Kingfish, with Bob Weir, on *Kingfish* (1976).

First performance: June 3, 1976, at the Paramount Theater in Portland, Oregon. "Lazy Lightnin'" was played fairly often through the early 1980s, but it was dropped from the repertoire in 1984.

Rope of fire ever tight'nin'
Rope of fire 'round my heart
It's either lunacy or lightnin'

Lazy lightnin'
The way you always 'lectrify me
Someday I know you'll satisfy me
And all that lightnin' will be my lightnin' too
My lightnin' too

SUPPLICATION

(Whoo-hoo-hoo) Dizzy ain't the word for the
   way that you're
Makin' me feel now
(Whoo-hoo-hoo) I need some indication if
All of this is real now
(Whoo-hoo-hoo) I've heard it said there could
   be something
Wrong in my head, now
(Whoo-hoo-hoo) Could it be infatuation or am
   I just
Bein' misled, now
Little bolt of inspiration, right beside me now
Sparkin' my imagination, lightnin' now
Causin' instant excitation, 'cause you're
   fright'nin' now
Come to heed my supplication, got to have
   it now
My light'nin' too, My light'nin' too

Words by John Barlow
Music by Bob Weir

might as well

Great North Special, were you on board?
You can't find a ride like that no more
1 Night the chariot swung down low
Ninety-nine children had a chance to go

One long party from front to end
Tune to the whistle going 'round the bend
No great hurry, what do you say?
Might as well travel the elegant way

Chorus:
2 Might as well, might as well (4x)

Ragtime solid for twenty-five miles
then slip over to the Cajun style
Bar car loaded with rhythm and blues
Rock and roll wailing in the old caboose

Long train running from coast to coast
bringing 'long the party where they need it
   the most
Whup on the boxcar, beat on the bell
Nothing else shaking so you might just
   as well

(Chorus)

Never had such a good time in my
   life before
I'd like to have it one time more
One good ride from start to end
I'd like to take that ride again
Again

Run out of track and I caught the plane
Back in the county with the blues again   3
Great North Special been on my mind
Might like to ride it just one more time

(Chorus)

Words by Robert Hunter
Music by Jerry Garcia

1 **chariot swung down low**
A reference to the spiritual "Swing Low, Sweet Chariot."

2 **Might as well**
Sometimes heard and/or transcribed as "mighty swell."

3 **county**
Possibly a reference to the band's home county, Marin, in California, just across the Golden Gate Bridge from San Francisco.

Notes:
Studio recording: *Reflections* (January 1976).

First performance: June 3, 1976, at the Paramount Theater in Portland, Oregon.

The song memorializes the Trans-Continental Pop Festival, or Festival Express tour, which saw the Dead, Janis Joplin, the Band, New Riders of the Purple Sage, Delaney and Bonney, and others joining forces to "bring on the party where they need it the most," in May 1970. Hunter wrote: "Everyone agreed we had just about the best time of our collective lives in that week of non-stop music and partying. Nearing her last days, Janis, for one, wished aloud that the ride would never have to stop." A documentary film from the tour, titled *Festival Express*, was released in 2004.

samson and delilah

1 Samson and Delilah
The biblical story of Samson is found in Judges, 14–16.
Delilah appears in Judges 16.

Notes:
Studio recording: *Terrapin Station* (July 27, 1977).

First performance: June 3, 1976, at the
Paramount Theater in Portland, Oregon. It
remained in the repertoire thereafter.

This was a popular Negro spiritual, usually
sung a capella until it was put on record in the
late twenties by Texas bluesman Blind Willie
Johnson. His version (titled "If I Had My Way
I'd Tear the Building Down") appears on most
CD compilations of Johnson's 78s. That version

Chorus:

If I had my way
If I had my way
If I had my way
I would tear this whole building down

Delilah was a woman, she was fine and fair
She had good looks—God knows—and coal
   black hair
Delilah she gained old Samson's mind
When first he saw this woman, she looked so fine

Delilah she climbed up on Samson's knee

Said tell me where your strength lies, if you please
Then she spoke so kind, she talked so fair
That Samson said, Delilah you cut off my hair
You can shave my head, cleanse my hand
My strength comes as natural as any other man

(*Chorus*)

You read about Samson, all from his birth
He was the strongest man ever had lived on earth
One day while Samson was walking along
Looked down on the ground he saw an old jawbone
Then he stretched out his arm and his chains broke
   like threads
And when he got to move, ten thousand were dead

(*Chorus*)

Now Samson and the lion, they got in attack
And Samson he walked up on the lion's back
You read about this lion, he killed a man with
   his paw
Samson got hands up 'round the lion's jaw
He ripped that beast, killed it dead
And the bees made honey in the lion's head

(*Chorus*)

    Words and music: traditional
    Arranged by Bob Weir

inspired Reverend Gary Davis to work out his own arrangements, and it is his recording of the tune that prompted people like Peter, Paul and Mary, Dave Van Ronk, and, later, the Dead to record it.

A sample verse from Negro spiritual transcription shows that it has changed little over the years: "They bound him with ropes and while walking along / He looked on the ground, he saw an old jawbone / He moved his arms, the ropes popped like threads/ When he got through killin', three thousand was dead." (Jackson: *Goin' Down the Road*). [94]

The wheeL

1 **The wheel**
Compare Hunter's "Lay of the Ring" from the "Eagle Mall Suite":

> Age by age the ancient wheel creaks and turns around

A potent symbol throughout human history (well, at least since the invention of the wheel).
In Buddhism, known as the *bhava-cakra,* from the Sanskrit "wheel [*cakra*] of becoming [*bhava*]."

Also called WHEEL OF LIFE . . . a representation of the endless cycle of rebirths governed by the law of dependent origination . . . , shown as a wheel clutched by a monster, symbolizing impermanence.
In the center of the wheel are shown the three basic evils, symbolized by a red dove (passion), a green snake (anger), and a black pig (ignorance). The intermediate space between the center and the rim is divided by spokes into five (later, six) sections, depicting the possible states into which a man can be reborn: the realm of gods, titans (if six states are shown), men, animals, ghosts, and demons. Around the rim of the wheel the twelve *nidanas,* or interrelated phases in the cycle of existence, are shown in an allegorical or symbolical manner—ignorance, karmic formations, rebirth consciousness, mind and body, sense organs, contact, sensation, craving, grasping, becoming, birth, and old age and death. *(Encyclopedia Britannica)*

The wheel is turning   1
and you can't slow down
You can't let go
and you can't hold on
You can't go back
and you can't stand still
If the thunder don't get you
then the lightning will   2

Chorus:
Won't you try just a little bit harder?
Couldn't you try just a little bit more?
Won't you try just a little bit harder?
Couldn't you try just a little bit more?

Round, round, robin run around   3
Gotta get back where you belong
Little bit harder, just a little bit more
Little bit farther than you than you've gone
    before

The wheel is turning
and you can't slow down
You can't let go
and you can't hold on
You can't go back
and you can't stand still
If the thunder don't get you
then the lightning will

Small wheel turn by the fire and rod
Big wheel turn by the grace of God   4

Every time that wheel turn round
bound to cover just a little more ground

The wheel is turning
and you can't slow down
You can't let go
and you can't hold on
You can't go back
and you can't stand still
If the thunder don't get you
then the lightning will

(Chorus)

> *Words by Robert Hunter*
> *Music by Jerry Garcia and Bill Kreutzmann*

See note on "wheel of fortune" under "Alice D. Millionaire."
In Roman mythology:

> Fortuna . . . the goddess of fortune or chance. She was identified with the Greek Tyche, and she was often depicted with a rudder, as the pilot of destiny, with wings, or with a wheel. The wheel of fortune was a widely used symbol in medieval art and literature, forming the concept which Lydgate's *Falls of Princes* (1494) and Chaucer's "Monk's Tale" from *The Canterbury Tales* were based. (Benet's) 71

In the Bible, the wheel appears several times, most notably in Ezekiel 1:15–16:

> Now as I beheld the living creatures, behold one wheel upon the earth by the living creatures, with his four faces. The appearance of the wheels and their work was like unto the color of a beryl: and they four had one likeness: and their appearance and their work was as it were a wheel in the middle of a wheel."

2 **If the thunder don't get you / then the lightning will**
Nearly a quote from Merle Travis's song "Sixteen Tons." "If the left one don't get you, then the right one will," speaking of his two fists, one of steel and one of iron.

3 **Round, round robin**
The robin:

> Perhaps the most abundant and conspicuous of all our western birds. . . . While the western robin, as a species, is highly migratory and moves south at the approach of cold weather, large numbers remain to winter in the protected valleys of the northwestern states. It is probable, however, that the winter robins of Washington and Oregon are the summer

birds of farther north, and that our own summer robins spend the winter in the sunshine of Southern California. (Eliot, Willard, *Birds of the Pacific Coast*)

A "round robin" competition, in athletic events, is one in which each team or participant competes against every other team or participant. Also, there is a research design used in biology and psychology called the round robin. Imagine four people, A, B, C, and D, who interact with one another. Each person's behavior in response to another (e.g., smiling) is measured. The data structure looks like this:

```
    A B C D
A   - x x x
B   x - x x
C   x x - x
D   x x x -
```

where x's are one person's response to another and dashes are diagonal elements. This is a very unusual design in sci- ence and indeed has a wheellike quality. Also, this is a structure used in athletic events (round robin tennis tournament).

Note also that rounds are a musical form unto themselves.

4 Small wheel turn by the fire and rod / Big wheel turn by the grace of God

Echoing a line from the African American spiritual "'Zekiel Saw De Wheel" (based upon the biblical passage from Ezekiel, quoted above):

De big wheel run by faith,
Little wheel run by de grace of God

Notes:
Studio recording: *Garcia* (January 1972).

First performance: June 3, 1976, at the Paramount Theater in Portland, Oregon. It occupied a steady spot in the repertoire thereafter.

mission in the rain

I turn and walk away
then I come 'round again
It looks as though tomorrow
I'll do pretty much the same

I must turn down your offer
but I'd like to ask a break
You know I'm ready to give everything
for anything I take

Someone called my name
You know I turned around to see
1   It was midnight in the Mission
and the bells were not for me

Chorus:

Come again
Walking along in the Mission
in the rain
Come again
Walking along in the Mission
in the rain

Ten years ago I walked this street
my dreams were riding tall
Tonight I would be thankful
Lord for any dream at all

Some folks would be happy
just to have one dream come true
but everything you gather
is just more that you can lose

(Chorus)

1 the Mission
The Mission District in San Francisco, so named because it surrounds the Spanish Mission Dolores. Mission Dolores is located on Dolores Street between 16th and 17th Streets: founded in 1776 by Father Junipero Serra. First named in honor of St. Francis of Assisi, common usage soon gave it the name of Mision de los Dolores from a nearby marsh known as Laguna de Nuestra Senora de los Dolores (Lagoon of Our Lady of Sorrows). The first mass was sung five days before the Declaration of Independence was signed at Philadelphia. The adobe building was begun in 1782 and is an unusual example of Spanish mission architecture.

Behind the mission in the high-walled, flower-covered graveyard are buried many of the famous dead of San Francisco's early days. . . . The graves of Casey and Cora, hanged by the vigilantes in 1856, are a reminder of lawless days. Many of the graves are unmarked. *(WPA Guide to California)*

Garcia, raised in the Excelsior District of San Francisco, was familiar with the area, which is largely Hispanic. He stated that the song was "autobiographical, though I didn't write it." 72

And Hunter, in an interview in *Relix:*

Well yeah. I used to live over in the Mission when I was just starting to write for the Dead full time. I wasn't living at 710, I was living over on 17th and Mission, and that was very much a portrait of that time: looking backward at ten years.

Notes:

Studio recording: *Reflections* (January 1976).

First performance: June 4, 1976, at the Paramont Theater in Portland, Oregon.

Performed for a very brief period in 1976 (five performances) by the Dead, then reserved for the Jerry Garcia Band

All the things I planned to do
I only did halfway
Tomorrow will be Sunday
born of rainy Saturday

There's some satisfaction
in the San Francisco rain
No matter what comes down
the Mission always looks the same

(Chorus)

Words by Robert Hunter
Music by Jerry Garcia

terrapin station (suite)

1 LADY WITH A FAN

2 Let my inspiration flow
in token rhyme suggesting rhythm
that will not forsake me
till my tale is told and done

3 While the firelight's aglow
strange shadows from the flames will grow
till things we've never seen
will seem familiar

Shadows of a sailor forming
winds both foul and fair all swarm

1 Lady with a Fan
The plot of this section of the piece is very similar to that of the ballad "Lady of Carlisle," known also as Sharp, #66, "The Bold Lieutenant," and as "The Lion's Den," or "The Lady's Fan." (Hunter recorded a version of this on his 1980 album, *Jack o' Roses.*)

Down in Carlisle there lived a lady,
Being most beautiful and gay;
She was determined to live a lady,
No man on earth could her betray.

Unless it were a man of honor,
A man of honor and high degree;
And then approached two loving soldiers,
This fair lady for to see.

One being a brave lieutenant,
A brave lieutenant and a man of war;
The other being a brave sea captain,
Captain of the ship that come from far.

Then up spoke this fair young lady,
Saying, "I can't be but one man's bride
But if you'll come back tomorrow morning,
On this case we will decide."

She ordered her a span of horses,
A span of horses at her command;
And down the road these three did travel
Till they come to the lion's den.

There she stopped and there she halted
These two soldiers stood gazing around,
And for the space of half an hour,
This young lady lies speechless on the ground.

And when she did recover,
Threw her fan down in the lion's den
Saying, "Which of you to gain a lady
Will return her fan again?"

Then up spoke the brave lieutenant,
Raised his voice both loud and clear,
Saying, "You know I am a dear lover of
    women,
But I will not give my life for love."

Then up spoke this brave sea captain,
He raised his voice both loud and high,
Saying," You know I am a dear lover of
    women,
I will return her fan or die. "

Down in the lion's den he boldly entered,
The lions being both wild and fierce;
He marched around and in among them,
Safely returned her fan again.

And when she saw her true lover coming
Seeing no harm had been done to him,
She threw herself against his bosom
Saying, "Here is the prize that you have won!"

down in Carlisle he loved a lady
many years ago

Here beside him stands a man
a soldier from the looks of him
who came through many fights
but lost at love

While the storyteller speaks
a door within the fire creaks
suddenly flies open
and a girl is standing there

Eyes alight with glowing hair
all that fancy paints as fair
she takes her fan and throws it
in the lion's den

"Which of you to gain me, tell
will risk uncertain pains of hell?
I will not forgive you
if you will not take the chance"

The sailor gave at least a try
the soldier being much too wise
strategy was his strength
and not disaster

The sailor coming out again
the lady fairly leapt at him
that's how it stands today
you decide if he was wise

The storyteller makes no choice
soon you will not hear his voice

4

his job is to shed light
and not to master

Since the end is never told
we pay the teller off in gold
in hopes he will come back
but he cannot be bought or sold

TERRAPIN STATION

Inspiration move me brightly
light the song with sense and color,
5   hold away despair
More than this I will not ask
faced with mysteries dark and vast
statements just seem vain at last
some rise, some fall, some climb
6   to get to Terrapin

7   Counting stars by candlelight
all are dim but one is bright:
8   the spiral light of Venus
rising first and shining best,
9   From the northwest corner
of a brand-new crescent moon
10   crickets and cicadas sing
a rare and different tune

Terrapin Station
11   in the shadow of the moon
Terrapin Station
and I know we'll be there soon

2 Let my inspiration flow and Inspiration, move me brightly
Hunter invokes the muse with a prayerlike suppli-cation in the manner of the Greek poets: He comments on this in Steve Silberman's interview, "Standing in the Soul":

Hunter: This band is known for dense subcon-sciousness. A lot of it is the Muse.

  I just started work on an essay last night, because I told Anne Waldman that I would go to Naropa, and I was informed that I had to give a ninety-minute lecture. And I went, "Me? Lecture?" I've got no retentive memory at all. I don't remember the names of poets. I don't remember anything but the feel of them. So I decided to write a lecture called "Courting the Muse." That's one thing I do know something about: Here, kitty, kitty, kitty!

Silberman: The Muse is often envisioned as female in lyric tradition, and you have delin-eated her garments more deliberately and elaborately than many poets. There's a very interesting female presence in your work. Can you talk about that?

Hunter: I saw my muses once. It was a very, very high time, many years back. There were three golden presences in the room. It was a visual. I don't say I was straight at the time, but I will say it had a lasting effect on me. I have a feeling that there's something that helps me, gives it to me, sometimes. "Terrapin" starts out with a shameless invoca-tion to the Muse.

  I know Muse is unfashionable now, but I think if people knew what it was, they couldn't throw it out. It's an informing joy in creation, in which one's verbal flow spills over the page with a great deal of ease and pleasure. That joy is there even in the communication of pain. The trick is to seek this out first, before anything else. William Burroughs has said something about, "A writer's business is to make his mind absolutely blank."

This is not literally so, but you could say something "comes into the ear,"* and moves around the head, and you know you're on. When you're on, you can do no wrong.

Silberman: Kerouac said, "Don't think of words when you stop, but to see the picture better." Thus an image-centered process. Do you feel more conscious of your writing being driven by the language, or by a set of images, or feelings? What does your Muse feel like?

Hunter: The language is little tricks that I play with my input, and if it delights the Muse, you hear a little bell [*laughing*]. Don't take this literally, 'cause we are talking about what can't be talked about. I'd say a lot of my poetry is about that, even. Milton found a very fine way to talk about it. Wallace Stevens is just chock-full of Muse. I feel that anything that doesn't have this central, singular focus is an exercise, and you wouldn't select it for your selected works. 73

*Compare Hunter's translation of Rainer Maria Rilke's second sonnet from *Sonnets to Orpheus*:

Something akin to a maiden strayed
from this marriage of song and string,
glowing radiant through veils of spring;
inside my ear a bed she lay.

And there she slept. Her dream was my
  domain:
the trees which enchanted me; vistas vast
and nearly touchable; meadows of a vernal
  cast
and every wondrous joy my heart could claim

She dreamed the world. Singing, God, how
  made

Terrapin—I can't figure out
Terrapin—if it's the end or beginning 12
Terrapin—but the train's put its brakes on
and the whistle is screaming: *Terrapin*

AT A SIDING

While you were gone
these spaces filled with darkness
The obvious was hidden
With nothing to believe in
the compass always points to Terrapin

Sullen wings of fortune beat like rain
You're back in Terrapin for good or ill again
For good or ill again

Words by Robert Hunter
Music by Jerry Garcia

you that primordial repose so sound she never felt a
need to waken? Upon arising she fell straight to dream.

Where is her death? O, will you yet discover
   her theme
before your song is eclipsed forever?—
Abandoning me, where does she go?—some
   thing akin to a maid. 74

Some examples of the invocation of the muse in literature:

Homer begins the *Iliad:* "Sing, goddess, the anger of
Peleus' son Achilleus. . . ."

Virgil's *Aeneid* borrows from Homer and begins in the
same fashion ("I sing of arms and a man"), but moves on
to a four-line invocation of the Muse. The footnote for
these lines in Clyde Pharr's edition of Virgil's *Aeneid* shows
the importance for classical poets of seeking inspiration
(the muse), when it states:

   It is the custom of epic poets to invoke the muse for
   inspiration and to assign to some such divine source the
   gift of being able to compose their poems.

Hesiod: "Pierian Muses whose songs glorify,
   hither!"
Solon: "O, ye splendid children of Memory and Zeus the
Olympian, Pierian Muses, hear! Heed
   me now as I pray!"

Inspiration is from the Latin for "breathing in." The entry
for "inspiration" in *The Princeton Encyclopedia of Poetry and
Poetics* states that:

   At least as early as Homer, inspiration holds a central
   place in Greek poetics, both as invocation to the gods,
   or, more often, the Muses for the gift of memorable
   speech, and also as claim that when the god does take
   possession, the poet enters a state of transcendant
   ecstasy or frenzy, a "poetic madness" or *furor poeticus.*
   Throughout most of archaic Greek thought, the creation of art is associated with ritual, religion, and sub-
   stance-induced *ecstasis.* 75

3 **While the firelight's aglow**
Compare Hunter's lines in "Lay of the Ring," from his
"Eagle Mall Suite":

   Josephus lately of the mountain wild,
   Seated before a desert fire,
   Led the men to silence
   While the fire told its tales . . .

Lewis Carroll's poem "Faces in the Fire" presents another
interesting comparison:

   The night creeps onward, sad and slow:
   In these red embers' dying glow
   The forms of Fancy come and go.

   The picture fadeth in its place:
   Amid the glow I seem to trace
   The shifting semblance of a face.

4 **all that fancy paints as fair**
Again, compare the Lewis Carroll poem:

   She's all my fancy painted him;
   (I make no idle boast);
   If he or you had lost a limb,
   Which would have suffered most?

5 **hold away despair**
Hunter's journal of September 24, 2001, contains this
entry:

   Later:
   After dark fell, I sat alone on the roof, fifteen stories
   high, of a building in Soho commanding a panoramic
   and unobstructed view of the skyscrapers of midtown
   Manhattan and the lights of the bridges. I had my guitar in hand and felt moved to sing "Terrapin Station"
   to the City. While I sang, rain began falling—I stood
   and edged around to the other side of the roof, still
   singing, to the corner of the roof facing the World
   Trade Center, some fifteen blocks away, where the sky
   is bright with floodlight illuminating the work of the
   excavation crew. A great plume of smoke continues to

rise from the site of the devastation. As I sang, a powerful wind blew up very suddenly—wind so strong it threatened to rip my guitar out of my hands—reminding me of the storm in which I first composed the words I now sang. I wondered if I was involved in some kind of sacrilege, singing like this in the face of all that had gone down—the wind roaring increasingly louder and stronger, as though filled with spirits, as though trying to blow me over, make me stop. I kept singing until the end, repeating the "hold away despair," expressing all the sorrow I felt for the lost loved ones and for the healing of this magnificent and resilient City. I hope it helped. Helped me, anyway. 76

6 Terrapin

From the Algonquian for "little turtle." Brought into the English language ca. 1672.

According to Cirlot:

The turtle has a variety of meanings, all of which are organically related. In the Far East its significance is cosmic in implication. As Chochod has observed: "The primordial turtle has a shell that is rounded on top to represent heaven, and square underneath to represent the earth." To the Negroes of Nigeria it suggests the female sex organ and it is in fact taken as an emblem of lubricity. In alchemy it was symbolic of the *massa confusa*. These disparate senses have, nevertheless, one thing in common: In every case, the turtle is a symbol of material existence and not of any aspect of transcendence, for even where it is a combination of square and circle it alludes to the forms of the manifest world and not to the creative forces, nor to the Origin, still less to the irradiating Centre. In view of its slowness, it might be said to symbolize natural evolution as opposed to spiritual evolution which is rapid or discontinuous to a degree. The turtle is also an emblem of longevity. 77

The Encyclopedia of Religion has an entry on turtles and tortoises—here's an excerpt:

There is a widespread belief that the earth rests on the back of a turtle or tortoise. This archaic idea is found not only among North American Indians but also in South Asia and Inner Asia. The turtle now appears even as a symbol of the entire universe (e.g., in China). Moreover, according to creation myths involving an earth diver, the turtle, sometimes as an incarnation of the divine being, plays a prominent part in the cosmogony of various cultures. (Eliade)

Other resonances occur: the naming of the North American continent as "Turtle Island" by the Native Americans; and the use of the terrapin as a character in the Uncle Remus tales of Joel Chandler Harris.

Turtles always make me think of the following story:

An old woman approached William James after he gave a lecture on the solar system. "We don't live on a ball rotating 'round the sun," she said. "We live on a crust of earth on the back of a giant turtle."

"If your theory is correct, Madam, what does the turtle stand on?" James asked gently.

"You're a clever man, Mr. James, and that is a good question, but I can answer it. The first turtle stands on the back of a second, far larger turtle."

"But what does this second turtle stand on?" asked James.

"It's no use, Mr. James!" the old woman crowed. "It's turtles all the way down."

William James did write at least once about turtles and elephants. In "Humanism and Truth" *Mind* 13 (N.S.): (October 1904), p. 472; reprinted as chapter III of *The Meaning of Truth,* he wrote:

> But is this not the globe, the elephant and the tortoise over again? Must not something end by supporting itself? . . .

This in turn seems to be an echo of comments by John Locke in *An Essay Concerning Human Understanding* (1690), Book II, Chapter XIII, Section 19:

> . . . Had the poor Indian philosopher (who imagined that the earth also wanted something to bear it up) but thought of this word *substance,* he needed not to have been at the trouble to find an elephant to support it, and a tortoise to support his elephant: the word *substance* would have done it effectually. And he that inquired might have taken it for as good an answer from an Indian philosopher,—that *substance,* without knowing what it is, is that which supports the earth, as we take it for a sufficient answer and good doctrine from our European philosophers—that *substance,* without knowing what it is, is that which supports accidents.

and Book II, Chapter XXIII, Section 2:

> . . . If any one should be asked, what is the subject wherein colour or weight inheres, he would have nothing to say but the solid extended parts; and if he were demanded, what is it that solidity and extension adhere in, he would not be in a much better case than the Indian before mentioned who, saying that the world was supported by a great elephant, was asked what the elephant rested on; to which his answer was—a great tortoise: but being again pressed to know what gave support to the broad-backed tortoise, replied—something, he knew not what.

7 Counting stars by candlelight
Vincent van Gogh famously painted *Starry Night Over the Rhone* on the banks of the Rhone River, with candles set on the brim of his hat.

8 spiral light of Venus
The motion of the position of the planet Venus, viewed over a period of eight years, describes a pentagram across the zodiac, progressing from one constellation to another every nineteen months: from Scorpio to Taurus, to Capricorn, to Cancer, to Pisces, and back to Scorpio. But is this motion a spiral? Not really.

The planet, named for the Roman goddess, has long been associated with the goddess of love, who in the Greek pantheon was Aphrodite.

The Greek poet Bion (ca. 100 B.C.E.) writes:

> Evening Star, gold light of Aphrodite born in the foam,
> Evening Star, holy diamond of the glass blue night,
> you are dimmer than the moon, brighter than another star.
> Hello, good friend!

And William Blake's "To the Evening Star":

> Thou fair-hair'd angel of the evening,
> Now, whilst the sun rests on the mountains, light
> Thy bright torch of love; thy radiant crown
> Put on, and smile upon our evening bed!

Smile on our loves, and while thou drawest
the
Blue curtains of the sky, scatter thy silver dew
On every flower that shuts its sweet eyes
In timely sleep. Let thy west wind sleep on
The lake; speak silence with thy glimmering
eyes,
And wash the dusk with silver. Soon, full soon,
Dost thou withdraw; then the wolf rages wide,
And the lion glares thro' the dun forest:
The fleeces of our flocks are cover'd with
Thy sacred dew: protect them with thine
influence.

Spiral Light was the title of a British Grateful Dead fan magazine ("The official newsletter of Deadheads in England") that ran for thirty-five issues, from Feburary 1984 through May 1996.

9 northwest corner
A possible Masonic allusion pertaining to a Masonic ritual in which all new Masons are placed in the northwest corner of the lodge, standing there a just and perfect mason (the implication is that you are as yet unsullied, much as an infant is considered innocent, having not yet experienced the world).

10 crickets and cicadas
In the *Phaedrus,* in a section called "The Myth of the Cicadas," Socrates relates a creation myth of how cicadas (or in some translations,

"locusts") came to be, in which, when the Muses were finally born, a curtain tribe of people were so overcome with happiness at being able to sing that they sang until they expired for lack of food and drink. From that time, they became cicadas, who need no sustenance from birth until they die, can sing constantly, and are taken to the Muses upon their deaths.

An American weather saying has it that "crickets are accurate thermometers; they chirp faster when warm and slower when cold." Sloane notes that.

> They are extremely accurate. Count their chirps for fourteen seconds, then add forty, and you have the temperature of wherever the cricket is.

11 in the shadow of the moon
An ambiguous line meaning either "within the dark portion of the brand-new crescent moon" or "on the dark side of the moon." The second reading reminds us, inevitably, of the Pink Floyd album *Dark Side of the Moon.* Or it may refer to a solar eclipse.

12 end or the beginning
Compare T. S. Eliot's oft-quoted lines from the *Four Quartets: Little Gidding:*

> What we call the beginning is often the end
> And to make an end is to make a beginning.

(Is it possibly significant that Terrapin Station's initials match Thomas Stearn's?)

Notes:
Studio recording: *Terrapin Station* (July 27, 1977).

First performance: February 26, 1977, at the Swing Auditorium in San Bernardino, California. It occupied a stable place in the repertoire thereafter.

Hunter:
> I wrote Terrapin, Part One, at a single sitting in an unfurnished house with a picture window overlooking San Francisco Bay during a flamboyant lightning storm. I typed the first thing that came into my mind at the top of the page, the title; "Terrapin Station." Not knowing what it was to be about, I began my writing with an invocation to the Muse and kept on typing as the story began to unfold.

On the same day, driving to the city, Garcia was struck by a singular inspiration. He turned his car around and hurried home to set down some music that popped into his head, demanding immediate attention. When we met the next day, I showed him the words and he said, "I've got the music." They dovetailed perfectly and Terrapin edged into this dimension. (Hunter: *A Box of Rain*) 78

The Grateful Dead's realization of the piece is, in Hunter's view, lamentably incomplete,

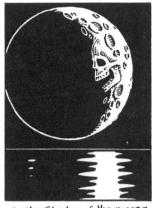

–In the Shadow of the moon– "Terrapin"

leaving out as it does the lyric's resolution. Garcia intentionally uses only a portion of Hunter's lyric. In *A Box of Rain,* Hunter writes more about "Terrapin" than about any other single piece, with the exception of "Amagamalin Street." Hunter's own recording of "Terrapin," on *Jack o' Roses,* is closer to being complete, and attempts to incorporate a plethora of imagery and iconography from all over the Grateful Dead map, especially in the "Ivory Wheels/Rosewood Track" portion of the song. See Hunter's *A Box of Rain* for the entire suite.

Estimated Prophet

1 time sure passin' slow
Compare the Bob Dylan song from 1970's *New Morning*: "Time Passes Slowly":

> Time passes slowly up here in the daylight,
> We stare straight ahead and try so hard to stay
>   right,
> Like the red rose of summer that blooms in
>   the day,
> Time passes slowly and fades away 79

2 golden door
A reference to the Golden Gate, the entrance to the San Francisco Bay. Also immortalized in the 1924 song "California, Here I Come," by Al Jolson, Bud DeSylva, and Joseph Myers:

> Open up that golden gate,
> California here I come

3 The sea will part before me...
Exodus 14:21–31:

> Then Moses
> stretched out his
> hand over the sea,
> and the Lord drove
> the sea away all
> night with a strong
> east wind and
> turned the seabed
> into dry land.

A familiar story, and one of the most powerful tales of the power of a prophetic presence. Invoked here, visions of Cecil B. DeMille's screen epic *The Ten Commandments* come to mind.

My time coming, any day, don't worry 'bout me, no
Been so long I felt this way, ain't in no hurry, no
Rainbows end down that highway where ocean
  breezes blow
My time coming, voices saying, they tell me where
  to go

Don't worry 'bout me, no no, don't worry 'bout
  me, no
And I'm in no hurry, no no no, I know where to go

California, preaching on the burning shore
California, I'll be knocking on the golden door
Like an angel, standing in a shaft of light
Rising up to paradise, I know I'm gonna shine

My time coming, any day, don't worry bout me, no
It's gonna be just like they say, them voices tell me so
Seems so long I felt this way and time sure passin' slow   1
Still I know I lead the way, they tell me where I go

Don't worry 'bout me, no no, don't worry 'bout me, no
And I'm in no hurry, no no no, I know where to go

California, a prophet on the burning shore
California, I'll be knocking on the golden door   2
Like an angel, standing in a shaft of light
Rising up to paradise, I know I'm gonna shine

You've all been asleep,
You would not believe me
Them voices telling me,

You will soon receive me
We're standing on the beach,
3   The sea will part before me
4   (Fire wheel burning in the air)
And you will follow me,
And we will ride to glory
(Way up the middle of the air)

And I'll call down thunder
And speak the same
And my word fills the sky with flame
And might and glory gonna be my name
And men gonna light my way

My time coming, any day, don't worry 'bout me, no
It's gonna be just like they say, them voices tell me so
Seems so long I felt this way and time sure passin' slow
My time coming, any day, don't worry 'bout me, no

Don't worry 'bout me . . .

Words by John Barlow
Music by Bob Weir

Moses also appears in Hunter's "Greatest Story Ever Told."

4 Fire wheel burnin' in the air
Daniel 7:9:

Flames of fire were his throne and its wheel blazing fire

Ezekiel 10:9–10:

They had the sparkle of topaz, and all four were alike, like a wheel inside a wheel.

These two Bible passages found life in a spiritual, "'Zekiel Saw De Wheel":

Wheel, oh wheel,
Wheel, in de middle of a wheel;
Wheel, oh wheel,
Wheel in the middle of a wheel.

'Zekiel saw de wheel of time,
Wheel in the middle of a wheel,
Ev'ry spoke was humankind,
Wheel in the middle of a wheel.

Way up yonder on de mountain top,
Wheel in de middle of a wheel,
My Lord spoke an de chariot stop,
Wheel in de middle of a wheel.

'Zekiel saw de wheel,
Way up in de middle of de air,
'Zekiel saw de wheel,
Way in de middle of de air.

De big wheel run by faith,
Little wheel run by de grace of God;

Wheel widin a wheel
Way in de middle of de air." (Johnson)

There is an echo here, as well, of the Robert Hunter lyric
"The Wheel" in the lines "De big wheel run by faith /
Little wheel run by de grace of God."

The reference on Weir and Barlow's part is to the
"Prophet" of the title, as reflected in the words of the
prophets Ezekiel and Daniel, via the traditional spiritual.

Notes:
Written in Cora, Wyoming, and Mill Valley, California,
January 1977.

Studio recording: *Terrapin Station* (July 27, 1977).

First performance: February 26, 1977, at the Swing
Auditorium in San Bernardino, California. A steady number in the repertoire thereafter.

According to Weir, he and Barlow wrote the song from
the perspective of a crazy, messianic zealot, a type
which one invariably encounters in Deadhead crowds
now and again. As Weir explains: "The basis of it is this
guy I see at nearly every backstage door. There's always
some guy who's taken a lot of dope and he's really
bug-eyed, and he's having some kind of vision. He's
got a rave he's got to deliver." In "Estimated Prophet,"
the psychopath claims "My time comin' any day, don't
worry about me," and Weir essentially *lets* him rave.
(Jackson: *Grateful Dead*) 80

Fire on the Mountain

Long-distance runner what you standing
  there for?
Get up, get off, get out of the door
You're playing cold music on the barroom floor,
drowned in your laughter and dead to the core
There's a dragon with matches loose on the town
Take a whole pail of water just to cool him down

1   Fire—fire on the mountain
Fire—fire on the mountain

Almost aflame still you don't feel the heat
Takes all you got just to stay on the beat
You say it's a living, we all gotta eat
but you're here alone there's no one to compete
If mercy's in business I wish it for you
More than just ashes when your dreams come true

Fire—fire on the mountain
Fire—fire on the mountain

Long-distance runner what you holding out for?
Caught in slow motion in your dash to the door
The flame from your stage has now spread to
  the floor
You gave all you got, why you wanta give more?
The more that you give, why, the more it will take
to the thin line beyond which you really can
  not fake

There's a fire
Fire on the mountain

Words by Robert Hunter
Music by Mickey Hart

1 fire on the mountain
A standard old-time country tune recorded by a large number of performers including Riley Puckett and Clayton McMichen, and Gid Tanner & his Skillet Lickers.

According to Alan Lomax's *Check-List of Recorded Songs in the English Language in the Archive of American Folk Song to July, 1940* (Library of Congress, 1942), a tune called "Fire in the Mountain" was played by G. G. Albritton and Cleo Wynn O'Berry on fiddle with straw beating in Sebring, Florida, in 1940.

Also included as a line in a nursery rhyme:

Hogs in the garden, catch 'em, Towser;
Cows in the cornfield, run, boys, run!
Cats in the cream-pot, run girls, run!
Fire on the mountain, run, boys, run!

In the *I Ching,* or the ancient Chinese *Book of Changes,* hexagram 56 is titled "The Wanderer" (or "The Traveler," "Travel," "The Stranger," and so on). It is represented by two trigrams, Fire (*Li*) and Mountain (*Ken*), with Fire resting on Mountain.

Notes:
Studio recording: *Shakedown Street* (November 15, 1978).

First performance: March 18, 1977, at Winterland Arena in San Francisco. "Fire" closed the first set, following its eternal partner, "Scarlet

Begonias." This combination of tunes, which often enclosed some wonderful jamming, came to be known as "Scarlet Fire." It remained steadily in the repertoire from then on.

Mount St. Helens, in Washington State, erupted during a performance of "Fire on the Mountain" by the Dead in Portland, Oregon, on June 12, 1980. As the crowd streamed out of the Memorial Coliseum, ashes were raining down.

—croaker—

sunrise

Gazing at the fire
Burning by the water
Before he speaks, the world around us quiets
With eyes as sharp as arrows
And turning to the fire
He clears the air and cuts it with a feather

Many in a circle
Slowly 'round the fire
When he is gone, I want to know him better
No one is forsaken
No one is a liar
1   He plants the tree of life on our foreheads
with water

He hums
There are drums
2   Four winds
Rising suns
We are singing and playing
I hear what he's saying
I remember breezes
From winds inside your body
Keep me high
Like I told you
I'll sing to them this story
And know why

Words and music by Donna Godchaux

1 **tree of life**
The tree planted by God in the Garden of Eden, along with the Tree of Knowledge. And more generally, the World Tree or axis mundi of many mythological systems.

2 **four winds**
See note under "Franklin's Tower."

Notes:
Studio recording: *Terrapin Station* (July 27, 1977).

First performance: May 1, 1977, at the Palladium in New York.

This song is about a Native American ceremony conducted by the Grateful Dead's shaman associate, Rolling Thunder, a Paiute, in honor of the passing of Rex Jackson, Grateful Dead roadie and road manager after whom the Rex Foundation is named. Jackson died in October 1976.

iko iko

Hey now (hey now)
Hey now (hey now)
Iko iko un day
Jockomo feeno ah na nay
Jockomo feena nay

My grandma see your grandpa
Sitting by the bayou
My grandma see your grandpa
Gonna fix your chicken wire

Hey now (hey now)
Hey now (hey now)
Iko iko un day
Jockomo feeno ah na nay
Jockomo feena nay

My spy dog see your spy dog
Sitting by the bayou
My spy dog see your spy dog
Gonna set your tail on fire

Hey now (hey now)
Hey now (hey now)
Iko iko un day

Jockomo feeno ah na nay
Jockomo feena nay

My little boy see your little boy
Sitting by the bayou
My little boy see your little boy
Gonna fix your chicken wire

Hey now (hey now)
Hey now (hey now)
Iko iko un day
Jockomo feeno ah na nay
Jockomo feena nay

My grandma see your grandma
Sitting by the Bayou
My grandma see your grandma
Gonna fix your chicken wire

Hey now (hey now)
Hey now (hey now)
Iko iko un day
Jockomo feeno ah na nay
Jockomo feena nay

Words and music: traditional

Notes:
First performance: May 15, 1977, at the St. Louis
Arena in St. Louis. It remained in the repertoire
thereafter.

This tune has an interesting and complicated
origin. It definitely derives from African call-and-
response chants, and it probably came over to
the Americas with the first slaves. In African,
people would put on ceremonial leaves for big
celebrations, but, initially, white plantation owners who
used slaves in the eighteenth and nineteenth centuries
prohibited that kind of behavior. Then, in the late eighteenth century, whites evidently became fascinated with
the black tribal chants and music and decided to allow

the slaves one day a week to strut their stuff and whoop it up in New Orleans' Congo Square while the gentry watched. Over the years, different groups of blacks formed Mardi Gras "tribes," and the leaves gave way to feathers, most likely because of the influence of the Seminoles and other Native Indian tribes (some of whom even owned slaves). The Mardi Gras tribes used their celebration days to fight each other as well as to get crazy, but the white powers that ruled put an end to the fighting in the 1890s and the "wars" evolved into battles of *style* and dressing up.

The song we know as "Iko-Iko" started out as two separate Mardi Gras chants. There is no real translation of the lyrics, but it adds up to gentle mocking of rival tribes; a thumbed nose as it were. "It was just something you grew up saying in the neighborhood," says the great New Orleans songwriter-producer Allen Toussaint. "You'd use it like a cocky argument. It has verses like 'My spy boy saw your spy boy sittin' by the fi-yo. / My spy boy told your spy boy, "I'm gonna set your flag on fi-yo."'" ("Spy boys" are supposed to alert other tribe members when an "enemy" tribe approaches on Mardi Gras day.)

Art Neville, of New Orleans' Neville Brothers, is more literal in his speculation about the meaning of *iko:* "I think it's a case where the pronunciation changed over the generations. It was 'iko' by the time it got to Chief Jolly. It may have come from the word *hike*, because that's what you'd do on Mardi Gras—hike all over the city, trying to see all the masks and the different parades. It was like you'd 'hike-o, hike-o all day.' I heard a couple of other definitions, too," he adds with a knowing, lascivious laugh, "but I don't know how true they are."

The first recorded version of "Iko-Iko" was "Jock-o-Mo," cut by a young New Orleans singer named James "Sugar Boy" Crawford for Checker Records in 1954. "I didn't really know much about the Indians and all that," he confessed when I reached him by phone at his New Orleans home, "but I'd heard these chants and I liked the sound of them, and so I just put a little tune to them. I can't take credit for the words, obviously, but I guess the tune is mine. I don't know, though. I never got any royalties."

Pianist Professor Longhair was undoubtedly the main influence on "Jock-o-Mo," which was a big regional hit for Sugar Boy Crawford. "I don't think people outside New Orleans knew what it was all about," Crawford says with a laugh. "But then, to be honest, I didn't, and still don't, have any idea what the words mean."

The next version of "Iko" worth noting was by the Dixie Cups, three New Orleans girls who had a fluke top twenty national hit with the song in 1965. The group members hadn't even intended to record the song and were actually just singing it casually in the studio—as any Mardi Gras–loving daughters of New Orleans might—when their producer, Phil Spector, surreptitiously turned on the tape machine. The trio, which still performs around New Orleans, is best remembered for the title tune of the album on which "Iko-Iko" appeared, *Chapel of Love.*

In the late sixties, an accomplished singer and instrumentalist named Mac Rebennack burst out of New Orleans as Dr. John the Night Tripper and was an immediate hit with fans of psychedelic music. Though his image—complete with feathered gowns and singers and dancers who seemed born of both Mardi Gras and Caribbean voodoo traditions—was somewhat contrived, his music was pure, based in Creole folk and New Orleans R&B. (Indeed, Rebennack did session work for Professor Longhair, Lee Allen, and other Crescent City greats, in the fifties and early sixties.) As his career went on, he dropped the *gris-gris* trappings and instead helped pioneer modern New Orleans funk along with Allen Toussaint, his sometime collaborator and producer, and musical colleagues such as the Meters, who later evolved into the Neville Brothers. This triumvirate exerted considerable influence on music in the mid-seventies, touching the Rolling Stones (who had the Meters open shows for them on one tour), Paul Simon, Paul McCartney, LaBelle, and numerous others. Dr. John's own recording of "Iko-Iko," which he says he recorded at the urging of J. Geils' Peter Wolf, strangely enough, appeared on his 1972 album *Gumbo.* (Blair Jackson. Excerpt from *Goin' Down the Road: A Grateful Dead Travelling Companion).* 94

passenger

Firefly,

can you see me?

Shine on, glowing

Brief and brightly

Could you imagine,

One summer day

That same night

Be on your way

Do you remember?

Hearts were too cold

Seasons had frozen us

Into our souls

People were saying

The whole world is burning

Ashes were scattered

Too hard to turn

Chorus:

Upside out

Or inside down

False alarm, the only game in town

No man's land, the only game in town   1

Terrible, the only game in town

Passenger

Don't you hear me?

Destination

Seen unclearly

What is a man

Deep down inside

But a raging beast

With nothing to hide

(Chorus)

Words by Peter Monk
Music by Phil Lesh

---

1 only game in town
See Hal Kant's essay on gambling, under "Loser."

Notes:

Studio recording: *Terrapin Station* (July 27, 1977).

First performance: May 17, 1977, at Memorial Coliseum, University of Alabama, Tuscaloosa, Alabama. "Passenger" remained in the repertoire fairly steadily through 1981 and was then dropped.

In an interview in *Dupree's Diamond News,* Lesh says:

> What's weird about that song is I sort of did it as a joke. It's a take on a Fleetwood Mac tune called "Station Man." I just sort of sped it up

and put some different chord changes in there.

Outtakes from the *Terrapin Station* album sessions reveal that when the song was being developed, the lyrics after the first chorus were sung in a different order and included additional verses:

> Jet plane shadows
> Under the sky
> Just like the elephant
> Planning to die
>
> Ask me no questions
> Sing you no names
> No more mysteries
> Simple games

equinox

She reclines, closing her eyes
The sun that set is bound to rise
Night birds and fireflies settle round her
Days grow long, spring is here
Waterfalls shine again
Our minds have gone downstream
Shooting the rapids

Bright as gold, the arms you gave
Bright as the eye of a hurricane
We're all just the sins growing children
Every moment is perfect, every sin is a jewel
Every man is a prophet at the mercy of a fool

Watch the seasons go, as sunshine turns to
   cold snow
Showers and rain
Numbers of tomorrow
The great globe spins, the music starts
Every beat knows its part
To keep it spinning in a circle
Every moment is perfect, every eye's a jewel
Every man is a prophet with the mercy of a fool

Words and music by Phil Lesh

Notes:
Studio recording: issued as an outtake from
Terrapin Station (July 27, 1977) with the *Beyond
Description* box set.

Never performed.

It is often called "Mercy of a Fool" in bootleg
lyric lists.

Bob Weir gave this account of its origins:

One tune that took the longest to get was one
that we didn't use. Another of Phil's originals.
It was just too long, the song itself was too
long to put on without crowding something
else off the record. It was just very long and
quite involved, and it was looking to require a
good deal of work, and we only had so much
time for what we could do on the record—you
can only put about nineteen minutes per side
on a record before you start losing fidelity.
Phil's tune was six minutes long or so, and it
would have put both sides well over that, so
we decided to axe it and bring it back some
other time. We got a great basic on it. (Gans,
Conversations) 81

I need a miracle

I need a woman 'bout twice my age
A lady of nobility, gentility, and rage
A splendor in the dark, lightning on the draw
Who'll go right through the book and break
    each and every law

I got a feelin'
And it won't go away, oh no
Just one thing and I'll be okay
I need a miracle every day

I need a woman 'bout twice my height
Statuesque, raven-tressed, a goddess of the
    night
A secret incantation, candle burning blue
We'll consult the spirits, maybe they'll know
    what to do

And it's real
And it won't go away, oh no
Can't get around and I can't run away
I need a miracle every day

I need a woman 'bout twice my weight
A ton of fun who packs a gun with all that
    other freight

Find her in a sideshow, leave her in L.A.
Ride her like a surfer riding on a tidal wave

And it's real
Believe what I say
Just one thing that I gotta say
I need a miracle very day

It takes dynamite to get me up
Too much of everything is just enough
One more thing that I gotta say
I need a miracle every day

Words by John Barlow
Music by Bob Weir

Notes:

Written in Mill Valley, California, July 1978.

Studio recording: *Shakedown Street* (November 15, 1978).

First performance: August 30, 1978, at Red Rocks Amphitheater in Morrison, Colorado.

Source of the iconic "miracle" ticket of Deadhead lore, whereby if you stood around long enough outside of a sold-out show and repeated, "I need a miracle," eventually someone would give you a ticket. It happened often enough for miracles to become, if not commonplace, at least accepted.

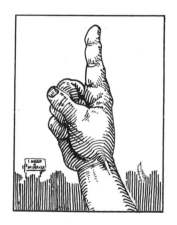

stagger Lee

1940 Xmas eve with a full moon over town
Stagger Lee met Billy DeLyon
and he blew that poor boy down
Do you know what he shot him for?
What do you make of that?

2 'Cause Billy DeLyon threw lucky dice,

3 won Stagger Lee's Stetson hat

4 *Baio, Baio, tell me how can this be?*
You arrest the girls for turning tricks
but you're scared of Staggerlee
Stagger Lee is a madman and he shot my Billy dead
Baio you go get him or give the job to me

Delia DeLyon, dear sweet Delia-D
How the hell can I arrest him when he's twice
    as big as me?
Don't ask me to go downtown—I won't
    come back alive
Not only is that mother *big* but he packs a .45

Baio Delia said just give me a gun
He shot my Billy dead now I'm gonna see him hung
She waded to DeLyon's Club through Billy
    DeLyon's blood
Stepped up to Stagger Lee at the bar

5 Said *Buy me a gin fizz, love*

As Stagger Lee lit a cigarette she shot him in
    the balls

1 Stagger Lee
A number of tunes titled "Stagger Lee" have been recorded over the years. They all derive from a series of tales and songs in African American folklore.

Cecil Brown's definitive study *Stagolee Shot Billy* should serve as a model for anyone wishing to do in-depth research into the factual background of traditional material. But Brown goes beyond historical research, exploring the cultural significance and influence of the Stagolee material since it was born, of actual events, in 1895. The ballad documents the historical fact of the murder, on Christmas Day, of Billy Lyons by Lee "Stack Lee" Shelton in a St. Louis bar. Brown tells the story compellingly, with sense and color. He examines dozens of versions of the ballad (including Hunter's) and discusses the variations and their implications.

Here's a partial list of other "Stagger Lee"s, in alphabetical order by performer:

Archibald: Imperial X5358
Bechet, Sidney: "Old Stack O'Lee Blues" on *The Best of Sidney Bechet* (Blue Note, CDP 7243 8 28891 2 0, 1994)
Bookbinder, Roy: "Stack O Lee" on *Ragtime Millionaire* (Yellow Bee Productions, 5BG-2023, 1977)
Brozman, Bob: "Stack o Lee Aloha" on *A Truck-load of Blues* (Rounder, CD 3119, 1992)
Calloway, Cab: "Stack O' Lee Blues" on *Cab Calloway and His Orchestra, 1931–1932* (Classics 526, 1990)
Clayton, Paul: *Bloody Ballads,* (Riverside RLP 12-615)
Dodds, Johnny: "Stack O'Lee Blues" on side B of *Melancholy* (Decca, 1676, 1938)
Domino, Fats: "Stack & Billy" on *Let's Play* (Imperial, LP-9065, 1959)

Dylan, Bob: "Stack a Lee" on *World Gone Wrong* (Columbia, CK 57590, 1993)

Edwards, Cliff: "Stack O' Lee, Part 1" and "Stack O' Lee, Part 2" (ca. 1924) on *I'm a Bear in a Lady's Boudoir* (Yazoo, L-1047, 1975)

English, Logan: (Riverside 12-643)

Fuller, Jesse: "Stagolee" on *Jazz, Folk Songs, Spirituals, and Blues* (Original Blues Classics, 2530 564 2, 1958)

The Green Mountain Boys: "Stagolee" on *The Green Mountain Boys* (Green Mountain Records, GMS 1053, 197?)

Guthrie, Woody: "Stagolee" on *Bound for Glory* (Smithsonian/Folkways Records, 02481, 1992; originally recorded 1956)

Houston, Cisco: "Stagolee" on *Hard Traveling* (Folkways, FA 2042, 1954)

Hull, Papa Harvey, Long "Cleve" Reed, and the Down Home Boys: "Original Stack O'Lee Blues" (ca. 1927) on *The Songster Tradition: Complete Recorded Works in Chronological Order (1927–1935)* (Document Records, DOCD-5045, 1991)

Hurt, Mississippi John: "Stack O' Lee Blues" on *1928 sessions* (Yazoo, 1065, 1990)

Hutchinson, Frank: on *American Folk Music,* vol. 1: Ballads (Folkways, FP 251, 1927)

Johnson, Tex: "Stack o Lee" on *Gunfighter Ballads* (Promenade, 2239, 1961)

Lester, Julius: "Stagolee" on *Julius Lester Accompanying Himself on the Guitar* (Vanguard, VRS-9199, 1965)

Lewis, Furry: "Billy Lyons and Stack O'Lee" on *Furry Lewis (1927–1929): Complete Recorded Works in Chronological Order* (Document Records, DOCD-5004, 1990); recording also includes "Kassie Jones, Part 1 and 2."

Lomax, Alan (comp.): "Stackerlee," by an unknown performer on *Negro Prison Songs from the Mississippi State Penitentiary* (Tradition, TLP 1020, 1947; recorded by Alan Lomax in

Blew the smoke off her revolver, had him
dragged to city hall
Baio, Baio, see you hang him high
He shot my Billy dead and now he's got to die

Delia went a-walking down on Singapore Street
A three-piece band on the corner played
  "Nearer My God to Thee"
But Delia whistled a different tune . . . what
  tune could it be?

  The song that woman sung was
    Look out Staggerlee
  The song that Delia sung was
    Look out Staggerlee
  The song that woman sung was
    Look out Staggerlee
  The song that Delia sung was
    Look out Staggerlee

6

  Words by Robert Hunter
  Music by Jerry Garcia

1947 at the Mississippi State Penitentiary at Parchman, Mississippi

Lomax, Alan: *Listen to Our Story* (BR-1024)

McCurdy, Ed: (Elektra 108)

Memphis Slim: "Stack Alee" on *Broken Soul Blues* (United Artists, UAL3137, 1961)

New Lost City Ramblers: "Stackerlee" on *The New Lost City Ramblers* (Folkways Records, FA 2399, 1962)

Noble, Ray: "Stack O' Lee" (ca. 1935) on *Ray Noble and His American Dance Orchestra* (Jazz Archives, JA-22, 1975)

Paley, Tom: "Stackerlee" on *Old Tom Moore and More* (Global Village, C 309, 1991)

Price, Lloyd: "Stagger Lee" by Harold Logan and Lloyd Price (based on traditional material) (1958)

Rainey, Ma: "Stack O'Lee Blues" on *Ma Rainey's Black Bottom* and on *The Complete Madam Gertrude "Ma" Rainey Mastertakes' Collection, 1923/28* (King Jazz, KJ-182 FS, 1994)

Senter, Boyd: "Original Stack O'Lee Blues" on *Solos and Senterpedes: 1927–1928* (Harlequin, HQ 2044, 1986)

Sol Hoopii's Novelty Trio: "Stack O'Lee Blues" on side B of *Farewell Blues* (Columbia, 797-D, 1926)

Stuart, Alice: "Stackerlee" on *All the Good Times* (Arhoolie, F 4002, 1964)

Travis, Merle: "Stack O'Lee" on *Rough, Rowdy, and Blue* CMH (CMH-C-6262, 1986.)

Turner, Titus: *Return of Stagolee* (King, 45-5186, 1959)

The Washingtonians (a pseudonym for Duke Ellington and his Orchestra): "Stack O'Lee Blues" on side B of *Red Head Blues* (Velvet Tone, 1601-V, 1927)

Watson, Doc: "Stack O'Lee" on *Ballads from Deep Gap* (Vanguard, VMD-6576, 1988)

Wheeler, Mary (comp.): "Stacker Lee" (Bertha Wenzel, singer; Bill Small, guitar) on *Folk Songs of the River* (Century Custom Recording Service, 20074, ca. 1982)

Three versions of "Stagger Lee":

STAGOLEE

Stagolee was a bad man,
Ev'rybody knows.
Spent one hundred dollars
Just to buy him a suit of clothes.
He was a bad man
That mean old Stagolee

Stagolee shot Blly de Lyons
What do you think about that?
Shot him down in cold blood
Because he stole his Stetson hat;

He was a bad man
That mean old Stagolee

Billy de Lyons said, Stagolee
Please don't take my life
I've got two little babes
And a darling, loving wife;
You are a bad man
You mean old Stagolee.

What do I care about your two little babes,
Your darling, loving wife?
You done stole my Stetson hat
I'm bound to take your life;
He was a bad man,
That mean old Stagolee.

The judge said, Stagolee,
What you doing in here?
You done shot Mr. Billy de Lyons,
You going to die in the electric chair;
He was a bad man
That mean old Stagolee.

Twelve o'clock they killed him
Head reached up high
Last thing that poor boy said,
"My six-shooter never lied."

He was a bad man,
That mean old Stagolee.

STAGALEE

Bad man Stagalee when he bad
He bad wid a gun
Stagalee, Stagalee——you must-a been a sinner
Ev'ry Christmas Eve they give Stagalee a dinner
Bad man Stagalee, when he bad
He bad wid a gun.

Don't you remember you remember
One dark stormy night
Stagalee and Bill O. Lion
Dey had dat noble fight.

Bill O. Lion tole Stagalee
Please don't take my life
I got three little children
And a dear lil' lovin'wife

Stagalee told Billy O. Lion
I don't care for your three lil' children
Or even your lovin' wife
You stole mah Stetson hat
And I'm goin to take yo' life

Stagalee pulled out his forty-four
It went boom boom boom
It wasn't long' fore Bill O. Lion
Were layin' on de flo'

Stagalee's woman she went to her boss
Said, "Please give me some change.
Dey got my baby in de station house
An' mah business mus' be 'ranged. "

Stagalee asked his woman
"How much change has you got?"
She run her han' in her stocking feet
And pulled out a hundred spot.
She had to get mo'money.

From *Southern Folk Ballads,* McNeill Collected from Vera
Hall, AL 1947
This variation of Stagalee was collected February 9,

1910, from a Miss Ella Scott Fisher, San Angelo, Texas,
and appears in *A Compilation of American Ballads and
Folk Songs* (1934) by John and Allan Lomax. It was
sung as a work song on the levees while loading and
unloading the river freighters.

STAGALEE

'Twas a Christmas morning,
The hour was about ten,
When Stagalee shot Billy Lyons
And landed in the Jefferson pen.
O Lordy, po' Stagalee!

Billy Lyons' old woman
She was a terrible sinner
She was home that Christmas mornin'
A-preparin' Billy's dinner.
O Lordy, po' Stagalee!

Messenger boy came to the winder,
Then he knocked on the door
An' he said "Yer old man's a lyin' there
Dead on the barroom floor."
O Lordy, po' Stagalee!

(Billy's old woman:)
"Stagalee, O Stagalee,
What have you gone and done?
You've gone and shot my husband
With a forty-four Gatlin' gun?"
O Lordy, po' Stagalee!

(Stagalee's friend:)
"Stagalee, O Stagalee
Why don't you cut and run
For here comes the policeman
And I think he's got a gun."
O Lordy, po' Stagalee!

(Policeman, a little scared of Stagalee:)
"Stagalee, O Stagalee
I'm 'restin' you just for fun
The officer jest wants you
To identify your gun."

O Lordy, po' Stagalee!

(Stagalee in jail:)
"Jailer, O Jailer
I jest can't sleep
For the ghost of Billy Lyons
Round my bed does mourn and weep."
O Lordy, po' Stagalee!

(Council for the defense:)
"Gentlemen of this jury
You must let poor Stagalee go
His poor and aged mammy
Is lyin' very low."
O Lordy, po' Stagalee!

(Counsel for the Prosecution:)
"Gentlemen of this jury
Wipe away your tears.
For Stagalee's aged mammy
Has been dead these 'leven years."
O Lordy, po' Stagalee!

Stagalee's old woman
She hung around the jail
And in three days she had him out
On a ten-thousand-dollar bail
O Lordy, po' Stagalee!

Mary Wheeler's collected version of the tune is included in her collection of songs *Roustabout Songs: A Collection of Ohio River Valley Songs:*

Stacker Lee is lookin' fo' de bully, de bully
   cain't be foun',
Now we gonna walk dis levee roun', roun',
Gonna walk dis levee roun',
I'm lookin' fo' de bully of dis town!
I'm lookin' fo' de bully, de bully mus' be foun'!
I'm lookin' fo' de bully boys, to lay de body
   down,
I'm lookin' fo' de bully of dis town!

2 lucky dice
Dice references are plentiful in Grateful Dead lyrics, being part of the overall gambling motif.

"Roll those laughing bones"—"Candyman"
"They say that Cain caught Abel / rolling loaded dice"—
"Mississippi Half-Step Uptown
   Toodeloo"
"Rat cat alley, roll them bones"—"Throwing
   Stones"
"Commissars and pinstripe bosses / Roll the
   dice"—"Throwing Stones"

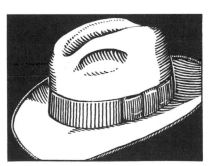

3 Stetson hat
The archetypal Western hat. Patrick Bousquet's article "The Hat of the West: John B. and His Stetson," tells the history of the hat and of its creator, John B. Stetson. Stetson was born in 1830 to a "master hatmaker, Stephen Stetson, of Orange, New Jersey." In about 1850, he invented what is now thought of as the classic Stetson, "a large hat with a broad brim for protection from the sun and rain, and it had a high crown." When he went into production with this hat, he christened it "Boss of the Plains."

Botkin has this story:

THE MAGIC HAT

You see, it happened like this: Stack was crazy about Stetson hats; specially them great big five-gallon hats with dimples in the crown. And he had a whole row of 'em hangin' on pegs, and you could look at em along the wall of his rickety shanty on Market Street, in St. Louis, where he lived with his woman, Stack o' Dollars, that I'm goin to tell you about later.

He had a dimpled and lemon-colored yaller hat, and a black Sunday one with two white eyes to wear to funerals with his new brogans, and lots of other ones, all kinds and colors.

But his favorite one was an oxblood magic hat that folks claim he made from the raw hide of a man-eatin' panther that the devil had skinned alive. And like I told you, how come Stack to have it was because he had sold his soul to old Scratch. You see, Satan heard about Stack's weakness, so he met him that dark night and took him into the grave yard, where he coaxed him into tradin' his soul, promisin him he could do all kinds of magic and devilish things long as he wore that oxblood Stetson and didn't let it get away from him. And that's the way the devil fixed it, so when Stack did lose it he would lose his head, and kill a good citizen, and run right smack into his doom.

Brown, quoting Nathan Young, describes the style of Stetson favored by the St. Louis underworld in 1895:

The hats had "a special high felt crown" but "were not as tall as the regular toppers. They came in colors, seldom black. The brims were slightly rolled with a silk binding. They had to be Stetsons, and no other brand!"

4 Baio, Baio
This name seems to be unique to Hunter's version of the story. However, Brown appears to have spoken with Hunter about the lyric, and he cites the passage as "Bail, Bail," Perhaps Garcia changed the name in his singing, leading Hunter to alter his original name for the song's representative of the law; *bail* could be short for "bailiff," and hence be a nickname relating to the job.

5 gin fizz
Blend:
5 oz gin
5 heaping teaspoons sugar
juice of a lemon
one egg

one tablespoon Cointreau
one teaspoon orange rind or one teaspoon
   orange flower water
Add 4 ice cubes—mix till they're gone
Add equal amount of milk and mix
Serve in chilled glasses. [82]

6 Nearer, my God, to Thee
The title of an old hymn (1859), by Sarah Adams and Lowell Mason, famously played by the ship's band on the *Titanic* as the boat sank.

Nearer, my God, to Thee,
Nearer to Thee!
E'en tho' it be a cross
That raiseth me;
Still all my song shall be—
Nearer, my God, to Thee,
Nearer, my God, to Thee,
Nearer to Thee!

Tho' like the wanderer,
The sun goes down,
Darkness be over me,
My rest a stone;
Yet in my dreams
I'd be nearer, my God, to Thee,
Nearer, my God, to Thee,
Nearer to Thee!

There let my way appear,
Steps unto heaven;
All that Thou sendest me,
In mercy given;
Angels to beckon me
Nearer, my God, to Thee,
Nearer, my God, to Thee,
Nearer to Thee!

Then with my waking thoughts,
Bright with thy praise,
Out of my stony griefs,
Bethel I'll raise;
So by my woes to be,

Nearer, my God, to Thee,
Nearer, my God, to Thee,
Nearer to Thee!

And if on joyful wing,
Cleaving the sky,
Sun, moon, and stars forgot,
Upward I fly;
Still all my song shall be—
Nearer, my God, to Thee,
Nearer, my God, to Thee,
Nearer to Thee!

Notes:

Studio recording: *Shakedown Street* (November 15, 1978).

First performance: August 30, 1978, at Red Rocks Amphitheater in Morrison, Colorado. The song has had a fairly consistent place in the repertoire over the years, disappearing now and then for extended periods.

In Hunter's *A Box of Rain,* the lyric is titled "Delia Delyon and Staggerlee."

If I Had the World to Give

If I had the world to give
I'd give it to you—long as you live
Would you let it fall
or hold it all in your arms?

If I had a song to sing
I'd sing it to you—as long as you live
Lullaby—or maybe a plain serenade
wouldn't you laugh, dance, and cry
or be afraid at the trade you made?

I may not have the world to give to you
but maybe I have a tune or two
Only if you let me be your world
could I ever give this world to you
could I ever give this world to you

But I will give what love I have to give
I will give what love I have to give
I will give what love I have to give
long as I live

If I had a star to give
I'd give it to you—long as you live
Would you have the time
to watch it shine—watch it shine
or ask for the moon and heaven, too?
I'd give it to you

Maybe I've got no star to spare
or anything fine or even rare
Only if you let me be your world
would I ever give this world to you
could I ever give this world to you

Words by Robert Hunter
Music by Jerry Garcia

Notes:
Studio recording: *Shakedown Street* (November 15, 1978).

First performance: August 30, 1978, at Red Rocks Amphitheater in Morrison, Colorado. It was performed only three times in concert, the final performance being November 20, 1978, in Cleveland.

From the Heart of Me

Voices slide down off the mountain
Sunlight turning red
Falls on the earth and it spreads
Even the families lower their head

As they ride
Age-old faces of the mountains
Looming naturally
I wonder if they're looking at me
Their monumental eyes I can feel
And the glow in the twilight
The dawn of hope
Reminds me
Now I'm reaching out to you
Anything I can do
To be safe and warm
In your arms
All I have is the heart of you

I'd meet you anywhere in the country
Or anywhere on the sea
All over the world it could be
I would follow you
With the heart of me

Love calls echo in the valley
Dream come true tonight
Remembering you hold me tight
In tomorrow morning's light
I will find you
When I awoke the stars were out
And shining, shining for you and me
All I ever want to be
Safe and warm
In your arms
All I have from the heart of me

Words and music by Donna Godchaux

Notes:
Studio recording: *Shakedown Street* (November 15, 1978).

First performance: August 31, 1978, at Red Rocks Amphitheater in Morrison, Colorado.

shakedown street

1 you can never tell
Reminiscent of the Chuck Berry tune "C'est la Vie (You Never Can Tell)"

2 sunny side of the street
"On the Sunny Side of the Street" is a song by Jimmy McHugh (1894–1969) with words by Dorothy Fields. Wilder's *American Popular Song* has this to say about the tune:

> One of [McHugh's] earliest and best-known songs is "On the Sunny Side of the Street," from *Lew Leslie's International Revue* (1930). It's one of the jazz musicians' favorites, having precisely the springboard from which they love to leap. Singers, as well, love it as much for its extremely fine lyric, by Dorothy Fields, as for its music. 83

Notes:
Studio recording: *Shakedown Street* (November 15, 1978).

First performance: August 31, 1978, at Red Rocks Amphitheater, Morrison, Colorado. It remained in the repertoire thereafter.

You tell me this town ain't got no heart
(Well, well, well—you can never tell)   1
The sunny side of the street is dark   2
(Well, well, well—you can never tell)
Maybe that's 'cause it's midnight
and the dark of the moon besides, or
maybe the dark is in your eyes
maybe the dark is in your eyes
maybe the dark is in your eyes
You know you got such dark eyes

Nothin' shakin' on Shakedown Street
used to be the heart of town
Don't tell me this town ain't got no heart
You just gotta poke around

You say you've seen this town clear through
(Well, well, well—you can never tell)
Nothin' here that could interest you
(Well, well, well—you can never tell)
It's not because you missed out
on the thing we had to start
Maybe you had too much too fast
Maybe you had too much too fast
Maybe you had too much too fast
and just overplayed your part

Nothin' shakin' on Shakedown Street
used to be the heart of town
Don't tell me this town ain't got no heart
You just gotta poke around

Since I'm passing your way today
(Well, well, well—you can never tell)
I just stopped in cause I want to say
(Well, well, well—you can never tell)
I recall your darkness
when it crackled like a thunder cloud
don't tell me this town ain't got no heart
don't tell me this town ain't got no heart

don't tell me this town ain't got no heart
when I can hear it *beat out loud*

Nothin' shakin' on Shakedown Street
used to be the heart of town
Don't tell me this town ain't got no heart
You just gotta poke around

Words by Robert Hunter
Music by Jerry Garcia

- warzone -

France

Way down in the south of France
All the ladies love to dance
Kick their heels up in the air
Snap their fingers for romance
While the gentlemen compare
Blond or black or auburn hair
Check the motion and the style
Ah, you know they take their while

To make the motion more complete
Just to make it more a treat
Love will show us where to go
Come on down and see the show
When the rhythm's really right

You can burn it down tonight
When the singing's really fine
Sweet as Spanish sherry wine

When the club can't contain the beat
It just rolls out in the street
Spills on down the avenue
Bringing dancers to their feet
When it's good as it can be
It gets better, wait and see
These folks don't never sleep
Till they're passed out in the street

Way down in the south of France
All the ladies love to dance
Clap their hands and walk on air
Yeah, the feeling's really there
Won't you take a little taste
Raise it to your charming face?
When the rhythm's really right
You can burn it down tonight

When the singing's really fine
Sweet as Spanish sherry wine
Go on, take a chance
The ladies *do* love to dance

Words by Robert Hunter
Music by Bob Weir and Mickey Hart

Notes:
Studio recording: *Shakedown Street* (November 15, 1978). Never performed live.

In *A Box of Rain,* Hunter published nine additional verses to "France" and wrote an explanatory note about its origins, as the words written to "tapes of a joyous afternoon Latin jam at Mickey Hart's ranch."

ALThea

1 I told Althea I was feeling lost
Lacking in some direction
Althea told me upon scrutiny
my back might need protection

I told Althea that treachery
was tearing me limb from limb
Althea told me: Now cool down boy—
2 settle back easy, Jim

3 You may be Saturday's child all grown
moving with a pinch of grace
4 You may be a clown in the burying ground
or just another pretty face
5 You may be the fate of Ophelia
6 sleeping and perchance to dream—
honest to the point of recklessness
self-centered to the extreme

Ain't nobody messing with you but you
your friends are getting most concerned—
loose with the truth
maybe it's your fire
but baby . . . don't get burned

When the smoke has cleared, she said,
that's what she said to me:
You're gonna want a bed to lay your head
and a little sympathy

1 Althea
Name by which Richard Lovelace (1618–1658)
poetically addressed a woman supposed to have
been Lucy Sacheverell, whom he also celebrated
by the name of Lucasta. *(New Century Cyclopedia
of Names)*

Lovelace's poem "To Althea from Prison" (1649):

When Love with unconfined wings
Hovers within my Gates;
And my divine Althea brings
To whisper at the Grates:
When I lye tangled in her haire,
And fetter'd to her eye;
The Birds, that wanton in the Aire,
Know no such Liberty.

When flowing Cups run swiftly round
With no allaying Thames,
Our carelesse heads with Roses bound,
Our hearts with Loyall Flames;
When thirsty griefe in Wine we steepe,
When Healths and draughts go free,
Fishes that tipple in the Deepe,
Know no such Libertie.

When (like committed Linnets) I
With shriller throat shall sing
The sweetness, Mercy, Majesty,
And glories of my KING;
When I shall voyce aloud, how Good
He is, how Great should be;
Inlarged Winds that curle the Flood,
Know no such Liberty.
Stone Walls doe not a Prison make,
Nor Iron bars a Cage;
Mindes innocent and quiet take
That for an Hermitage;
If I have freedome in my Love,
And in my soule am free;

Angels alone that soar above,
Injoy such Liberty.

This is the second name in a Hunter song that has been used as a pseudonymous form of address by a poet addressing a real-life woman; the other is "Stella," used by Jonathan Swift as his poetic name for Esther Johnson, as well as by Philip Sidney, in his sonnet series "Astrophel and Stella," in addressing Lady Penelope Devereux.

The meaning and derivation of the word *althea,* according to *The Oxford English Dictionary:*
> *Bot.* [L. *althaea,* a marsh mallow, f. [the Greek] to heal.] A genus of the plants of which the Marsh Mallow and Hollyhock are species; by florists often extended to the genus *Hibiscus.*

In Greek mythology, Althea was the mother of Meleager. From *Bulfinch's Mythology* (1913):
> One of the heroes of the Argonautic expedition was Meleager, son of Œneus and Althea, king and queen of Calydon. Althea, when her son was born, beheld the three destinies, who, as they spun their fatal thread, foretold that the life of the child should last no longer than a brand then burning upon the hearth. Althea seized and quenched the brand, and carefully preserved it for years, while Meleager grew to boyhood, youth, and manhood. It chanced, then, that Œneus, as he offered sacrifices to the gods, omitted to pay due honors to Diana; and she, indignant at the neglect, sent a wild boar of enormous size to lay waste the fields of Calydon. Its eyes shone with blood and fire, its bristles stood like threatening spears, its tusks were like those of Indian elephants. The growing corn was trampled, the vines and olive trees laid waste, the flocks and herds were driven in wild confusion by the slaughtering

There are things you can replace
and others you cannot
The time has come to weigh those things
this space is getting hot—
you know this space is getting hot

I told Althea
I'm a roving sign—
that I was born to be a bachelor—
Althea told me: Okay, that's fine—
So now I'm trying to catch her

Can't talk to you without talking to me
We're guilty of the same old thing
Talking a lot about less and less
And forgetting the love we bring

Words by Robert Hunter
Music by Jerry Garcia

7

foe. All common aid seemed vain; but Meleager called on the heroes of Greece to join in a bold hunt for the ravenous monster. Theseus and his friend Pirithous, Jason, Peleus, afterwards the father of Achilles, Telamon the father of Ajax, Nestor, then a youth, but who in his age bore arms with Achilles and Ajax in the Trojan war,—these and many more joined in the enterprise. With them came Atalanta, the daughter of Iasius, king of Arcadia. A buckle of polished gold confined her vest, an ivory quiver hung on her left shoulder, and her left hand bore the bow. Her face blent feminine beauty with the best graces of martial youth. Meleager saw and loved.

But now already they were near the monster's lair. They stretched strong nets from tree to tree; they uncoupled their dogs, they tried to find the footprints of their quarry in the grass. From the wood was a descent to marshy ground. Here the boar, as he lay among the reeds, heard the shouts of his pursuers, and rushed forth against them. One and another is thrown down and slain. Jason throws his spear, with a prayer to Diana for success; and the favoring goddess allows the weapon to touch, but not to wound, removing the steel point of the spear in its flight. Nestor, assailed, seeks and finds safety in the branches of a tree. Telamon rushes on, but stumbling at a projecting root, falls prone. But an arrow from Atalanta at length for the first time tastes the monster's blood. It is a slight wound, but Meleager sees and joyfully proclaims it. Anceus, excited to envy by the praise given to a female, loudly proclaims his own valor, and defies alike the boar and the goddess who had sent it; but as he rushes on, the infuriated beast lays him low with a mortal wound. Theseus throws his lance, but it is turned aside by a projecting bough. The dart of Jason misses its object, and kills instead one of their own dogs. But Meleager, after one unsuccessful stroke, drives his spear into the monster's side, then rushes on and despatches him with repeated blows.

Then rose a shout from those around; they congratulated the conqueror, crowding to touch his hand. He, placing his foot upon the head of the slain boar, turned to Atalanta and bestowed on her the head and the rough hide which were the trophies of his success. But at this, envy excited the rest to strife. Plexippus and Toxeus, the brothers of Meleager's mother, beyond the rest opposed the gift, and snatched from the maiden the trophy she had received. Meleager, kindling with rage at the wrong done to himself, and still more at the insult offered to her whom he loved, forgot the claims of kindred, and plunged his sword into the offenders' hearts.

As Althea bore gifts of thankfulness to the temples for the victory of her son, the bodies of her murdered brothers met her sight. She shrieks, and beats her breast, and hastens to change the garments of rejoicing for those of mourning. But when the author of the deed is known, grief gives way to the stern desire of vengeance on her son. The fatal brand, which once she rescued from the flames, the brand which the destinies had linked with Meleager's life, she brings forth, and commands a fire to be prepared. Then four times she essays to place the brand upon the pile; four times draws back, shuddering at the thought of bringing destruction on her son. The feelings of the mother and the sister contend within her. Now she is pale at the thought of the proposed deed, now flushed again with anger at the act of her son. As a vessel, driven in one direction by the wind, and in the opposite by the tide, the mind of Althea hangs suspended in uncertainty. But now the sister prevails above the mother, and she begins as she holds the fatal wood: "Turn, ye Furies, goddesses of punishment! turn to behold the sacrifice I bring! Crime must atone for crime. Shall Œneus rejoice in his victor son, while the house of Thestius is desolate? But, alas! to what deed am I borne along? Brothers forgive a mother's weakness! my hand fails me. He deserves death, but not that I should destroy him. But shall he then live, and triumph, and reign over Calydon, while you, my brothers, wander unavenged among the shades? No! thou hast lived by my gift; die, now, for thine own crime. Return the life which twice I gave thee, first at thy birth, again when I snatched this brand from the flames. O that thou hadst then died! Alas! evil is the conquest; but, brothers, ye have conquered." And, turning away her face, she threw the fatal wood upon the burning pile.

It gave, or seemed to give, a deadly groan. Meleager, absent and unknowing of the cause, felt a sudden pang. He burns, and only by courageous pride conquers the pain which destroys him. He mourns only that he perishes by a bloodless and unhonored death. With his last breath he calls upon his aged father, his brother, and his fond sisters, upon his beloved Atalanta, and upon his mother, the unknown cause of his fate. The flames increase, and with them the pain of the hero. Now both subside; now both are quenched. The brand is ashes, and the life of Meleager is breathed forth to the wandering winds.

Althea, when the deed was done, laid violent hands upon herself. The sisters of Meleager mourned their brother with uncontrollable grief; till Diana, pitying the sorrows of the house that once had aroused her anger, turned them into birds.

2 easy, Jim

Jim n. (1940s–1950s) term of address to a male. (Major)

From Miles Davis's autobiography, *Miles* (1989):

But Dexter didn't think my dress style was all that hip. So he used to always tell me, "Jim" ("Jim" was an expression a lot of musicians used back then), "you can't hang with us looking and dressing like that. Why don't you wear some other shit, Jim? You gotta get some vines. You got to go to F&M's," which was a clothing store on Broadway in midtown.

3 Saturday's child

The proverbial rhyme goes:

Monday's child is fair of face,
Tuesday's child is full of grace,
Wednesday's child is full of woe,
Thursday's child has far to go,
Friday's child is loving and giving,
Saturday's child works hard for its living,
And a child that's born on the Sabbath day
Is fair and wise and good and gay.

Also the title of a song recorded by the Monkees, written by David Gates.

4 clown in the burying ground

The first of three references in the song to Shakespeare's *Hamlet,* this line is apparently in reference to a pair of minor characters, listed as First Clown and Other, or as First Gravedigger and Other, the undertakers in the play, who do serve the purpose of providing comic relief in the midst of tragedy. It has also been suggested that the phrase might refer to Yorick himself, as the "clown." Hamlet finds Yorick's skull in an open grave (which turns out to be for Ophelia) and laments over the death of his friend, the former court jester (i.e., clown). His speech concludes with the passage that includes the lines "There are more things in heaven and earth, Horatio, / Than are dreamt of in your philosophy."

5 Ophelia
In Shakespeare's *Hamlet,* the daughter of Polonius. She loses her mind after Polonius's death.

6 sleeping and perchance to dream
    Compare *Hamlet* (iii, 1, 65), from Hamlet's "To be or not to be" soliloquy: "To sleep, perchance to dream. . . ."

7 Can't talk to you without talking to me
"Hunter wrote: Can't talk to me without talking to you."

Notes:
Studio recording: *Go to Heaven* (April 28, 1980).

First performance: August 4, 1979, at the Oakland Auditorium Arena in Oakland, California. It remained in the repertoire thereafter.

Hunter and Garcia discuss "Althea":

Garcia: [To Hunter] What is she—the anima? The helpful lady, big sister kind of . . .

Hunter: I don't know if it's the anima, I'm not a Jungian.

Garcia: Me neither. [*Laughs*] I don't know. I see her out there.

Hunter: You evoke her; you don't say what she is.

Garcia: She's beyond description.

Hunter: Minerva.

Garcia: Right. Your helpful god-woman.

Hunter: Or Athena. Sure.

(Jackson, *Goin' Down the Road*) 84

LOST Sailor

1 Compass card
Mariner's compass in the form of a card that rotates so that 0 degrees, or north, points to magnetic north.

2 dog star
The star is Sirius, often used as a navigational aid by sailors because of its brightness.

The line has frequently been misconstrued as "Where's the Dark Star?" There's even an entry for this in *Skeleton Key,* which serves as an opening for a mini-essay, with examples, of the wonderful opportunities for mis-hearing the words of Grateful Dead songs.

Compass card is spinning   1
Helm is swingin' to and fro
Ooh, where's the dog star?   2
Ooh, where's the moon?
You're a lost sailor
You've been too long at sea

Some days the gales are howling
Some days the sea is still as glass
Ooh, reef the mainsail
Ooh, lash the mast
You're a lost sailor

You've been too long at sea

Now the shore lights beckon
Yeah there's a price for being free

Yeah the sea birds cry
There's a ghost wind blowin'
It's calling you to that misty swirling sea
Till the chains of your dreams are broken
No place in this world you can be

You're a lost sailor
You've been way too long at sea
Now the shore lights beckon
Yeah there's a price for being free

3   Drifting yeah drifting
Yeah drifting and dreaming

'Cause there's a place you've never been
Maybe a place you've never seen
You can hear her calling on the wind
Go on and drift your life away
Yeah just drifting and dreaming
Maybe drift your life away
Drifting and dreaming
Yes I'm going on a dream
Maybe going on a dream
Maybe going on a dream
Maybe going on a dream

*[The end is largely improvised. An example
of a variation:]*

3 **drifting and dreaming**
The title of a song: "Drifting and Dreaming
(Sweet Paradise) (A Hawaiian Love Song)" (1925)
words by Haven Gillespie; music by Egbert van
Alstyne, Erwin R. Schmidt, and Loyal Curtis. I will
spare you a complete quote of the text, which is
of the "Moon, June, spoon" variety. Another
song was titled "Dreaming and Drifting" (1877),
words by Arthur W. French, music by C. M. Pyke.

4 **Freedom from and freedom to**
Another common distinction made between
kinds of freedom is the difference between
"freedom from" social and political ills (which,
some argue, is really more accurately
described as safety or security) and "freedom
to" do what one wants (for which some consider the term *liberty* more precise). *(Wikipedia:
The Free Encyclopedia)*

Notes:
Written in Mill Valley, California, July 1979.

Studio recording: *Go to Heaven* (April 28, 1980).

First performance: August 4, 1979, at the
Oakland Coliseum Arena in Oakland, California.
It remained in the repertoire through the early
part of 1986, then disappeared.

Every day you got to pay
Some more time you got to pay
Two kinds of freedom
4 Freedom from and freedom to be
One you may know where you're going
Or maybe you're just drifting to the sea
Drifting and dreaming

Is this a place you've never seen?
Maybe a voice you've never heard or a face
you've never seen
But you can hear them calling on the way to
    [hell?]
Drifting and dreaming

Words by John Barlow
Music by Bob Weir

easy to love you

Good, good morning, so good to see you
You weren't just a dream of mine
1 Real as a raven, real as thunder
Real as the sun shining
But still so very hard to find
I can't imagine what's behind those sleepy eyes

Little stranger, don't try to hide now
You look so young and you're afraid
There is no danger but from the devil
And he may want you but I'm in his way
You don't know how easy it is
You don't know how easy it is to love you

And come the moonrise, when the dew falls
Don't be the sun that fades away
Don't leave me darkness, she is no lover
She hides the day
You don't know how easy it is
You don't know how easy it is to love you

Words by John Barlow
Music by Brent Mydland

1 Real as a raven

Arista Records president Clive Davis lobbied for a change from the original "real as a bluebird." He complained about Brent's lyrics—thought they weren't 'Grateful Dead' enough.

Notes:
Studio recording: *Go to Heaven* (April 28, 1980).

First performance: August 14, 1979, at the McNichols Sports Arena in Denver. It remained in steady rotation through 1980, then dropped away for a decade, reappearing in 1990 for a number of performances.

saint of circumstance

1 sirens
In Greek mythology, the sirens were sea nymphs, luring unsuspecting sailors, with music,
to their deaths. Eventually, Orpheus (see "Reuben and Cerise") triumphed over them by playing more sweetly, and they were turned into a group of rocks in the Mediterranean.

2 Dog Star
Sirius. Compare the line in "Saint of Circumstance"'s companion song, "Lost Sailor": "Where's the Dog Star?"

3 tiger in a trance
The title of a 2003 novel by Max Ludington, about a Deadhead ca. 1985.

Notes:

Written in Mill Valley, California, July 1979.

Studio recording: *Go to Heaven* (April 28, 1980).

First performance: August 31, 1979, at Glens Falls Civic Center, Glens Falls, New York.

The song title was used, at Steve Silberman's suggestion, as the title of Sheila Weller's 1997 book, *Saint of Circumstance: The Untold Story Behind the Alex Kelley Rape Case: Growing Up Rich and Out of Control.*

This must be heaven—
Tonight I crossed the line
You must be the angel
I thought I might never find
Was it you I heard singin'
While I was chasin' dreams?
Driven by the wind
Like the dust that blows around
And the rain fallin' down . . .

But I never know,
(Sure don't know)
Never know
Never know
(Sure don't know)

This must be heaven—
'Cause here's where the rainbow ends
At last it's the real thing . . .
Or close enought to pretend
When that wind blows
When the night's about to fall
I can hear the sirens call   1
It's a certain sort of sound
In the rain fallin' down
Rain fallin' down . . .
Rain fallin' down . . .
Rain fallin' down . . .
Rain fallin' down . . .

Holes in what's left of my reason
Holes in the knees of my blues,

Odds against me been increasin'
But I'll pull through

Never could read no road map
And I don't know what the weather
    might do
But hear that witch wind whinin'
See that dog star shinin'
I've got a feelin' there's no time to lose
No time to lose!

Maybe goin' on a feelin' maybe goin' on
    a dream
Maybe goin' on a feelin'

Well I never know
(Sure don't know)
Never know
Never know
(Sure don't know)

Well it's been heaven
But even rainbows end
Now my sails are fillin'
And the wind's so willin'
That I'm good as gone again

I'm still walkin', so I'm sure that I can
    dance
Just a saint of circumstance
Just a tiger in a trance
In the rain fallin down

Rain fallin' down . . .
Rain fallin' down . . .
Rain fallin' down . . .
Rain fallin' down . . .

Well I never know, just don't know, just
    don't know

Sure don't know
What I'm goin' for
But I'm gonna go for it
For sure

Maybe goin' on a feelin'
Maybe goin' on a dream
Maybe goin' on a feelin'

Words by John Barlow
Music by Bob Weir

Alabama Getaway

This number includes the wisdom teeth.

2 Alabama
The name seems to be used here as both a personal name and the name of the state—see the line "Forty-nine sister states / Had Alabama in their eyes." This is reminiscent of the line in Neil Young's song "Alabama": "You've got the rest of the Union to help you along." This song provoked the wonderful response from Lynyrd Skynyrd in "Sweet Home Alabama," in which the band tells off Neil Young:

> Well, I hope Neil Young will remember
> A Southern man don't need him around any
> how.

3 Billy Bojangles
Bill "Bojangles" Robinson, May 25, 1878–November 25, 1949. Excerpts from his entry in *The Dictionary of American Biography:*

> The publicity that gradually came to surround him included the creation of his famous "stair dance," his successful gambling exploits, his prodigious charity, his ability to run backward at great speed and to consume ice cream by the quart, his argot—most notably the neologism *copacetic* [used so nicely in "West L.A. Fadeaway"]—and such stunts as dancing down Broadway in 1939 from Columbus Circle to 44th Street in celebration of his sixty-first birthday.
> . . . blacks and whites developed differing opinions of him. To whites, for example, his nickname "Bojangles" meant happy-go-lucky, while

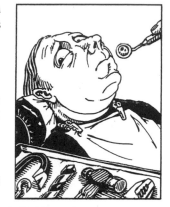

Thirty-two teeth in a jawbone   1
Alabama's tryin' for none   2
Before I have to hit him
I hope he's got the sense to run

Reason the poor girls love him
Promise them everything
Why they all believe him?
He wears a big diamond ring

Alabama getaway, getaway
Alabama getaway, getaway
Only way to please me
Just get down and leave and walk away

Majordomo Billy Bojangles   3
Sat down and had a drink with me
Said what about Alabama
That keeps a-coming back to me?

I heard your plea in the courthouse
Witness box began to rock and rise
Forty-nine sister states
Had Alabama in their eyes

Alabama getaway, getaway
Alabama getaway, getaway
Only way to please me
Just get down and leave and walk away

Major said why don't we give him
Rope enough to hang himself?
No need to worry the jury
They'll probably take care of themselves

4   Twenty-third Psalm Majordomo
Reserve me a table for three
Down in the Valley of the Shadow
Just you, Alabama and me

Alabama getaway, getaway
Alabama getaway, getaway
Only way to please me
Just get down and leave and walk away

Words by Robert Hunter
Music by Jerry Garcia

the black variety artist Tom Fletcher claimed it
was slang for "squabbler."

   Robinson died of a chronic heart condition,
. . . His body lay in state at an armory in
Harlem, schools were closed, thousands lined
the streets waiting for a glimpse of his bier,
and he was eulogized by politicians, black and
white—perhaps more lavishly than any other
Afro-American of his time. [85]

The line that refers to "Majordomo Billy
Bojangles" may be alluding to the role Robinson
often played in films, as the head of staff for
antebellum estates, particularly in Shirley Temple
movies.

Many of us know the name from the famed
1968 song by Jerry Jeff Walker, "Mr. BoJangles."

Jerry Garcia's namesake, Jerome Kern, also wrote
a song, with Dorothy Fields, titled "Bojangles of
Harlem," for the 1936 Fred Astaire movie, *Swing
Time.* (Dennis McNally's *A Long Strange Trip* veri-
fies that Garcia was named for the composer, a
favorite of his mother's.)

**4 Twenty-third Psalm, and Valley of the
Shadow**
Two references to the Twenty-third Psalm. See
note under "Ripple."

Also compare "John Silver," from Hunter's *Eagle
Mall Suite:* "Through the Valley of the Shadow
ran he."

Notes:
Studio recording: *Go to Heaven* (April 28, 1980).

First performance: November 4, 1979, at the
Civic Center in Providence, Rhode Island. It
remained in the repertoire through June 1989,
then revived in 1995 for several shows.

far from me

1 close your eyes to see
Reminiscent of the line in "Attics of My Life":
"And closed my eyes to see."

Notes:
Studio recording: *Go to Heaven* (April 28, 1980).

First performance: March 30, 1980, at the
Capitol Theater in Passaic, New Jersey. It
appeared in a fairly regular rotation in the live
repertoire until Mydland's death.

You say you want to try again
Wear it down between the lines
Well I have a better end in mind
It doesn't seem you really have to close your
    eyes to see   1
Though I know you don't mean to be
You are so far from me

There was something I had caught inside
Screaming hard to make it known
In time it died alone
It doesn't seem you really have to close your
    eyes to see
You have been all you'll be to me
It's just too late; and we can't relate at all

It doesn't seem you really have to close your
    eyes to see
Though I know you don't mean to be
You are so far from me

This time's the last time I want to say so long
This song's my last song for you
There's nothing here to hold on to
Nothing to hold on to

Words and music by Brent Mydland

Feel Like a Stranger

Inside you're burning
I can see clear through
Your eyes tell more than you mean
  them to
Lit up and flashing
Like the reds and blues
Out there on the neon avenue

But I feel like a stranger
Feel like a stranger

Well the music's thundering
We're restless and hot
You keep firing glances across the room

And I can't stop wondering
Just what you got
Get the feeling I'm gonna find out real
  soon

Still I feel like a stranger
Feel like a stranger

Well you know it's gonna get stranger
So let's get on with the show

Yes and the wheel
Gets smoking 'round midnight
You shoot me a look that says let's go

Yes and it feels
Just like running a red light
There ain't no point in looking behind us, no

Still I feel like a stranger
Feel like a stranger
You know it keeps getting stranger and stranger
If it's love then how would I know?

Yes and it's gonna get stranger
Some things you just know

If this were love then how would I know?
(Feel like a stranger)
(Feel like a stranger)
(Feel like a stranger)
(Feel like a stranger)
It's gonna be a long hot crazy night
It's gonna be a long long crazy crazy night
Yeah crazy night
Silky silky, crazy crazy night

Words by John Barlow
Music by Bob Weir

Notes:
Written in Mill Valley, California, January 1980.

Studio recording: *Go to Heaven* (April 28, 1980).

First performance: March 31, 1980, at the Capitol Theater in Passaic, New Jersey. It remained in the repertoire thereafter.

never trust a woman

Gonna see some good times
Gonna get to ring that bell
Gonna see some good times
Some times to make up for when I'm not
    feeling well
I must be due some great times
'Cause right now I feel like hell

Never trust a woman who wears her pants
    too tight
Never trust a woman who wears her pants
    too tight
She might love you tomorrow
But she'll be gone tomorrow night

Come tomorrow I get my pay and I'm gonna
    leave this town
Come tomorrow I get my pay and I'm gonna
    leave this goddamn town
'Cause she don't really love me

There ain't no reason to stick around

Gonna see some good times
Gonna get to ring that bell
Gonna see some good times
Some times to make up for when I'm not
    feeling well
Must be due some great times
'Cause right now I feel like hell

[ad-lib]
But if they don't come
Well if they never come around
If they don't come to me
If they don't come to me tonight
If they don't come to me next week
If they don't come to me next year
What the hell

Words and music by Brent Mydland

Notes:
Recording: *Dozin' at the Knick* (October 1996).

First performance: August 28, 1981, at the Long
Beach Arena in Long Beach, California.

The song is often referred to as "Good Times."

keep your day job

Maybe you collect or maybe you pay
Still got to work that eight-hour day
Whether you like that job or not
Keep it on ice while you're
1 Lining up your long shot
Which is to say
hey-ey

Chorus:
Keep your day job
Don't give it away
Keep your day job
Whatever they say

Ring that bell for whatever it's worth
When Monday comes don't forget about work
By now you know that the face on your dollar
Got a thumb to its nose and a
Hand on your collar
Which is to say
hey-ey

(Chorus)

Punch that time card
Check that clock
When Monday comes
You gotta run, run, run
Not walk

1 Lining up your long shot
From the pool/billiards argot. Compare line in "Here Comes Sunshine": "Line up a long shot. . . ."

2 V-8 'Vette
The first two years of production of the Chevrolet Corvette, beginning in 1953, resulted in a beautiful car but one without sufficient power. According to James Schefter:

Zora Arkus-Duntov fixed it. . . . He immediately put a V-8 into 1955 Corvettes. Only seven hundred cars were built in 1955, but they sold. Arkus-Duntov went on to become Corvette's first chief engineer.

The engine was a 210-horsepower machine, and the 1956 Corvette was the first American car to reach the 150-mile-per-hour mark at Daytona. The car had its trademark V-8 engine until 1990, when a V-6 model was introduced.
   The horsepower of the Corvette's V-8 engine ramped up gradually from the initial 195-horsepower machine, in 1955, until it peaked, in 1967, with the optional 435 horsepower engine.

3 God bless the child
Compare the Billie Holiday song "God Bless the Child" (A. Herzog Jr./Billie Holiday).

Notes:

First performance: August 28, 1982, at the Oregon Country Fair Site, Veneta, Oregon (the second "Field Trip" with Ken Kesey and the Merry Pranksters).

No studio recording.

Hunter, in his *A Box of Rain,* notes that "this song was dropped from the Grateful Dead repertoire at the request of fans. Seriously."

(Chorus)

Steady, boy, study that eight-day hour
But don't underrate that paycheck power
If you ask me, which I know you don't,
I'd tell you to do what I know you won't
Which is to say
Hey-ey

(Chorus)

Daddy may drive a V-8 'Vette   2
Mama may bathe in champagne yet
God bless the child with his own stash   3
Nine to five and a place to crash
Which is to say . . .

Keep your day job
Don't give it away
Keep your day job
Whatever they say
Keep your day job
Until your night job pays

Words by Robert Hunter
Music by Jerry Garcia

WEST L.A. FADEAWAY

1 Looking for a château
Twenty-one rooms but one will do
Looking for a château
Twenty-one rooms but one will do
I don't want to buy it
I just want to rent it for an hour or two

I met an old mistake
Walking down the street today
I met an old mistake
Walking down the street today
I didn't want to be mean about it
But I didn't have one good word to say

West L.A. fadeaway
West L.A. fadeaway
Little red light on the highway
Big green light on the speedway, hey, hey, hey

I had a steady job
Hauling items for the mob
I had a steady job
Hauling items for the mob
Y'know the pay was pathetic
It's a shame those boys couldn't be more
2   copacetic

I meet a West L.A. girl
Already know what I need to know
I meet a West L.A. girl
I already know what I need to know
Name, address, and phone number
Lord, and just how far to go

1 chateau
A reference to the Chateau Marmont, the hotel
on Sunset Strip in Los Angeles, where John
Belushi died on March 5, 1982. The entire song
could be taken as being about Belushi's death,
but as usual, Hunter throws in some curveballs,
skewing the character of the song so that it
becomes someone else.

2 copacetic
A word coined by Bill "Bojangles" Robinson, the
famous dancer (mentioned in "Alabama
Getaway"); its meaning is, roughly, "cool."

Notes:
Studio recording: *In The Dark* (July 6, 1987).

First performance: August 28, 1982, at the
Oregon Country Fair Site in Veneta, Oregon. The
song remained in steady rotation thereafter.

Early performances of the song included this
verse:

> Here's what Ginger says, she talks like she ain't
>   nobody's fool
> Here's what Ginger says, she tries to live by
>   the golden rule
> She says you treat people all right,
> other people will probably treat you cool

West L.A. Fadeaway
West L.A. Fadeaway
Little red light on the highway
Big green light on the speedway, hey, hey, hey

Looking for a château
Twenty-one rooms but one will do
Looking for a château
Twenty-one rooms but one will do
I don't want to rent it
I just want to use it for a minute or two

West L.A. Fadeaway
West L.A. Fadeaway
Little red light on the highway
Big green light on the speedway, hey, hey, hey

Words by Robert Hunter
Music by Jerry Garcia

touch of grey

Must be getting early
Clocks are running late
Paint-by-number morning sky
Looks so phony

Dawn is breaking everywhere
1   Light a candle, curse the glare
Draw the curtains
I don't care 'cause
It's all right

I will get by / I will get by
I will get by / I will survive

I see you've got your list out
Say your piece and get out
Yes, I get the gist of it
but it's all right

Sorry that you feel that way
The only thing there is to say
Every silver lining's got a
2   Touch of grey

I will get by / I will get by
I will get by / I will survive

It's a lesson to me
3   The Ables and the Bakers and the Cs
The ABCs we all must face
And try to keep a little grace

1 light a candle, curse the glare
Hunter notes in *A Box of Rain* that this line was by Garcia.

It is a play on the saying, coined by Adlai Stevenson in 1962 in reference to the death of Eleanor Roosevelt, that "She would rather light a candle than curse the darkness."
   The line also provides a nice resonance with, and may be the source of, the album's title, *In the Dark.*

2 Every silver lining's got a / Touch of grey
A play on the saying "Every cloud has a silver lining."

The earliest usage of the concept in literature is from John Milton's 1631 poem "Il Penseroso"

> Was I deceiv'd or did a sable cloud
> Turn forth her silver lining on the night?

Used in the 1915 song "Keep the Home Fires Burning," words by Lena Guilbert Ford, music (and the song's first line) by Ivor Novello:

> Keep the home fires burning,
> While your hearts are yearning;
> Though your lads are far away
> They dream of home.
> There's a silver lining
> Through the dark cloud shining;
> Turn the dark cloud inside out,
> Till the boys come home.

This saying was also the basis for the 1920 song "Look for the Silver Lining," with words by P. G. Wodehouse and Buddy G. de Sylva and music by Garcia's namesake, Jerome Kern.

> So always look for the silver lining
> And try to find the sunny side of life

3 The Ables and the Bakers and the Cs

Able and *Baker* are the first two words in the military communication alphabet, used to make spelling more intelligible over radio communications devices. So they are literally "ABCs." Here's a table comparing the old and new standard phonetic alphabets. The new one is used by the International Civil

	Old Military	New International		Old Military	New International
A	Able	Alfa	N	Nan	November
B	Baker	Bravo	O	Oboe	Oscar
C	Charlie	Charlie	P	Peter	Papa
D	Dog	Delta	Q	Queen	Quebec
E	Easy	Echo	R	Roger	Romeo
F	Fox	Foxtrot	S	Sugar	Sierra
G	George	Gold	T	Tare	Tango
H	How	Hotel	U	Uncle	Uniform
I	Item	India	V	Victor	Victor
J	Jig	Juliet	W	William	Whiskey
K	King	Kilo	X	X-ray	X-ray
L	Love	Lima	Y	Yoke	Yankee
M	Mike	Mike	Z	Zebra	Zulu

It's a lesson to me
The Deltas and the East and the Freeze
The ABCs we all think of
Try to give a little love.

I know the rent is in arrears
The dog has not been fed in years
It's even worse than it appears
but it's all right

The cow is giving kerosene
Kid can't read at seventeen
The words he knows are all obscene
but it's all right

I will get by / I will get by
I will get by / I will survive

The shoe is on the hand it fits   4
There's really nothing much to it
Whistle through your teeth and spit
'cause it's all right

Oh well a touch of grey
Kind of suits you anyway
That was all I had to say
It's all right

I will get by / I will get by
I will get by / I will survive
We will get by / We will get by
We will get by / We will survive

Words by Robert Hunter
Music by Jerry Garcia

Aviation Organization, a U.N. agency. (Note that "Delta," from the song's next bridge, is the only other easily identifiable alphabet letter.)

Interestingly, there are two streets in Palo Alto (the Grateful Dead's original home base), named Abel and Baker. According to the Palo Alto Historical Association's website, "Abel Avenue was named soon after World War II; *Abel* was the first letter of the military phonetic alphabet in use at that time. The next street, Baker, the second letter of the military phonetic alphabet, was named for the property owners, Linda and Clark Baker, who bought the land from George and Georgia Reed." Note that the street name is spelled "Abel" as in "Cain and Abel," but seems to have been named for the military alphabet nonetheless.

Able and Baker were also the names of two pioneering animal astronauts—monkeys. They were launched into space on May 28, 1959, in the nose cone of Jupiter Missile AM-18. They reached an altitude of three hundred miles and a distance of fifteen hundred miles while traveling at speeds over ten thousand miles per hour on their brief trip into space. This mission marked the first successful recovery of living beings after their return from space. Able was a seven-pound rhesus monkey; Baker an eleven-ounce squirrel monkey.

4 The shoe is on the hand it fits
A play on the saying "If the shoe fits, wear it." See note under "If the Shoe Fits."

Notes:
Studio recording: *In the Dark* (July 6, 1987). The song became the Grateful Dead's first top-ten hit, and propelled the band into the spotlight.

First performance: September 15, 1982, at the Capital Center, Landover, Maryland.

throwing stones

1 ashes, ashes, all fall down
From the nursery rhyme "Ring a ring a rosie."
Also echoed in two other Dead tunes: "Doin'
That Rag" (q.v. for a full note) and "Till the
Morning Comes."

2 jones
From *The Oxford English Dictionary:*

> Jones . . . 2. *slang.* A drug addict's habit. 1968
> *Sun Mag.* (Baltimore) 13 Oct. 19/4 Soon
> you're out to keep from getting the Jones.
> 1970 C. MAJOR *Dict. Afro-Amer. Slang* 71 *Jones,*
> a fixation; drug habit; compulsive attachment.

No one seems to have a theory on the origin of
the word, but it appears to have appeared quite
recently in its current meaning, say, about 1965.

3 throwin' stones
Echoes the biblical saying, also found in "Playing
in the Band," against casting stones unless you
are without sin.

**4 Commissars and pinstripe bosses . . .
Selling guns 'stead of food today**
Weir changed these words on occasion, singing:

> Anymore the pinstripe bosses
> *Own* the dice.
> Any way they roll,
> Guess who gets to pay the price.
> Money green . . .
> It's the only way.

Weir has sung the final line of this verse variously
as "Blood for oil, dropping bombs today," "Drop
them bombs, grab that oil today," and "Sell
them guns, rape the earth today."

**5 If the spirit's sleeping / Then the flesh
is ink**
Compare the biblical reference "The spirit is willing, but the flesh is weak" (Matthew 26:41).

Picture a bright blue ball, just spinning,
    spinning free
Dizzy with eternity
Paint it with a skin of sky
Brush in some clouds and sea
Call it home for you and me
A peaceful place or so it looks from space
A closer look reveals the human race
Full of hope, full of grace
Is the human face
But afraid we may lay our home to waste

There's a fear down here we can't forget
Hasn't got a name just yet
Always awake, always around
Singing ashes, ashes, all fall down   1
Ashes, ashes, all fall down

Now watch as the ball revolves
And the nighttime falls
Again the hunt begins
Again the bloodwind calls
By and by, the morning sun will rise
But the darkness never goes
From some men's eyes
It strolls the sidewalks and it rolls
    the streets
Staking turf, dividing up meat
Nightmare spook, piece of heat
It's you and me
You and me

Click flash blade in ghetto night
Rudies looking for a fight
Rat cat alley, roll them bones
2 Need that cash to feed that jones
3 And the politicians throwin' stones
Singing ashes, ashes, all fall down
Ashes, ashes, all fall down

4 Commissars and pinstripe bosses
Roll the dice
Any way they fall
Guess who gets to pay the price
Money green or proletarian gray
Selling guns 'stead of food today

So the kids they dance
And shake their bones
And the politicians throwin' stones
Singing ashes, ashes, all fall down
Ashes, ashes, all fall down

Heartless powers try to tell us
What to think
If the spirit's sleeping
5 Then the flesh is ink
History's page will thus be carved in stone
6 And we are here, and we are on our own
On our own
On our own
On our own

If the game is lost
Then we're all the same
No one left to place or take the blame

6 we are on our own
Reminiscent of the Neil Young song "Ohio,"
which includes the lines:

Tin soldiers and Nixon's coming
We're finally on our own
This summer I hear the drumming
Four dead in Ohio.

7 Shipping powders back and forth
In *Conversations with the Dead,* David Gans
reveals that he himself wrote these lines about
cocaine and gunpowder.

Notes:
Written in Cora, Wyoming, August through
December 1982.

Studio recording: *In the Dark* (July 6, 1987).

First performance: September 17, 1982, at the
Cumberland County Civic Center in Portland,
Maine. It remained in the repertoire thereafter.

We can leave this place an empty stone
Or that shinin' ball we used to call our home

So the kids they dance
And shake their bones
And the politicians throwin' stones
Singing ashes, ashes, all fall down
Ashes, ashes, all fall down

7 Shipping powders back and forth
Singing black goes south and white comes north
In a whole world full of petty wars
Singing I got mine and you got yours
And the current fashion sets the pace
Lose your step, fall out of grace
And the radical, he rant and rage
Singing someone's got to turn the page
And the rich man in his summer home

Singing just leave well enough alone
But his pants are down, his cover's blown . . .

And the politicians throwin' stones
So the kids they dance
And shake their bones
And it's all too clear we're on our own
Singing ashes, ashes, all fall down
Ashes, ashes, all fall down

Picture a bright blue ball
Just spinnin', spinnin', free
Dizzy with the possibilities
Ashes, ashes, all fall down

[*ad lib*]

Words by John Barlow
Music by Bob Weir

MY BROTHER ESAU

My brother Esau killed a hunter

2

Back in 1969
And before the killing was done
His inheritance was mine
But his birthright was a wand to wave
Before a weary band
Esau gave me sleeplessness
And a piece of moral land

My father favored Esau
Who was eager to obey
All the bloody wild commandments
The Old Man shot his way
But all this favor ended
When my brother failed at war
He staggered home
And found me in the door

Esau skates on mirrors anymore . . .
He meets his pale reflection at the door
Yet sometimes at night I dream
He's still that hairy man
Shadowboxing the Apocalypse
And wandering the land
Shadowboxing the Apocalypse
And wandering the land

Esau holds a blessing
Brother Esau bears a curse

1 Esau

The Biblical character Esau is told of in Genesis 25, 27, and 33. He was, according to *The Anchor Bible Dictionary*:

> Isaac and Rebecca's firstborn son, and Jacob's older twin. In the OT, he is described both as an individual person who represents a specific lifestyle (the hunter) and as the eponymous ancestor of a people (Edomites or Idumeans).

The entry continues:

> The contrast between the twins is already anticipated before their birth in God's proclamation that the older brother will serve the younger. . . . The older son is his father's favorite while the younger is favored by his mother. . . . The younger brother bargained for the older brother's birthright . . . and deceitfully obtained the firstborn's blessing from Isaac. . . . Jacob fled to Harran to escape Esau's vengeance. . . . After Jacob's return, the brothers reconciled and settled in different regions. [21]

2 Killed a hunter / Back in 1969

Possibly a reference to Altamont, where the man knifed by the Hell's Angels was Meredith Hunter.

Notes:

Written in Cora, Wyoming, August through December 1982.

First performance: March 25, 1983, at Compton Terrace Amphitheater, Tempe, Arizona. It remained fairly steadily in the repertoire through October 1987.

I would say that the blame is mine
But I suspect it's something worse
The more my brother looks like me
The less I understand
The silent war that bloodied both our hands
Sometimes at night, I think I understand

It's brother to brother and it's man to man
And it's face to face and it's hand to hand . . .

We shadowdance the silent war within
The shadowdance, it never ends . . .
Never ends, never ends
Shadowboxing the Apocalypse, yet again . . .
Yet again
Shadowboxing the Apocalypse
And wandering the land

Words by John Barlow
Music by Bob Weir

FRIEND OF THE DEVIL

Words by Robert Hunter, music by Jerry Garcia and John Dawson.

Illustration by Jim Carpenter, 2005.

Throwing Stones
Words by John Barlow, music by Bob Weir.
Illustration by Tim Truman, 2005.

maybe you know

Have you ever wanted something
Wanted it so fuckin' bad
That you'd lie, that you'd cheat
That you'd fight in the street
A chance to lose what little you had?

Maybe you know how I'm feeling
Maybe you know how I feel
Maybe you know how I'm feeling
But maybe to you, I don't seem so real

I've been hearing for a long time
I still hear about some long-term plan
I ain't gettin' younger
Got tired of wandering
1   I was promised a rock and all I own is this
         sand

Maybe you know how I'm feeling
Maybe you know how I feel
Maybe you know how I'm feeling
But maybe to you, I don't seem so real

Time is only wasted
On talking that is taking life
When it all comes down
You're really covering ground
I know I'll get more done tonight

1 I was promised a rock and all I own is this sand
An allusion to the biblical parable of stability versus instability found in Matthew 7:24–27:

> Therefore whosoever heareth these sayings of mine, and doeth them, I will liken him unto a wise man, which built his house upon a rock: And the rain descended, and the floods came, and the winds blew, and beat upon that house; and it fell not: for it was founded upon a rock. And every one that heareth these sayings of mine, and doeth them not, shall be likened unto a foolish man, which built his house upon the sand: And the rain descended, and the floods came, and the winds blew, and beat upon that house; and it fell: and great was the fall of it.

Notes:
No studio recording.

First performance: April 13, 1983, at the Patrick Gym, University of Vermont, Burlington, Vermont. Garcia, Weir, and Lesh had left the stage prior to the song's performance.

Maybe you know how I'm feeling
Maybe you know how I feel
Maybe you know how I'm feeling
But maybe to you, I don't seem so real

Now you don't owe me nothing
So don't take it so personally
There's only one way
To make it today
And I'm doing all I can for me

Maybe you know how I'm feeling
Maybe you know how I feel
Maybe you know how I'm feeling
But maybe to you, I don't seem so real

Maybe you know how I'm feeling
Maybe you know how I feel
Maybe you know how I'm feeling
But maybe to you, I don't seem so real

Words and music by Brent Mydland

Little star

Long as we got to be
Long as we are
I just wanna be
One of them little stars

One of them little stars
That'd just be fine
All you gotta do now
Just hang up there and shine
Hang up there and shine

Hang up there and shine
Hang up there and shine
Hang up there and shine

Words and music by Bob Weir

Notes:
No studio recording.

First of three total performances with the
Grateful Dead was on April 15, 1983, at
Community War Memorial in Rochester, New
York. AKA "Bob Star."

HeLL in a Bucket

1 **hell in a bucket**
Conjures up the line from "Saint Stephen":
"Bucket hanging clear to Hell."

The phrase in American colloquial speech is
"going to hell in a handbasket."

2 **at least I'm enjoying the ride**
One of my favorite "mis-hearings" of a Grateful
Dead lyric came when Alice Kahn, the Bay Area
writer, wrote in a review in the *East Bay Express*
that this song was "Police on a Joyride."

3 **Catherine the Great**
A reference to the Empress of Russia, 1762–96,
who was an intellectual and, as hinted at in the
song, a famous libertine.

Hunter also uses her name in his song "Do Deny
(Lying Man)":

   I who ate with Kate the Great
   On Chinese silver plate . . .

4 **When the snakes come marching in**
A reference to the spiritual "When the Saints Go
Marching In."

Notes:
Written in Cora, Wyoming, August through
December 1982.

Studio recording: *In the Dark* (July 6, 1987).

First performance: May 13, 1983, at the Greek
Theater, University of California at Berkeley,
Berkeley, California. It remained in the repertoire
thereafter.

Well, I was drinking last night with a biker
And I showed him a picture of you
I said, "Pal, get to know her. You'll like her"
Seemed like the least I could do . . .

'Cause when he's driving his chopper
Up and down your carpeted halls,
You will think me by contrast quite proper
Never mind how I stumble and fall
Never mind how I stumble and fall

You imagine me sipping champagne from
   your boot
For a taste of your elegant pride
I may be going to hell in a bucket, babe,   1
But at least I'm enjoying the ride   2
At least I'm enjoying the ride
At least I'm enjoying the ride

Now miss sweet little soft-core pretender,
Somehow baby got hard as it gets
With her black leather chrome-spiked
   suspenders,
Her chair and her whip and her pets

Well we know you're the reincarnation
Of the ravenous Catherine the Great   3
And we know how you love your ovations
For the Z-rated scenes you create
The Z-rated scenes you create

You analyze me, pretend to despise me,
You laugh when I stumble and fall

There may come a day I will dance on your grave
If unable to dance, I will crawl across it
Unable to dance, I'll still crawl

You must really consider the circus
'Cause it just might be your kind of zoo
I can't think of a place that's more perfect
For a person as perfect as you

And it's not like I'm leaving you lonely
'Cause I wouldn't know where to begin
But I know that you'll think of me only
4   When the snakes come marching in
When the snakes come marching in

Words by John Barlow
Music by Bob Weir

-crash-

DON'T NEED LOVE

1 nowhere slow
A nice reversal of the cliché "going nowhere fast."

Notes:
No studio recording.

First performance: March 28, 1984, at the Marin County Veterans Auditorium in San Rafael, California. Garcia and Lesh did not stay onstage for the performance. It dropped out of rotation in 1986, after sixteen performances.

I don't need love anymore
I don't need love anymore
I don't need anyone to tell me that I do
I don't need love and I don't need you

I try and I try to make it work
I try and I try to make it work
I try and I try again, I won't forget, I know
Love gets you nowhere slow   1

I want no more heartaches
No more good-byes
Ain't no more real good love
Only new love
But old love dies

Ain't worth the time that it takes
Ain't worth the time that it takes
Ain't worth the endless hours of changes
    I go through
I don't need love and I don't need you

I don't need love anymore
I don't need love anymore
I don't need anyone to tell me that I do
I don't need love and I don't need you

Words and music by Brent Mydland

tons of steel

I know these rails we're on like I know my
    lady's smile
Re-see a dozen dreams in every passing mile
Can't begin to count the trips
That she and I have made
1 But I wish I had a dollar
For each time we both been down this grade

Nine hundred thousand tons of steel
Made to roll
Her brakes don't work and this grade's so steep
Her engine's sure to blow
Nine hundred thousand tons of steel
Out of control
She's more a roller coaster than the train I used
    to know

It's one hell of an understatement to say she
    can get mean
She's temperamental, more a bitch than a machine
She wasn't built to travel at
The speed a rumor flies
These wheels are bound to jump the tracks
Before they burn the ties

Nine hundred thousand tons of steel
Made to roll
Her brakes don't work and this grade's so steep
Her engine's sure to blow
Nine hundred thousand tons of steel
Out of control

1 But I wish I had a dollar
Compare line from "Loser": "If I had a gun for every ace I've drawn."

2 Murphy
A reference to Murphy's Law: "What can go wrong, will," which has many corollaries. Murphy himself remains shrouded in mystery—sources list this saying as being of uncertain origin, dating roughly from the 1950s.

Notes:
Studio recording: *In the Dark* (July 6, 1987).

First performance: December 28, 1984, at the Civic Auditorium in San Francisco.

She's more a roller coaster than the train I used
  to know

2 Murphy's sure outdone himself to pick this
  stretch of track
I can only hope my luck is riding in the back
Well I have prayed to God
This ain't the day we meet
I've done about everything
But try dragging my feet

Nine hundred thousand tons of steel
Made to roll
Her brakes don't work and this grade's so steep

Her engine's sure to blow
Nine hundred thousand tons of steel
Out of control
She's more a roller coaster than the train I used
  to know

Oo, oo, I wanna go down slow
Oo, oo, oo, oo, oo
Nine hundred thousand tons of steel
Out of control
She's more a roller coaster than the train I used
  to know

Words and music by Brent Mydland

Revolutionary Hamstrung Blues

Halfway past cool on Monday for the sight of her
Rode in town while he built afar [a fire?] with the
    riders and then the poor
Hot damn, it's a mother's day, don't you all look
    fine
Promenading down long car ocean, yes it's mine
    and it's sniffing white

They got poets, shuckers and Godzillas 'round
Mother's sweet little frozen no suit
1 We got Speed Racer and his archaic as words
Revolutionary Hamstrung Blues

Bringin' all the mares hide in your cabs, honey
    now loosen your load
You belong to this has-no-name, what
I remember some chicks from the sciz would
    come along and sit and squeeze too
Silly says, I say it once, for you it's cold steel
    and slow
Its sounds have all ruptured, it sounds just
    like glass
Suspect out in the corners, sounding verse and
    kickin' ass
I felt the city have a narly, don't make the six
    o'clock news
Speed Racer and the band here playing

1 Speed Racer
A 1970s cartoon character still alive in the world
of anime.

Notes:
No recordings.

Only performance: March 27, 1986, at
Cumberland County Civic Center in Portland,
Maine.

Christian Crumlish and Nicolas Meriwether have
done considerable work in deciphering this lyric,
and the results of their efforts can be found in
their article "Revolutionary Hamstrung Blues:
A First Transcription," which is replete with
notes and annotations, in *Dead Letters,* vol. 1
(inaugural issue, 2001). This version of the lyrics
is theirs, because the original probably went
through the wash in somebody's back pocket.

As I recall I went for the window, but I never did
    get me there
Hit me hard with his hickory stick was the last
    thing I saw, met you
Drag me down and tangle, you carry the charges
    if you feel
Pray for the day that one yourself, but then figure
    we'll lick a few

But when I try to look up, don't want to let me
    loosen your load

Here alone take this grenade for me, well I
The forerunner radiates wild help up far now, gun
    ships pass so far
Pass me a vote, silly, and how we did it all over
Did it all over, did it all over the road

We got broads, suckers, and guys in this jail
    mother sweet little frozen no suit
We got Speed Racer and his archaic A.M. words
Revolutionary Hamstrung Blues

Words by Robert M. Petersen
Music by Phil Lesh

Black Muddy River

1 When the last rose of summer pricks my finger
2 And the hot sun chills me to the bone
   When I can't hear the song for the singer
3 And I can't tell my pillow from a stone

   I will walk alone by the black muddy river
   And sing me a song of my own
   I will walk alone by the black muddy river
   And sing me a song of my own

   When the last bolt of sunshine hits the mountain
   And the stars start to splatter in the sky
   When the moon splits the southwest horizon
   With the scream of an eagle on the fly

   I will walk alone by the black muddy river
4 And listen to the ripples as they moan
   I will walk alone by the black muddy river
   And sing me a song of my own

   Black muddy river
   Roll on forever
   I don't care how deep or wide
   If you got another side
5 Roll muddy river
   Roll muddy river
   Black muddy river roll

   When it seems like the night will last forever
   And there's nothing left to do but count the years
   When the strings of my heart start to sever
6 And stones fall from my eyes instead of tears

1 last rose of summer
A reference to the 1813 song by the Irish poet
Thomas Moore (1779–1852), "'Tis the Last Rose
of Summer.":

> 'Tis the last rose of summer,
> Left blooming all alone,
> All her lovely companions
> Are faded and gone.
> No flower of her kindred,
> No rose bud is nigh,
> To reflect back her blushes,
> Or give sigh for sigh.
>
> I'll not leave thee, thou lone one,
> To pine on the stem;
> Since the lovely are sleeping,
> Go sleep thou with them;
> Thus kindly I scatter
> Thy leaves o'er the bed
> Where thy mates of the garden
> Lie scentless and dead.
>
> So soon may I follow
> When friendships decay,
> And from love's shining circle
> The gems drop away!
> When true hearts lie withered
> And fond ones are flown
> Oh! who would inhabit
> This bleak world alone?

For roses generally, see note under "That's It for
the Other One."

2 hot sun chills
Compare the line in the 1848 song by Stephen
Foster (1826–64) "Oh, Susanna": "The sun so
hot I froze to def." This was the

first song for which Foster received any cash
payment. "Imagine my delight," he wrote, "in

receiving one hundred dollars in cash! The two
fifty-dollar bills I received for it had the effect
of starting me on my present vocation as a
songwriter." (Ewen)

3 can't tell my
pillow from a
stone
Compare the story of
Jacob in Genesis 28:

Jacob left
Beersheba and set
out for Haran.
When he reached
a certain place, he
stopped for the
night because the
sun had set. Taking one of the stones there, he
put it under his head and lay down to sleep.

4 ripples
Robert Hunter cannot use the word *ripple*
without invoking his own song of that title.

5 Roll muddy river
A song called "Roll Muddy River" was a hit for
the Osborne Brothers in the late 1960s and starts
"Roll muddy river, roll on."

6 stones fall from my eyes instead of
tears
Compare Shakespeare's *Richard III,* Act 1,
Scene 8:

First Murderer: Tut, tut, my lord! We will not
stand to prate;
Talkers are no good doers. Be assured:
We go to use our hands, and not our tongues.

Gloucester: Your eyes drop millstones when

I will walk alone by the black muddy river
And dream me a dream of my own
I will walk alone by the black muddy river
And sing me a song of my own   7
And sing me a song of my own

Words by Robert Hunter
Music by Jerry Garcia

fools' eyes fall tears.
I like you, lads: about your business straight.
Go, go, dispatch.

7 sing me a song of my own

Compare the lines containing the phrase "songs of our own" or "songs of its own" from "Eyes of the World."

Notes:

Studio recording: *In the Dark* (July 6, 1987).

First performance: December 15, 1986, at the Oakland Coliseum Arena in Oakland, California. It remained in the repertoire thereafter.

Hunter, in an interview with Steve Silberman, made these comments:

Silberman: Both "Standing on the Moon" and "Black Muddy River" came into the repertoire after Garcia's coma, and both seem to be uncannily appropriate for what he had been through. Were you conscious of that at all when you were writing those tunes?

Hunter: Not specifically, but Jerry and I have been hanging out since we were eighteen and nineteen respectively, and I know him as well as I know any other human being. We were folksingers together, and I know what kind of song he loves. So when I give him something, I'll give him something that I have a high degree of suspicion that he will love—and sometimes I'm right. "Standing on the Moon" was one of those neat, sweet, quick things, like "It Must Have Been the Roses," where the whole picture just came to me, and I grabbed a piece of paper and got it down. No changes, no nothin'. Out of the head of Zeus, full-born and clad in armor.

Silberman: There's a great poem by William Carlos Williams that I thought of when I heard "Black Muddy River"—it's the first poem in his selected poems— called "The Wanderer." He talks about being anointed as a young man by the Passaic River, as a kind of initiation, or permission, to be a poet. Did you ever read that poem? And it's not the clean, pristine Passaic, it's full of muck and mire and . . .

Hunter: The "filthy Passaic."

Silberman: Exactly. It seems as if you guys have walked along the banks of similar rivers.

Hunter: The black muddy river is a dream that I've had maybe three or four times over my life, and it is one of the most chilling experiences that I've had. It's enough to turn you religious. I've burrowed under this incredible mansion, gone down into the cellars, and I find myself down at this black, lusterless, slow-flowing Stygian river. There are marble columns around, and cobwebs. It's vast and it's hopeless. It's death, it's death, with the absence of the soul. It's my horror vision, and when I come out of that dream I do anything I can to counter it.

Silberman: And yet in "Black Muddy River," you're not saying flee the banks of this dark place. You're saying walk along the banks, and sing a song of your own making.

Hunter: Right. And what's on the other side of it is . . . whatever it is. It's a bit of whistling in the dark. I'll face whatever it is, because I wouldn't have any choice, would I? So you might as well go for it. 87

when push comes to shove

1 Here there may be
A phrase borrowed from old maps. "Here there may be monsters"

indicated that the mapmaker was in uncharted territory. At least, that's the common wisdom. Trying to find an actual map that employed this phrase proves difficult—maybe impossible. Rather than a bona fide phrase from mapmaking antiquity, it may be a phrase used by modern mapmakers creating pseudoantique maps.

2 bullets made of glass
In Jules Verne's 1870 novel, *20,000 Leagues Under the Sea,* Captain Nemo invites Professor Aronnax on an undersea hunting expedition, which, among other marvels, will employ guns powered by compressed air, firing glass bullets:

> On the contrary, sir, with this rifle every shot is fatal; and as soon as the animal is hit, no matter how lightly, if falls as if struck by lightning."
>
> "Why?"
>
> "Because this rifle doesn't shoot ordinary bullets but little glass capsules invented by the Austrian chemist Leniebroek, and I have a considerable supply of them. These glass capsules are covered with a strip of steel and weighted with a lead base; they're genuine little Leyden jars charged with high-voltage electricity.

Shaking in the forest, what have you to fear?
Here there may be tigers to punch you in the ear
Gloves of stainless steel, bats carved out of brick,
Will knock you down and beat you up and give
    your ass a kick
When push comes to shove
You're afraid of love

Shaking in the desert, wherefore do you cry?
Here there may be rattlesnakes to punch you   **1**
   in the eye
Shotguns full of silver, bullets made of glass,   **2**
String barbed wire at your feet and do not let
   you pass
When push comes to shove, you're afraid of love

Chorus:
When push comes to shove
When push comes to shove
You're afraid of love
When push comes to shove

Shaking in the bedroom, covers on your head
Cringing like a baby at the hand beneath the bed
Phantom in the closet, scratching at the door
The latest mystery killer that you saw on
   Channel Four

When push comes to shove, you're afraid of love

Shaking in the garden, the fear within you grows

3 Here there may be roses to punch you in the nose
Twist their arms around you, slap you till you cry,
Wrap you in their sweet perfume and love you
  till you die
When push comes to shove, you're afraid of love

When push comes to shove
When push comes to shove
You're afraid of love
When push comes to shove

Words by Robert Hunter
Music by Jerry Garcia

3 roses
See note under "That's It for the Other One."

Notes:
Studio recording: *Built to Last* (October 31, 1989).

First performance: December 15, 1986, at the Coliseum Arena in Oakland, California. It remained in the repertoire through July 17, 1989.

victim or the crime

1 Patience runs out on the junkie
Gerrit Graham, from an essay written for *The Annotated Grateful Dead Lyrics:*

The j-word! Good God, the hue and cry. Desperate wails of scandalized sensibility! Indignant bellows of outraged morality! And not just, or even mostly, from the band. . . . [Bob] did finally broach the subject with Garcia, and Jerry said, "I don't give a fuck, sing what you want." How predictable is that? And the reference had *nothing* to do with Garcia.

All that noise over one little word—seems like your standard teapot tempest now. But as Bob points out, it gave the teapot a good stir: The furor made it plain that we were onto something of value, something about which folks had actual feelings, even if they wouldn't say what those feelings really were. In the event, the band recorded the song and played it regularly for the next five or so years, as everyone knows, and soon enough the down-front Deadheads were singing along with Weir. Brent, who hated the lyric but told me that the song "sure is fun to play," pestered Bob and me for a while to change "junkie" to something — anything — else; so once, just to get everybody to shut up about it, Bob sang "Patience runs out on the bunny." I don't remember the gig, and that was the only time Bob did it, but it became a running joke of sorts for a while. I'm sure there are lots of other iterations of the story in the annals of GD arcana.

. . . Regardless of what anyone thinks about the words, the tune, while not exactly cuddly, remains one of Bob's most sophisticated and arresting compositions, a striking piece of work for which he deserves real credit. Bob says the song's scarcity in the catalog is due to a lingering prejudice against the horrible j-word. Tut, tut. 88

Patience runs out on the junkie   1
The dark side hires another soul
Did he steal his fate or earn it?
Was he force-fed, did he learn it?
Whatever happened to his precious self-control
Like him I'm tired of trying to heal
This tomcat heart with which I'm blessed
Is destruction loving's twin
Must I choose to lose or win?   2
Maybe when my turn comes I will have guessed

These are the horns of the dilemma   3
What truth is proof against all lies?
When sacred fails before profane
The wisest man is deemed insane
Even the purest of romantics compromise

What fixation feeds this fever
As the full moon pales and climbs?
Am I living truth or rank deceiver?
Am I the victim or the crime?
Am I the victim or the crime?
Am I the victim or the crime
Or the crime?

And so I wrestle with the angel   4
To see who'll reap the seeds I sow
Am I the driver or the driven?
Will I be damned to be forgiven?
Is there anybody here but me who needs to know?

What it is that feeds this fever
As the full moon pales and climbs?

Am I living truth or rank deceiver?
Am I the victim or the crime?
Am I the victim or the crime?
Am I the victim or the crime
Or the crime?

Words by Gerrit Graham
Music by Bob Weir

2 Must I choose to lose or win
See "Deal" for a companion sentiment:

> Since it costs a lot to win
> And even more to lose
> You and me bound to spend some time
> Wonderin' what to choose

3 horns of the dilemma
First recorded use of the cliché/metaphor is by Laurence Sterne, in his *Tristram Shandy* (1760): "One of the two horns of my dilemma." (Book IV, chapter 26)

4 And so I wrestle with the angel
A reference to Genesis 32:24–32, in which Jacob wrestles with a supernatural being, often rendered as an angel, who is trying to prevent him from crossing a stream. Jacob's thigh is put out of joint in the melee, but eventually he prevails and insists on receiving the being's blessing. The being blesses Jacob (under duress) and names him Israel.

Worth noting is that this story follows immediately the story of Jacob and his brother Esau. (See "My Brother Esau.")

Notes:
Studio recording: *Built to Last* (October 31, 1989).

First performance: June 17, 1988, at the Metropolitan Sports Center in Bloomington, Minnesota. It remained in the repertoire steadily thereafter.

Foolish Heart

1 Search for where the rivers end / Or where the river start

More than one hundred years ago, the world was still filled with wonders and unknown places waiting to be discovered. A popular undertaking of the time was the search for the source of the Nile, in Africa, the mother river. One of the most famous efforts at finding "where the rivers start" was the one made together by Dr. David Livingstone and Henry Morton Stanley in 1869, after Stanley found Livingstone, a missionary who had been missing in Africa (hence the famous greeting "Dr. Livingstone, I presume?"). They never found the source of the Nile, though they did everything but. Stanley recorded their adventures together in *How I Found Livingstone* (1872). The source of the Nile was later discovered by John Speke, along with Sir Richard Burton, the adventurer and translator of *The Arabian Nights,* who also visited the Mountains of the Moon.

2 Speak with wisdom like a child

Compare the expression "out of the mouths of babes," an expression meaning that sometimes innocence can give birth to great wisdom (or if you prefer, "kids say the darnedest things"). This expression comes from the Bible, Psalms 8:2:

> Out of the mouth of babes and sucklings hast thou ordained strength because of thine enemies, that thou mightest still the enemy and the avenger.

3 Crown yourself the king of clowns

A famous clown named Lou Jacobs billed himself "The King of Clowns." Jacobs was born in 1903 and died in 1992. He joined the Ringling Bros. and Barnum & Bailey Circus in 1925. There he created one of the most famous clown gags ever: the midget car.

4 Never look around the bend

Legend has it that Neal Cassady could see around

Carve your name
Carve your name in ice and wind
Search for where
Search for where the rivers end
Or where the rivers start   1
Do everything that's in you
That you feel to be your part
But never give your love, my friend,
Unto a foolish heart

Leap from ledges
Leap from ledges high and wild
Learn to speak
Speak with wisdom like a child   2
Directly from the heart
Crown yourself the king of clowns   3
Or stand way back apart
But never give your love, my friend
Unto a foolish heart

Shun a friend
Shun a brother and a friend
Never look
Never look around the bend   4
Or check a weather chart
Sign *The Mona Lisa*
With a spray can, call it art
But never give your love, my friend
Unto a foolish heart

A foolish heart will call on you
To toss your dreams away
Then turn around and blame you

For the way you went astray
A foolish heart will cost you sleep
And often make you curse
A selfish heart is trouble
But a foolish heart is worse

5   Bite the hand
    Bite the hand that bakes your bread
    Dare to leap
6   Where the angels fear to tread
    Till you are torn apart
    Stoke the fires of paradise
    With coals from Hell to start
    But never give your love, my friend
    Unto a foolish heart

    Unto a foolish heart. . . .

Words by Robert Hunter
Music by Jerry Garcia

corners while driving through city streets at high speeds. Compare the lines in "A Box of Rain": "Around some corner / Where it's been waiting to meet you.")

Recalls the Creedence Clearwater Revival song "Up Around the Bend."

5 Bite the hand

The saying "bite the hand that feeds them" first appeared in Edmund Burke's *Thoughts and Details on Scarcity* (1800):

And having looked to Government for bread, on the very first scarcity they will turn and bite the hand that fed them.

6 Where the angels fear to tread

This refers to a line by Alexander Pope, in his poem "An Essay on Criticism" (1711), in which Pope takes critics, with their easy slander, to task:

The bookful blockhead, ignorantly read,
With loads of learned lumber in his head,
With his own tongue still edifies his ears,
And always list'ning to himself appears.

No place so sacred from such fops is barred,
Nor is Paul's church more safe than Paul's
  churchyard:
Nay, fly to Altars ; there they'll talk you dead:
For Fools rush in where Angels fear to tread. [Italics added]

Notes:

Studio recording: *Built to Last* (October 31, 1989).

First performance: June 19, 1988, at the Alpine Valley Music Theater in East Troy, Wisconsin. The song remained in the repertoire thereafter.

Blow away

1 Maker
"Wharf Rat" uses the same designation for God.

2 Empty bottles
that can't be
filled
Echoes of "Ripple":
"Reach out your
hand if your cup be
empty," and of
"Comes a Time":
"You've got an
empty cup / only
love can fill."

Notes:
Written in Martinez, California, February 1988.

Studio recording: *Built to Last* (October 31, 1989).

First performance: June 20, 1988, at Alpine Valley Music Theater, East Troy, Wisconsin.

A man and a woman come together as strangers
When they part they're usually strangers still
It's like a practical joke played on us by our Maker 1
Empty bottles that can't be filled   2

Chorus:
Baby who's to say it could have been different now
     that it's done
Baby who's to say that it should have been, anyway
Baby who's to say that it even matters in the
     long run
Give it just a minute
And it will blow away
It'll blow away

You fancy me to be the master of your feelings
You barely bruise me with your looks to kill
Though I admit we were sometimes brutal in
     our dealings
I never held you against your will

(Chorus)

Your case against me is so very clearly stated
I plead no contest, I just turn and shrug
I've come to figure all importance overestimated
You must mean water when you beg for blood

(Chorus)

Like a feather in a whirlwind
Blow away
Just as sure as the world spins
Blow away . . .

Words by John Barlow
Music by Brent Mydland

I will take you home

Little girl lost   1
In a forest of dreams
It's a dark old wood
And it's damp with dew
Hoot owl hoots
For a moment it seems
Something big and cold
Just got ahold of you.
Just when everything gets scary,
Daddy's come 'round for his darlin' again
Hold my hand with your little fingers
Daddy's loving arms gonna gather you in

Ain't no way the Bogeyman can get you,   2
You can close your eyes, the world is gonna
    let you,
Your daddy's here and never will forget you,
I will take you home   3
I will take you home
Gonna carry you back home
In my arms
I will take you home

Long is the road
We must travel on down
Short are the legs
That will struggle behind
I wish I knew for sure
Just where we're bound,
What we will be doin'
And what we're gonna find

O'er this desert bright,
Let thy moon arise,
While I close my eyes.

Sleeping Lyca lay;
While the beasts of prey,
Come from caverns deep,
View'd the maid asleep

The kingly lion stood
And the virgin view'd,
Then he gambold round
O'er the hallowd ground.

Leopards, tygers play
Round her as she lay;
While the lion old,
Bow'd his mane of gold.

And her bosom lick,
And upon her neck,
From his eyes of flame,
Ruby tears there came;

While the lioness,
Loos'd her slender dress,
And naked they convey'd
To caves the sleeping maid.

Also the title of a 1932 novel by Temple Bailey.
According to *The Book Review Digest* of that year:

Sentimental love story about a young girl of
19 who takes a year to make up her mind
just which man she wants to marry—the fasci-
nator who doesn't really believe in marriage,
and hasn't a nickel, or the fine-looking young
man who wants terribly to marry her, and is
incidentally worth several millions. She arrives
at her momentous decision after a number of
adventures, and promises to marry the nice
young man with the millions.

Wherever we go, there will be birds to cheer you
Flowers to color in the fields around
Wherever we go, I'll be right here near you
You can't get lost when you're always found

Ain't no fog that's thick enough to hide you
Your daddy's gonna be right here beside you
If your fears should start to get inside you
I will take you home
I will take you home
Gonna carry you back home
In my arms
I will take you home

Words by John Barlow and Brent Mydland
Music by Brent Mydland

Other excerpts from reviews indicate that Temple Bailey was the Danielle Steel of her time.

The title has since been used repeatedly, including recently by Drew Barrymore for her 1990 autobiographical account of drug abuse.

2 Bogeyman
boogerman n. Also sp. *boogarman, buggerman*
1 also *boog man:*
(Note: *boogeyman* is the more frequently used term throughout the U.S. except in the South, where it is slightly less common than *boogerman.* A spirit of the dark that carries off children *(Dictionary of American Regional English)*

This is one of those words whose etymology is, perhaps appropriately, very murky.

3 I will take you home
Compare the line from "Ripple": "If I knew the way, I would take you home."

Notes:
Written in Martinez, California, February 23, 1988.

Studio recording: *Built to Last* (October 31, 1989).

First performance: June 22, 1988, at Alpine Valley Music Theater, East Troy, Wisconsin.

1 Believe it or not
Ripley's Believe It or Not is a regular cartoon featuring strange and amazing factoids, started by Robert Leroy Ripley in 1919. Ripley died in 1949, but the feature continues to this day.

2 with my heart in my shoes

His heart sank into his boots. In Latin, *cor illi in genua decidet;* in French, *avoir la peur au ventre.* The last two phrases are very expressive: Fear makes the knees shake, and it gives one a stomach-ache; but the English phrase suggests that his heart or spirits sank as low as possible short of absolutely deserting him. *(Brewer's)*

3 Whippoorwill
Camprimulgus vociferus. Robin-size bird. Brown (hmm, not gray . . .), the male has broad white-tipped feathers. The female has brown feathers on its tail. Found in dry open woodland near fields. Breeds from Saskatchewan east to maritime provinces and south to Kansas, north Louisiana, and north Georgia. Its call is a loud rhythmic "whippoorwill." The eggs are most often hatched when the moon is full.

One or two moments
a piece of your time
is all I am asking
and I'll give you mine
One or two moments
out of all you have got
to show how I love you
believe it or not

Remember the day
I rolled into town
with my heart in my shoes,
my head hanging down?
Now my only trouble
the rest I forgot
is to show how I love you
believe it or not

Done time in the lockup
Done time in the street
Done time on the upswing
and time in defeat
I know what I'm asking
and I know it's a lot
when I say that I love you
believe it or not

I know I'm no angel
my prospects are high
as the flood line in summer
when the river's gone dry
but I'll roll up my shirtsleeves
and make my best shot
to show how I love you
believe it or not

Right now while the sun shines
on the crest of the hill
with a breeze in the pines
3   and a gray whippoorwill
making music together
that guitars never caught
let me show how I love you
believe it or not

Words by Robert Hunter
Music by Jerry Garcia

Notes:
Recorded in the studio for *Built to Last* (October 31, 1989) but not included. Eventually released on the box set compilation *So Many Roads.*

First performance: June 23, 1988, at Alpine Valley Music Theater in East Troy, Wisconsin.

Gentlemen, start your engines

1 combat zone
A seedy section of Boston in a downtown area bordering Chinatown, known for prostitution and "adult," or pornographic, bookstores. Fired up in the late seventies and peaking out in the eighties as a center of prostitution. Interesting parallel to "Picasso Moon," which is set in the South of Market area of San Francisco.

2 Gentlemen, start your engines
The phrase that kicks off the Indianapolis 500 racing event. According to the official Indy 500 website,

Wilbur Shaw's first Indianapolis 500 win came in 1937, but his second and third wins at the Indianapolis Motor Speedway—in 1939 and 1940—put him in the history books as the first driver to win back-to-back Indianapolis 500-Mile races. He ranks fifth on the all-time list for laps led, leading the Indianapolis 500 for 508 laps. Shaw became president of the Indianapolis Motor Speedway in 1945 and would later popularize the tradition of announcing "Gentlemen, start your engines," in the early 1950s.

3 seven-grand red-line
A reference to the 7,000 rpm level—a danger point on a tachometer.

4 The dead can do my sleepin'
Perhaps the earliest literary text comparing sleep and death is found in Homer's *Iliad:* "There she met sleep, the brother of death."

It's three A.M. in the combat zone. **1**
Gentlemen, start your engines! **2**
You can close this bar, but baby I ain't going
Gentlemen, start your engines!
If you lock up the whiskey, give me gasoline
I got a seven-grand redline on the black machine **3**
The dead can do my sleepin', if you know what **4**
   I mean

Chorus:
Gentlemen, start your engines!
Ge-Ge-Ge-Gentlemen, start your engines! **5**
Gentlemen, start
Gentlemen, start
Ge-Ge-Ge-Gentlemen, start your engines!

Got a little girl here in a pinafore
Gentlemen, start your engines!
She's gonna do us all and then beg for more
Gentlemen, start your engines!
It's dark outside, but it's darker within
Check the back of my jacket just to see my grin **6**
They don't write poems about the state that I'm in

(Chorus)

One of these days I'm gonna pull myself together **7**
Soon as I finish tearin' myself apart
Like the Devil's Mustangs,
I've been ridden hell for leather,
Put away wet and angry in the dark.

When the police come you better let 'em in,
Gentlemen, start your engines!
Don't forget to tell 'em what a sport I've been
Gentlemen, start your engines!
I got a head full of vintage TNT,
They're gonna blow me up 'stead of burying me
If you don't like trouble, better leave me be

(Chorus)

One of these days I'm gonna pull myself together
Soon as I finish tearin' myself apart
Let me tell you, honey,
8 There's some mighty stormy weather
Rolling 'round the caverns of my heart

Words by John Barlow
Music by Brent Mydland

Hamlet, in Shakespeare's famous "To be or not to be" soliloquy, equates sleep with death in the lines

> To die, to sleep;
> No more; and, by a sleep to say we end
> The heartache and the thousand natural
>   shocks
> That flesh is heir to, 'tis a consummation
> Devoutly to be wish'd. To die, to sleep;
> To sleep, perchance to dream: ay, there's the
>   rub;

> For in that sleep of death what dreams may
>   come
> When we have shuffled off this mortal coil,
> Must give us pause.

Warren Zevon's song "I'll Sleep When I'm Dead" has a similar message and tone to this Barlow-Mydland song.

5 Ge-ge-ge-gentlemen
Calls to mind the famous stutter line from the Who's 1965 song "My Generation": "talkin' bout my ge-ge-generation."

6 Check the back of my jacket just to see my grin
A probable reference to the insignia, or colors, of the Hell's Angels jacket, which depicts a grinning skull. Or, perhaps, the Dead's very own "Steal Your Face" insignia!

7 One of these days, I'm gonna pull myself together
Resonates with the line from "Wharf Rat": "But I'll get back / on my feet someday."

8 stormy weather
Title of a 1933 song, words by Ted Koehler, music by Harold Arlen.

Notes:
Written in Martinez, California, February 23, 1988.

First performance: June 26, 1988, at Pittsburgh Civic Arena in Pittsburgh. It was only performed live one more time. The version on the box set *So Many Roads* was recorded as a demo for *Built to Last*.

BuiLt to Last

1 All these trials/Soon be past
Compare the traditional hymn "All My Trials, Lord":

> Hush, little baby, don't you cry
> You know your mama was born to die
> All my trials, Lord, soon be over

> Too late, my brothers
> Too late, but never mind
> All my trials, Lord, soon be over

> If religion were a thing that money could buy
> The rich would live and the poor would die
> All my trials, Lord, soon be over

> I've got a little book that was given to me
> And every page spells liberty
> All my trials, Lord, soon be over

> There is a tree in Paradise
> And the pilgrims call it the Tree of Life
> All my trials, Lord, soon be over

2 Here comes the sun
Evokes George Harrison's "Here Comes the Sun," from the Beatles' *Abbey Road.*

Notes:

Studio recording: title track from *Built to Last* (October 31, 1989).

First performance: October 20, 1988, at the Summit, Houston, Texas. It was performed infrequently through early 1990.

There are times that you can beckon
There are times when you must call
You can take a lot of reckoning
But you can't take it all
There are times when I can help you out
And times that you must fall
There are times when you must live in doubt
And I can't help at all

Three blue stars/Rise on
    the hill
Say no more, now/Just
    be still
All these trials/Soon   1
    be past
Look forsomething/Built
    to last
Wind held by the collar
Yes, a cloud held by the breeze
You can walk on coals of fire
But sometimes you must freeze
There are times when you offend me
And I do the same to you
If we can't or won't forget it,
I guess we could be through

One blue star/Sets on the hill
Call it back/You never will
One more star/Sinks in the past
Show me something/Built to last

Built to last till time itself
Falls tumbling from the wall
Built to last till sunshine fails
And darkness moves on all
Built to last while years roll past
Like cloudscapes in the sky
Show me something built to last
Or something built to try

There are times when you get hit upon
Try hard but you cannot give
Other times you'd gladly part
With what you need to live
Don't waste the breath to save your face
When you have done your best
And even more is asked of you
Let fate decide the rest.

All the stars/Are gone but one
Morning breaks/Here comes the sun
Cross the sky/Now sinking fast
Show me something/Built to last

Three blue stars rise on the hill
Sing no more now just be still
All these trials soon be past
Look for something built to last

One blue star sets on the hill
Call it back you never will
One more star sinks in the past
Show me something built to last

All the stars are gone but one
Morning breaks here comes the sun   2
Cross the sky now sinking fast
Show me something built to last

Words by Robert Hunter
Music by Jerry Garcia

standing on the moon

1 indigo

The color indigo, often associated with political power or religious ritual, has held a significant place in many world civilizations for thousands of years. In the excavation of Thebes, an indigo garment dating from ca. 2500 B.C.E. was found, for example — furthermore, the Hindu god Krishna is most often depicted in blue, human sacrifices were often painted blue in ancient Mayan culture, and the Virgin Mary is regularly imagined draped in blue clothes in Christian art.

The indigo dye comes from a leguminous plant of the *Indigofera* genus, of which over three hundred species have been identified. Only two species are named frequently in the commercial history of the dye, namely: *Indigofera tinctoria* (native to India and Asia) and *Indigofera suffructiosa* (native to South and Central America). Indigo plants have a single semiwood stem, dark green leaves that are oval-shaped in most species, and clusters of red flowers that look like butterflies and turn into pea-pods. The plants can grow from two to six feet in height and the dye is obtained mainly from the leaves through a process of fermentation. (Mattson) 89

2 A scrap of age-old lullaby / Down some forgotten street

Compare the lines in "Stella Blue":

In the end there's still that song
comes crying like the wind
down every lonely street
that's ever been

3 But I'd rather be with you

An emotionally charged line, often sung over and over by Garcia in concert. Proposed by some as an appropriate epitaph for him.

Standing on the moon
I got no cobweb on my shoe
Standing on the moon
I'm feeling so alone and blue
I see the Gulf of Mexico
As tiny as a tear
The coast of California
Must be somewhere over here—
Over here

Standing on the moon
I see the battle rage below
Standing on the moon
I see the soldiers come and go
There's a metal flag beside me
Someone planted long ago
Old Glory standing stiffly
Crimson, white, and indigo—
Indigo

I see all of Southeast Asia
I can see El Salvador
I hear the cries of children
And the other songs of war
It's like a mighty melody
That rings down from the sky
Standing here upon the moon
I watch it all roll by—
All roll by

1

Standing on the moon
I see a shadow on the sun
Standing on the moon
The stars go fading one by one
I hear a cry of victory
Another of defeat
2   A scrap of age-old lullaby
Down some forgotten street

Standing on the moon
Where talk is cheap and vision true
Standing on the moon
But I would rather be with you
Somewhere in San Francisco
On a back porch in July
Just looking up at heaven
At this crescent in the sky
In the sky

Standing on the moon
With nothing left to do
A lovely view of heaven
3   *But I'd rather be with you—*
Be with you

Words by Robert Hunter
Music by Jerry Garcia

Notes:
Studio recording: *Built to Last* (October 31, 1989).

First performance: February 5, 1989, at Henry J. Kaiser Convention Center in Oakland, California. It remained steadily in the repertoire thereafter.

we can run but we can't hide

1 We can run / But we can't hide from it
A turn of phrase coined by boxer Joe Louis (Joseph Louis Borrow, 1914–1981), who, prior to a heavyweight title bout with Billy Conn in June 1946, said, "He can run, but he can't hide."

The turn of phrase implemented here by Barlow also recalls Porcupine's maxim, "We have met the enemy and he is us!" The phrase is widely believed to have appeared in Walt Kelly's *Pogo* cartoon strip on Earth Day, 1971, but, in fact, it appears dated "8-8" (August 8) in a collection of *Pogo* strips from 1970, *Impollutable Pogo*, which bears the subtitle *Don't Tread on Me.*

2 Of all possible worlds
Compare the often quoted line from Voltaire's *Candide* (1759): "In this best of all possible worlds . . . everything is for the best" (chapter 1) and its more modern corollary by James Branch Cabell, in *The Silver Stallion* (1926): "The optimist proclaims that we live in the best of all possible worlds; and the pessimist fears this is true."

3 oil for the rich and babies for the poor
Compare the folk saying "The rich get richer, and the poor get babies."

4 till the night-time
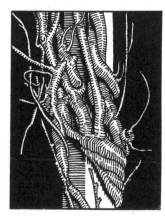
Barlow originally wrote "like a bad vine." This sounded like a biblical reference of which Barlow is very fond, and, indeed, there are many such references in the Bible, though not specifically to a "bad" vine as such; rather, there are numerous

We don't own this place, though we act as if
  we did
It belongs to the children of our children's kids
The actual owners haven't even been born yet

But we never tend the garden and rarely we pay
  the rent
Some of it is broken and the rest of it is bent
Put it all on plastic and I wonder where we'll be
  when the bills hit

Chorus:
We can run
But we can't hide from it   1
Of all possible worlds   2
We only got one
We gotta ride on it
Whatever we've done
We'll never get far from what we leave behind
Baby, we can run, run, run, but we can't hide
Oh no, we can't hide

I'm dumpin' my trash in your backyard
Makin' certain you don't notice really isn't so hard
You're so busy with your guns and all of your
  excuses to use them

Well, it's oil for the rich and babies for the poor   3
They got everyone believin' that more is more
If a reckoning comes, maybe we'll know what
  to do then

(Chorus)

All these complications seem to leave no choice
I heard the tongues of billions speak with just
  one voice
Saying, "Just leave all the rest to me
I need it worse than you, you see"
And then I heard . . .
The sound of one child crying

Today I went walking in the amber wind
There's a hole in the sky where the light pours in
I remembered the days when I wasn't afraid of
  the sunshine

But now it beats down on the asphalt land
Like a hammering blow from God's left hand
What little still grows cringes in the shade till the
4   nighttime

Words by John Barlow
Music by Brent Mydland

analogies using vines that bear no fruit, or bitter
fruit, as in Psalms 80:8-9:

> There was a vine: You uprooted it from Egypt;
> to plant it, you drove out other nations,
> you cleared a space where it could grow,
> it took root and filled the whole country. . . .

Isaiah 5:1:

> . . . planted choice vine in it.
> He expected it to yield grapes,
>   but sour grapes were all that it gave.

Jeremiah 2:21:

> Yet I had planted you, a choice vine,
>   a shoot of soundest stock.
> How is it you have become a degenerate
>   plant, you bastard vine?

Notes:
Studio recording: *Built to Last* (October 31,
1989).

First performance: February 5, 1989, at the
Henry J. Kaiser Convention Center in Oakland,
California.

Just a Little Light

1 armies of the night

Norman Mailer used this phrase as the title of his 1968 "nonfiction novel" about an antiwar march on the Pentagon in 1967, and it won the National Book Award and the Pulitzer Prize. He took it from the last line of Matthew Arnold's "Dover Beach":

> And we are here as on a darkling plain
> Swept with confused alarms of struggle and
>   flight,
> Where ignorant armies clash by night.

Arnold, in turn, was probably referring to a specific battle, fought at night and usually assumed to be Thucydides' account of the Battle of Epipolae in his *Peloponnesian Wars* (chapter XXII):

> The Athenians now fell into great disorder and perplexity, so that it was not easy to get from one side or the other any detailed account of the affair. By day certainly the combatants have a clearer notion, though even then by no means of all that takes place, no one knowing much of anything that does not go on in his own immediate neighbourhood; but in a night engagement (and this was the only one that occurred between great armies during the war) how could any one know anything for certain?

Some critics think, however, that Arnold may have been making a reference to Tennyson's *Morte d'Arthur*, in which he recounts the "last, dim, weird battle of the west," the battle of Camlann (ca. A.D. 540):

> Nor ever yet had Arthur fought a fight
> Like this last, dim, weird battle of the west.
> A deathwhite mist slept over sand and sea:
> Whereof the chill, to him who breathed it,
>   drew

Well, there ain't nobody safer than someone who
    doesn't care
And it isn't even lonely when no one's ever there
I had a lot of dreams once, but some of them
    came true . . .
The honey's sometimes bitter when fortune falls
    on you

So you know I've been a soldier in the armies of
    the night   1
And I'll find the fatal error in what's otherwise   2
    alright
But here you're trembling like a sparrow, I will try
    with all my might
To give you just a little sweetness . . .
Just a little sweetness . . .
Just a little light   3

I have always heard that virtue oughta be its
    own reward,   4
But it never comes so easy when you're living by
    the sword   5
It's even harder to be heartless when you look at
    me that way
You're as mighty as the flower that will grow
    the stones away

Even though I been a stranger, full of irony
    and spite
Holding little but contempt for all things
    beautiful and bright,   6

Something shines around you and it seems, to
    my delight
To give me just a little sweetness . . .
Just a little sweetness . . .
Just a little sweetness . . .
Just a little light

This could be just another highway, coiled up in
    the night
7 You could be just another whitetail, baby,
        stranded on my brights,
There's a tingling recognition
Like the sound of distant thunder
And I begin to wonder
If the love I've driven under
Won't ignite

So you know I've been a soldier in the armies of
    the night
And I'll find the fatal error in what's otherwise
    alright
Something shines around you that seems, to
    my delight
To give me just a little sweetness . . .
Just a little sweetness . . .
Just a little sweetness . . .
Just a little light

Words by John Barlow and Brent Mydland
Music by Brent Mydland

Down with his blood, till all his heart was cold
With formless fear; and ev'n on Arthur fell
Confusion, since he saw not whom he fought.

2 fatal error
A computer-screen message indicating that
something is very wrong. *The McGraw-Hill
Dictionary of Electronics and Computer Technology*
has this definition: "An error in a computer program which causes running of the program to be
terminated."

3 sweetness . . . / Just a little light
Another reference to Arnold: In his *Culture and
Anarchy,* the first chapter is called "Sweetness
and Light."

**4 virtue oughta
be its own reward**
From a quote by
Ralph Waldo
Emerson in his essay
"Friendship," pub-
lished in his *Essays:*
"The only reward of
virtue is virtue."

**5 living by the
sword**
Matthew was the
only writer of the Gospels to report the words of
Jesus, "Those who live by the sword will die by
the sword." (Matthew 26:52)

6 all things beautiful and bright
This is the second use by Barlow of a line from
the hymn "All Things Bright and Beautiful"
(1848) by Cecil Frances Alexander (1818–95):

All things bright and beautiful,
All creatures great and small,
All things wise and wonderful,
The Lord God made
    them all."

The other is in "Weather Report Suite, Part 2": "Let It Grow."

7 whitetail, baby, stranded on my brights
Whitetail deer are known to stare, as if hypnotized, into the lights of oncoming traffic, especially in rural areas. They will stand still and often get hit.

Notes:

Written in Martinez, California, January 27, 1989.

Studio recording: *Built to Last* (October 31, 1989).

First performance: February 7, 1989, at the Henry J. Kaiser Auditorium in Oakland, California.

picasso moon

1 South of Market in the land of ruin
You'll find all manner of action
Got your tinsel tigers in the Metal Room
Stalking satisfaction
They got 'em packaged up for love and money
Tatooed tots, chrome-spike bunnies
Pop on my mirrored shades, the better to see
And roll on in, gonna roll in it, honey

I get a feeling like when big things collide
Like the crack before the thunder, like I really
ought to hide
Here comes metal angel, she looks ready to ride
What's that she's tryin' to show me?
What's that she's tryin' to show me?

2 Picasso moon, shattered light
Diamond bullets ripping up the night
Picasso moon, liberate me
Ah, life's infinite diversity
Great, amazing, majesty
And it's bigger than a drive-in movie, oo-wee
Bigger than a drive-in movie, oo-wee

3 Hanging ten out on space and time
Redefining distance
The next skull on your necklace is mine
Cheap for such assistance
I had a job trading bits for pieces
We'd make wrinkles, advertise them as creases
Please find my resignation enclosed
Roll with it, go on, let's roll with it, honey . . .

Dark angel, what's bothering you

1 South of Market
The area of San Francisco to the south of the main drag, Market Street. The area was notorious at the time of the song's writing as a haven for junkies. The Mission District, immortalized in "Mission in the Rain," is also south of Market, but there is little ambiguity here regarding the district sometimes known as SoMa.

2 Picasso Moon
An interview with Weir, included on a promotional CD for the *Built to Last* album, includes a hilarious retelling of the origin of this phrase, which just popped out of Phil Lesh's mouth one day while the band was sitting around in the studio: 'Picasso moon.' I don't know why I said that!" The phrase came back repeatedly in Weir's mind, haunting him one day during a bike ride so that he nearly fell off his bike.

Deconstructing the little phrase allows almost too many references: to the famous artist himself and to the moon, one of the band's favorite and oft-recurring symbols, in songs from "Terrapin Station" to "Standing on the Moon."

3 Hangin' ten
A reference to the surfing maneuver in which a surfer is at the front of the board with all ten toes hanging over the front end.

4 I guess it doesn't matter . . .
Compare the line in "Morning Dew": "I guess it doesn't matter anyway..."

5 Heart of darkness
Title of a Joseph Conrad novel (1899), the inspiration for the 1979 Francis Ford Coppola film *Apocalyspe Now,* which featured a percussion underscore by Mickey Hart.

6 Wheels within wheels
Compare the line (and its source) in "Estimated Prophet": "Fire wheel burning in the air."

Notes:
Written in Mill Valley, California, February through May, 1989.

Studio recording: *Built to Last* (October 31, 1989).

First performance: April 28, 1989, at Irvine Meadows Amphitheater in Irvine, California. It remained in the repertoire thereafter.

So strange, you do me all that you do
Dark angel, you're making me blue
I guess it doesn't matter
I guess it doesn't matter   4

Picasso moon, blinding ball
I feel the quickening, I hear the call
Picasso moon, fill the sky
Amaze and blaze and mystify
With the lunar wind, I want to fly
And it's bigger than a drive-in movie, oh my
And it's bigger than a drive-in movie, oh my

Strikes the morning, the atomic dawn
Scramble back to cover
Quick, pop your mirrored sunglasses on
My little leather-winged lover
I see your face printed on my money
Your brazen ways really move me, honey
Heart of darkness, yeah, yeah   5
Why am I laughing, this ain't funny

Dark angel, now just don't start
You'll break my spirit, you'll wreck my heart
You must have a license for practicing that art
I don't presume to imagine
No, I don't presume to imagine

Picasso moon, fractal flame
Blazing lace filling every frame
Picasso moon, wheels within wheels   6

The bells are ringing, it's way unreal
Trying to tell y'all about just how it feels
And it's bigger than a drive-in movie, for real
Bigger than a drive-in movie, for real

Picasso moon, shattered light
Diamond bullets ripping up the night
Picasso moon, illuminate me
Picasso moon, blinding ball
I feel the quickening, I hear the call
Picasso moon, fill the sky
Picasso moon, fractal flame
Blazing lace filling every frame
Picasso moon, wheels within wheels
Picasso moon, shining bright
The universe is working fine tonight
Picasso moon, illuminate me

Words by John Barlow, with Bob Weir
and Bob Bralove
Music by Bob Weir

reuben and cérise

1 Cérise

Cerise is French for "cherry" and also used to refer to the color, cherry red. The word is also used in English for the color. Garcia sang "cherise."

2 carnival

Hunter has set the story in New Orleans, so this reference must be to Mardi Gras, the pre-Lent blowout celebration. This places the time in February, on Shrove Tuesday, which falls on a date determined by the date of Easter in any given year. It is the final night of the traditional worldwide celebration of Carnival, which is a season of celebration beginning with Twelfth Night, January 6.

Cérise was brushing her long hair gently down   1
It was the afternoon of Carnival   2
as she brushes it gently down

Reuben was strumming his painted mandolin   3
It was inlaid with a pretty face in jade
Played the Carnival Parade   4

Cérise was dressing as Pirouette in white   5
when a fatal vision gripped her tight
Cérise beware tonight

Reuben, Reuben tell me truly true   6

I feel afraid and I don't know why I do
Is there another girl for you?

If you could see in my heart
you would know it's true
there is none Cérise except for you except for you
I swear to it on my very soul
If I lie may I fall down cold

When Reuben played on his painted mandolin
the breeze would pause to listen in
before going its way again

Masquerade began when nightfall finally woke
Like waves against the bandstand dancers broke
to the painted mandolin

Looking out on the crowd, who is standing there?
7   Sweet Ruby Claire at Reuben stared
    At Reuben stared
8   She was dressed as Pirouette in red
    and her hair hung gently down

The crowd pressed 'round
Ruby stood as though alone
Reuben's song took on a different tone
and he played it just for her

The song he played was the Carnival Parade
Each note cut a thread of Cérise's fate
It cut through like a blade

Reuben was playing his painted mandolin
When Ruby froze and turned to stone
for the strings played all alone

The word *carnival* derives from the renunciation of meat (*carne vale,* or "farewell to meat"), which is a traditional way of observing Lent.

3 Reuben
According to *American Given Names:*

> From the oldest son of Jacob; also a tribal name. . . . The name is uncommon and approaches extinction after 1850. (Stewart)

4 Carnival Parade
"The Carnival Parade" was written in 1929 by the Cuban composer Ernesto Lecuona (1896–1963). The English lyric is by Albert Gamse.

> We were torn apart in the crowd.
> That very moment,
> I lost you,

It is interesting to note that there are three main parades at the New Orleans Mardi Gras: Endymion, Bacchus, and Orpheus.

5 Pirouette
The Pierrot clown character in the French clowning tradition has a female counterpart called Pirouette. This is a whiteface clown character, usually dressing in black and white. The character's origins lie in the commedia dell'arte tradition.

6 Reuben, Reuben
Calls to mind the song by Harry Birch, "Reuben and Rachel":

> Reuben, Reuben, I've been thinking,
> What a queer world this would be
> If the men were all transported
> Far beyond the Northern Sea.

7 Ruby Claire

Again, a name meaning "red." The addition of *claire* to the name indicates "bright red."

8 dressed . . . in red

Ruby dresses in red. Reminiscent of the lines in "Casey Jones": "Trouble ahead / The Lady in Red!"

9 unsung song

Compare "Attics of My Life": "seeking all that's still unsung."

10 without a look behind

In the version of the song published in *A Box of Rain,* Hunter includes a number of verses that flesh out the song's plot a bit, making it clearly a parallel to the tale of Orpheus, in which the hero makes a trip to the underworld in order to rescue his wife, Eurydice. He is told that he may have her back as long as he does not look behind to make sure that she is following him.

In the context of the *Cats Under the Stars* album, there is a nice echo of this idea in "Gomorrah," in which Lot is allowed to escape the doomed city with his family as long as he does not turn around. Of course, his wife does so, and is turned into a pillar of salt. The positioning of the songs on the album puts brackets around the entire set of songs, with "Reuben and cerise" opening the album, and "Gomorrah" closing it.

The setting of the Orpheus legend in the context of Carnival also echoes the 1949 Jean Cocteau film, *Orphée.*

Notes:
Studio recording: *Cats Under the Stars* (1978), Jerry Garcia Band.

First performance: Performed only four times by the Dead March 17, 1991, at the Capital Center in Landover, Maryland.

The voice of Cérise from the face of
the mandolin
singing: Reuben, Reuben tell me true
for I have no one but you
If you could see in my heart
you would know it's true
There is none Cérise, except for you—except
for you

I swear to it on my very soul
If I lie, may I fall down cold

The truth of love
an unsung song must tell   9
The course of love must follow blind
without a look behind   10
Reuben walked through the streets
of New Orleans till dawn,
Cérise so lightly in his arms
and her hair hung gently down

Words by Robert Hunter
Music by Jerry Garcia

so many roads

1   Thought I heard a blackbird singin'
     up on Bluebird Hill

2   Call me a whinin' boy if you will

3   Born where the sun don't shine

4   and I don't deny my name

5, 6   Got no place to go, ain't that a shame?

     Thought I heard that KC whistle

7   moanin' sweet and low
     Thought I heard that KC when she blow
     Down where the sun don't shine

8   Underneath the Kokomo
     Whinin' boy—got no place else to go

     So many roads I tell you
     So many roads I know
     So many roads—
     So many roads—

9   *Mountain high, river wide*
     So many roads to ride
     So many roads
     So many roads

     Thought I heard a jug band playin'

10   "If *you* don't—who else will?"
     from over on the far side of the hill

11   All I know the sun don't shine,
     the rain refuse to fall

12   and you don't seem to hear me when I call

     Wind inside and the wind outside
     tangled in the window blind

1 blackbird singin'
Possible reference to the Beatles' "Blackbird," by John Lennon and Paul McCartney (but mostly McCartney): "Blackbird singin' in the dead of night."

2 whinin' boy
Compare "Winin' Boy Blues" by Jelly Roll Morton, ca. 1938:

3 Born where the sun don't shine
Compare the 1947 song "Sixteen Tons," written by Merle Travis and made famous by Tennessee Ernie Ford:

     I was born one mornin' when the sun didn't shine
     I picked up my shovel and I walked to the mine

4 and I don't deny my name
See lyrics from "Whinin' Boy Blues," mentioned above: "I'm a whinin' boy, I don't deny my name."

Big Brother and the Holding Company also did a traditional song called "Easy Rider," whose chorus was

     Easy rider, don't you deny my name

5 Got no place to go
Compare "No Particular Place to Go" by Chuck Berry

6 ain't that a shame
Compare "Ain't That a Shame" by Fats Domino.

7 KC whistle / moanin' sweet and low
Compare the traditional tune "KC Moan," performed once by the Grateful Dead and now part of the Ratdog repertoire. Performed by The Dead in

2004. And, of course, the line brings to mind the Grateful Dead's own "Casey Jones."

8 Kokomo

Kokomo is a town in Indiana. It was named after an Indian: In the Miami Indian tribe of the Ohio Valley a local leader named his sons after trees. One was Ko-ko-mo-ko

(black walnut), who was thought to have become a war chief of the Miami Tribe.

Mentioned in "No Particular Place to Go" (1964) by Chuck Berry.

"Kokomo" is also a Beach Boys song, written by Terry Melcher and John Phillips for the sound-track to the Tom Cruise movie *Cocktail* (1988).

Kokomo Arnold (1901–1968) was a Delta bluesman.

During the four-month hiatus in 1986 (August to December), while Jerry was recovering from his diabetic coma, Kreutzman and Myland toured the East Coast in September, calling themselves "KOKOMO."

9 Mountain high, river wide

Compare "River Deep, Mountain High," written by Ellie Greenwich, Jeff Barry, and Phil Spector and recorded by Keith and Donna Godchaux (among many others, including, most famously, Ike and Tina Turner) on their 1975 eponymous LP. The Grateful Dead sound-checked the song on December 31, 1976.

Tell me why you treat me so unkind
Down where the sun don't shine
Lonely and I call your name
No place left to go, ain't that a shame?

So many roads I tell you
New York to San Francisco
All I want is one
to take me home
From the high road to the low   13
So many roads I know
So many roads—So many roads

From the land of the midnight sun   14
where ice blue roses grow   15
'long those roads of gold and silver snow
Howlin' wide or moanin' low   16
So many roads I know
So many roads to ease my soul

Words by Robert Hunter
Music by Jerry Garcia

10 "If *you* don't—who else will?"
Compare the line in Doctor John's "Such a Night": "If I don't do it, somebody else will."

11 All I know the sun don't shine
Compare "In the Pines," an old folk tune:
> In the pines, in the pines, where the sun never
>   shines

and "Dark Hollow," another standard bluegrass tune:
> "I'd rather be in some dark hollow, where the
>   sun don't ever shine

12 and you don't seem to hear me when I call
Compare Al Smith and Luther Dixon's "Big Boss Man" (part of the Grateful Dead repertoire): "Big boss man, can't you hear me when I call."

13 From the high road to the low
Compare "Loch Lomond," quintessential Scottish song: "You take the high road and I'll take the low road and I'll be in Scotland afore ye."

14 midnight sun
Compare line in "China Cat Sunflower": "proud walking jingle in the midnight sun."

15 ice-blue roses
"The blue rose is a symbol of the Impossible."
—Juan-Eduardo Cirlot

Compare the Mouse and Kelley poster "Blue Rose" for the closing of Winterland. Also reminiscent of "Dark Star": "ice-petal flowers / revolving."

For roses in general, see note under "That's It for the Other One."

16 Howlin' wide or moanin' low
"Moanin' Lo" (possibly by Howard Dietz and Ralph Rainger, 1929) was a song performed in the 1930s by Billie Holiday.

Notes:
No studio recording. Included on the box set *So Many Roads.*

First performance: February 22, 1992, at the Coliseum Arena in Oakland, California.

wave to the wind

1 rolling thunder
Evokes the name of the band's shaman associate.
See note under "Sunrise."

2 Say, can you see / By the dawn's early light
A reference to Francis Scott Keye's words to the U.S. national anthem, "The Star-Spangled Banner." The Grateful Dead, in the persons of Garcia, Weir, and

Welnick, sang the national anthem to open the San Francisco Giants' home opener baseball game at Candlestick Park in 1993. The national anthem also served as an occasional time-killing piece during Dead shows in the late sixties and early seventies.

Notes:
No studio recording.

First played February 22, 1992, at the Oakland Coliseum Arena in Oakland, California.

Gonna wave, gonna wave
Gonna wave to the wind
Gonna wave my way
My way on through the wind
Gonna wave, gonna wave
Gonna wave to the wind
Gonna wave my way to
Places I never have been

Gonna wave to the curious people
Looking on from the side of
The road as I'm rolling on by
Wave goodbye to the trouble
That's always on my mind
Gonna jump-start my life
Or go down trying

Gonna wave to the memories
I carry in my heart and the
New ones I'll find along my way
To the new millennium
Reeling 'round the bend like
A dove or some dark-winged bird of prey

Gonna wave, gonna wave
Gonna wave to the wind
Gonna wave my way
My way on through the wind
Gonna wave, gonna wave
Gonna wave to the wind
Gonna wave my way to the
Edge of the world and jump in

Gonna snap like a rippling banner
Sailing sheets to the breeze over
Cloudy oceans to the moon
I could hold out forever
Keeping it together
Or wish upon a star and call the tune

Lift my voice like the young man
Broken in the war who
Cries out to know the reason why
Gonna stand and deliver
A passionate song to the
High wide and handsome morning sky

Gonna wave, gonna wave
Gonna wave to the wind
Gonna wave my way
My way on through the wind
Gonna wave, gonna wave
Gonna wave while the wind
Plays the stars, the sky, the
Moon and the night like a hymn

1   Gonna ride with the rolling thunder
    Let the sky crack assunder

As lightning cries out of the rain
Gonna wade across rivers
Gathered in the stream from the
Mountains that rise above the plain

Wave away my confusion
That drives this delusion
So long I forgot that I could fly
Soar aloft like a songbird
Dancing in the wind
Singing long, singing loud, singing high

Gonna wave, gonna wave
Gonna wave to the wind
Gonna wave my way
My way on through the wind
Gonna speak to the breeze
Add my voice to the wind
Singing: Say, can you see
By the dawn's early light streaming in?   2

Words by Robert Hunter
Music by Phil Lesh

corrina

1 Corrina

The most familiar reference, for American listeners, is the folk blues "Corinna, Corinna," sung and recorded by innumerable performers.

> Corinna, Corinna, where'd you stay last night? (2x)
> Your shoes ain't buttoned, girl, don't fit you
>   right.
>
> Corinna, Corinna, where you been so long? (2x)
> Ain't had no lovin' since you been gone.
>
> Corinna, Corinna, what's the matter now? (2x)
> You done gone bad, babe, ain't no good
>   nohow.
>
> Corinna, Corinna, way cross the sea, (2x)
> Ain't done no good, babe, since you left me.
>
> I love Corinna, God know I do, (2x)
> And I hope some day, she come to love me,
>   too.

The version by the Blue Sky Boys includes the first verse from "Midnight Special" as well.

A tune called "Corrine, Corrina" (1932) by Bo Chatman, Mitchell Parish (Grateful Dead roadie Steve Parish's uncle), and J. M. Williams was popularly revived in 1961.

The original Corinna was a Greek lyric poetess, ca. 200 B.C.E. or possibly ca. 500 B.C.E. Little is known about her, but some fragments of her poetry have survived:

> According to an ancient anecdote, Corinna criticized the absence of myth from one of Pindar's poems; when he thereupon went to the other extreme, she remarked that one

Chorus:

Corrina . . . Wake it up baby   1
Corrina . . . Shake it on down
Corrina . . . Corrina . . .

Hog of a Sunday
Dog of a Monday
Get it back some day
What'd I say?
Movin' in closer
Cut from a long shot
Fade on a down beat
Ready or not

(Chorus)

Cruise thru a stop sign
Loggin' up short time
Bird on a phone line   2
Soakin' up sun
Salt on the crowtail   3
What can I do?
I'm down by law
But true to you

(Chorus)

If, what, where, and when
Told at the proper time
Big black wings beat at the wind
But they don't hardly climb
There's a silver ocean

Silver clouds and silver sea
A bird on the horizon
Silver wingin' back to me

(Chorus)

Wake it up baby
Shake it down easy
Bring it back someday
What'd I say?
Movin' in closer
Cut from a long shot
Fade on a downbeat
Ready or not

(Chorus)

Corrina/wake it up baby
Corrina/Shake it down easy
Corrina/Shake it on up now
Corrina/Shake it back down Corrina . . .

If, who, how and why
don't mean that much to me
long as it don't hurt too much
believe we'll let it be
Outside major darkness
where the circle is complete
there is no fear that lovers born
4   will ever fail to meet

[*Addendum: Ways in which it might be shaken*]

should "sow by handfuls, not with the whole sack," an expression which became proverbial. (*Oxford Companion to Classical Literature*)

Ovid, the Roman poet, wrote numerous poems about a Corinna.

Jonathan Swift wrote a poem titled "Corinna" (ca. 1711), which was probably about either a Mrs. Manley or Mrs. Eliza Haywood—there seems to be some dispute. Swift, as evidenced by his other poems to "Stella," was fond of assigning pseudonyms to women of his acquaintance.

One of Robert Herrick's two poems about a Corinna is "Corinna's Going A-Maying" (1648). After berating his beloved for staying in bed too long on a beautiful spring day, the poet concludes:

> Come, let us go, while we are in our prime;
> And take the harmless folly of the time.
> We shall grow old apace, and die
> Before we know our liberty.
> Our life is short, and our days run
> As fast away as does the sun;
> And as a vapour, or a drop of rain,
> Once lost, can ne'er be found again,
> So when or you or I are made
> A fable, song, or fleeting shade,
> All love, all liking, all delight
> Lies drown'd with us in endless night.
> Then while time serves, and we are but
>   decaying,
> Come, my Corinna, come, let's go a-Maying.

The other Herrick poem is "Upon the Loss of His Mistresses," in which he laments a series of names, Corinna and Electra (see "Mountains of the Moon") among others.

2 Bird on a phone line
Compare with the line in "Loose Lucy."

3 Salt on the crow-tail
Children wishing to catch a bird are advised to put salt on its tail. While this may be a commonsense piece of advice (if you can get that close to a bird, you can probably catch it), it may also reflect some more ancient belief in the magical powers of salt.

Jonathan Swift: "As boys do sparrows, with flinging salt upon their tails." (*A Tale of a Tub,* 1704)

In the Swedish folktale "Salt on a Magpie's Tail," a young boy is told by a wise old man that he will get his wish if he sprinkles salt on the tail-feathers of a magpie. After going through a great deal of work to be able to communicate with a magpie and sprinkle the salt, he finds that he is in need of nothing, and the salt falls off the bird's tail before he can think of something he needs, so he loses his wish. The magpie is a member of the crow family.

4 there is no fear that lovers born will ever fail to meet
Hunter notes in *A Box of Rain* that these two lines were lifted from the portion of the "Terrapin Station" suite that was never set to music, as he despaired of otherwise hearing them sung.

Notes:
No official Grateful Dead recording.

First performance: February 23, 1992, at the Oakland Coliseum Arena in Oakland, California. "Corrina" remained in the repertoire thereafter.

Corrina/Wake it up baby
Corrina/Shake it down easy
Corrina/Shake it on up now
Corrina/Shake it back down

Corrina/Makin' me crazy
Corrina/C'mon baby
Corrina/Shake it all day
Corrina/Tell me what'd I say

Corrina/Shake it up closer
Corrina/Shake it away
Corrina/Shake it in the shadow
Corrina/Shake it in the shade

Corrina/Shake it on the shakedown
Corrina/Shake it uptown
Corrina/Shake it in the short haul
Corrina/Shake it around

Corrina/Shake it at the window
Corrina/Shake it at the door
Corrina/Shake it on the stairwell
Corrina/Shake it on the floor

Corrina/Shake it in the mornin'
Corrina/Shake it in the dawn
Corrina/Shake it all night babe
Corrina/Shake it on down

Words by Robert Hunter
Music by Bob Weir and Mickey Hart

way to go home

Who—do you think you are?
What do you mean
when you put us all down
Walking 'round in circles
Your nose to the ground
You think you're saying something
Because you're making a sound?

You say you've seen it all
You don't care to see no more
But you don't get up and go
until they throw you out the door

Chorus:
It's a long long long long way to go home
It's a long long long long way to go home
Any which way you are tempted to roam
It's a long long long long long long way
Way to go home

Who—'s it you remind me of?
What do you do
when you do your own time?
Did you run away
from the scene of your crime?
I feel as though I know you
1   Could you spare me a dime

It's a lot less than prison
but it's more than a jail
I'd tell you all about it
but that's another tale

1 **Could you spare me a dime?**
Compare "Wharf Rat":
"asked me for a dime— / a dime for a cup of coffee."

Notes:
No official Grateful Dead recording.

First performance: February 23, 1992, at the Oakland Coliseum Arena in Oakland, California. The song remained in the repertoire thereafter.

(Chorus)

You say you've seen it all
You don't care to see no more
of the hungry, the homeless,
the sick, and the poor

You say you've seen enough
to last you all your days
like the moon in high heaven
you're just going through a phase

(Chorus)

Who—do you want to be?
What do you need

to set your body free?
I don't mean to pry
this ain't no third degree
but looking at you baby
you remind myself of me

There's any way to tell you—
Any way, any way to persuade—
I'd really love to spare you
the mistakes I've made

(Chorus)

Words by Robert Hunter
Music by Vince Welnick, Bob Bralove

Eternity

I'm lookin' out my window
I watch the clouds go by
I look to see eternity
The endless rolling sky

You cannot think of eternity
Think of it like time
You try to think, you try to count
You just mess up your mind

Eternity, eternity
Honey, I love you, you love me
Let's love each other through eternity

Since before man could see
There was eternity
After man is come and gone
Eternity lingers on, eternity lingers on

Everything crawl, creep, or fly
Just live until they die
I love you, honey, you love me
Let's love each other through eternity

Eternity, eternity
I love you, you love me
Let's love each other through eternity
Through eternity

Well I think about life, we don't know
Whether it all could be in vain
Look through time, it's for sure
It's the greatest gift to man

Notes:

No official Grateful Dead recording.

First performance: February 21, 1993, at the Oakland Coliseum Arena in Oakland, California.

Blues bass player and composer Willie James Dixon was born on July 1, 1915, in Vicksburg, Mississippi. He was the seventh of fourteen children. He left Vicksburg for Chicago at age seventeen to become a boxer but only fought four matches as a pro after attaining the title of Illinois State Golden Gloves Heavyweight Champion. He formed a musical group, the Five Breezes, in 1940 and was arrested a year later for refusing to serve in the armed forces. In 1945 he formed a new group, the Big Three Trio, and they played blues clubs in Chicago, occasionally teaming up with Muddy Waters. Dixon began to work for Chess Records as a composer and arranger in the early 1950s, and stayed through 1971. He wrote some of the best-known blues songs, which were recorded by a wide variety of artists: "Hoochie Coochie Man" and "I Just Want to Make Love to You" for Muddy Waters; "Wang Dang Doodle" for Koko Taylor; and "Back Door Man" for Howlin' Wolf. He died in Burbank, California, on January 19, 1992. He wrote an autobiography, *I Am the Blues,* published in 1989.

Music and love, you can't explain
Try and understand
The greatest thing could ever be
We make love through eternity
Make love through eternity

When the world think our defeat
Think that we are gone
We'll still have our place of peace
Our love will linger on, linger on

We won't care just what who said
If it's truth or lie
We'll still have our greatest gift
Our love won't ever die
Love won't ever die
Love won't ever die

Words by Willie Dixon
Music by Bob Weir and Rob Wasserman

lazy River Road

1, 2 Way down upon Sycamore Slough
     a white man sings the blues
3   selling roses of papier-mâché
     with flecks of starlight dew
     I swiped a bunch and threw it your way
     where hazy moonlight glowed
     Way down
          down along
4   Lazy River Road

     Way down upon Shadowfall Ward
     End of the avenue
     Run, hide, seek in your own backyard
     Mama's backyard won't do
     All night long I sang Love's Sweet Song
     down where the water flowed
     Way down
          down along
              Lazy River Road

     Moonlight wails as hound dogs bay
     but never quite catch the tune
     Stars fall down in buckets like rain
     till there ain't no standin' room
     Bright blue boxcars train by train
     clatter while dreams unfold
     Way down
          down along
              Lazy River Road

1 Way down upon The opening words to one of America's best-known songs, Stephen Foster's "Old Folks at Home" (1852):

Way down upon the Swanee River, far, far
    away
That's where my heart is turning ever
That's where the old folks
    stay

All up and down the whole creation, sadly I
    roam
Still longing for the old plantation
And for the old folks at home

All the world is sad and dreary everywhere I
    roam
Oh, darkies, how my heart grows weary
Far from the old folks at home

All 'round the little farm I wandered, when I
    was young
Then many happy days I squandered, many
    the songs I sung
When I was playing with my brother, happy
    was I
Oh, take me to my kind old
    mother, there let me live
    and die

One little hut among the bushes,
    one that I love
Still sadly to my mem'ry rushes,
    no matter where I rove
When shall I see the bees a-hum-
    ming, all 'round the comb
When shall I hear the banjo
    strumming,
    down by my good old home

2 Sycamore Slough, Shadowfall Ward, Seminole Square
These three alliterative places appear to be fictitious.

3 roses
See note under "That's It for the Other One."

4 Lazy River
Compare the lines in "Mississippi Half-Step Uptown Toodleoo": "Across the Rio Grande-eO / Across the lazy river."

5 Thread the needle . . . I let pass by
Compare the party game "The Needle's Eye," similar to "London Bridge" :

> The needle's eye that doth supply
> The thread that runs so true
> Many a lass have I let pass
> Because I wanted you

> Mama taught me how to sew
> And how to thread the needle;
> Every time my finger slips,
> Pop goes the weasel.

There is also a slightly different version of this, where the speaker is female and "Many a lass / have I let pass" is replaced by "Many a beau / Have I let go." (Owens)

Way down upon Seminole Square
belly of the river tide
call for me and I will be there
for the price of the taxi ride
Night time double-clutches into today
like a truck downshifting its load
Way down
      down along
           Lazy River Road

Thread the needle   5
right through the eye
The thread that runs so true
All the others I let pass by
I only wanted you
Never cared for careless love   6
but how your bright eyes glowed
Way down
      down along
           Lazy River Road

Words by Robert Hunter
Music by Jerry Garcia

Echoes of the line from "Scarlet Begonias": "I had to learn the hard way / to let her pass by."

6 careless love
The title of a folk song formalized in 1921 by W. C. Handy, Spencer Williams, and Martha Koenig.

Love, oh love, oh careless love,
Love, oh love, oh careless love,
Oh, it's love, oh love, oh careless love
You see what careless love has done.

Once I wore my apron low
Once I wore my apron low
Oh, it's once I wore my apron low,
You'd follow me through rain and snow.

Now I wear my apron high
Now I wear my apron high
Oh, it's now I wear my apron high,

You'll see my door and pass it by.

I cried last night and the night before,
I cried last night and the night before,
Oh, I cried last night and the night before,
Going to cry tonight and cry no more.

Love, oh love, oh careless love,
Love, oh love, oh careless love,
Oh, it's love, oh love, oh careless love
You see what careless love has done.

Notes:
Studio recording: A studio rehearsal dated February 18, 1993, was released on the box set *So Many Roads (1965–1995)*.

First performance: February 21, 1993, at the Oakland Coliseum Arena in Oakland, California.

Liberty

1 Liberty
Hunter's liner notes to his release of *Liberty* carried this quote:

> We must all be foolish at times It is one of the conditions of liberty.
> —Walt Whitman

2 To find my own way home
Compare "Ripple": "If I knew the way I would take you home."

3 Whole lotta shakin'
Title of a Top 10 hit for Jerry Lee Lewis in 1957, written by Dave Williams and Roy Hall.

Notes:
Original version was the title track of Robert Hunter's 1988 album and was eventually rewritten by Garcia for performance by the Grateful Dead. No Grateful Dead studio recording. The March 30, 1994, performance was included on the *So Many Roads (1965–1995)* box set.

First performance: February 21, 1993, at the Oakland Coliseum Arena in Oakland, California. The song remained in steady rotation thereafter.

Saw a bird with a tear in his eye
Walking to New Orleans my oh my
Hey now Bird, wouldn't you rather die
Than walk this world when you're born to fly?

If I was the sun, I'd look for shade
If I was a bed, I would stay unmade
If I was a river I'd run uphill
If you call me you know I will
If you call me you know I will

Chorus:
Ooo, freedom—ooo, liberty   1
O . . . Leave me alone
To find my own way home   2
To find my own way home

Say what I mean and I don't give a damn
I do believe and I am who I am
Hey now Mama come and take my hand
Whole lotta shakin' all over this land   3

If I was an eagle I'd dress like a duck
Crawl like a lizard and honk like a truck
If I get a notion I'll climb this tree
or chop it down and you can't stop me
Chop it down and you can't stop me

(Chorus)

Went to the well but the water was dry
Dipped my bucket in the clear blue sky
Looked in the bottom and what did I see?
The whole damned world looking back at me

If I was a bottle I'd spill for love
Sake of mercy I'd kill for love
If I was a liar I'd lie for love
Sake of my baby I'd die for love
Sake of my baby I'd die for love

(Chorus)

Words by Robert Hunter
Music by Jerry Garcia

Ties/Pics

Days Between

1 August
Evoking the month of Garcia's birth.

2 headless horsemen

A reference to Washington Irving's tale "The Legend of Sleepy Hollow."

Notes:

First performance: February 22, 1993, at the Coliseum Arena in Oakland, California. It appeared regularly thereafter.

From Lesh's autobiography:

> Achingly nostalgic, "Days Between" evokes the past. The music climbs laboriously out of shadows, growing and peaking with each verse, only to fall back each time in hopeless resignation. When Jerry sings the line "when all we ever wanted / was to learn and love and grow" or "gave the best we had to give / how much we'll never know," I am immediately transported decades back in time, to a beautiful spring morning with Jerry, Hunter, Barbara Meier, and Alan Trist—all of us goofing on the sheer exhilaration of being alive. I don't know whether to weep with joy at the beauty of the vision or with sadness at the impassable chasm of time between the golden past and the often painful present. 95

A brief, speculative note on the song's structure: Hunter has laid out the lyric in an interesting manner, comprising four verses of fourteen lines each. While fourteen lines is the traditional

There were days
and there were days
and there were days between
Summer flies and August dies   1
the world grows dark and mean
Comes the shimmer of the moon
on black infested trees
the singing man is at his song
the holy on their knees
the reckless are out wrecking
the timid plead their pleas
No one knows much more of this
than anyone can see
anyone can see

There were days
and there were days
and there were days besides
when phantom ships with phantom sails
set to sea on phantom tides
Comes the lightning of the sun
on bright unfocused eyes
the blue of yet another day
a springtime wet with sighs
a hopeful candle lingers
in the land of lullabies
where headless horsemen vanish   2
with wild and lonely cries
lonely cries

There were days
and there were days

and there were days I know
when all we ever wanted
was to learn and love and grow
Once we grew into our shoes
we told them where to go
walked halfway around the world
on promise of the glow
stood upon a mountain top
walked barefoot in the snow
gave the best we had to give
how much we'll never know
we'll never know

There were days
and there were days
and there were days between
polished like a golden bowl
the finest ever seen
Hearts of Summer held in trust
still tender, young and green
left on shelves collecting dust
not knowing what they mean
valentines of flesh and blood
as soft as velveteen
hoping love would not forsake
the days that lie between
lie between

Words by Robert Hunter
Music by Jerry Garcia

length of the sonnet form, Hunter's lines are much shorter than strict sonnet form would allow, but this may nevertheless be an homage to the form. More significant than the number of lines in each verse is the subtle reference to one season of the year in each verse, in the manner of a poet using the seasons as a metaphor for the cycles of life. The first verse is autumn; the second, spring; the third, winter; and the fourth, summer. So it's a nonlinear year.

Easy Answers

Notes:

Studio recording: Rob Wasserman's *Trios* (1994).

First performance: June 5, 1993, at Giants Stadium in East Rutherford, New Jersey.

From an interview with Bob Weir in the liner notes to *Weir Here:*

> I had some lyrics that Hunter had given me for that, but there weren't enough of them to make a whole song out of. So Neil [Young] said, "Let me see what you've got. It needs one more verse." We got two verses in, and I sang the first verse again. Neil says, "Shut your eyes and listen to the colors of your mind." He throws his head back and says, "Get yourself a breath of air, let your soul unwind. You don't have to say a word . . ." and he was thinking, and I said, "If you've got dick to say?" And he said, "'Cause no one ever said there's going to be an easy way." And we had the song.

Promises made in the dark dissolve by light of day
Easy answers
Ain't no saying what will be, it's always been that way
Only thing I know for sure, someone got to pay
Easy answers
Ain't no easy answers, is what I got to say

Easy answers
I don't wanna hear
Ain't nobody cares
C'mon let's go
I don't wanna know
I don't wanna know
I don't wanna know
I don't wanna know
I don't wanna know

Love is an easy word to say, roll's right off the tongue
Easy answers
Seems to crop up like a weed, in every song that's sung
It always sounds so easy, the way it falls upon the ear
Easy answers
Plenty easy answers now, listen to me here

Easy answers
Find 'em anywhere
Easy answers
Easy answers
Easy answers
Easy answers
I don't wanna know
I don't wanna know

Shut your eyes and listen to the colors of your mind
Easy answers
Give yourself a breath of air, let your soul unwind
Easy answers
You don't have to say a word, you got dick to say
'Cause no one ever said there's gonna be an easy way
Easy answers

Find them anywhere
Easy answers
Ain't nobody care
Easy answers
I don't wanna know

Easy answers
I don't wanna know
Easy answers
I don't wanna know
I don't wanna know

Promises made in the dark dissolve by light of day
Easy answers
Ain't no saying what we'll be, it's always been that way
Only thing I know for sure, someone got to pay
Easy answers
Ain't no easy answers, that's all I got to say
Easy answers

Easy answers
I don't wanna hear
Easy answers
Easy answers
Ain't nobody there
Easy answers
Easy answers
C'mon now, let's go
I don't wanna know
I don't wanna know
I don't wanna know

Easy answers
Easy answers
Feel alright
Easy answers
Easy answers
Feel alright
Easy answers
Easy answers

Words by Robert Hunter
Music by Bob Weir, Bob Bralove,
Rob Wasserman, and Vince Welnick

samba in the rain

1 sweet and low
"Sweet and Low-Down," a song by George and Ira Gershwin (1925). According to David Ewen's *American Popular Songs*:

> the phrase "sweet and low-down" had earlier been coined by Ira Gershwin for a discarded song, "Little Jazz Bird." This phrase was listed in *The American Thesaurus of Slang*.

2 cellophane
Hunter's use of this brand name recalls Cole Porter's use of the same word in "You're the Top" (1934):

> You're the purple light of a summer night in
>   Spain,
> You're the National Gall'ry,
> You're Garbo's sal'ry,
> You're Cellophane

3 Samba
The Samba (or *Mesemba*), which means "to Pray" is an Afro-Brazilian dance from Bahia, Brazil. It is said to have been derived from a dance called the Lundu (adding a ballroom hold), the West African slaves, Portuguese songs, and Indian rituals. When different body motions and Carnival steps were added to the dance, it would be called the Zemba Queca, which was described as "a graceful Brazilian dance" way back in 1885 and later became known as the Mesemba and, finally mixing with the Maxixe during the 1900s, became known as the Samba. (Dance History Archives)

4 the dirty bop
Bop was a popular form of swing dancing during the 1950s as well as done as a solo dance (especially when the melody divorced

Ten and ten is thirty
If you tell me it is so
Let's get down and dirty, baby
Let's get sweet and low   1

Any way you call the shot
That's how it's gonna be
You can serve it cold or hot
It's all okay by me

Tie me with a ribbon bow
Wrap me in cellophane   2
Send me out to steal the show
  or Samba in the rain   3

Chorus:
Samba in the rain oh baby
Samba in the rain
Let's get down and dirty
Don't bother to explain
Don't care if they call a cop
and say we are insane
we'll keep goin' till we drop
Samba in the rain

How many hours in a day
They tell me twenty-four
There could be a couple less
I know there ain't no more

4　We can do the dirty bop
5　The Darktown Strutter's Ball
　　Just as long as we don't stop
　　We'll dance right up the wall

　　We can do the bump and grind
6　The Apache in Spain
　　We can do the never mind
　　or Samba in the rain

(Chorus)

Words by Robert Hunter
Music by Vince Welnick

5 Darktown Strutter's Ball
A 1917 song, with words and music by Shelton Brooks, made popular by Sophie Tucker on the vaudeville circuit. It was selected by ASCAP in 1963 for its All-time Hit Parade. (Note the reference to the "Jelly Roll blues" found in "Dupree's Diamond Blues.")

6 The Apache
The Apache *(pronounced A-Posh or A-Poe-Shay)* dance originated in the Parisian lower classes. A domestic street fight between two men and a woman in the Montmartre section of Paris, in front of a nightclub, was indirectly responsible for the name *Apache*. A local gazette journalist reported that "the fury of a riotous incident between two men and a women rose to the ferocity of savage Apache Indians in battle." These participants, proud of their deed, formed "Apache Bands," which were actually street gangs. These gangs created their own type of dancing, which reenacted the actions of that night. The Apache was billed as the "Dance of the Underworld." (Dance History Archives)

itself from traditional dance rhythms). Its style was slightly different than its predecessor the Jitterbug. The term *bop* was also used as slang for a type of careless movement, such as "Bop on over." The dance style was a form of Jitterbug, or more recently East Coast Swing. Bop was mainly eight counts with a hip-twisting, body-swaying, double-rhythm style. The basic step is done in open position, Follower mainly staying in front of the Leader: *Originally: "Tap-Step—-Walk-Walk—-Tap-Step—-Walk-Walk"*—swaying from his left to right. Today a basic East Coast triple rhythm is all that's needed. (Dance History Archives)

Notes:
No Grateful Dead recordings.

First performance: June 8, 1994, at Cal Expo Amphitheater in Sacramento, California.

If the shoe Fits

Will your high hopes get you there
Goal so far and yet so near
You can't ignore the writing on the wall
Every time you rise you fall
End's nowhere in sight at all

1 If the shoe fits
The proverb from which the song takes its title is
characterized as follows:

> If something belongs or pertains to you,
> accept it. This proverb first appeared as "if the
> cap fits," which may have referred to a fool's
> cap. The later version has become more com-
> mon and is associated with the glass slipper in
> the fairy tale "Cinderella." (Hirsch)

2 take your ball and go home
A cliché of indeterminate origin that's often but
not always used in an athletic context.

3 Friends in need are never really true
A play on the saying "A friend in need is a friend
indeed."

Notes:
No official recording.

First performance: June 9, 1994, at Cal Expo
Amphitheater in Sacramento, California.

Andrew Charles is a self-taught musician born
and raised on the island of Barbados, the West
Indies. After moving to the Bay Area in 1993, he
played with several local Caribbean bands and
then expanded his musical talent to songwriting.
Jill Lesh introduced Phil to Andrew. Phil listened
to a few songs and asked if he could play around
with "If the Shoe Fits," which was originally titled
"Give It Up."

Why should you pick it up and try again

Chorus:
Give it up, 'cause you can't win
Let it go while you still can
Gave it all you had, now you're feelin' bad
So you're gone, ready to roam
You come on so strong with that same sad
   song
Wherever you go
Run along, take your ball and go home   2

Promised yet another chance
Forbidden just a single glance
So much rides on what you say and do
Discarded truths and famous myths
Tales that life deceives you with
Certain things you always thought you knew

(Chorus)

Helpful hands that pull you down
Smaller minds turn you around
Friends in need are never really true   3
So why should you put trust in this
The bridge above the dark abyss
You never learned you can't make all the rules

(Chorus)

Run along, take your ball and go home
Take a hike, we ain't got all night
Take your ball, get out my house, go home

Words by Andrew Charles
Music by Phil Lesh

childhood's end

1, 2 When I was hoppin' freights and makin' payments
      on the farm

3 Here between the angels and the deep blue sea
      You were runnin', laughin', growin' sheltered from

4   the storm
      Dreamin' of the day the moon would set you free
      Yeah, to sing your siren song so sweet and warm

      River run deep
      River run slow
      Get a little restless
      Wanna see some whales blow

5 River run cold
      River run clear
      That feeling always gets to me
      'Round about this time of year

      Scoutin' unknown borders under multi-colored
        moons
      In the wildest flights of cosmic mystery
      Rang a single soarin' tone that strung the sky
        in tune
      As the silence in my heart rose from the sea
      Aaah, to greet you in the dawn with a
        pale harpoon

      River run restless
      River run high
      Runnin' thru a hailstorm
      Try to catch a star on the fly

1 hoppin' freights
This led to one of Phil's greatest early adventures: hitchhiking to Calgary, Alberta, Canada to work in the oil fields. He only made it as far as Spokane before learning that the job in Alberta didn't exist. So he rode in a boxcar from Spokane to Seattle—thirty-six hours—and borrowed money from some friends of his parents to take a Greyhound back to the Bay Area: "My parents picked me up, and boy, did I catch shit then! They made me get a job in a bank and I worked there just long enough for school to be starting again in San Mateo." (Jackson and Gans, unpublished material for *Garcia: An American Life*) 90

2 makin' payments on the farm
The phrase "bought the farm" is slang for dying suddenly. Its origin is undetermined, though there are a number of theories floating around, including the idea that a soldier killed in combat will bring enough of a death benefit to his family back home that they can finally purchase the farm.

3 between the angels and the deep blue sea
A new take on the old expression "between the devil and the deep blue sea," which carries the meaning, roughly, of "between a rock and a hard place."

The first recorded use of the expression, according to *The Oxford Dictionary of English Proverbs* (3rd ed.), was in Bartholemew Robinson's 1621 work *Adagia in Latine and English:* "Betwixt the Deuill and the dead sea." This version of the saying was modified over the years into the familiar expression.

Perhaps the best-known use of the phrase in popular song is in Gram Parsons' "Return of the Grievous Angel" (1974):

And I saw my devil,
And I saw my deep blue sea

4 sheltered from the storm
Compare the Bob Dylan song "Shelter from the Storm."

5 River run
Reminiscent of the first line of James Joyce's *Finnegans Wake:*

riverrun, past Eve and Adam's, from swerve of shore to bend of bay, brings us by a commodius vicus of recirculation back to Howth Castle and Environs.

Notes:
No official recordings.

First performance: July 20, 1994, at Deer Creek Music Center in Noblesville, Indiana.

The song's title is reminiscent of the 1953 Arthur C. Clarke novel, though Lesh stated, "It has nothing to do with that." It was also the title of a song by Pink Floyd, recorded on their soundtrack album for the 1972 film *La Vallée,* released as *Obscured by Clouds.*

River run muddy
River flow like tears
Cocoon of life surroundin' us
Holdin' all our hopes and fears

Reach behind the wind
Search beyond the stars
We're the life on Mars

When the day grows dark and scary scatterin'
    the light
All the colors run away and hide behind your
    knees
The same sweet thunder tumbles rollin' down
    the night
Like a mothership that calls for you and me
Come on, and drift along that sky river bright

River run swiftly
River run wide
Feel like sailin'
On the morning tide

River run golden
River run true
Set a course and follow
Ooooh, the star that leads to you

Words and music by Phil Lesh

coda:
original songs played by the dead

Note from the editors: Throughout this book, the Grateful Dead are occasionally referred to as the Dead. When the post-Garcia incarnation of the band is referred to, it is always with a capitalized *T* as in The Dead.

After Jerry Garcia's death, on August 9, 1995, the remaining band members formally dissolved the Grateful Dead. They continued to write songs and play in various bands (Weir in Ratdog; Lesh in Phil and Friends; Hart in various groups, including Planet Drum and Mystery Box; Kreutzmann in Backbone and the Trichromes), even, on occasion, together as the Other Ones. It was in February 2003 that all four regrouped to tour as The Dead.

ALL that we ARE

Black book of night
Flip back the pages
Thread of inner sight
Saw my dream
Spinning out of control
Believe in yesterday
Today is all you really need to know

Open the door
Take a look around
Veil of sunbeam
Tears come rainin' down
Where have they gone
Those I left behind
Stranded at a crossroad
Under empty sky
All that we are
All that we are

I got to keep movin'
I got to get home
I got to keep movin'
I got to keep on

All that we are
All that we are

Open your eyes
Back through the years
Ocean of sorrow
Drown a river of tears
Winding road
Call me in the dawn
Unknown land
Over far horizon walk alone

Where the winds rage
Where the ice falls
Where the sky moves
To shake me apart
Silent axis of the turning world
Glows in the flame
In the flame of our hearts

Throw the windows open wide
See the dawn outrace the tide
Let the past slip away
On the wings of yesterday

But me, I got to keep movin'
I got to get home
I got to keep movin'
I got to keep on

I got to keep movin'
I got to get home
I got to keep movin'
I got to keep on

Words and music by Phil Lesh

Notes:
First played by The Dead (sung by Joan Osborne)
on August 5, 2003, at the Verizon Wireless
Amphitheater, Indianapolis. Subsequently played
by Phil and Friends with Warren Haynes on vocals.

A Little Piece for you

I will never get out in one piece
Those aren't the terms of my release
Since that's the case, I've thought it through
And decided to leave a piece for you

A piece of my vision, a piece of my brain
To fight your battles once I am slain
A piece of my heart I never touched
A piece of my soul, though I can't spare much

A piece of blue from me to you
See the sky when night is through
See the moon hanging full and low
Off the coast of China, or wherever you go

I'll be with you, in spirit at least
Every time glory rises in the east
When sunlight splatters down Rampart Street
And the last cool breeze tastes oh so sweet

Down Memory Lane, today is still tomorrow
Yesterday another source of sorrow
Come what may, today is only borrowed
It may not be returned from whence it came

Here's a piece for you, another for your friend
Here's a piece for everyone, line forms at the end
Here's a little piece for you
A little piece for you
A little piece for you

Salt and sand and river tide
Ties that bind but to divide
A drunk passed out on the Lower East Side

Trailer park in flames
Identifying marks of blame
Dissolved in sudden rain

Warmed in the cradle by the hammer of
    the sun
I never looked up to see what I had won
It wasn't much in silver, smaller yet in gold
It could soothe the heat, but never touch
    the cold
Never touch the cold

Here's a piece for you
Just a piece from me to you
Here's a piece of blue
When the night is through

Words by Robert Hunter
Music by Phil Lesh

1 Rampart Street
A famed New Orleans street located in the
French Quarter and associated with music.

Notes:
First performance: June 21, 2003, at the
Meadows in Hartford Connecticut.

Night of a Thousand Stars

1 Alcatraz

The island in the San Francisco Bay, used for years as a federal prison. Now a national park. On November 9, 1969, a group of Native Americans began an occupation of the island that lasted until June 11, 1971. The National Park Service history of the island acknowledges that:

> As a result of the occupation, either directly or indirectly, the official government policy of termination of Indian tribes [a policy adopted under the Eisenhower administration, whereby all federal treaties with Indian tribes would be eliminated, along with all federal support] was ended and a policy of Indian self-determination became the official U.S. government policy. (National Park Service)

2 Jehosophat

A ninth-century B.C.E. Judean king who formed an alliance with Israel. He appears in the Bible primarily in Chronicles 2:17–21 but also, to a lesser extent, in Kings 1:22. Of his daughter, nothing is to be found in the Bible; however, his daughter-in-law, the wife of his son and successor, Joram, was the daughter of Ahab, an earlier enemy.

3 B minor masses

Johann Sebastian Bach's *Mass in B Minor* (ca. 1733) is one of the great works of choral literature.

Notes:

Studio recording: *There and Back Again* (2002), Phil and Friends.

First performance by The Dead: June 21, 2003, at the Meadows in Hartford, Connecticut.

Full moon rising over Alcatraz   1
Hangin' there like a big topaz
Ruling this night of a thousand stars
With a backseat full of broken guitars
Raised in chains by Jehosaphat's daughter   2
Served twenty years for walkin' on the water
Just out fishin' for love in the rain
From an easy chair in the passing lane
If I had forgotten, I'd remember well
The fruit and the tree from which it fell
Many long years rollin' homeward bound
Goin' hell-for-leather on this merry-go-round

Night of a thousand stars
The sound of sweet guitars
On this night *(on this night)*
On this night *(on this night)*
On this night *(on this night)*
On this night of a thousand blazing stars

Down in the laundry with my head in my hands
Doin' whatsoever the Lord commands
Poppin' the hood off a Ford V8
Disguised with an out-of-state licence plate
Payin' my taxes in whiskey and blood
Mixed in a barrel floating on the flood
Doing my penance for a life of crime
Singing B-minor masses in double time   3
The tiger and the lion hanging on the wall

Between the head of a saint and a bocci ball
I've been rebuked and I've been scorned
But I can't ever say that I haven't been
    warned

Night of a thousand stars
The sound of sweet guitars
On this night *(on this night)*
On this night *(on this night)*
On this night *(on this night)*
On this night of a thousand blazing stars
I tried to serve you right

I tried to serve you well
It looked all right by morning light
In hindsight—who can tell?
I don't know what to tell
Truth or farewell

Flipping though the pages of my soul
My heart rears up and swallows me whole
These were moments of my life
Since dissected with a thick blunt knife
If I could recapture one moment of truth
From the firm foundation of a misspent
    youth

I'd fall like rain on this thirsty earth
A testament of beauty and worth
But if it don't happen because it can't
I hope and pray this wish you grant
From one man's heart to a falling star
We always remember who we are

Remember the night of a thousand stars
When love swam naked in the reservoir
Writing mad sonnets in the midnight park
Leaving tracks of tears for her watermark
Drums of the jungle on the edge of night
Only you could see with your perfect sight
If you don't remember you can be excused
'Cause it could never be reproduced

Night of a thousand stars
The sound of sweet guitars
On this night *(on this night)*
On this night *(on this night)*
On this night *(on this night)*
On this night of a thousand blazing stars

Words by Robert Hunter
Music by Phil Lesh and Warren Haynes

NO MORE DO I

Meet me under painted thunder
Lift me up to gospel skies
Let me live in your blue heaven
When I die, when I die
When I die, when I die

Let me love you without ending
Don't say no I beg of you
Let me give all I got to give
While I live, while I live
While I live, while I live

Never give me cause to doubt you
I'll lay all my cards down too
Learn to trust the things you tell me
Loving you, loving you

Where we're going, I can't tell you
Somewhere on the other side

Driving blind across the border
Born to ride, born to ride
Born to ride, born to ride

I will stand by you forever
If you'll always stand by me
On the shifting sand or water
Take my hand, take my hand

No more, no more, no more do I
Seek reflection in a dead man's eye
Seek my fortune in shades of black
Run down spinning on the outside track
Ice-cold wind screaming at my back
Lightning fails at the thunder's crack

Words by Robert Hunter
Music by Phil Lesh

Notes:
Studio recording: *There and Back Again* (2002),
Phil and Friends.

First performance by The Dead: June 17, 2003,
at the Verizon Wireless Amphitheater in Virginia
Beach, Virginia.

strange world

Strange world
Time's running out
It's crazy
Make me want to shout

No escape
Nowhere to turn
Clock keep ticking, ticking, ticking
No money to burn
Living in a strange world
Oh, oh, oh
Living in a strange world
Oh, oh, oh
Living in a strange world
Oh, oh, oh

Heartbreak
And desolation
It's a cruel world
There's so much frustration

Anger
The world's going mad
Contamination
It's getting real bad
Oh, it's getting real bad

Living in a strange world
Oh, oh, oh
Living in a strange world
Oh, oh, oh

Living in a strange world
Oh, oh, oh

Don't give up without a fight
You know everything's gonna be all right
You got to be strong to survive
Got to keep hope alive
Keep hope alive

Destiny
Is an act of fate, an act of fate
The sun comes up tomorrow, up tomorrow
It's never too late, it's never too late
Never too late

Living in a strange world
Oh, oh, oh
Living in a strange world
Oh, oh, oh
Living in a strange world
Oh, oh, oh

Words by Mickey Hart
Music by Mickey Hart and Warren Haynes

Notes:
First performance by The Dead: June 15, 2004,
at Red Rocks Amphitheater in Morrison,
Colorado. Sung by Warren Haynes and Bob Weir.

1 banyan tree
A tree native to South and Southeast Asia, with branches that send shoots out that grow downward, eventually rooting in the soil to form secondary trunks. It grows higher than one hundred feet, and as it forms secondary trunks, it becomes impossible, often, to tell which was the original trunk. A single tree eventually resembles a forest, with circumferences up to hundreds of yards.

Notes:
First performance by The Dead: August 4, 2004, at the Ford Pavilion in Scranton, Pennsylvania.

Running down the muddy road
A hundred miles from hope
Dangling from a banyan tree
I see a length of rope

Behind me is a tiger
And a killer with a knife
One wants me for supper
And the other wants my life

I got no choice but to grab
The rope and start to climb
The situation here is such
The choice was never mine

Hand by hand I pull my body
From the mucky ground
Up into the sunshine
Where the birds are flying round

I just keep on climbing 'cause
There's nothing else to do
My hands are getting tired
But my spirit pulls me through

Don't know if the tree is high
Or if the clouds are low
Pretty soon I'm looking down
A hundred miles below

The earth is spinning blue and green
Beneath my dizzy eyes
But I leave caution to the faint
And reason to the wise

I see another climber and
I think it could be you
Climbing up a length of rope
Where stars come shining through

Was it hope of freedom
Or panic born of fear
Sent you climbing for your life
Up in the stratosphere?

I got no fear of falling
And I got no fear to fly
I believe my soul will live
Although my body die

Maybe I am right in that
And maybe I am wrong
I just keep on climbing
And sometimes I make a song

This is not the way I chose
The way has chosen me
Dangling to the muddy road
Beneath the banyan tree

Words by Robert Hunter
Music by Mickey Hart and Bob Weir

onLy the strange Remain

Notes:

Studio recording: *Mystery Box* (1997), Mickey
Hart.

First performance by The Dead: June 22, 2003,
at the Tweeter Center, Great Woods, Mansfield,
Massachusetts.

I've been searching in sectors both private
  and dark
With the eye of a witness—silent and stark
Seen everything that goes on in the night
Things that are twisted and hide from the light
Things that live under the rock and the stone
Flesh like a fever on a platter of bone
Blacker than blackness and whiter than white
Things that live only on the edges of sight

So I pack my sack with a fistful of fire
There are cutthroats and thieves in this night
  of desire
Who steals this treasure must contend with
  its flame?
Where only the strange remain

Yeah, only the strange remain

Only the strange remain
Only the strange remain
Only the strange remain

Looking deep and then deeper into every face
Past beauty and wisdom, past gender and race
I see a lone hungry wolf in a shining blue flame
And only the strange remain

I'm dying of thirst with a drink in my hand
Praying for something that I don't understand
One foot on the gravel, one foot in the sky
Too reckless to live and too careful to die

When the moment has passed
With death at the door?
Will I still look for answers?
Will I still beg for more?
Will I slip into silence or ride with the pain?
Where only the strange remain

Yea, yea, yea
Only the strange remain
Only the strange remain
Only the strange remain

Tell me friend, have you noticed of late?

How only the strange remain?
I'm speaking about the cream of the strange
Not the merely weird, out of sight or insane
No, only the strange remain
Only the strange remain

They keep on talking just to rattle their teeth
A light coat of surface and nothing beneath

They're fishing for answers with love as the bait
Related to something that time doesn't date
Soon as it's spoken, it no longer applies
Words twist and stutter and deliver up sighs

If truth is impossible, so is the lie
There's no in-between, you can't swim, you
   can't fly
At the uttermost link at the end of our chain
Only the strange remain
Only the strange remain

In the dark of silence the strange remain
Yea, only the strange remain

Only the strange remain
Only the strange remain
Only the strange remain

Words by Robert Hunter
Music by Mickey Hart

october queen

Evokes the Jimi Hendrix song "Purple Haze."

Notes:
Studio recording: *Evening Moods* (September 2000), Ratdog.

First performance by The Dead: June 24, 2003, at PNC Bank Arts Center in Holmdel, New Jersey.

Andre Pessis has written lyrics for Huey Lewis ("Walking on a Thin Line"), Bonnie Raitt ("Slow Ride"), Journey, Mr. Big (coauthoring with Eric Martin), and Waylon Jennings. Pessis was vocalist for the 1960s band Circus (formerly Flying Circus), joining in 1969 after leaving New York, where he lived till then. Circus frequently played double bills with Huey Lewis's band Clover. Bob Weir met Pessis through Mark Karan, of Ratdog.

Well, I spend my tomcat nights in New Orleans
Always 'round this red moon time of year
Just let it go, and fall right off the deep end
'Cause you sure don't look for soul salvation here

Bars and alleys are running wild with fat brass
And your three-piece bottled-up conventioneers
And your drag queens and your strip bars
And your hazy purple streetlights   1
All steaming up the atmosphere

She always waits for me right down there in
    the lobby
A little shopworn but sure not the worst I've seen
And I nod across the way to Bon Temps Billy's
    Black Water Lounge
And she nods back, 'cause we both know what
    that means

She follows me on in like we're both strangers
'Cause I kind of can't afford, y'all, to be seen
She's got that far-off, smoky, leaves-are-falling
    look in her eyes
A true last-chance October Queen

And I know it's gonna be one hell of an evening
Just like the year before, and the year before,
    and the year before
Still something about it, something about her
Something that always evades my memory
I don't know what it is
There's so little I recall, little I recall

So we small talk and drink our way through
   the motions
And then the lights dim for the big show up
   in my room
On a threadbare bed with feathers and
   scented lotions
Like some kind of carnival gin-soaked
   dream cartoon

Well I guess you can chalk up one more night
   up for the ages
And I wake up in a haze of sweat and
   cheap perfume
But she's way long gone, way long gone at the
   cottonmouth sunrise
And I don't know if it's way too late or way
   too soon

Down the street, the hose wagon's
Washing last night on down the storm drain
And I'm lying here and my head's on fire and
   my body's flat
Guess it's gonna take a long hot shower or two
   to wash it away, wash it away
We just won't talk about that

And I think about the life that I'll go back to
And the congregation that pays my country
   club and rent
But at 1:55 Delta flight 648 gonna take off
   and fly
And I'll have one more full year to repent

And I bet it was one hell of an evening
Just like the year before, and the year before,
   and the year before
Still there's something about it, something
   about her
Something always evades my memory
I don't know what it is
There's so little I recall, little I recall

Something about, something about her
Something about, something about her
Something about, something about her
Something about, something about her

Words by Bob Weir and Andre Pesses
Music by Bob Weir and Ratdog

Even so

Midnight perdition
Bad news, the wolfman's at the door
I hold my position
I know I can't fall off the floor
Even so—I guess I best lay low
Even so—yeah but I don't know, I don't know
But, no, no, no no, oh no no

Begging your pardon
But I don't think that I can stay
This particular garden
Ain't never seen the light of day
Even so—talkin' and touch and go
Even so—hey but I don't know, I don't know
Even so
No, no, oh no no, oh no no, oh no no, oh
   no no

Wish you were naked
Wish you were wholesome and sincere
Wish I could fake it
Wish I were anywhere but here
Even so—you make yes look like no
Even so—you've been so nice to know, been so
nice to know
But no, but no, oh no, no no, no, no

Bring back the wolfman
He tell me I'm his long lost son
I say "suit yourself man"
Looks like this night has just begun
Even so
Even so—he ain't no kitty cat no, no
Even so—been one hell of a, hell of a show
Talkin' midnight rodeo
Well you been so nice to know
Nice to know
Nice to know
But no, no, oh no, oh no, no, no

Words by Gerritt Graham
Music by Bob Weir & Ratdog

1 wolfman
See note under "Ramble On Rose."

Notes:
Studio recording: *Evening Moods* (September
2000), Ratdog.

First performance by The Dead: June 24, 2003,
at PNC Bank Arts Center, Holmdel, New Jersey.

baba jingo

Chorus:

1, 2 Baba Jingo, Baba Jingo, voices in the wind

Run the circle to the end and roll it back again

Run it 'round the midnight 'til the bell of
    morning peals

Seven miles to the step with wings upon your heels

Seven miles to the step with wings upon your heels

Burn the water, freeze the fire, spin the molten silk

Squeeze the butter from the stone and rubies from
    the milk

In the land of amber skies where the sun shines
    from the ground

You draw a circle in the sand and you pass that
    cup around

Now pass that cup from lip to lip but never spill
    a drop

Sip the foam and lick the brine from the bottom
    to the top

Ask the lizard on the stone the way to No-man's
    Land

Right by night and left by day, just as the wind
    commands

Up the mountain, down the pass beside the
    waterfall

If you're thirsty fill your flask but do not drink
    it all

1 Baba

The *Oxford English Dictionary* defines this as "an infantile variant of papa."

Also, in the intersecting world of rock music and Eastern spirituality, the song by the Who, "Baba O'Reilly" comes to mind—a song by Pete Townshend that referred at least obliquely to Townshend's own spiritual guru, Meher Baba. *Baba* in this context is an honorific, from the Persian for "father" or "grandfather." So the root is the same, but the meaning expanded to include all human gurus.

2 Jingo

According to the *OED:*

> Appears first circa 1670 as a piece of conjuror's gibberish, usually *Iheyl* or *high jingo!* prob. a mere piece of sonorous nonsense with an appearance of mysterious meaning. In 1694 *by jingo* occurs in Motteux's transl. of Rabelais, where the Fr. has *par Dieu:* this, being contemporary with the conjuror's terms, may be presumed (though not proved) to be the same word, substituted, as in many other cases, for a sacred name: cf. *by Golly, Gock, Gom, Gosh, Jabers,* etc. In Scotland, *by jing* has long been in common use.

And another meaning given by the *OED:*

> one who brags of his country's preparedness for fight and generally advocates or favors a bellicose policy in dealing with foreign powers: a blustering or blatant "patriot"; a chauvinist.

Notes:

Played by the Other Ones in 1998. First performance by The Dead: June 20, 2003, at SPAC in Saratoga Springs, New York.

When the song was being developed, this was sung as the first verse:

> Baba Jingo fly by night, break those bones
>   in two
> Suck the marrow, chew the gristle, boil 'em
>   down to glue
> Raggle Daggle, king of mustard, peppercorns
>   and salt
> Add your spices to the brew beneath the
>   starry vault

Save a healthy swallow for the blue wind of
    the vale
To take you home by midnight on wings that
    never fail
To take you home by midnight on wings that
    never fail

Baba Jingo, king of mustard, pepper corns
    and salt
Add your spices to the brew beneath the starry
    vault

(Chorus)

Run it 'round the midnight 'till the bell of
    morning peals
Seven miles to the step with wings upon your heels
Seven miles to the step with wings upon your heels

(Chorus)

Run it 'round the midnight 'til the bell of
    morning peals
Seven miles to the step with wings upon your heels
Seven miles to the step with wings upon your heels

(Chorus)

Words by Robert Hunter
Music by Mickey Hart

seLf-defense

I can't tell you nothing except for what I've said
Shut down by exhaustion, just want to go to bed
No, I don't expect to sleep, just beg to be excused
I don't mean to dump on you, just need to sing
    the blues

1   I was from Orlando West, the good side of
     the town
2   You lived in Mandelaville, I guess you've
     been around
    Working in the gold mine, over in the rand
3   Hanging in the Shabine, when time was on
     your hands

Chorus:
It makes no difference if I'm wrong or if I'm right
I've got no self-defense, I've got no will to fight
If they are unable to see it through my eyes

I'll plead my case to angels in the court of paradise
I'll plead my case to angels in the court of paradise

Soweto in the summer heat, Soweto in the rain
Tin shack down in shantytown, down on
4   Kliptown lane
You could barely hide your smile, inflicting
    pointless pain

1 Orlando West, et al.
The places mentioned in this song are all in or near Soweto, the township near Johannesburg in South Africa. Orlando West is the suburb of Soweto where many of the leaders of the African National Congress live.

2 Mandelaville
Was the site of a squatter camp, removed in 2002 by the city council.

3 Shabine
Synonym for "bar."

4 Kliptown
Where antiapartheid organizations signed the Freedom Charter in 1955 but also the site of squatter camps.

Notes:
First performance by The Dead: June 18, 2003, at Merriweather Post Pavilion, Columbia, Maryland.

According to Mickey Hart: "I wrote it with Hunter, and Bob wrote the bridge."

Sympathy is not your style, that much at least
  is plain

I can keep from crying by staring straight ahead
I can keep from dying by pretending that
  I'm dead
To all the tender feelings that I still have for you
Despite the double dealings that you have put
  me through

(Chorus)

It makes no difference now, except for when
  it does

All the things our love could be were never
  what it was
Starting from your pickup line until the last
  goodbye
None of it makes any sense, no point to
  even try

Now if I cop to self-defense, no jury
  would convict
If they have a notion of the pain that you inflict
If they are unable to see it through my eyes
I'll plead my case to angels in the court
  of paradise

(Chorus)

Words by Robert Hunter
Music by Mickey Hart and Bob Weir

TIME NEVER ENDS

Stepping through the midnight sun
To a life that never ends
Snowflakes fall, winter comes
Time to make amends

God of wind, god of time
I give my heart to thee
Take me to a better place
Let my soul fly free
Let my soul fly free

Beyond the moon, beyond the stars
A wizard guiding me
Beyond the moon, beyond the stars
Beyond the galaxy
A secret place, a gentle space
A land beyond pretend
Where time stands still and always will
Time stands still
Time never ends

Chorus:
Time goes on forever
Time never ends
No, time never ends

Footprints in the sea of time
We watch and do our thing
But all we leave behind us
Is the loving that we bring
Mother nature, northern lights
All that life can bring
The mountain spirit dances and
The evening owls sing

The evening owls sing
God of dreams, of life supreme
Come to me tonight
Guide me to a better place
Beyond this starry night
Take me to a better place
On golden spirit wings
Where time stands still and always will
Time stands still
Time never ends

(Chorus)

Time goes on forever
Time never ends
No, time never ends

(Chorus) (2x)

Where gods and angels sing
Where gods and angels sing

Words by Mickey Hart
Music by Mickey Hart and Warren Haynes

Notes:
First performance by The Dead: August 10, 2004,
at the PNC Arts Center in Holmdel, New Jersey.

Mickey Hart described the origin of the song in
his road journal:

> Tonight we introduced a new one I wrote; it is
> called "Time Never Ends." This song is very
> powerful. I wrote it as a sort of prayer and
> then I decided not to play it soft and sweet
> but go the opposite way with the music, to
> give it a ska and high-life kinda groove. I think
> it works well in this form.

YOU Remind Me

See note under "That's It for the Other One."

2 Sam Cooke
Singer and composer (1931–1964) from the
1950s and 1960s whose brand of soul was highly
influential. His 1956 song "You Send Me" sold
more than two million copies.

Notes:
First performance by The Dead: June 22,
2004, at the Cricket Pavilion, Phoenix.

A song played in 2002 by Mickey Hart and
Bembe Orisha. This was Robert Hunter's comment in his road journal:

> Mickey is doing a very hot show with his best
> band ever, outside of the Dead, and doing a
> bunch of new songs we cowrote. He has three
> excellent singers to give them full impact. Phil
> and Jimmy Herring joined him yesterday and
> they tore the roof off. One of our new tunes,
> "You Remind," actually gave me goosebumps
> that lasted for several minutes. A no-nonsense
> sweet, sweet love song that struck home with
> the audience in a way rarely seen with an
> unfamiliar mid-tempo ballad.

You remind me of feather pillows
Georgia dawns and weeping willows
Days of summer, long ago
Angel wings in new-fallen snow

You remind me of radio plays
In the "Golden Age of Radio" days
When imagination still was king
You didn't actually need to see everything

You remind me
How sweet it all can be
How to whisper, how to sing
Of the passion we brought to everything
Of the promise that was spring
You remind me love is nothing
But the best that life can bring

You remind me of shooting stars
Life was a joy, if the living was hard
Rewards were few, and patience thin
Still it was easy to start all over again

You remind me of piano keys
Little bit sharp on the middle C
Dust of the soundboard, a vase of roses
A roaring fire where a hound dog dozes

You remind me
How sweet it all can be
How to whisper, how to sing
Of the passion we brought to everything
Of the promise and the spring
You remind me love is nothing
But the best that life can bring

1

You remind me how the more things change
The more it's sure they'll remain the same
How everything old again is new
That serves in the end
To remind me of you

You remind me of feather pillows
Georgia dawns, and weeping willows
Days of summer, long ago
2 Sam Cooke singing on the radio

You remind me
How sweet it all can be
How to whisper, how to sing
Of the passion we brought to everything
Of the promise that was spring
You remind me

How to whisper, how to sing
Of the passion we brought to everything
Of the promise that was spring
You remind me

How to whisper, how to sing
Of the passion we brought to everything
Of the promise that was spring
You remind me love is nothing
But the best that life can bring

You remind me
You remind me
You remind me
You remind me

Words by Robert Hunter
Music by Mickey Hart and Warren Haynes

DOWN THE ROAD

1 **Fiddler's Green**
The happy land imagined by sailors where there is perpetual mirth, a fiddle that never stops playing for dancers who never tire, plenty of grog, and unlimited tobacco. (*Brewer's*)

2 **bought the store**
A reworking of the "bought the farm" phrase. See "Childhood's End" for a discussion of the origin of this phrase.

3 **a smile on empty space**
Evoking the Cheshire Cat, referred to in "China Cat Sunflower" and "Can't Come Down." See "Can't Come Down" for a full discussion of the renowned cat.

Notes:
Studio recording:
Mickey Hart's Mystery Box (June 1996).

First performance by The Dead: July 10, 2003, at Red Rocks Amphitheater in Morrison, Colorado.

The song at one time had an additional verse. Hunter sang it in a solo performance on March 1, 1997:

> Driving down the road all night, the sun is rising red
> [Reciting] old stories, and conversing with the dead
> I rode into Selma, low on gasoline
> Been so long on empty, I been ridin' on a dream
> The fellow at the station looked like Martin Luther King

Down the road to Union Station running through
the fog
I thought I saw Joe Hill last night grinning like
a dog
"I understand they did you in for everyone to see"
He smiled—shook his head—"that's a lie,"
said he
"I been on a mountain top observing from a cloud
Been in the hearts of workers milling with
the crowd
My tears are shed for freedom and equality
of means
My blood and perspiration oil the gears of your
machine"

Down the road again
Down the road again

Down the road to Massachusetts driving
through the night
I thought I saw Jack Kennedy hitchhiking by
a light
I hit the brakes—backed up slow, and
Kennedy got in
I said, "It's nice to see you lookin' back in
shape again
Correct me if I'm wrong but I believe they
gunned you down"
He just shook his head and looked off sadly
with a frown
Said, "bullets are like waves, they only rearrange
the sand

History turns upon the tides and not the deeds
   of man"

Down the road again
Down the road again

1 Driving down to Fiddler's Green to hear a tune
      or two
   I thought I saw John Lennon there, looking kind
      of blue
   I sat down beside him, said "I thought you bought
2   the store"
   He said "I heard that rumor, what can I do
      you for?"
   "Have you written anything I might have
      never heard?"
   He picked up his guitar and strummed a
      minor third
   All I can recall of what he sang, for what it's
      worth
   "Long as songs of mine are sung I'm with you
      on this earth"

Down the road again
Down the road again

"You're low on oil," he said, with an old
   familiar ring
"How far to the mountain, friend," I asked him
   face to face
"You're standing on it now," he said, "you just
   don't know the place"

In a 1996 interview with David Gans, Mickey
Hart explained the background to how this verse
came to be replaced with the verse about Garcia:

Gans: ["Down the Road"] must have been one
of the last ones that got written?
Hart: Oh, yeah, well, it got written, but then
Hunter came in and changed the last verse. He
said, "You know the fourth verse? I've got a
better verse."
Gans: Who was it before?
Hart: The fourth verse? It was a Martin Luther
King verse, you know.
Gans: Uh-huh.
Hart: I said, "Okay, write it down, let me see
it." He said, "No." He said, "Let me sing it." I
go, "Okay, man—go in there, and you know,
the mike's set up, go ahead. Let's hear it." And
as soon as he was halfway through it, you
know, I just looked at him. I realized what he
had just done, you know. It was just right on; I
mean, you can imagine what the control room
was like at that very moment.
Gans: Yeah.
Hart: You know, just Hunter—he just went
outside, you know, [and] lightning struck. It
came to him like it usually does, and he just
poured it right out. I think he was still writing
while he was singing. It's like one of those kind
of magical moments, just "shoop"—"oh, boy,
this is exactly perfect." My sentiments exactly,
and you know, it couldn't have been—it was

exactly how we were feeling, and of course we were all grieving and everything at this time, it happened right after Jerry went. So this was a, like, real spontaneous act on Hunter's part. I mean, I would have never asked him to do it—it entered my mind, but I couldn't imagine anything that wouldn't be corny, you know, and he managed to do it *very* well. Great sentiment. 91

From the corner of my eye I saw the sun explode
I didn't look directly 'cause it would have burned
   my soul
When the smoke and thunder cleared enough to
   look around
I heard a sweet guitar lick, an old familiar sound
I heard a laugh I recognized come rolling from
   the earth
Saw it rise into the skies like lightning giving birth
It sounded like Garcia but I couldn't see the face
Just the beard and the glasses and a smile on
   empty space   3

      Words by Robert Hunter
      Music by Mickey Hart

notes on the instrumentals

he Grateful Dead's music over the past 40 years can be described in countless ways, using just about every adjective known to our language at one time or another, good and bad. Primary among these descriptions, to me, is "poetic." This applies to both the poetic and lyrical way in which the band's songs are structured, and, more literally, to the poetry that is such an essential element of this music, namely the words of Robert Hunter and John Barlow. However, the canon includes several songs for which this explicit poetry is not present, the instrumental songs. Although few in number, they more than make up for their dearth in quantity with variety and substance.

Most of the beloved Grateful Dead early jam vehicles, such as "Dark Star," "Alligator" etc, are songs with, as their heart and soul, lyrics. However, one of their earliest improvisational vehicles, "That's It For The One," included the sections "Quadlibet for Tenderfeet" and "We Leave the Castle," the band's earliest instrumental songs. This would begin a tradition in the band's recorded history of including occasional instrumental interludes amongst the more traditional "songs." What offers such a unique insight into the Grateful Dead's impressive dynamic is that these instrumental pieces are as diverse in length, structure, tempo, time signature and vision as are the songs with words. They are instrumental narratives, poetic. Amongst the studio performances are the masterful "Sage and Spirit" from *Blues For Allah,* one of the most melodic and poignant songs in the entire oeuvre. Also on that 1975 masterpiece are the instrumentals "Slipknot!" (and what a well-deserved

413

exclamation point!) and Phil and the drummers' "King Solomon's Marbles" suite. Although *Blues For Allah* was really the height of the band's in-studio instrumental experimentation, they would continue to include shorter instrumentals on their studio albums, such as *Shakedown Street's* "Serengetti" or the quirky-but-essential "Antwerp's Placebo" from *Go To Heaven*, as well as the more elaborate instrumental segments from the "Terrapin Station" suite. Similarly, some of the Grateful Dead's most admired live albums contain instrumental passages that are not at all considered separate from the songs-with-words on those albums, such as "Feedback" (*Live/Dead*), "Space" and "Rhythm Devils" (both *Dead Set*), and, perhaps most impressive of all, "Prelude/Epilogue" from *Europe 72*.

It's always been best to accept the Grateful Dead's output from 1965 to 1995 as a whole, not as a fragmented body of work. Likewise, within this whole, if we accept that there is psychedelic music, country music, jazz music and just about every other form of music, we're best off integrating the instrumental songs into the entire canon. Although lacking a distinct and essential element of Grateful Dead music, the words, these instrumental passages are integral to the band's legacy.

—David Lemieux
Grateful Dead Prod. / Music Archivist
San Rafael, California
June 2005

Quadlibet for Tenderfeet

Music by the Grateful Dead

We Leave the Castle

Music by Tom Constanten

QUADLIBET

Though the Grateful Dead playfully misspell it, the word *quodlibet* is a combination of the Latin *quod* (meaning "what") and *libet* ("it pleases"). Over time, *quodlibet* acquired a more specialized meaning. In medieval times, there would be certain days when professors of theology would open up the class and answer questions on any theological topic. In fact, people not even enrolled in the school scould come in off the street and pose questions. The professors would be required to answer any and all questions. The quodlibet was, thus, the opportunity for posing important, sometimes difficult questions to the masters of theology. Some theologians shunned quodlibets, while others loved them. Saint Thomas Aquinas was among this latter group. Still later, building on both earlier meanings of *quodlibet,* the word began to be applied to certain types of musical compositions. The *Oxford Companion* defines the word as "a collection of different tunes or fragments brought together as a joke." The device was introduced by J. S. Bach in the *Goldberg Variations.* It is suggested that the word comes from the practice of allowing performers to "work into the web of the music any tune they liked." The word came to be used for certain kinds of jazz improvisations, as well. Thus, Kurt Weill's op. 9, composed in 1923, is titled *Quodlibet.*

TENDERFEET

Tenderfoot, used in the American West for a newly arrived immigrant. Some sources also say that cowboys first used the word to refer to cattle not yet used to the trail, then began to apply it to beginning cowhands or newcomers in general.

Notes:

Interludes between sections of the suite "That's It for the Other One."

Studio recording: *Anthem of the Sun* (July 18, 1968).

Sage and Spirit

Music by Bob Weir

Notes:

Studio recording: *Blues for Allah* (September 1, 1975).

First performance: August 13, 1975, at the Great American Music Hall, San Francisco, California. This is the performance captured on *One from the Vault.*

Rock Scully:

> Bobby wrote "Sage and Spirit" while my daughters, named Sage and Spirit, were jumping on his bed and generally trashing his hotel room. He was trying to play his guitar and came up with the rhythm for this from their jumping. The flute mimics their laughter. (Scully) 92

Slipknot!

Music by Jerry Garcia, Keith Godchaux, Phil Lesh, Bob Weir and Bill Kreutzmann

Notes:

Studio recording: *Blues for Allah* (September 1, 1975)

First performance: June 20, 1974, at the Omni in Atlanta. The piece dropped in and out of regular rotation but was played fairly frequently from 1989 on.

"Slipknot!"
Beautiful lie
You can pray

You can pay
Till you're buried alive
Blackmailer blues
Everyone in the room
Owns a part of the noose
Slipknot gig
Slipknot gig
Slipknot gig
Did someone say
Help on the way
Well, I know
Yeah, I do
That there's help on the way

Hunter, asked about these lyrics, which were sent to me as
the missing lyrics to "Slipknot!," replied:

David,
Most of the *Blues for Allah* material was written on the
spot on the fly, while engineers stood by waiting to
record the vocals. Those lyrics are my style and seem
familiar—there were lots of throwaways and I doubt not
those were among them. There's always a taker for throw
away pages, and I believe someone was collecting them,
possibly Ramrod.
The lines are, of course, rejects from "Help on the Way."
"Slipknot Gig" would be in the space of: "I will stay / one
more day,"
There's no cutting it out. But it's neither permanent nor
serious.
rh 93

Woody Guthrie wrote a hard-hitting song called "Slip Knot,"
about capital punishment, with the slipknot in question, of
course, being a hangman's knot.

King Solomon's Marbles
Part 1: King Solomon's Marbles
Part 2: Stronger than Dirt or Milkin'
the Turkey

Music by Phil Lesh, Mickey Hart, and Bill Kreutzmann

Hank Harrison's *The Dead Book* reproduces a "handwriting
sample" from Phil Lesh dating from 1962. It includes the
words *Stronger Than Dirt* (in block capitals). The note in the
book says this "was an allusion to an Ajax scouring-powder
commercial of the day. Phil has mentioned that he often
heard classical riffs in commercials and this is probably one
of them."

Notes:
Studio recording: *Blues for Allah* (September 1, 1975)

Infrared Roses
Infrared Roses is a collection of tracks of drums/space/jams
from 1989 and 1990, put together by Bob Bralove. His
liner notes say that some tracks are put together from
performances on several different nights. The tracks were
whimsically titled by Robert Hunter.

I.
Crowd Sculpture
Parallelogram
Little Nemo in Nightland

II.
Riverside Rhapsody
Post-Modern Highrise Table Top Stomp
Infrared Roses

III.
Silver Apples of the Moon
Speaking in Swords
Magnesium Night Light

IV.
Sparrow Hawk Row
River of Nine Sorrows
Apollo at the Ritz

LITTLE NEMO IN NIGHTLAND

Little Nemo in Slumberland was an early comic strip.
Jerry Robinson's *The Comics: An Illustrated History of Comic Strip Art* has the following to say about the strip:

> A world of magic, dreams, and whimsy, enhanced by a superb craftmanship that some think has not been equaled in the comics since, appeared in 1905: *Little Nemo in Slumberland* by Winsor McCay. Each of Nemo's weekly adventures was a story of the dream of a tousle-haired boy of about six that concluded with his waking up or falling out of bed (reminiscent of the back-to-reality ending of *Alice's Adventures in Wonderland*). His dreamworld was peopled by Flip, a green-faced clown in a plug hat and ermine-collared jacket; a cannibal; a certain Dr. Pill; and a vast array of giants, animals, space creatures, queens, princesses, and policemen. There were sky bombs, wild train and dirigible rides, exotic parades, bizarre circuses, and festivities of all kinds in Byzantine settings and rococo landscapes. (Robinson)

The U.S. Post Office included it in its set of comics stamps issued in 1995.

SILVER APPLES OF THE MOON

A line from a William Butler Yeats poem. See note in "Pride of Cucamonga" for more details.

afterword

fterword. Afterward. After. Words. This is an intimidating task. So much has been said and sung —and not said yet, and never sung—but now it seems we've reached the end of it, and I've been asked to say a few words afterward. There is so much to say that only silence seems eloquent enough to make a proper closing bookend. But silence would also seem like a cop-out. After so many acts of courage, great and small, this is no time to be fainthearted.

I think now that no more Grateful Dead songs will be written. It appears that after forty years, we can say, truly and finally, that the words are yours. That we are done with ours. (Not that they ever really belonged to anyone in the first place.)

Of course, Hunter and I and the others whose works are included here will still write songs, and even some for those voices that sang these who, being still alive, can sing. But they won't be Grateful Dead songs. All the Grateful Dead songs that will ever be written are in your hands.

Of course—and more to the point—these songs here will continue to expand and grow as others come along and fill them with their own imaginings and annotations, explicit or tacit. We've always tried (and Hunter, being subtler, more than I) to give you plenty of room to flesh your own song around the bones of what we gave you.

Every time someone would ask me, over the years, what I meant by this line or that, I would say, "What does it mean to you?" I'm glad I did that. I have heard some marvelous things following that question. The answers were often utterly unrelated to anything that I, or Bobby or Brent might have meant, but yet they would *fit* somehow. Depending on whether I was drunk or not, I would say either, "No, that's not what I was thinking, but that's pretty good," or, conspiratorially, "Yes. That's it exactly. But please don't tell anyone. Let's leave them room for interpretation. Let's give them a chance to make up their own songs." With each interpretation, the song became new again.

The fact is, one doesn't really know himself sometimes. Some stanza is suddenly there in your head and with it there sometimes is, as Dylan said, "a terrible roaring sound." Someone once said to me that "art is what happens when God speaks through a human being." I wouldn't claim that I've been that sort of oracle very often, but Hunter has, and there is no question that there were many moments when God, or whatever you want to call the Holy Whoknows, would zap Its stunning meaningfulness at you through the Grateful Dead. And it was as much a gift to us as it was to you. The good stuff just appeared, like grace. No, not like grace. Grace.

Dylan is a pretty good case in point. I remember one night in 1987, when the Dead were touring with Dylan for the first time and I was herding an ancient Cadillac filled with Ken Kesey and other old Pranksters down the Left Coast, following the tour

down to Anaheim, of all places. There, not far from Disneyland, Dylan was singing, and Kesey turned to me and said, "I've just figured out who this weird little fuck is." "And?" my eyes inquired. "Same guy who wrote the Book of Revelations." Dead right, I thought. There have been times when Hunter also was, for sure. Sometimes I came pretty close to being that.

And what is being *that* like? It's like being a faucet or a crack in the rocks from which the water emerges. The spring doesn't make the water. At best, it knows how to get out of the way and open itself wide to the flow. If it's really blessed and happens to be connected to some sweet, clear water, then it will taste like a revelation to those who encounter it.

But in the end, it's just the song. It's not the guy who writes the words, or the guy who writes the melody, or even the guys who work up the chords and improvise the fresh miracles that occur in that space for years and years. It's the song itself. Again, I think of Dylan.

One time during the early nineties when Bobby and I hadn't written anything for a while, I was at a concert at Shoreline and a freshly minted young Deadhead came up to me in the audience. He was about sixteen, and I expect some older, more experienced Deadhead had pointed me out to him.

"Hey," he said, "I really like that new song you wrote for Bobby." I cocked an eyebrow, sorry that there was no such thing.

"And what song might that be?" I inquired.

"That one about the watchtowers and stuff." I gritted my teeth in a moment of involuntary humility.

"I wish I could tell you I wrote that song, but I didn't."

"Oh, yeah. Who did?"

"Bob Dylan."

"Who's Bob Dylan?" he asked.

This was a great moment for me. I realized, as I should have known all along, that if the song is any good, it detaches from its apparent source and enters into the hearts and minds of those who hear it to make its own home there, leaving behind everyone except for, say, the person you were making love with the first time you heard it. Or the folks who were in the microbus with you that night you threw a rod outside of Winnemucca and still managed to make it to the Sacramento show in time to hear it at the beginning of the second set.

Authorship and pride has been a tricky matter for me in this context. It has been no picnic for the ego to spend these decades writing songs in the tall shadow of Robert Hunter. Talk about intimidating. You cannot imagine how humbling (and occasionally humiliating) this has been. T. S. Eliot dedicated *The Wasteland* to Ezra Pound and called him, as he did so, *il miglior fabbro.* The better maker.

(At least T. S. Eliot got to be T. S. Eliot, a better faucet than almost anyone who ever channeled poetry in English.) But I was just me, a trickle of almost brackish, certainly at times hackish, water next to a torrent of what has always felt to me—and continues to feel—like revealed truth. Hunter was the better maker, as any fool could hear. There is no false humility in that recognition. It is simply how things have been.

And yet I knew why I was there. I knew why it was important to continue to persevere with my own far less immortal output. Had it not been for me, and my other junior-varsity colleagues, this ecosystem you behold here would have been a monoculture, a brilliant garden in which all the flowers were roses but which lacked in the diversity that is essential to ecological health. Furthermore, on a good night, when God (or whatever you want to call It) had shown up, the Grateful Dead could make everything I'd ever written for them sound transforming and true.

Still, if someone asked me to name my favorite twenty Grateful Dead songs, they would all consist of words that entered the conscious world through Hunter's head. He has written over a hundred of the greatest short novels that have ever been sung and taught me a huge amount about what it is to be merely what one is, equipped with ordinary tools, beavering on in relative mediocrity, adding my own meager but necessary weeds to his rose garden. Making it real.

And then there is always that question. "Who's Bob Dylan?"

Personally, I have been incredibly blessed by the songs in this book, in more ways than I know so far. As Deadheads know, these songs are continuously growing and revealing themselves. Resonating with frequencies unheard at the time of their writing. Being imbued with all that received belief, collateral and yet vital as anything that happened in the silence of our own minds or in the hugeness of two hundred thousand people dancing.

The songs revealed themselves over time, even to us. I'll tell you a story and make an essential admission. I thought I wouldn't do this, but I will anyway. It's as good a way as I know of conveying an essential point about all these lovely collections of phonemes, belief, and meaning.

When I wrote "Looks Like Rain," I had never fallen in love. I had certainly heard a lot of love songs. I had been to an opera or six. I was not unfamiliar with the huge literature of amorous

helplessness. But I remained skeptical. I secretly believed that "falling in love" was a conceit that people had made up in order to make themselves even more miserable for their perceived insufficiencies. People do stuff like that. Nevertheless, there this song was on a winter day in Wyoming, and I didn't try to stop it from coming into existence merely because it trafficked in emotions I hadn't quite experienced. I didn't know who these people in the song were or, really, what they were experiencing, but as it arrived, it seemed as genuine as any other love song.

That was in 1972. Twenty-one years later, I fell in love for the first time in my life. I looked across a crowded room and saw somebody's back and *knew*. Don't ask me how I knew. Don't even ask me what it was that I knew.

Now, mind you, this was after I'd had about two hundred people come up to me in various contexts and tell me that "Looks Like Rain" was the song they fell in love to, or was the song that was played at their wedding, or was the song that changed their lives and helped them feel like one person. I would nod and smile as if I knew what they were talking about.

In any event, I was instantaneously in love with some person whose face I hadn't seen yet. She turned around and fell in love with me. We were both so convinced of this emotional reality that a week after we met, we were living together, even though she was freshly married at the time to a far likelier candidate for the positon.

She was also an improbable Deadhead, a sleek young psychiatrist who preferred black Armani suits to tie-dyes and had never smoked pot in her life. In fact, she'd grown up making particular fun of hippies, particularly old ones like me.

After we'd been together almost a year, enjoying a relationship so radiant that others would gather around it like cats to a fireplace, we were at a Dead concert in Nassau Coliseum (of all grim places). Bobby started to sing "Looks Like Rain," and I started singing it to her myself so that she would get all the words. About halfway through, I realized that *I* was getting all the words for the first time. I finally knew what the song was about. I finally meant it. Or perhaps one could say more accurately that it finally meant me. Both of us were crying by the time it was over. And we didn't even know why we were crying yet.

About three weeks later, I put her on a plane in Los Angeles, two days before her thirtieth birthday. She went to sleep almost immediately. When the flight steward tried to wake her up to tell her to put her seat belt on as they descended into JFK, he found that she was dead and had been for a while. The flu we'd both been suffering from when I sang that song in her ear had attacked her heart and given her viral cardiomyopathy. She fibrillated in her sleep. She flew away, as angels sometimes do. And I still sing her love songs. . . .

I tell you this story not as a mere self-indulgence (though it probably is that) but to make a point about these songs. I can't really speak for any of the other songwriters whose babies nestle in these covers, but I suspect that all of us learned some startling things about our own words as time proceeded, and, evolving in the primordial soup of Deadhead consciousness, they became themselves.

I could tell you lots of stories about all these songs, and not just my own. I have had at least one memorable experience that I could associate with every song in this volume. And collectively, you could tell me enough stories about your own experiences with them to fill many books this size.

Also, David Dodd has done, with your help, a marvelous job over the years of identifying the references and resonances buried in them, whether intentionally or not, and making them richer for everyone. I hope this book will not be the end of that enterprise. You and he have barely scratched the surface of what we extracted from the Bible alone. . . . In other words, there is a lot of ore still unmined here. And yet, at the same time, it's over. Gems may be discovered, but no new ones will be formed.

Afterword. And after everything else, I guess.

After the most remarkable tapestry of sagas—as all these frayed threads wove themselves in afterthought —after all these experiences that could never be trapped in words, whether for being ineffable or unspeakable, here I am gazing back on the words themselves. For me, for Hunter, for Robbie Peterson, Gerrit Graham, "McGannahan Skejellyfetti," and all the rest, every one of these songs has a story that surrounded its creation, known only to us and a few others. (Elsewhere in this volume, you will find my own little creation myth for the writing of "Cassidy," but generally we left that to your imagination as well.)

As improbable as it seems that this is actually the end of all that, the greater improbability is that it went on so long.

Hell, we thought it had been a long, strange trip in *1969!* We didn't know from long or strange, as things turned out. It was a hazardous environment, socially and physically. Many of us actually *are* dead now, having departed earlier than we would have if we'd taken up a safer undertaking. Many more of us would be, had we not developed such an astonishingly facility for spitting in the Devil's eye and laughing. And, mostly, loving each other in our own weird, dysfunctional way and somehow hanging together. Hanging out. Hanging on.

A big part of what we leave lies between these covers. It's a long epitaph. It is as beautiful as it deserves to be.

Thank you for summoning it forth, you Deadheads.

Thank you wordsmithies, particularly Hunter, for rising so magnificently and often to the call.

Thank you, Whatever You are, for issuing it so abundantly.

It was long, it was strange, but we really did enjoy the ride.

—John Barlow
New York
June 2005

the Lyricists

The chief lyricists of the Grateful Dead were Robert Hunter, who collaborated primarily with Jerry Garcia but wrote with all the band members, and John Barlow, who collaborated primarily with Bob Weir. Phil Lesh collaborated occasionally with old family friends Robert M. Petersen and Peter Monk, and Bob Weir with Gerrit Graham.

JOHN BARLOW
Born October 3, 1947, Jackson Hole, Wyoming. A friend of Bob Weir's since high school, when they met at Fountain Valley High, a prep school in Colorado Springs, Colorado, where each had been sent to shape up from an early life of misbehavior. Barlow studied literature and theology at Wesleyan, then reunited with Weir in 1967. It was not until several years later that he began writing lyrics for

Pen and Ink drawing by Jerry Garcia

Weir's songs. He also wrote for Brent Mydland. Since the end of the Grateful Dead's career he has been writing songs with The String Cheese Incident.

He is a co-founder of the Electronic Frontier Foundation, which advocates for freedom in cyberspace, and travels internationally to lecture in service of that cause and to consult with Internet-related business. In 1988, he was elected a Fellow at Harvard Business School's Berkman Institute for Internet and Society. He lives in Pinedale, Wyoming, and New York City. He has three daughters: Leah, Anna Winter, and Amelia.

ROBERT HUNTER
Born June 23, 1941,
in Arroyo Grande,
California. The family
lived in San Francisco
and Palo Alto, where
he played trumpet in
addition to guitar and
violin. He attended

Pen and Ink drawing by Jerry Garcia

the University of Connecticut briefly in 1958. He
met Garcia in 1961 in Palo Alto, where they became
part of the early Peninsula bohemian scene and musical collaborators, playing together in several early
bluegrass and folk bands. Hunter was adopted as the
lyricist member of the Grateful Dead in 1967 and
remained in this role throughout the band's career.
His work outside the band includes a string of solo
albums and several volumes of poetry, including a
translation of Rainer Maria Rilke's *Duino Elegies* and
Sonnets to Orpheus. He published his collected lyrics in
A Box of Rain, in 1990. He has continued to write,
producing lyrics for a range of musicians from the
band Zero to country singer Jim Lauderdale. He lives
in Marin County, California. He has three children,
Charlotte, Jesse, and Kate.

PETER RICHARD ZIMELS, aka PETER MONK
Born on March 21, 1937, in New York City. He
majored in Philosophy and graduated from the
University of Michigan in 1958. He served in the
U.S. Navy from 1958 to 1962. On leaving the Navy,
he again made his way around the world from New
York, through Europe to Asia and eventually to Sri
Lanka and Thailand, where he became an ordained
Buddhist monk, a calling he took seriously for the
rest of his life. Returning to the United States in
late 1967, he served as some kind of spiritual force
during his years in the Grateful Dead's extended
family, attending many births and performing many
marriages. He tried to minister to the suffering and
the dying. He had three children, Bodhi, Eva, and
Johnny Violet. Peter died in 1992.

Peter wrote songs recorded by the Grateful Dead,
Mickey Hart, the Dinosaurs, Richie Havens, and
Peter, Paul, and Mary. He wrote poetry throughout
his life. Peter also made collages that reflected the
complexity of his worldview and that sometimes just
gathered together the extended family of the Dead for
a calendar, a book, or an album cover.

ROBERT M. PETERSEN
Born in 1936, of a solid middle-class background in
Klamath Falls, Oregon. In the fifties, he hopped

freights, played jazz saxaphone, and attended San Mateo College, in California, where he met Phil Lesh, with whom he later wrote several songs for the Dead. Sometimes, he lived on the mountain. He served time. He knew the lore of the West, its local and natural history. He practiced freedom. He bridged the Beat scene of San Francisco to the rock era, like his sometime companion, Neal Cassady. He was a constant presence in the Grateful Dead's world, from its earliest days in Palo Alto. He published one volume of poetry during his lifetime, *Far Away Radios.* A posthumous edition of his collected poems, *Alleys of the Heart,* was published by Hulogosi. Petersen died in 1987. He has one son, Didrik.

GERRIT GRAHAM

Born in New York, New York, November 27, 1948, and grew up in St. Louis, Detroit, and Chicago.

Graduated from Groton School in 1966. He attended Columbia University through spring 1968, studying French literature. Caught up in the events of that spring, Graham heard the Grateful Dead when they played for striking students who opposed the war in Vietnam. He dropped out of Columbia to become a professional actor, cast opposite Robert De Niro in the Brian De Palma movie *Greetings.* He moved to Hollywood when Andy Leonard, who worked for Grateful Dead Records (and shot the cover photo for *Grateful Dead from Mars Hotel*), introduced Graham to Weir, in the fall of 1974, and they became close friends. Weir asked Graham to take a stab at writing lyrics for the incipient song "Victim or the Crime." Pleased with the results, they wrote four songs for Ratdog's Evening Moods, and are still collaborating. Graham continues to act, with a lengthy resumé in TV, movies, and stage.

Bibliography

Grateful Dead Sources

Brandelius, Jeryn Lee. *Grateful Dead Family Album*. NY: Warner, 1989.

Constanten, Tom. *Between Rock and Hard Places: A Musical Autobiodyssey*. Eugene, OR: Hulogosi Press, 1992.

Dodd, David G., and Robert G. Weiner. *The Grateful Dead and the Deadheads: An Annotated Bibliography*. Westport, CT: Greenwood Press, 1996.

Dodd, David G., and Diana B. Spaulding, eds. *The Grateful Dead Reader*. NY: Oxford University Press, 2000.

Gans, David. *Conversations with the Dead: The Grateful Dead Interview Book*. NY: Citadel Underground, 1991. Reissued March 2002, Da Capo Press.

————*Playing in the Band: An Oral and Visual Portrait of the Grateful Dead*. NY: St. Martin's Press, 1985.

Garcia: The Rolling Stone Interview by Charles Reich and Jann Wenner; Plus a Stoned Sunday Rap with Jerry, Charles and Mountain Girl. San Francisco: Straight Arrow Books, 1972.

Garcia: By the Editors of Rolling Stone. Boston: Little, Brown, 1995.

Getz, Michael M., and John R. Dwork. *The Deadhead's Taping Compendium, vols. 1–3*. NY: Henry Holt, 1998, 1999, 2000.

Getz, Michael M., et al. *The Deadhead's Taping Addendum*. San Francisco: Pepper Tonic Productions, 2001.

Grateful Dead: The Illustrated Trip. NY: DK, 2003.

Grateful Dead Anthology I & II. Miami: Warner Bros. Publications, 1979, 1996.

Greenfield, Robert. *Dark Star: An Oral Biography of Jerry Garcia*. NY: Morrow, 1996.

Grushkin, Paul. *Grateful Dead: The Official Book of the Dead Heads*. NY: Quill, 1983.

Harrison, Hank. *The Dead Book: A Social History of the Haight-Ashbury Experience*. San Francisco: Archives Press, 1985.

Hart, Mickey, with Fredric Lieberman. *Spirit into Sound: The Magic of Music*. Acid Test Productions, 1999.

Hart, Mickey, with Fredric Lieberman and D.A. Sonneborn. *Planet Drum: A Celebration of Percussion and Rhythm*. San Francisco: HarperSanFrancisco, 1991.

Hart, Mickey, with Jay Stevens and Fredric Lieberman. *Drumming at the Edge of Magic: A Journey into the Spirit of Percussion*. San Francisco: HarperSanFrancisco, 1990.

Hunter, Robert. *A Box of Rain: The Collected Lyrics of Robert Hunter*. NY: Viking, 1991.

————. *A Box of Rain*, 2nd ed. with additional lyrics. NY: Penguin, 1993.

————. *All Good Things: Jerry Garcia Studio Recordings*, LA: Rhino Records, 2004.

————. *Glass Lunch*. NY: Penguin, 1997.

————. *Night Cadre*. NY: Viking, 1991.

————. *Sentinel*. NY: Penguin, 1993.

Jackson, Blair. *Garcia: An American Life*. NY: Viking, 1999.

————. *Goin' Down the Road: A Grateful Dead Traveling Companion*. NY: Crown, 1992.

————. *Grateful Dead: The Music Never Stopped*. NY: Delilah, 1983.

Lesh, Phil. *Searching for the Sound: My Life with the Grateful Dead*. NY: Little, Brown, 2005.

McNally, Dennis. *A Long Strange Trip*. NY: Broadway, 2002.

Parish, Steve. *Home Before Daylight: My Life on the Road with the Grateful Dead*. NY: St. Martin's, 2003.

Peters, Stephen. *What a Long, Strange Trip: The Stories Behind Every Grateful Dead Song*. NY: Thunder's Mouth Press, 1999.

Peterson, Robert M. *Alleys of the Heart: The Collected Poems of Robert M. Peterson*. Eugene, OR: Hulogosi, 1988.

Scott, John W., Mike Dolgushkin, and Stu Nixon. *DeadBase I–XI: The Complete Guide to Grateful Dead Song Lists*. Hanover & Cornish, NH: DeadBase, 1987–1999.

Scully, Rock, with David Dalton. *Living with the Dead: Twenty Years on the Bus With Garcia and the Grateful Dead*. NY: Little, Brown, 1995.

Shenk, David, and Steve Silberman. *Skeleton Key: A Dictionary for Deadheads*. NY: Doubleday, 1994.

Trager, Oliver. *The American Book of the Dead*. NY: Fireside, 1997.

Trist, Alan. *The Water of Life: A Tale of the Grateful Dead*. Illustr. by Jim Carpenter. Eugene, OR: Hulogosi, 1989.

Troy, Sandy. *Captain Trips: A Biography of Jerry Garcia*. NY: Thunder's Mouth Press, 1994.

————. *One More Saturday Night: Reflections with the Grateful Dead, Dead Family, and Dead Heads*. NY: St. Martin's, 1991.

Weiner, Robert G., ed. *Perspectives on the Grateful Dead: Critical Writings*. Westport, CT: Greenwood Press, 1999.

Womack, David. *The Aesthetics of the Dead*. Palo Alto, CA: Flying Public Press, 1991.

Periodicals

Dead Letters. Edited by Nicholas Meriwether. Irregular. 2001–

Dupree's Diamond News. Edited by John Dwork and Sally Ansorge Mulvey. Quarterly. 1986–1996.

The Golden Road. Edited by Blair Jackson and Regan McMahon. Quarterly. 1984–1993.

Grateful Dead Almanac. Edited by Gary Lambert. Quarterly. 1993 Also available on the WWW at: http://www.dead.net/almanac/index.html.

Krassner, Paul. "Interview: Jerry Garcia." *The Realist*, 99 (Sept.–Oct. 1985): 6–7.

Relix Magazine. Edited by Les Kippel and Jerry Moore, 1974–1979; Toni Brown 1979–. Irregular.

Spiral Light. "The Official Newsletter of Deadheads in England." 1984–1996.

Unbroken Chain. Edited by Laura Paul Smith 1986–1994; 1994–1996 by Dave Serrins.

Electronic Resources

Allan, Alex. *The Grateful Dead Lyric and Song Finder*. http://www.whitegum.com/intro.htm

Barlow, John. *Songs For the Dead*. http://www.eff.org/Misc/Publications/John_Perry_Barlow/HTML/barlows_lyrics.html

The Grateful Dead (official website). http://www.dead.net

Grateful Dead newsgroup. rec.music.gdead available via groups.google.com

Hart, Mickey. *Road Journal, 2004*. http//www.dead.net

Hunter, Robert. *Robert Hunter Personal Archives*. http://www.dead.net/RobertHunterArchive/hunterarchive.html

Jackson, Randy. *The Roots of the Grateful Dead*. http://taco.com/roots/roots.html

Slabicky, Ihor W. *The Compleat Grateful Dead Discography*. The Eleventh Revision. http://tcgdd.freeyellow.com/tcgdd.html 1993-2000.

The Well. deadlit and deadsongs.vue conferences. http://well.com

Other Works:

Abrahams, Roger D. *Deep Down in the Jungle: Negro Narrative Folklore From the Streets of Philadelphia*. Chicago: Aldine, 1970.

————. *Positively Black*. Englewood Cliffs, NJ: Prentice-Hall, 1970. *The American Heritage Dictionary of the English Language*. Boston: Houghton Mifflin, 2000.

American Places Dictionary: A Guide to 45,000 Populated Places, Natural Features, and Other Places in the United States. Frank R. Abate, ed. Detroit: Omnigraphics, 1994.

Anchor Bible Dictionary. NY: Doubleday, 1992.

Apostolos-Cappadona. *The Dictionary of Christian Art*. NY: Continuum, 1994.

Arrien, Angeles. *The Tarot Handbook: Practical Applications of Ancient Visual Symbols*. Sonoma, CA: Arcus, 1987.

Baum, Joseph. *The Beginner's Handbook of Dowsing: The Ancient Art of Divining Underground Water Sources*. NY: Crown, 1974.

Beall, Pamela. *Wee Sing Silly Songs*. Los Angeles: Price/Stern/Sloan, 1982.

Benet, William Rose. *The Reader's Encyclopedia*, 2nd ed. NY: Thomas Y. Crowell, 1965.

Benet's Reader's Encyclopedia of American Literature. George Perkins,

Barbara Perkins, and Phillip Leininger, eds. NY: HarperCollins, 1991.

Blake, Fay M. and H. Morton Newman, *Verbis non factis: Words Meant to Influence Political Choice in the United States, 1800-1980.* Metuchen, NJ: Scarecrow Pr., 1984.

Botkin, B. A. *A Treasury of American Folklore: Stories, Ballads, and Traditions of the People.* NY: Crown, 1944.

Bousquet, Patrick. "The Hat of the West: John B. and His Stetson," in *Western Horseman,* May, 1993, pp. 18–20.

Brewer's Dictionary of Phrase and Fable. 14th ed. (Fourteenth Edition). NY: Harper and Row, 1989.

Brewer's Dictionary of Phrase and Fable. NY: Harper and Row, 1968.

Bronson, Bertrand Harris, ed. *The Singing Tradition of Child's Popular Ballads.* Princeton, NJ: Princeton University Press, 1976.

Brown, Cecil. *Stagolee Shot Billy.* Cambridge, MA.: Harvard University. Press, 2003.

Bulfinch, Thomas. *Bulfinch's Mythology.* NY: Avenel Books, 1978.

Burns, Robert. *Poems and Songs.* London: Oxford University Press, 1969.

Cambridge Gazetteer of the United States and Canada: A Dictionary of Places. Archie Hobson, ed. NY: Cambridge, 1995.

Cannings, Richard J. "Northern Saw-Whet Owl," in *The Birds of North America,* no. 42, 1993. Philadelphia, PA: The American Ornithologists' Union and the Academy of Natural Sciences.

Carroll, Lewis. *The Annotated Alice: Alice's Adventures in Wonderland & Through the Looking-Glass.* With an introduction and notes by Martin Gardner. NY: Clarkson Potter, 1960.

Child, Francis James. *The English and Scottish Popular Ballads.* NY: Dover, 1965. (Reprint of Houghton Mifflin edition of 1882–1898.)

Cirlot, J. E. *A Dictionary of Symbols.* NY:, Philosophical Library, 1971.

Cities of the World: A Compilation of Current information on Cultural, Geographical, and Political Conditions in the Countries and Cities of Six Continents, Based on the Department of State's "Post Reports." Monica M. Hubbard and Beverly Baer, ed. Detroit: Gale Research, 1993.

Clarke, Charlotte Bringle. *Edible and Useful Plants of California.* Berkeley: University of California Press, 1977.

Clunn, Harold P. *The Face of London.* NY: Spring Books, 1956.

Coats, Alice M. *Flowers and Their Histories.* NY: McGraw-Hill, 1968.

Cooper, B. Lee. *Popular Music Perspectives: Ideas, Themes, and Patterns in Contemporary Lyrics.* Bowling Green, OH: Bowling Green State University Popular Press, 1991.

Courlander, Harold. *A Treasury of Afro-American Folklore.* NY: Crown, 1976.

Crow, Bill. *Jazz Anecdotes.* NY: Oxford University Press, 1990.

Crowley, Aleister. *The Book of Thoth: A Short Essay on the Tarot of the Egyptians, Being the Equinox Volume III No. V.* York Beach, ME: Samuel Weiser, 1969. (Originally published 1944)

Cruden, Alexander. *Cruden's Complete Concordance to the Old and New Testaments.* Philadelphia, Toronto, The John C. Winston Company 1930.

Cudden, J. A. *A Dictionary of Literary Terms.* NY: Doubleday, 1977.

Cullen, Tom A. *When London Walked in Terror.* Boston: Houghton Mifflin, 1965.

Cummings, E. E. *100 Selected Poems.* NY: Grove Press, 1959.

Dance, Daryl Cumber. *Shuckin' and Jivin': Folklore from Contemporary Black Americans.* Bloomington: Indiana University Press, 1978.

The Dictionary of American Regional English. Frederic G. Cassidy, chief editor. Cambridge, MA: Belknap Press, 1985–

A Dictionary of Americanisms on Historical Principles. Mitford M. Mathews, ed. Chicago: University of Chicago Press, 1951.

Dictionary of the History of Ideas: Studies of Selected Pivotal Ideas. Philip P. Wiener, editor in chief. NY: Scribner's, 1973.

Dictionary of the Middle Ages. Joseph R. Strayer, editor in chief. NY: Scribner's, 1982.

Dudar, Helen. "It's Home Sweet Home for Geniuses, Real Or Would-Be," in *The Smithsonian,* December 1983, p. 94. [Chelsea Hotel]

Dunning, John. *Tune in Yesterday: The Ultimate Encyclopedia of Old-time Radio, 1925–1976.* Englewood Cliffs, NJ: Prentice-Hall, 1976.

Dylan, Bob. *Lyrics, 1962–1985.* NY: Knopf, 1985.

Eckert, Allan W. (Text) *The Owls of North America (North of Mexico): All the Species and Subspecies Illustrated in Color and Fully Described.* Garden City, NY: Doubleday, 1974.

Eliot, T. S. *Collected Poems 1909–1962.* NY: Harcourt, Brace & World, 1963.

———. *Selected Essays.* NY: Harcourt Brace Jovanovich. 1978.

Eliot, Willard Ayre. *Birds of the Pacific Coast.* NY: G. P. Putnam's Sons, 1923.

The Encyclopedia of Birds. Christopher M. Perrins and Alex L.A. Middleton, eds. NY: Facts on File, 1985.

The Encyclopedia of Religion. Mircea Eliade, editor in chief. NY: MacMillan, 1987.

Evans, Tom. *Guitars: Music, History, Construction, and Players from the Renaissance to Rock.* NY: Facts on File, 1977.

Ewen, David. *American Popular Songs: From the Revolutionary War to the Present.* NY: Random House, 1966.

Flexner, Stuart Berg. *I Hear America Talking: An Illustrated Treasury of American Words and Phrases.* NY: Van Nostrand Reinhold, 1976.

The Folklore of World Holidays. Margaret Read MacDonald, ed. Detroit: Gale Research, 1992.

Foucault, Michel. *Madness and Civilization: A History of Insanity in the Age of Reason.* Translated from the French by Richard Howard. NY: Vintage Books, 1973.

Freeman, Scott. *Midnight Riders: The Story of the Allman Brothers Band.* Boston: Little, Brown, 1995.

Fuld, James J. *The Book of World-Famous Music: Classical, Popular and Folk.* NY: Crown, 1966.

Funk & Wagnalls Standard Dictionary of Folklore, Mythology and Legend. Maria Leach, ed. NY: Funk & Wagnalls, 1972.

Galland, China. *Longing For Darkness: Tara and the Black Madonna, A Ten-Year Journey.* NY: Viking, 1990.

Grahame, Kenneth. *The Wind in the Willows.* NY: Charles Scribner's Sons, 1908.

Greek Lyric Poetry. Translated by Willis Barnstone. Bloomington, IN: Indiana University. Press, 1962.

Green, Jonathan. *The Dictionary of Contemporary Slang.* NY: Stein and Day, 1985.

Green, Percy B. *A History of Nursery Rhymes.* London: Greening & Co., 1899.

Gribbin, John and Martin Rees. *Cosmic Coincidences, Dark Matter, Mankind and Anthropic Cosmology* NY: Bantam, 1989.

Griffin, Rick, and Gordon McClelland. *Rick Griffin.* NY: Perigree, 1980.

Grzimek, Bernhard. *Grzimek's Animal Life Encyclopedia.* NY: Van Nostrand Reinhold, 1972.

Gunnell, John A., ed. *Standard Catalog of American Cars, 1946–1975.* Iola, WI: Krause Publication, 1987.

Han-shan. *Cold Mountain: 100 Poems by the T'ang Poet Han-shan.* Translated and with an introduction by Burton Watson. NY: Columbia University Press, 1970. (First published 1962 by Grove Press.)

Haynes, Robert V. *A Night of Violence: The Houston Riot of 1917.* Baton Rouge, Louisiana: Louisiana State University Press, 1976.

Hirsch, E. D., Joseph F. Kett, and James Trefil. *The New Dictionary of Cultural Literacy.* Boston: Houghton Mifflin, 2002.

The Holy Bible: Containing the Old and New Testaments. Translated Out of the Original Tongues, with the Former Translations Diligently Compared and Revised. Cleveland: World Publisher., n.d.

Hortus: A Concise Dictionary of Gardening, General Horticulture and Cultivated Plants in North America. L. H. Bailey and Ethel Zoe Bailey. NY: MacMillan, 1935.

The Illustrated Dictionary of Place Names: United States and Canada. Edited by Kelsie B. Harder. NY: Van Nostrand Reinhold, 1976.

Jasen, David A. *Rags and Ragtime: A Musical History.* NY: Dover, 1989, 1978.

Jepson, Willis Linn. *A Manual of the Flowering Plants of California.* San Francisco: California School Book Depository, 1925.

Jerde, Judith. *Encyclopedia of Textiles.* NY: Facts on File, 1992.

Johnson, James Weldon, and J. Rosamond Johnson. *The Books of American Negro Spirituals: Including the Books of American Negro Spirituals and the Second Book of Negro Spirituals.* NY: Viking, 1969.

Jones, Arthur C. *Wade in the Water: The Wisdom of the Spirituals.* Maryknoll, NY: Orbis Books, 1993.

Jones, Bessie, and Bess Lomax Hawes. *Step It Down: Games, Plays, Songs, and Stories from the Afro-American Heritage.* NY: Harper & Row, 1972.

Kaplan, S. R. *Tarot Cards for Fun and Fortune Telling.* NY: U.S. Games Systems, 1970.

Knight, Stephen. *Jack the Ripper: The Final Solution.* London: Harrap, 1976.

Kurten, Bjorn, and Elaine Anderson. *Pleistocene Mammals of North America.* NY: Columbia University Press, 1980.

The Larousse Dictionary of World Folk Lore. Edited by Alison Jones. NY: Larousse, 1995.

Lax, Roger, and Frederick Smith. *The Great Song Thesaurus.* NY: Oxford University Press, 1989.

Lenz, Lee W. *Native Plants for California Gardens.* Claremont, CA Rancho Santa Ana Botanic Garden, 1956.

Levine, Lawrence W. *Black Culture and Black Consciousness: Afro-American Folk Thought from Slavery to Freedom.* NY: Oxford University Press, 1977.

Lomax, Alan. *Check-List of Recorded Songs in the English Language in the Archive of American Folk Song to July 1940.* Washington, D.C.: Library of Congress, 1942.

Lomax, Alan. *The Folk Songs of North America in the English Language.* NY: Doubleday, 1960.

Lomax, John. *Folk Song USA.* NY: Duell, Sloan and Pearce, 1947.

Lomax, John A. and Alan Lomax, comps. *American Ballads and Folk Songs.* NY: Macmillan, 1934.

Lydon, Michael. *Rock Folk: Portraits from the Rock 'n' Roll Pantheon.* NY: Dial, 1971.

Major, Clarence. *Juba to Jive: A Dictionary of African-American Slang.* NY: Penguin, 1994.

Manguel, Alberto, and Gianni Guadalupi. *The Dictionary of Imaginary Places.* NY: Macmillan, 1980.

Marcus, Greil. *Invisible Republic: Bob Dylan's Basement Tapes.* NY: Henry Holt, 1997.

Marschall, Richard. *America's Great Comic-Strip Artists.* NY: Abbeville, 1989.

McGraw-Hill Dictionary of Electronics and Computer Technology. Edited by Sybil B. Parker, NY: McGraw-Hill, 1984.

McKenna, Richard. *The Left-handed Monkey Wrench.* Annapolis, MD: Naval Institute Press, 1984.

Mitchell's School Atlas: Comprising the Maps and Tables Designed to Accompany Mitchell's School and Family Geography. Philadelphia: Thomas, Cowperthwait & Co., 1853.

Morris, William and Mary. *Dictionary of Word and Phrase Origins:* NY: Harper & Row, 1962.

Mother Goose. *The Annotated Mother Goose: Nursery Rhymes Old and New.* Arranged and explained by William S. Baring-Gould and Ceil Baring-Gould. Illustrated by Walter Crane [and others]. NY: Bramhall House, 1962.

Mother Goose. *The Real Mother Goose.* Chicago: Rand, McNally, 1916.

New Catholic Encyclopedia. Catholic University of America. Palatine, Il: J. Heraty, 1981

The New Century Cyclopedia of Names. Edited by Clarence L. Barnhart. NY: Appleton-Century-Crofts, 1954.

The New Grove Dictionary of American Music. H. Wiley Hitchcock and Stanley Sadie, eds. NY: Grove's Dictionaries of Music, 1986.

The New Grove Dictionary of Jazz. Barry Kernfeld, ed. NY: Grove's Dictionaries of Music, 1988.

New Lost City Ramblers Song Book. John Cohen and Mike Seeger, eds. NY: Oak, 1964.

The New Princeton Encyclopedia of Poetry and Poetics. Alex Preminger and T. V. F. Brogan, eds. Princeton: Princeton University Press, 1993.

A Nonsense Anthology. Carolyn Wells, comp. NY: Scribner's, 1902.

Oakley, Giles. *The Devil's Music: A History of the Blues.* NY: Harcourt Brace Jovanovich, 1978.

Odum, Howard Washington and Guy B. Johnson. *Negro Workaday Songs.* NY: Negro Universities Press, 1969.

The Official Rules of Card Games. Cincinnati: United States Playing Card Company, 1969.

Oman, Charles. *The Great Revolt of 1381.* Oxford: Clarendon, Press, 1969.

Owens, William A. *Swing and Turn: Texas Play-Party Games.* Dallas: Tardy Publishing Company, 1936.

The Oxford Book of Ballads. James Kinsley, ed. Oxford: Clarendon Press, 1969.

The Oxford Book of Seventeenth Century Verse. H. J. C. Grierson and G. Bullough, eds. Oxford: Clarendon Press, 1934.

The Oxford Companion to the Bible. Bruce M. Metzger and Michael D. Coogan, eds. NY: Oxford University Press, 1993.

The Oxford English Dictionary. J. A. Simpson and E .S. C. Weiner, eds. Oxford: Clarendon Press, 1989.

The Oxford English Dictionary of Nursery Rhymes. Iona Archibald Opie and Peter Opie, eds. Oxford: Clarendon Press, 1951.

Partridge, Eric. *A Dictionary of Slang and Unconventional English: Colloquialisms and Catch-phrases, Solecisms and Catachreses, Nicknames and Vulgarisms.* NY: MacMillan, 1984.

Picturesque Expressions: A Thematic Dictionary. Laurnece Urdang, editorial director, Nancy LaRoche, editor in chief. Detroit: Gale Research Co., 1980.

Porter, Katherine Anne. *Ship of Fools.* Boston: Little, Brown, 1962.

Random House Historical Dictionary of American Slang. J. E. Lighter, ed. NY: Random House, 1994

Regan, Gary and Mardee Haidin Regan. *The Book of Bourbon and Other Fine American Whiskeys.* Shelburne, Vermont: Chapters Pub., 1995.

Rilke, Rainer Maria. *Duino Elegies; The Sonnets to Orpheus.* Translated by Robert Hunter. Eugene, OR: Hulogosi, 1993.

Robbins, Chandler S., Bertel Bruun and Herbert S. Zim. *Birds of North America.* NY: Golden Press, 1966.

Roberts, Leonard Ward. *In the Pine: Selected Kentucky Folksongs.* Pikeville, KY: Pikeville College Press, 1978.

Robinson, Jerry. *The Comics: An Illustrated History of Comic Strip Art.* NY: Putnam's, 1974.

The Rolling Stone Illustrated History of Rock & Roll: The Definitive History of the Most Important Artists and Their Music. Anthony DeCurtis and James Henke, with Holly George-Warren, eds. Original Editor: Jim Miller. NY: Random House, 1992.

The Rolling Stone Rock 'n' Roll Reader. Ben Fong-Torres, ed. NY: Bantam, 1974.

Rombauer, Irma S. and Marion Rombauer. *Joy of Cooking.* Indianapolis, IN: Bobbs-Merrill, 1962.

Royce, Anya Peterson. *The Anthropology of Dance.* Bloomington, IN: Indiana University Press, 1977.

Rumbelow, Donald. *The Complete Jack the Ripper.* London: W. H. Allen, 1975.

Sackheim, Eric. *The Blues Line: A Collection of Blues Lyrics.* NY: Grossman, 1969.

Schefter, James. *All Corvettes Are Red: The Rebirth of an American Legend.* NY: Simon & Schuster, 1996.

Scholes, Percy Alfred. *The Oxford Companion to Music.* NY: Oxford University Press, 1970.

Shannon, Bob. *Behind the Hits.* NY: Warner, 1986.

Sharp, Cecil James. *English Folk Songs from the Southern Appalachians: Comprising Two Hundred and Seventy-three Songs and Ballads with Nine Hundred and Sixty-eight Tunes. Including thirty-nine tunes con tributed by Olive Dame Campbell.* Maud Karpeles, ed. London: Oxford University Press, 1932.

Silber, Irwin. *Folksinger's Wordbook.* Woodstock, NY: Oak Publications, 1973.

Silberman, Steve. "Standing in the Soul: Robert Hunter inter view." in *Poetry Flash,* December 1992.

Sloane, Eric. *Folklore of American Weather.* NY: Duell, Sloan and Pierce, 1963.

Snyder, Gary. *Riprap and Cold Mountain Poems.* Berkeley, CA: North Point Press, 1990. (Cold Mountain Poems first published in the *Evergreen Review,* no. 6, 1958.)

Spiering, Frank. *Prince Jack.* NY: Doubleday, 1978.

Stewart, George R. *American Given Names: Their Origin and History in the Context of the English Language.* NY: Oxford University Press, 1979.

Strong, Martin C. *The Great Rock Discography: Complete Discographies Listing Every Track Recorded by More Than 1,200 Artists.* Edinburgh: Cannongate, 2004.

The Sutra of the Lotus Flower of the Wonderful Law. Translated by Bunno Kato. Tokyo: Rissho Kosei-kai, 1971.

Tergit, Gabriele. *Flowers Through the Ages.* London: Oswald Wolff, 1961.

Tolman, Beth, and Ralph Page. *The Country Dance Book: The Old-fashioned Square Dance, Its History, Lore, Variations & Its Callers. Complete & Joyful Instructions.* Weston, VT: The Countryman Press, 1937.

Waldo, Terry. *This Is Ragtime.* NY: Da Capo Press, 1991, 1976.

Walheim, Lance. *The World of Trees.* San Francisco: Ortho Books, 1977.

Weisberger, Bernard A., *They Gathered at the River: The Story of the Great Revivalists and Their Impact upon Religion in America.* Boston: Little, Brown, 1958.

Wheeler, Mary, comp. *Roustabout Songs: A Collection of Ohio River Valley Songs.* NY: Remick Music Corp., 1939.

White, Newman Ivey. *American Negro Folk-Songs.* Cambridge, MA: Harvard University Press, 1928.

Wilder, Alec. *American Popular Song: The Great Innovators, 1900–1950.* NY: Oxford, 1972.

Wolfe, Tom. *The Electric Kool-Aid Acid Test.* NY: Farrar, Straus and Giroux, 1968.

The World Atlas of Birds. NY: Random House, 1974.

The WPA Guide to California. The Federal Writers' Project Guide to 1930s California. Written and compiled by the Federal Writers' Project of the Works Progress Administration for the State of California. NY: Pantheon, 1984. (Originally copyrighted in 1939 by Mabel R. Gillis, California State Librarian)

Electronic Resources

The All-Music Guide. http://www.allmusic.com

Alpert, Stephen P. *A Dictionary of Hobo Slang.* http://www.hobonick els.org/alpert04.htm

Asher, Levi. *Literary Kicks* http://www.litkicks.com.

Callerlab. The International Association of Square Dance Callers. http://www.callerlab.org

Dance History Archives. http://www.streetswing.com/histmain.htm

Digital Tradition Folk Song Database. Greenhaus, Dick, and friends, site maintainers. http://www.mudcat.org/

The Internet Movie Database. Hartill, Rob, site maintainer. http://www.imdb.com

Levick, Ben and Mark Beadle. *Games of the Viking and Anglo-Saxon Age.* http://mahan.wonkwang.ac.kr/link/med/folk/game/games.htm.

Mattson, Anne. "Indigo in the Early Modern World." http://www.bell.lib.umn.edu/Products/Indigo.html

Morton, J. L. *Color Matters.* http://www.colormatters.com.

RoJaRo Index: an online index to popular music magazines. http://www.notam02.no/rojaro/

Samuel Taylor Coleridge Home Page. http://etext.lib.virginia.edu/stc/Coleridge/index.html

Smith, Jennifer. *Sacred Woods and the Lore of Trees.* http://www.tarahill.com/treelore/trees.html

U.S. Gazetteer. http://www.census.gov/cgi-bin/gazetteer

Wikipedia. http://en.wikipedia.org/wiki/Main_Page

Yahoo. http://www.yahoo.com

credits and permissions

1 *The Annotated Alice*, by Marin Gardner. W.W. Norton & Co. Reprinted by permission.

2 Blair Jackson, in *Dupree's Diamond News*, "In Phil We Trust: A Conversation." Spring 1994, pp. 12–22. Used by kind permission.

3 Excerpt from *Tarot Cards for Fun and Fortune Telling*, by Stuart R. Kaplan © U.S. Games Systmes Inc. 1970. Further reproduction prohibited.

4 Excerpt from Rock Scully and David Dalton's *Living with the Dead*. © 1996 Little, Brown, and Company. Used with kind permission.

5 Tom Wolfe. *The Electric Kool-Aid Acid Test*. Farrar, Straus & Giroux, 1968. Reprinted by permission.

6 Tom Wolfe. *The Electric Kool-Aid Acid Test*. Farrar, Straus & Giroux, 1968. Reprinted by permission.

7 Gates of Eden. Copyright © 1965 by Warner Bros. Inc. Copyright renewed 1993 by Special Rider Music. All rights reserved. International copyright secured. Reprinted by permission.

8 Blair Jackson, in *The Golden Road*, 1993 annual. Used by kind permission.

9 *A Dictionary of Symbols*, by Juan Eduardo Cirlot. Routledge, 1983. Used by permission.

10 Gabriele Tergit. *Flowers Through the Ages*, Material originally published by: Berg Putlishers, Oxford, New York. www.berg publishers.com.

11 Blair Jackson, in *Grateful Dead: The Music Never Stopped*. Used by kind permission.

12 David Gans. Used by kind permission.

13 Tom Wolfe. *The Electric Kool-Aid Acid Test*. Farrar, Straus & Giroux, 1968. Reprinted by permission.

14 Tom Wolfe. *The Electric Kool-Aid Acid Test*. Farrar, Straus & Giroux, 1968. Reprinted by permission.

15 Dennis McNally, in *A Long Strange Trip*. Random House, Inc. Used by permission.

16 Interview by Blair Jackson in *The Golden Road* magazine, Spring 1991, p. 30. Used by kind permission.

17 It Takes a Lot to Laugh It Takes a Train to Cry. Copyright © 1965 by Warner Bros. Inc. Copyright renewed 1993 by Special Rider Music. All rights reserved. International copyright secured. Reprinted by permission.

18 Quoted with permission from Robert Hunter. All rights reserved by the author.

19 David Gans, in *Conversations with the Dead*. Used by kind permission.

20 From *Benet's Reader's Encyclopedia of American Literature*, ed. by George Perkins, Barbara Perkins. Copyright © 1991 by Harper & Row Publishers Inc. Reprinted by permission of HarperCollins Publishers Inc.

21 From *The Anchor Bible Dictionary*, edited by David Noel Freeman. Random House, Inc. Used by permission.

22 From *Benet's Reader's Encyclopedia of American Literature*, ed. by George Perkins, Barbara Perkins. Copyright © 1991 by Harper & Row Publishers Inc. Reprinted by permission of HarperCollins Publishers Inc.

23 Gabriele Tergit. *Flowers Through the Ages*, Material originally published by: Berg Putlishers, Oxford, New York. www.berg publishers.com.

24 Gabriele Tergit. *Flowers Through the Ages*, Material originally published by: Berg Putlishers, Oxford, New York. www.berg publishers.com.

25 From *Benet's Reader's Encyclopedia of American Literature*, ed. by George Perkins, Barbara Perkins. Copyright © 1991 BY Harper & Row Publishers Inc. Reprinted by permission of HarperCollins Publishers Inc.

26 Quoted with permission from Robert Hunter. All rights reserved by the author.

27 Arthur C. Jones. *Wade in the Water: The Wisdom of the Spirituals*. Used by kind permission.

28 David Gans, from an interview on KPFA's *Dead to the World*. Used by kind permission.

29 *A Dictionary of Symbols*, by Juan Eduardo Cirlot. Routledge, 1983. Used by permission.

30 Excerpt from *Tarot Cards for Fun and Fortune Telling*, by Stuart R. Kaplan © U.S. Games Systmes Inc. 1970. Further reproduction prohibited.

30a Quoted with permission from Robert Hunter. All rights reserved by the author.

31 Blair Jackson, in *Goin' Down the Road: A Grateful Dead Traveling Companion*. Used by kind permission.

32 From *Benet's Reader's Encyclopedia of American Literature*, ed. by George Perkins, Barbara Perkins. Copyright © 1991 by Harper & Row Publishers Inc. Reprinted by permission of HarperCollins Publishers Inc.

33 *Ballin' the Jack*. James Henry Burris & Chris Smith. © 1913. Renewed Christie-Max Music. Permission secured. All rights reserved.

34 Blair Jackson, in *Goin' Down the Road: A Grateful Dead Traveling Companion*. Used by kind permission.

35 Quoted with permission from Robert Hunter. All rights reserved by the author.

36 Blair Jackson, in *Goin' Down the Road: A Grateful Dead Traveling Companion*. Used by kind permission.

37 Quoted with permission from Robert Hunter. All rights reserved by the author.

38 Excerpt from *The Fellowship of the Ring* by J. R. R. Tolkien. Copyright © 1954, 1965 by J. R. R. Tolkien. Copyright © renewed 1982 by Christopher R. Tolkien, Michael H.R. Tolkien, John F.R. Tolkien and Priscilla M.A.R. Tolkien. Copyright © renewed 1993 by Christopher R. Tolkien, John F. R. Tolkien and Priscilla M. A. R. Tolkien. Reprinted by permission of Houghton Mifflin Company. All rights reserved. Reprinted by permission of HarperCollins Publishers Inc. © 1954, 1965 by J. R. R. Tolkien.

38a Jennifer Smith and Colleen Whittaker, "Sacred Woods and the Lore of Trees." Used by kind permission.

39 Used by permission of Songs of Universal, Inc.

40 *A Dictionary of Symbols*, by Juan Eduardo Cirlot. Routledge, 1983. Used by permission.

41 *Downstream from Trout Fishing in America*. Copyright © Keith Abbott 2005.

41a Quoted with permission from Robert Hunter. All rights reserved by the author.

42 "Shuffle Off to Buffalo," by Al Dubin and Harry Warren. Used by permission of M. Witmark and Sons.

43 Quoted with permission from Robert Hunter. All rights reserved by the author.

44 From *The Anchor Bible Dictionary*, edited by David Noel Freeman.

Random House, Inc. Used by permission.

45 Quoted with permission from Robert Hunter. All rights reserved by the author.

46 Copyright © 2000 by Houghton Mifflin Company. Reproduced by permission from *The American Heritage Dictionary of the English Language, Fourth Edition*.

47 Quoted with permission from Robert Hunter. All rights reserved by the author.

48 Copyright © 2000 by Houghton Mifflin Company. Adapted and reproduced by permission from *The American Heritage Dictionary of the English Language, Fourth Edition*.

49 By Dylan Thomas, from The Poems of Dylan Thomas, copyright © 1939 by New Directions Publishing Corp. Reprinted by permission of New Directions Publishing Corp.

50 Dennis McNally, in *A Long Strange Trip*. Random House, Inc. Used by permission.

51 From *American Popular Song: The Great Innovators, 1900-1950* by Alec Wilder, edited by James T. Maher, copyright © 1972 by Alec Wilder. Used by permission of Oxford University Press, Inc.

52 David Gans, in *Conversations with the Dead*. Used by kind permission.

53 From *The Collected Poems of Wallace Stevens* by Wallace Stevens, copyright 1954 by Wallace Stevens and renewed 1982 by Holly Stevens. Used by permission of Alfred A. Knopf, a division of Random House, Inc.

54 Dr. J. L. Morton, in *Color Matters*. Used by kind permission.

55 David Gans, in *Playing in the Band*. Used by kind permission.

56 *A Dictionary of Symbols*, by Juan Eduardo Cirlot. Routledge, 1983. Used by permission.

57 David Gans, in *Conversations With the Dead*. Used by kind permission.

58 Reprinted with permission of Callerlab, The International Association of Square Dance Callers.

59 From *Benet's Reader's Encyclopedia of American Literature*, ed. by George Perkins, Barbara Perkins. Copyright © 1991 by Harper & Row Publishers Inc. Reprinted by permission of HarperCollins Publishers Inc.

60 From *Benet's Reader's Encyclopedia of American Literature*, ed. by George Perkins, Barbara Perkins. Copyright © 1991 by Harper & Row Publishers Inc. Reprinted by permission of HarperCollins Publishers Inc.

61 Katherine Anne Porter. *Ship of Fools*. Little, Brown and Company.

62 Used by kind permission of John Perry Barlow. All rights reserved by the author

63 Blair Jackson, in *Goin' Down the Road: A Grateful Dead Traveling Companion.* Used by kind permission.

64 From *American Popular Song: The Great Innovators, 1900-1950* by Alec Wilder, edited by James T. Maher, copyright © 1972 by Alec Wilder. Used by permission of Oxford University Press, Inc.

65 Robert Petersen. *Alleys of the Heart.* © 1988, Robert M. Petersen. Used with permission of Hulogosi Publishers.

66 Used by permission of author, Allan W. Eckert, May 6, 2005, from *The Owls of North America . . .* (Doubleday, 1974)

67 Blair Jackson, in *Goin' Down the Road: A Grateful Dead Traveling Companion.* Used by kind permission.

68 Blair Jackson, in *Goin' Down the Road: A Grateful Dead Traveling Companion.* Used by kind permission.

69 Van Morrison, "Astral Weeks." Used by permission.

70 "All in green went my love riding." Copyright 1923, 1951, © 1991 by the Trustees for the E. E. Cummings Trust. Copyright © 1976 by Geroge James Firmage, from *Complete Poems: 1904–1962* by E. E. Cummings, edited by George J. Firmage. Used by permission of Liveright Publishing Corporation.

71 From *Benet's Reader's Encyclopedia of American Literature,* ed. by George Perkins, Barbara Perkins. Copyright © 1991 BY Harper & Row Publishers Inc. Reprinted by permission of HarperCollins Publishers Inc.

72 Blair Jackson, in *Goin' Down the Road: A Grateful Dead Traveling Companion.* Used by kind permission.

73 "Standing in the Soul," by Steve Silberman. Used by kind permission.

74 Robert Hunter's translation of Rainer Maria Rilke's *Duino Elegies* and *The Sonnets to Orpheus.* ©1993, Robert Hunter. Used with permission of Hulogosi Publishers.

75 © 1993 Princeton University Press. Reprinted by permission of Princeton University Press.

76 Quoted with permission from Robert Hunter. All rights reserved by the author.

77 *A Dictionary of Symbols,* by Juan Eduardo Cirlot. Routledge, 1983. Used by permission.

78 Quoted with permission from Robert Hunter. All rights reserved by the author.

79 *Time Passes Slowly.* Copyright © 1970 by Big Sky Music. All rights reserved. International copyright secured. Reprinted by permission.

80 David Gans, in Blair Jackson's *Grateful Dead: The Music Never Stopped.* Used by kind permission.

81 David Gans. *Conversations with the Dead.* Used by kind permission.

82 Courtesy Roger Felton. Thanks, Roger!

83 From *American Popular Song: The Great Innovators, 1900-1950* by Alec Wilder, edited by James T. Maher, copyright © 1972 by Alec Wilder. Used by permission of Oxford University Press, Inc.

84 Blair Jackson, in *Goin' Down the Road: A Grateful Dead Traveling Companion.* Used by kind permission.

85 From *The Dictionary of American Biography,* by Thomas Cripps, Gale Group, Reprinted by permission of The Gale Group.

86 From *The Anchor Bible Dictionary,* edited by David Noel Freeman. Random House, Inc. Used by permission.

87 "Standing in the Soul," by Steve Silberman. Used by kind permission.

88 Gerrit Graham. "The Crime, and Its Victims." Essay for the *Annotated Grateful Dead Lyrics.* Used with the author's permission.

89 By Anne Mattson, copyright by the Regents of the University of Minnesota, Twin Cities, University Libraries, James Ford Bell Library.

90 Blair Jackson and David Gans, from unpublished material for Jackson's *Garcia: An American Life.* Used by kind permission.

91 David Gans. Used by kind permission.

92 Excerpt from Rock Scully and David Dalton's *Living w ith the Dead.* © 1996 Little, Brown, and Company. Used with kind permission.

93 Quoted with permission from Robert Hunter. All rights reserved by the author.

94 Blair Jackson, from *Goin' Down the Road: A Grateful Dead Traveling Companion.* Used by permission. Copyright Blair Jackson. All rights reserved.

95 Phil Lesh. Excerpts from *Searching for the Sound: My Life with the Grateful Dead.* © 2005 Little, Brown, and Company. All rights reserved.

96 Richard Cannings, from "Northern Saw-wWhet Owl," in *The Birds of North America.* used by permission of the American Ornithologists' Union and the Academy of Natural Sciences.

97 John Kessler. Excerpt from "On Cloud 9, Cream Puffs Revive Classics." *Denver Post,* May 31, 1995. Reprinted by permission of the *Denver Post.*

acknowledgments

Contributors to the Annotated Grateful Dead Lyrics website;
many thanks to each of you!

Aric Ahrens, Jeff Aitken, Bob Aldrich, Doug Allaire, Alex Allan, John Allen, Daniel Yairi Alth, Carl Anderson, John B. Andrews, Jonathan Baker, Scott Baldwin, Trevor Balmer, Larry Bartram, Charlie Bass, Andrew Bear, Jonathan Beers, Melinda Belleville, Jeff Bentch, Joe Berentes, Michael Berger, Jeff Bernstein, Joshua Bernstein, Erik Berry, Aaron Bibb, Steve Biederman, Brooke Borner, Brandi Bowen, John Bowers, Joshua P. Boyd, Ray Brizzi, David Brown, Ed Brown, Emily Brown, Wally Bubelis, Joe Burke, Gary Burnett, Valentine Cadieux, David Callaway, Matthew Carl, Adam Cerny, Joe Cesare, Ira Chernus, Eight Way Wesley Cherry, Oz Child, Ives Chor, Jim Chrzan, Paul Chumsky, F. Scott Clugston, Orchard Marie Coffin, Mike Cowperthwaite, Christian Crumlish, Peter Darling, Keith David, Daniel Dawdy, Carl Desenberg, Steven Doellefeld, Bill Doggett, Patrick Donnelly, Craig Dudley, Chuck Duncanson, Richard Clay Dunham, Eric Elliot, Dean Esmay, Andrew Estroff, Doug Everitt, Todd Brendan Fahey, Jurgen Fauth, Andria Daacon Fiegel, Steven Finney, Mark D. Firestone, Andy Fische, John Flanigan, Michael W. Fleming, Vic Flick, David Foyt, Josh Frankel, Suzanne Franks, Daniel Freeman, Carmen Fulford, Alisa Gaylon, Linda Gershon, Bill Gillispie, Jane Glass, Neil Glazer, David Gold, Anne Graham. Dave Harding, Gary Hartman, Ryan M. Hastings, Jeff Hedrick, Dave Hegland, Mike Hennessy, John Henrikson, Adam Hilliard , Craig Hillwig, Ben Hollin, Edward Brough Holzwanger , Dale G. Hoyt, Warren Hurley, Scott Hyatt, Blair Jackson, Steven Jernigan, Jerry Grau Jessup, Ken Johnson, Ken Johnson, Ken Johnson, Lane Kelley Kahn, Max Kaplan, Anastasia Karel,

Dick Katz, Ivon Katz, Richard Katz, Chris Keiner, Avtar Singh Khalsa, Lion Kimbro, Kieran Kirsten, Aaron J. Klamer, Walt Kohnke, Dave Kopel, Dan Kravitz, John Krulish, David Kudrav, Claude Kuhnen , Tony Kullen, Andy Kurzon, Greene Lawson, David Leach, Dana Leighton, Randy Lewi, Jeff Lifson, Candice Y. Lin, Lauren Lee Lindgren, Vincent Liota, Jay S. Lipsey, Sam Lopez, John Low, Luke Meade Lynn, Mike Maddux, Thomas E. Malloy, Dave Manoni, Dom Mastroianni, Miles Mathieu, Scott Matter, Kevin Matthews, John P. McAlpin, Arthur McCullough, Tom McKnight, Rob Meador, Ed Mechem, Conrad Miller, Matthew Mitchell, Mike Mnichowicz, James Molenda, Marty Mary-Ellen Mort, Andrew Murawa, Tom Murphy, Joe Newcomb, Aaron Nielsenshultz, Deb Nison, Scott Odell, Brett Orlob, Barbara Ortagus, Julie Ostoich, Tom Parmenter, Bill Parry, Tom Parsons, Andrea Jean Patten, Michael Patrick, Tim Paulman, Laurae Pearson, Brian Penney, Chris Perkins, Sebastian Petsu, John Edward Philips, Brad Phillips, S. Polczer, Dave Pruett, Ann Mary Quarandillo, Ken Rattenne, Timm Rebitzki, Roger Renken, Tom Richards, Brendan Riley, Chris Robbins, Matthew Robertson, Scott Robertson, Rollie Smith Roserunner, H. Ross, Maziar Sadri, Barbara Saunders, Joel Schneier, Matt Schofield, Matty Schultheis, David Schwarm, Chamberlain Segrest, John Shahabian, Andrew Shalit, Meg Shear, Timothy Sheehan, Doug Shipley, Steve F. Steve Silberman, Richard B. Simon, Daniel Sittner, Keven Skelton, Ihor Slabicky, Robert Steinhilber, Ray Stell, Clifford Stephens, Roger Stomperud, Duane Streufert, Isaac Sublett, Ian Szekeres, Adam Taylor, Bruce Thomas, Mike Tisdale, Bob Trudeau, Lee Tyson, Guy Urban, William Vidrine, Chad Walker, Rick Waters, Ed Watson, Roy Webb, Art Weller, April M. West, Justin Wetherell, David Whiteis, Alex Whitney, Josh Wilson, Erin Wolfe, Jill Zarazinski, Michael Zelner, Joe Zomerfeld, Tom Zubal.

general index

Aubrey, John, 190
Auditorium Theater (Chicago), 163, 164
August West (Wharf Rat) (artwork), 152
August, William, 98
Augustine, 236
"Auld Lang Syne", xv
Austria, 64
Autry, Gene, 230
Avalon Ballroom (San Francisco)
    performances at, 17, 18, 21, 34
    song references to, 36, 38
Azarian, Tom, 76–77

B

"Baba O'Reilly" (Townshend), 403
Babbs, Ken (Merry Prankster), 45
Babylon, 122
Bach, J. S., 392, 415
Bach, P. D. Q., 180
"Back Door Man" (Howlin' Wolf/Dixon), 373
Backbone (musical group), 389
Baez, Joan, 217
Bahamas, 60
Bailey, Temple, 342–343
Baja California State, 170
Baker, Josephine, 242
Baker, Pearly (song character), 150
Baker, Purley, 152
Baker, Thomas, 170
Bakersfield, California, 170
Bakongo religion, 79
Baldwin, Count of Flanders, 77
Baldwin, James, 158
"Ballad of Casey Jones" (Seibert/Newton), 87-88
"Ballin' the Jack" (Smith/Burris), 95–96
"Banbury Cross," 229

The Band (musical group), 253
Barcelona, Spain, 166
Barchilon, Jose, 223
Barlow, John, 46, 59, 232
    about, 424
    "Cassidy" essay by, 224–228
    father's death, 227–228
    Hunter viewed by, 420–421
    "Looks Like Rain" comments by, 421–422
    lyric authorship viewed by, 418–423
    as lyricist, xxii, xxiii, xxv, 32, 37, 186, 190, 213,
        214, 352–353, 355
Barnes, F.J., 229
Barnett, Dan, xii
Barnum & Bailey Circus, 220, 338
Barnum, P. T., 219–220
Barri, Steve, 25
Barrie, Sir James Matthew, 46
Barry, Jeff, 364
Barrymore, Drew, 343
The Basement Tapes, 120
Bass, Charles E., 137–138
Bates, Katherine Lee, 168
Baton Rouge International Speedway (Louisiana), 96
Baum, Joseph, 143–144
Beach Boys (musical group), 364
Bear *see* Owsley
Beastie Boys (musical group), xxx
The Beatles (musical group), xxiii, 5, 29, 46, 157 *see
    also individual album and song titles*
Bechet, Sidney, 70, 242
Beck, Jeff, 33
Beckett, Samuel, 101
Beckinsale, Kate, 122
"Been on the Cholly So Long," 88
Behan, Brendan, 197
Beijing, China, 92

Bellarmine College, Louisville, Kentucky, 69

"The Bells of London Town," 180

Belushi, John, 311

Belvedere Island, California, 62

Ben Hur, 251

Benson, Mr. (slang fictional character), 115

Berio, Luciano, xii

Berkeley, California, 29, 324

Berlin, Irving, 81, 124, 177–178

Bernhardt, Sarah, 196

Berrigan, Bunny, 70

Berry, Chuck, 124, 179, 290, 363, 364

Bertha (office fan), 141

Bester, Alfred, 249

"Betty and Dupree" (traditional), 70–73

"Big Boss Man" (Smith, Dixon), 365

Big Brother and the Holding Company (musical group), 363

"Big Iron" (Robbins), 144

"Big Railroad Blues" (Cannon's Jug Stompers), 21

Big Three Trio (musical group), 373

Bigfoot, Texas, 162

"Billy Grimes the Rover" (traditional), 104

Binford, T. A., 115

Binion, Benny "Deadman," 147

Bion (poet), 267

Birch, Harry, 361

"Bird in a Cage" (traditional), 48

"Bitter Olives" (Petersen), 234

Black Madonna, 34

Black Peter, 100

Black Peter (film), 100

"Blackbird" (Lennon, McCartney), 363

Blackmore, Richie, 203

"Blackwaterside" (traditional), 48

Blake, "Blind," 194

Blake, Eubie, 184

Blake, William, 267–268, 341–342

Blakesburg, Jay, 173

Bland, Bobby "Blue," 40

Bland, Len, 124

"Blest Be the Tie That Binds" (Fawcett), 191

Bloom, Rube, 131

Bloomington, Minnesota, 337

"Blow Away the Morning Dew" (Child #112), 245

Blue River, 211

Blue Sky Boys (musical group), 368

"Blue Suede Shoes" (Perkins), 215, 218

"Blue Yodel No. 9." *See* "Standin' on the Corner"

"Blueberry Hill" (Lewis, Stock, Rose), 230

"Blues for Alice" (Parker), 241

Blues for Mr. Charlie (Baldwin), 158

"Bo' Hog Blues" (Alexander), 39

Boar's Head Coffee House, Jewish Community Center (San Carlos, California), 104

Bob & Jerry (musical group), xxii

Bob Dylan and the Band (musical group), 120

Bojangles. *See* Robinson, Bill

"Bojangles of Harlem" (Kern, Fields), 305

"The Bold Lieutenant" (traditional), 261–262

Bolinas, California, 129

"Boneyard Shuffle" (Carmichael, Mills), 184

Bonneau, Annie (song character), 152

"The Bonnie Lass of Fenario" (traditional), 82

"The Bonnie Lass of Fyvie-O" (traditional), 82, 217

"Boogie Stop Shuffle" (Mingus), 184

Borrow, Joe Louis, 352

Boston, Massachusetts, 346

Botkin, B. A., 86, 87, 285–286

Bourbon Street (New Orleans, Louisiana), 132

Bousquet, Patrick, 285

A Box of Rain

    lyric variations in, 362

    notes from, 38, 52, 57, 67, 108, 110, 123, 130,

Camden, William, 200
Camlann, Battle of, 354–355
"Camptown Races" (Foster), 131
Candide (Voltaire), 352
Candlestick Park (San Francisco), 366
"Candy Man Blues" (Mississippi John Hurt), 114
Cannon Ball Express, 87
Cannon, Gus, 21
"Cannonball Blues" (traditional), 104
Cannon's Jug Stompers, 21
Canterbury Tales (Chaucer), 257
Capital Center (Landover, Maryland), 315, 362
Capitol Theater (New Jersey), 306, 307
Capitol Theater (New York), 119, 141, 144, 146, 147, 149, 152, 153, 155
The Captain and Tenille (musical group), xxiii
"Careless Love" (Handy, Williams, Koenig), 377
Caribbean, 60, 156, 386
Carlyle, Thomas, 100–101
Carmichael, Hoagy, 184
"The Carnival Parade" (Lecuona), 361
Carousel Ballroom (San Francisco), 38, 48, 57, 59, 65
"The Carrion Crow" (Sharp #222), 76
Carroll, Lewis, 3–5, 196, 265
Carter, A. P., 166
Carter, Michelle, 137
Carus, Emma, 177
Cash, Johnny, 182
"The Cask of Amontillado" (Poe), 107
Cassady, Neal, 44, 46, 224–226, 228, 338–339
Cat on a Hot Tin Roof, 169–170
Catherine the Great (Russia), 324
Cat's Cradle (Vonnegut), 247
Cats Under the Stars, 362
Cavanaugh, Ellen, 106
Cayce, Kentucky, 86

"C'est la Vie (You Can Never Tell)" (Berry), 290
Chan, Charlie (fictional character), 220
Chandrasekhar, Subrahmanyan, 50
Chaney, Lon, Jr., 181
Chapala, Lake (Mexico), 57
Chapel of Love (Dixie Cups), 277
Chaplin, Charlie, 102
Charles, Andrew, 386
Charleston, South Carolina, 104, 179
Charlie (slang fictional character), 115, 157–158
Charlotte Coliseum (North Carolina), 217
Chateau Marmont (Los Angeles), 311
Chatman, Bo, 368
"Chattanoogie," Tennessee, 165–166
Chaucer, Geoffrey, 109, 169, 257
Chelsea Hotel (New York), 196–197
Cherokee, (various towns), 113
  Cherokee Nation, 113
Cherry Creek, Arizona, 113
Cheshire-Cat, 3–5, 56, 410
Cheshire County, England, 4, 23
Chess Records, 373
Chicago, Illinois, 40, 168, 373, 426. *See also specific venues in Chicago, Illinois*
Childhood's End (Clarke), 388
"Children, Go Where I Send Thee" (traditional), 59
China, 55, 56, 74, 92, 139, 143
China Camp, California, xix, 159
"China Doll" (Hornsby), 201
Chino, California, 112–113
Chino Valley (Arizona), 113
Chisholm Trail (Texas), 145
Christian, Charlie, 114
Christianity, 44, 61–62, 79
Cincinnati, Ohio, 115
Circus (musical group), 400
Cirlot, J. E., 42, 85, 128, 200, 266, 365

Civic Auditorium (San Francisco), 327
Civic Center (Providence, Rhode Island), 305
Clarke, Arthur C., 196, 388
Clarke, Shirley, 197
Classic Albums: American Beauty, 140
"Clementine" (traditional), 53–54
Cleveland, Ohio, 180, 288
"Clinch Mountain Home" (Carter), 166
The Cloud of Unknowing (St. Denis), 116
Clover (musical group), 400
Clytemnestra (mythological character), 76
Cocktail (film), 364
Cocteau, Jean, 92, 362
Cohan, George M., 107
Cohen, John, 76, 106
Cold Mountain (poet). *See* Han-Shan (poet)
Colden Auditorium (New York), 136
Cole, Nat "King," 102, 179
Cole, Natalie, 179
Cole, "Old King," 36–37, 126
Coleman, Ornette, 38
Coleridge, Samuel Taylor, 90–92, 128, 150
Collins, Judy, 30–31
Cologne, 69, 232
Colorado, 11, 30, 43, 424
    performances in, 235, 280, 287, 288, 289, 290,
        301, 395, 410
Coltrane, John, xxii
Columbia, Maryland, 405
Columbia University (New York City, New York),
    426
"Come all ye" tunes, xix, 106, 114
Community War Memorial (Rochester, New York),
    323
Compton Terrace Amphitheater (Tempe, Arizona),
    319
Congo, Democratic Republic of, 74

Congregationalist, 168
Conn, Billy, 352
Connecticut. *See specific venues in Connecticut*
Conrad, Joseph, 358
Constanten, Tom, 52, 415
"Coo Coo Bird" (Ashley/traditional), 120
Cook, (Curly) Jim, 31
Cook, Shelley, 105
Cooke, Sam, 408
"Cool Drink of Water Blues" (Johnson), 143
"Cool Water" (Robbins), 144
Coon Creek Girls (musical group), 139
Cooper, B. Lee, 37, 124
Coots, J. Fred, 81
Copenhagen, Denmark, 193
Coppola, Francis Ford, 358
Cora, Wyoming, 186, 190, 228, 232, 249, 272, 317,
    319, 324
Coral (record label), 65
Corinna (poetess), 368–369
"Corinna" (Swift), 369
"Corinna, Corrina" (traditional), 368
"Corrina's Going A-Maying" (Herrick), 369
"Corrine, Corrina" (Chatma, Parish, Williams), 368
Cotten, Elizabeth, 159
Cotton Club, 66
Cotton, James, 40
"Courting the Muse" (lecture), 263
Cow Palace (Daly City, California), 228, 231
Cowley, John, 157–158
Crane, Hart, 196
Crawford, James "Sugar Boy," 277
Crazy Fingers. *See* Hopkins, Claude
"Crazy Fingers" (Maddox), 242
Crazy Fingers: Claude Hopkins' Life in Jazz (Hopkins), 242
Crazy Otto. *See* Maddox, Johnny; Schulz-Reichel,
    Fritz

"The Crazy Otto Medley" (Maddox), 180
Crazy Otto Piano, 181
Crazy Otto Plays Crazy Tunes, 242
"Creation" (traditional), 198
Creedence Clearwater Revival (musical group), 339
Creeley, Robert, 129–130
Cricket Pavilion (Phoenix, Arizona), 408
Croce, Jim, 125
"Cross-eyed Blues" (Humes), 48
Crow, Bill, 73
"Crow Black Chicken" (traditional), 104
"The Cruel Mother" (Sharp #10, version D), 64
Cruise, Tom, 364
Crumb, R., 66
Crumlish, Christian, 329
"Cry, Cry, Cry" (Bland), 40
Cucamonga, California, 233–234
"Cuckoo Song" (anon.), 35
Culture and Anarchy (Arnold), 355
Cumberland County Civic Center (Portland, Maine), 317, 329
"Cumberland Gap" (traditional), 98
Cumberland, references to, 97–99
Cummings, E. E., 56, 247
Curtis, Loyal, 299
Cushing, William O., 200

D

Dade Coal Company, 13
Daly City, California, 228, 231
Dance steps and dances
    African American, 101–102, 115, 156–157, 183–184
    Apache, 385
    Ballin' the Jack, 95–96
    Big Apple, 67
    Bop, 384–385
    Bow and Balance, 76
    Brazilian, 384
    Buck-and-Wing, 102–103, 156
    Caribbean, 156
    Contra, 76
    Do Paso, 209-210
    Irish Jig, 34
    Jitterbug, 36, 385
    Jive, 115
    Juba, 156–157
    Ring, 80
    Shake, 160–161
    Shuffle, 183–184
    Square Dance, 209–210
    Strutting, 66
    Swing, 384–385
    Truckin', 66
    Water, 103
    Zudie-O, 66
Danes, Claire, 122
Danish Center (Los Angeles), 12, 13
Danko, Rick, 211
Danko/Fjeld/Andersen, 211
Dante Alighieri, xxxi
Dardanus (god), 76
"Dark Hollow" (traditional), 139, 365
Dark Side of the Moon, 268
Dark Star (film), 51
Dark Star (race horse), 51
"Dark Star" (Oldfield), 51
"Dark Star" (Stills), 51
"Darktown Strutter's Ball" (Brooks), 385
David, King of Israel, xv
David Nelson Band, 24

Curtis/Gillespie), 299

Dubin, Al, 133, 184

Duino Elegies, 425

Duke (record label), 40

Dundes, Alan, 158

Dupree, Frank, 70–71

Dupree, Reese, 73

"Dupree's Blues" (Dupree), 73

Dupree's Diamond News, 278

Duvall, Robert, 179

Dylan, Bob, xxiii, 34, 56, 196, 217, 270, 388, 419, 420. *See also* Bob Dylan and the Band

E

Eagle Mall Suite, 56, 75, 128, 256, 265, 305

"Easin' In" (Cadillac), 22

East Palo Alto, California, xii

East Rutherford, New Jersey, 382

"East St. Louis Toodleloo" (Ellington), 199

East Troy, Wisconsin, 339, 340, 343, 345

Easy Rider, 227

"Easy Rider" (traditional), 363

Easy Street (film), 102

"Easy Street" (Jones), 102

Edda (Scandinavian epic), 179

"Edward" (Child #13), 167

Eisenhower, Dwight, 224

"El Paso" (Robbins), 144

El Salvador, 350

"Eldorado" (Poe), 75

Electra (mythological character), 76, 369

Electric Theater (Chicago), 93

Electronic Frontier Foundation, 424

Elektra Records, 33

Elgin, B., 125

Eliot, T. S., xxvii, 51, 196, 213, 268, 420

Ellen, R., 124

Ellington, Duke, 184, 199

Emergency Crew (musical group), 46. *See also* Grateful Dead

Emerson, Ralph Waldo, 355

"The Empty Cup" (Yeats), 173

Endgame (Beckett), 101

England, 29, 33. *See also specific place names in England*
  Alfred the Great's reign of, 77
  Great Revolt in, 169
  Hunter's first visit to, 121
  marshes in, 83
  religious music of, 60
  rosemary rites in, 68
  slang of, 198, 246

English Proverbs (Ray), 192

"An Enigma" (Poe), 189

Ephesus, Greece, 34

Epipolae, Battle of, 354

Epistulae ad Lucilium (Seneca), 100

Esau (biblical character), 319, 337

An Essay Concerning Human Understanding (Locke), 267

"An Essay on Criticism" (Pope), 339

Essays (Emerson), 355

Essex, England, 169

Ethelflaed, Lady of the Mercians, 77

Ethelgifu (nun), 77

Ethelred, Count of the Mercians, 77

Eureka, California, 54

Eurydice (mythological character), 362

Evans, David, 136

Evening Moods, 400, 402, 426

The Evergreen Review, 74

"Everybody's Doing It Now" (Berlin), 81

Ewen, David, 384

Ewing, James S., 84

Excelsior District (San Francisco), 259

"Eyes of the World" (various), 203
Ezekiel (prophet), 258, 271–272

F

"Fable of a Chosen One" (David Nelson Band), 24
"Faces in the Fire" (Carroll), 265
"Fair to Even Odds" (Hunter), 210
Fairy Sybil, 77
Falls of Princes (Lydgate), 257
"The False Knight upon the Road" (Sharp #2), 63
"False True Love" (traditional), 48
"False Young Man" (traditional), 48
The Family Dog at the Great Highway (San Francisco), 95, 113
Far Away Radios (Petersen), 426
"Fare Thee Well Marianne" (traditional), 122–123
Farina, Johann Maria, 69
Farrar, Straus, and Giroux, 227
Fawcett, John, 191
"F.D.R.'s Back Again" (traditional), 115
"Feelin' Groovy." *See* "59th Street Bridge Song"
Fellowship of the Ring (Tolkien), 118
de Feminis, Paul, 69
Fennario (mythological place), xx, 77, 82–84, 217
"Fennario" (traditional), 82
Fenris (mythological beast), 85
Ferrer, Jose, 223
Festival Express, 253
Festival Express Tour, 211, 253
Fiddler's Green (fictional place), 410
Field House (Cincinnati), 115
Fields, Dorothy, 80, 290, 305
"59th Street Bridge Song (Feelin' Groovy)" (Simon), 48
Fillmore Auditorium (San Francisco)
    performances at, 15, 22, 23, 40, 99, 108, 110

song references to, 36, 38
Fillmore East (New York), 70, 89, 94, 135
Fillmore West (San Francisco), 38, 101, 105, 120, 123, 125, 129, 133
Finnegans Wake (Joyce), 388
"Fire and Ice" (Frost), 104
"Fire on the Mountain" (traditional), 273
Fitzgerald, F. Scott, 196
Five Breezes (musical group), 373
Fjeld, Jonas, 211
Fleetwood Mac (musical group), 203, 278
Fletcher, Tom, 305
Flying Circus (musical group). *See* Circus (musical group)
Folkways Records, 105, 106
Fonda, Jane, 197
Ford, Lena Guilbert, 313
Ford Pavilion (Scranton, Pennsylvania), 396
Ford, Lena Guilbert, 313
Ford, Tennessee Ernie, 363
Forman, Milos, 100, 197
Fortuna (goddess), 257
Fortunado (fictional character), 107
Foster, Paul, 23
Foster, Stephen, xv, 109, 131, 331–332, 375
Foucault, Michel, 223
Fountain Valley High (Colorado Springs, Colorado), 424
Four Lads (musical group), 25
Four Quartets: Little Gidding (Eliot), 268
Fox, Matthew, 62
Foyle, Gulliver (fictional character), 249
Fragment (Aeschylus), 138
Franken, Al, 188
Frankenstein (castle of Germany), 182
Frankenstein (Shelly), 181–182
Frankenstein Meets the Wolf Man, 181

Frankenstein, Victor (fictional character), 182
Freemasons. *See* Masons
French, Arthur W., 299
Fresno, California, 170
"Friendship" (Emerson), 355
Frost, Robert, 104
Fuld, James L., 177–178
Fuller, Jesse, 13–14
Funny Girl, 251
Furthur (Kesey's bus), 45, 224–225
"Futuristic Shuffle" (Savitt), 184
Fyvie-O (imaginary place), 82, 84

G

Gaddy, Bob, 125
Gadsden, Christopher, 104
da Gama, Vasco, 67
Gamse, Albert, 361
Gans, David, interviews with, 44–45, 83–84, 317,
    411–412
"A Gaping Wide-mouthed Waddling Frog" (tradition-
    al), 59
Garcia, Jerry
    about, 52, 259, 305, 380, 425
    "Althea" comments by, 297
    artwork by, 152
    car accident memory of, 199
    "Casey Jones" comments by, 89
    in coma, 332–333, 364
    as composer, 34, 52, 89, 105, 269
    "Dark Star" comments by, 52
    death of, 62, 101, 153, 192, 389, 411–412
    "Dire Wolf" comments by, 84
    "Friend of the Devil" comments by, 113
    as lyricist, xxi, 5, 47, 84, 85, 105, 243, 360, 378
    "Mindbender" comments by, 46

New Lost City Ramblers and, 106
on *Reflections* cover, 11
as singer, 69, 163, 169, 202, 219, 230, 286, 350,
    366, 380
in Sleepy Hollow Hog Stompers, 104
solo albums and side projects
    Reflections, 11, 173, 208, 221, 253, 260
    Garcia, 52, 121, 146, 147, 153, 155, 159, 161,
        258
"That's It for the Other One" comments by, 47
tribute to, 411–412
"Turn On Your Love Light" comments by, 39
"Uncle John's Band" comments by, 34, 52, 89, 105
"Victim or the Crime" comments by, 336
Gates, David, 296
"Gates of Eden" (Dylan), 34
Georgia, 13, 415
Gerde's Folk City (New York), 33
Germany, 43, 49, 68, 69, 182, 188
Gershwin brothers, 384
Ghengis Khan, 92
Giants Stadium (East Rutherford, New Jersey), 382
The Giaour: A Fragment of a Turkish Tale (Byron), 5
Gibson, Bob, 145
Gid Tanner & His Skillet Lickers (musical group),
    273
Gideon (Jewish tribal leader), 143
Giessen University (Germany), 182
Gillespie, Dizzy, 206
Gillespie, Haven, 299
Ginsberg, Allen, xvi, xxiii, 224
Gleason, Ralph J., 110
Glens Falls Civic Center (New York), 302
Glover, Roger, 203
Gluck, Joyce, 106
"God Bless the Child" (Herzog Jr./Holiday), 309
Godchaux, Brian, 248

Steal Your Face, 192, 347
Steppin' Out with the Grateful Dead: England '72, 191
Terrapin Station, 254, 272, 275, 278, 279
Wake of the Flood, 197, 199, 204, 205, 210, 211, 212, 215
What a Long Strange Trip It's Been, 52
Workingman's Dead, 85, 89, 94, 96, 99, 101, 105, 106, 110
Grateful Dead Records, 426
Great American Music Hall (San Francisco), 249, 415
Great Highway. *See* The Family Dog at the Great Highway
The Great Jug Bands, 21
Great Northern Railroad, 168
Great Revolt (England), 169
Greatest Story Ever Told (film), 142
Greatest Story Ever Told (Oursler), 142
Greece, 34, 43, 246.
Greek Theater (University of California, Berkeley), 324
Green, Al, 124
Green, Eddie, 21
"Green, Green" (McGuire, Sparks), 182
"Green Grow the Rushes, Ho!" (Burns), 58
Green, Percy, 180
Greenacre, Phyllis, 4
Greenaway, Kate, 80
Greenhill, Manny, 33
Greenwich, Ellie, 364
Greetings, 426
Gregory XIII (Pope), 246
Grisman, David, 35, 89
Grogan, Emmett, 197
Groos, Arthur, 49
Grosvenor, Richard, 229
Grosvenor Square (London, England), 229

Groton School, 426
El Grotto (Chicago), 125
Gumbo, 277
Guthrie, Woody, 416
Gypsies, 6, 34

H

Hagar, Sammy, 207
Haight-Ashbury district (San Francisco), 28, 46
1/2 Set in Harlem, 125
Hall, Benjamin, 97
Hall, Roy, 378
Hamlet, 69, 296–297
Hamm (fictional character), 101
Hampstead Heath, England, 121
Hampton, Virginia, 139
Handy, W. C., 186, 377
The Hangman's Beautiful Daughter (Incredible String Band), 60
Han-Shan (poet), 74
"Happy Birthday to You", xv
Harbor Lights (Hornsby), 201
"Harlem Shuffle" (Relf, Nelson), 184
Harris, Charles K., 124
Harris, Joel Chandler, 266
Harrison, George, 348
Harrison, Hank, 416
Harrison, Michael, 176
Hart, Lenny, 192
Hart, Mickey, 13, 214, 292, 389, 425
    as composer, 34, 358
    "Down the Road" comments by, 411–412
    Hunter's comments about, 408
    "Self-Defense" comments by, 405
    solo albums and side projects of, 144, 148, 149 *see also* Mystery Box, Planet Drum

Humes, Helen, 48
Hunter, Meredith, 109, 319
Hunter, Robert
  about, 424–425
  "Althea" comments by, 297
  "Attics of My Life" comments by, 116
  Barlow's comments on, 228, 420–421
  "Bird Song" comments by, 153
  "Black Muddy River" comments by, 332–333
  "Box of Rain" comments by, 138, 139–140
  "Candyman" comments by, 115
  "Casey Jones" comments by, 89
  "China Cat Sunflower" comments by, 56–57
  "Crazy Fingers" comments by, 243
  as composer, 95, 221
  "Cumberland Blues" comments by, 97
  "Dark Star" comments by, 52
  dark v. light motifs of, 132, 173
  "Days Between" composition by, 380–381
  "Dire Wolf" comments by, 85
  "Eagle Mall Suite" by, 56, 75
  Festival Express Tour comments by, 253
  "France" comments by, 292
  "Friend of the Devil" comments by, 113
  "Greatest Story Ever Told" comments by, 144
  "Here Comes Sunshine" comments by, 205
  "Infrared Roses" titling by, 416
  "Keep Your Day Job" comments by, 310
  "Liberty" comments by, 378
  as lyricist, 37, 38, 54, 123, 132, 163, 174, 203,
      240, 286, 311, 324, 332, 360, 405
  marsh motif used by, 83
  Mission District comments by, 259
  "Mountains of the Moon" comments by, 77
  muses viewed by, 263–265
  Orpheus used by, 93
  Phil and Friends opening by, 231
  psalms used by, 128
  "Ramble on Rose " comments by, 180, 182
  "Reuben and Cérise" changes by, 362
  rose symbolism viewed by, 44
  "Row Jimmy" comments by, 209, 210
  "Saint Stephen" comments by, 61
  as singer, 83, 410–411
  "Slipknot!" comments by, 416
  solo albums by, xxv, 56, 75, 128, 256, 261, 269,
      378
    Jack o' Roses, 261, 269
    Tales of the Great Rum Runners, xxv
    Tiger Rose, xxv
  "Sugaree" comments by, 159
  "Tennessee Jed" comments by, 166
  "Terrapin Station" comments by, 265–266,
      268–269
  "To Lay Me Down" comments by, 121
  "Touch of Grey" comments by, 311
  "Truckin'" comments by, 131, 133, 134
  "Uncle John's Band" comments by, 105, 106
  Weir v., 119, 174
  "You Remind Me" comments by, 408
"Hurdy Gurdy Man" (Donovan), 201
Hurt, Mississippi John, 89, 114
Hussein, Zakhir, xii

I

"I Am a Pilgrim" (Travis), 129
I Am the Blues (Dixon), 373
"I Am the Walrus" (Beatles), 5, 157
"I Asked for Water (She Gave Me Gasoline)"
    (Howlin' Wolf), 143
"(I Can't Get No) Satisfaction" (Jagger/Richards), xv
I Ching (Book of Changes), 273
"I Just Want to Make Love to You" (Muddy

Waters/Dixon), 373
"I Pity the Fool" (Bland), 40
"I Walk the Line" (Cash), 182
Ice Nine Publishing Company, xxviii, 247
    logo, 247
Iliad (Homer), 265, 346–347
"I'll Fly Away" (traditional), 152
"I'll Sleep When I'm Dead" (Zevon), 347
Illinois Central Railroad, 86, 87
"I'm All Out and Down" (traditional), 84
In Concert, vol. 2 (Baez), 217
"In the Pines" (traditional), 13, 365
"In the Sweet Bye-and-Bye" (Tilzer/Bryan), 48
Incredible String Band (musical group), 60
India, 67
Indiana, 364, 388, 390
"Indianapolis 500," 346
International Civil Aviation Organization, 314–315
Intrepid Trips, Inc., 45
Invisible Republic (Marcus), 120
Irvine Meadows Amphitheater (California), 358
Irving, Washington, 380
Islam, 240
"It Takes a Lot to Laugh, It Takes a Train to Cry"
    (Dylan), 56
"I've Got a Secret (Shake Sugaree)" (Cotten), 159
"I've Got Rings on My Fingers" (Watson, Barnes),
    229
"Ivory Wheels/Rosewood Track" (Hunter), 83, 269

J

"Jack and Jill, and Old Dame Dob," 179–180
Jack Straw (fictional character), 169
Jack the Ripper, 176
"Jack-a-Roe (Jack the Sailor)", 74

Jackson, Al, Jr., 124
Jackson, Blair, 35
Jackson, Bruce, 11, 228
Jackson, Charles, 197
Jackson Hole, Wyoming, 424
Jackson, Rex, 226, 227, 275
Jackson, Rudy, xii
Jacob (biblical character), 332, 337
Jacobs, Lou, 338
James, William, 266–267
Jan & Dean (musical group), 233
Japan, 55
Jazz Giants (musical group), 242
Jefferson Airplane (musical group), 5, 38
Jehosophat, King of Judea, 392
"Jelly Roll Blues" (Morton), 70, 73
Jennings, Waylon, 400
Jericho, 178–179
Jerry Garcia Band (musical group), 260, 362
Jesus, 236
    eye of a needle quote by, 239–240
    film about life of, 142
    first miracle performed by, 143
    Mount of Olives sermon by, 148
        Jethro Tull (musical group), xxx
Jewish traditions, 161
"Jock-o-Mo" (Crawford), 277
Johannesburg, South Africa, 405
"John Silver" (Hunter), 128, 305
Johns, Jasper, 196
Johnson, "Blind Willie," 254
"The Johnson Boys" (traditional), 104
Johnson, Esther, 196, 294
Johnson, James Weldon, 185–186
Johnson, Robert, 18, 112
Johnson, Tommy, 143

Jolson, Al, 270
Jonah (biblical character), 59
Jones, Alan Rankin, 102
Jones, Arthur, 79, 178–179
Jones, Bessie, 156
Jones, Delilah (song character), 162
Jones, Jack (song character), 162
Jones, John Luther "Casey," 86
Jones, Mrs. John Luther, 86
Jones, R., 125
Joplin, Janis, 28, 153, 190, 253
Jordan, Louis, 234
Joshua (biblical character), 178–179
"Joshua Fit the Battle of Jericho" (traditional), 178
Journey (musical group), 400
Joyce, James, xxii, 388
The Judy Collins Concert, 31
Juno (goddess), 43
Jupiter (god), 43

K

Kahn, Alice, 324
Kali (goddess), 34
Kant, Hal, 147, 278
Kanzan (poet). *See* Han-Shan (poet)
Karan, Mark, 400
Kato, Banno, 185
Kazan, Elia, 151
"KC Moan" (traditional), 363–364
"Keep the Home Fires Burning" (Novello/Ford), 313
Keith and Donna, 248
Kelley, Alton, 365
Kelly, Walt, 352
Kennedy, John F., 410
Kentucky, 29, 47, 69, 97

Kentucky Colonels (musical group), 106
Kepler's Books (Palo Alto, California), xxvii
Kern County, California, 170
Kern, Jerome, 184, 305, 313
Kerouac, Jack, 224, 264
Kesey, Ken, 29, 224–225, 226, 310
    acid tests and, 204
    bus bought by, 45
    Dylan on tour and, 419
    house sign of, 23
    at Human Be-In, 28
    "on the bus" explained by, 46
    son's death, 123
    University of Virginia lecture by, 123
Kessler, John, 16
Keye, Francis Scott, 366
Kezar Stadium (San Francisco), 67
Khan, Ali Akbar, xii
King, B. B., 194
King, Martin Luther, Jr., 410-411
Kingfish (album), 251
Kingfish (musical group), xxv, 48, 251
Kirkwood, Missouri, 117
Klages, Raymond, 81
Klamath Falls, Oregon, 425
Kliptown (Johannesburg, South Africa), 405
Knight, Gladys, 125
Knossos, Greece, 43
Koehler, Ted, 131, 347
Koenig, Martha, 377
Kogan, Alice, 106
"Kokomo" (Beach Boys/Melcher, Phillips), 364
Kokomo, Indiana, 364
Korner, Alexis, 124
Krazy Kat (comic strip), 56
Kreutzmann, Bill, xxvi, 364, 389

Mali, 20

Malloy, Terry (fictional character), 151

"Mama Tried" (Haggard), 170

The Mamas and Papas (musical group), 31

"The Man of Constant Sorrow" (traditional), 47, 104

"The Man with the Blue Guitar" (Stevens), 194–195

Mandelaville (Johannesburg, South Africa), 405

Manhattan Transfer (musical group), 125

Mann, Barry, 182

Mann, Michael Norman, 99

Mansfield, Massachusetts. *See* Tweeter Center

Manson, Charles, 226

Marco Polo, 92

Marcus, Greil, 120

Marin County, California, 62, 174, 226–227, 253, 425

Marin County Veterans Auditorium (San Rafael, California), 326

Mariposa Folk Festival (Ontario, Canada), 33

Market Street (San Francisco), 357

Marre, Jeremy, 140

"The Marsh King's Daughter" (Andersen), 77

"Marta (Rambling Rose of the Wildwood)" (Gilbert, Simons), 179

Martin guitars, 115

Martin, Vince, 33

Martinez, California, 340, 343, 347, 356

Marvin, Lee, 223

Marx, Groucho, 198

Maryland. *See specific venues in Maryland*

Mason, Lowell, 286

Masons, 107–108, 268

Mass in B Minor, 392

Massachusetts, 77, 346, 398

Masters, Edgar Lee, 197

"Materna" (Ward), 168

Matrix (San Francisco), 5, 8, 9, 30, 67, 121

Matter, E. Ann, 212

Matthew (prophet), 355

McCarthy, Joseph, 179

McCartney, Paul, 277, 363

McCay, Winsor, 416

McCormick, Mack, 22, 39

McGoohan, Patrick, 25

McGuire, Barry, 182

McHugh, Jimmy, 80, 290

McIntyre, James, 102

McKenna, Richard, 142

McKernan, Ron
  Bland's influence on, 40
  as composer, 34, 40
  death of, 40, 197
  Joplin's relationship with, 190
  last show by, 197
  as lyricist, xxi, 38, 39
  as singer, 196

McKnight, Tom, 123

McMahon, Regan, 35

McMichen, Clayton, 273

McNally, Dennis, 174, 305

McNichols Sports Arena (Denver, Colorado), 301

McTell, "Blind Willie," 194

"Me and My Uncle" (Collins), 31

Meadows (Hartford, Connecticut), 391, 392

The Meaning of Truth, 267

Meher Baba (guru), 403

Meier, Barbara, 380

Melcher, Terry, 364

Meleager (mythological character), 294–295

Melinda (namesake), 97

Memorial Coliseum (Portland, Oregon), 274

Memorial Coliseum (University of Alabama), 278

Memphis State, 136

"Memphis, Tennessee" (Berry), 124

Menglewood, Tennessee, 20

Menlo Park, California, 45, 204

Meramec Community College (St. Louis, Missouri), 117

Mercia province, Britain, 77

Meriwether, Nicolas, 329

Merriweather Post Pavilion (Columbia, Maryland), 405

Merry Pranksters, 225 *See also* Kesey, Ken; Babbs, Ken; Sandy

The Meters (musical group), 277

Metropolitan Sports Center (Bloomington, Minnesota), 337

Mexicali, Mexico, 170

Mexico
Black Madonna of, 34
Cassady in, 44, 46, 226
dire wolves in, 84
marijuana from, 235
steel guitar origin in, 196
XERF radio station in, 181

Miami Indian tribe, 364

Michel, John, 49–50

Michigan, 425

Mickey Hart's Mystery Box. See Mystery Box

Middletown, Connecticut, 170

"Midnight Rider" (Allman), 96

"Midnight Special" (Leadbelly), 115, 368

A Midsummer Night's Dream, 179, 245–246

Milan, Italy, 69

Miles (Davis), 296

Mill Valley, California, 232, 249, 272, 280, 299, 302, 307, 358

Miller, Arthur, 196

Miller, Glenn, 230

Mills, Irving, 184

Milton, John, 313

Mimir (raven of memory), 92

Minglewood, 20–21

"Minglewood Blues" (Cannon's Jug Stompers), 21

Mingus, Charles, 184

Minnesota. *See specific venues in Minnesota*

Mission District (San Francisco), 259, 357

Mission Dolores (San Francisco), 259

Mississippi River, 36, 108, 158, 160

Mr. Big (musical group), 400

"Mr. Bojangles" (Walker), 305

Mitchell, Albert, 64

"Moanin' Lo" (Dietz, Rainger), 365

Moby-Dick, 59

"The Mocking Bird Song" (Sharp #234), 161

Monk, Thelonius, 102

Monkees (musical group), xxiii, 296

"Monk's Tale," 257

Monroe, Marilyn, 218

Montresor (fictional character), 107

"Moonshiner" (traditional), 162

Moore, Thomas, 68, 331

Morrison, Colorado. *See* Red Rocks Amphitheater

Morrison, Van, xxx, 40, 245

Morte d'Arthur (Tennyson), 354

Morton, "Jelly Roll," 70, 73, 209, 363

Morton, Jill L., 196

Moses (biblical character), 142, 144, 213, 236, 270–271

Mother Goose, xv

Mother Goose (Greenaway), 80

Mother McCree's Uptown Jug Champions (musical group), xxii–xxiii. *See also* Grateful Dead

"Mother Night" (Johnson), 185–186
Mother Night (Vonnegut), 185
Mother's (San Francisco), 7
"Mountain Jam" (Allman), 38
Mountains of the Moon, 74, 338
Mouse, Stanley, 365
Mud Creek, Texas, 145
Muddy Waters (musical group), 373
Murphy's Law, 327
Muses, 64, 263–265, 268
Muskrat, place references to, 233
Muslims, 240
"My Generation" (The Who), 347
Mydland, Brent, xxvi
    Barlow's collaboration with, 424
    death of, 306
    as lyricist, 301
    on tour, 364
    "Victim or the Crime" comments by, 336
Myers, Joseph, 270
The Mysteries of Harris Burdick (Van Allsburg), 127
Mystery Box, 398, 410
Mystery Box (musical group), 389

N

Nabokov, Vladimir, 195, 196-197
Das Narrenschiff [Ship of Fools] (Brant), 43, 222–223
Nash, John Henry, xxxi
Nassau Veterans Memorial Coliseum (Uniondale, New York), 211, 215, 422
National Guard Armory (St. Louis, Missouri), 64, 174
Native American Cherokee Nation, 113
Native Americans
    Alcatraz occupation by, 392
    Mardi Gras chants of, 277

memorial ceremony, 275
    Miami Tribe of, 364
    turtle symbolism to, 266
Nazareth (musical group), 33
"Nearer, My God, To Thee" (Adams, Mason), 286–287
Neil, Fred, 33, 159
Nelson, Earl, 184
Nelson, Willy, 179
Nemo, Captain (fictional character), 334
Nevada, 111–112
Nevada County, California, 113
Never-ever land, 46
Neville, Art, 277
Neville Brothers (musical group), 277
New Christy Minstrels (musical group), 182
New Jersey. *See specific venues in New Jersey*
New Lost City Ramblers (musical group), 76, 106, 165
New Mexico, xxii, 210
"New Minglewood Blues" (Lewis), 21
New Morning (Dylan), 270
New Orleans, Louisiana, 36, 133, 160, 391.
New Riders of the Purple Sage (musical group), 253
New York, xvi, 227, 400, 423, 424, 425, 426. *See also specific place names and venues in New York*
Newport Folk Festival (1964), 139
Newton, Eddie, 87, 88
Nicasio Valley (Marin County, California), 226
Nietzsche, Friedrich, 129
Nile River (Africa), 74–75, 338
Nina Music, 33
Nixon, Richard, xxiii, 226
No, No, Nanette, 231
"No Particular Place to Go" (Berry), 363, 364
Noblesville, Indiana, 388
Nonesuch Records, 105, 235

Pop-o-Pies (musical group), 132
Port Chester, New York. *See* Capitol Theater
Porter, Cole, 384
Porter, Katherine Anne, 223
Portland, Maine, 317, 329
Portland, Oregon. *See specific venues in Portland, Oregon*
Pound, Ezra, 420
Presley, Elvis, 218
"Pretty Peggy of Derby" (traditional), 82, 217
"Pretty Peggy-O" (Sharp #95), 82, 83, 217
"The Prickly Bush" (Child #95), 180
Pringle, Bob, xii
The Prisoner (television show), 25
"Promontory Rider" (Hunter), xxv
Providence, Rhode Island. *See* Civic Center
Prufrock, Alfred, 51
Psalm 23, 127–128, 305
Psalms, 127–128, 242, 305, 353
Ptolemy, 74
Puckett, Riley, 273
"Purple Haze" (Hendrix), 400
Pushkin, Alexander, 85
Pyke, C. M., 299

Q

Queen of Diamonds, 146
"The Queen of Spades" (Pushkin), 85
Queens College (Queens, New York), 136

R

"Rabbit Chase" (traditional), 104
Rackstraw, John, 169
Radio City Music Hall (New York), halloween at, 188
Ragtime Texas. *See* Thomas, Henry

Rail Talk, 56
Raim, Ethel, 106
"Rain, Rain, Go Away," 190
Rainbow (musical group), 203
Rainger, Ralph, 365
Raitt, Bonnie, 400
"Ramblin' Rose" (Sherman, J., Sherman, N.), 179
"Ramblin' Rose" (Wilkin, Burch), 179
Rambling Rose (film), 179
"Rambling Rose" (McCarthy, Burke), 179
Ramsey, Obray, 10
Rancho Cucamonga, California, 233–234
Randall, Bill, 180
Ratdog (musical group), 389, 426
    "KC Moan" performed by, 363
    studio recordings by, 400, 402
Ray, John, 192
Raye, Don, 125, 196
Raynor, Hal, 80
RCA, 33
Reagan, Ronald, 174
The Real Bahamas, 60
Rebennack, Mac, 277
Red Rocks Amphitheater (Morrison, Colorado), 235, 280, 287, 288, 289, 290, 395, 410
"The Red Shoes" (Andersen), xiv
Redding, Otis, 218
Reich, Charles, 52, 89
Relf, Bob, 184
R.E.M. (musical group), xxx
Remains Concerning Britain (Camden), 200
Reno, Jesse Lee, 111–112
Reno, Nevada, 111–112
The Return of Sherlock Holmes (Doyle), 100
"Return of the Grievous Angel" (Parsons), 388
"Reuben and Rachel" (Birch), 361
Revel, Harry, 81

Southern California Music Company, 88

Southern Pacific Railroad, 14

SPAC (Saratoga Springs, New York), 404

Sparks, Lee, 115

Sparks, Randy, 182

Spector, Phil, 277, 364

Spectrum (Philadelphia), 238

Speed Racer (cartoon character), 329

Speedway Meadows (San Francisco), 109

Speegle, Paul, 199

Speke, John, 338

Spence, Joseph, 60

Spiral Light, 268

Spivey, William, 125

"The Springhill Mine Disaster" (Seeger), 97

Sri Lanka, 425

St. Louis, Missouri, 64

"Stagger Lee" (traditional), 281–285

Stagolee Shot Billy (Brown), 281–285

"Standin' on the Corner (Blue Yodel No. 9)"
        (Rodgers), 25

"Standing in the Soul" (interview), 263–264

"Standing on the Corner" (Four Lads), 25

Stanford University (Stanford, California), 201, 204,
        205, 206, 208, 210

Stanley, Augustus Owsley, III. *See* Owsley

Stanley Brothers, 139

Stanley, Henry Morton, 338

"Stardust", xv

Starry Night Over the Rhone (painting), 267

The Stars My Destination (Bester), 249

"The Star-Spangled Banner" (Keye), 366

"Station Man" (Fleetwood Mac), 278

"Stealin'" (traditional), 35

"Steamboat Bill" (traditional), 108

Stearn, Thomas, 268

Steel, Danielle, 343

Steely Dan (musical group), 199

Stella (poetic pseudonym), 195–196, 294, 396

Stephen I, King of Hungary, 62

Stephen, J. K., 176

Sterne, Laurence, 337

Stevens, George, 142

Stevens, Ray, 229

Stevens, Wallace, 194–195

Stevenson, Adlai, 313

Stiff Dead Cat (musical group), 84

Stills, Stephen, 31

Stock, Larry, 230

Stoddard, Joshua C., 64

Stoker, Bram, 5

"Stormy Monday Blues" (Bland), 40

"Stormy Weather" (Arlen/Koehler), 347

Stormy Weather (Hiaasen), 140

"The Story the Crow Told Me" (traditional), 105

A Streetcar Named Desire, 195

Strong, Martin C., 131

"Study War No More" (traditional), 104

Subotnick, Morton, 235

"Subterranean Homesick Blues" (Dylan), xv

"Such a Night" (Doctor John), 365

Sugaree, Liberia, 160

The Summit (Houston, Texas), 348

Sun (record label), 40

Sunday, Billy, 177

"Sunflower Cat (Some Dour Cat) (Down with
        That)" (Hornsby), 57

The Sutra of the Lotus Flower of the Wonderful Law, 185

"Sweet and Low-Down" (Gershwin brothers), 384

"Sweet Home Alabama" (Lynyrd Skynyrd), 304

"Sweet Jane" (Velvet Underground), 133

"Sweet Sunny South" (traditional), 104

Swift, Jonathan, 195–196, 294, 369, 370

Swing Auditorium (San Bernardino, California), 268

"Swing Low, Sweet Chariot" (traditional), 109, 253
Swing Time (film), 305
Sycamore Slough (fictitious place), 376
de Sylva, Buddy G., 313
Sylvie and Bruno (Carroll), 196
"Syncopated Shuffle" (Ellington), 184

T

Taft, William Howard, 193
Tao te Ching, 129
Tara (goddess), 34
Taylor, Koko, 373
"Tea for Two" (Youmans/Caesar), 231
Tear Down the Walls (Martin and Neil), 33
Tell, William, 64
Tempe, Arizona, 319
Temple, Shirley, 305
The Ten Commandments, 270
Tennessee, 20, 21, 35
Tennessee Jed (radio show character), 165
Tennyson, Alfred, 354
Tergit, Gabriele, 42–43, 59, 69
Texas, 20, 22, 30, 115. *See also specific place names in Texas*
"Texas Flood," 125
Texas-Pacific Railroad, 22
Thailand, 425
"That's the Way Love Is" (Bland), 40
Them (musical group), 40
There and Back Again (Phil Lesh & Friends), 392, 394
"There is a Mountain" (Donovan), 38
"There is a Tavern in the Town" (anonymous), 242
"There's a Hole in the Bucket" (traditional), 54
Theseus (mythological character), 294–295
Theseus (Shakespearean character), 245–246
"Thirsty Boots" (Andersen), 211
Thomas, A. J. "Fatty," 86–87

Thomas, Bob, 192
Thomas, Dylan, 172, 197
Thomas, F. W., 198
Thomas, Henry, 22
Thompson, Ashley, 21
"Those Old Cumberland Mountain Farm Blues" (traditional), 98-99
Thoughts and Details on Scarcity (Burke), 339
"Three Men Went A-Hunting" (traditional), 104
Tiger in a Trance (Ludington), 302
Till, Emmett, 158
Tilzer, Harry von, 48
Timbuktu, 20
"Time Passes Slowly" (Dylan), 270
"'Tis the Last Rose of Summer" (Moore), 331
Tivoli Gardens (Copenhagen, Denmark), 193
"To the Evening Star" (Blake), 267–268
Today Is the Highway (Andersen), 211
Tolkien, J. R. R., 51, 118
Tom Banjo (nickname), 76–77
Toussaint, Allen, 277
Trans-Continental Pop Festival. *See* Festival Express Tour
Travis, Merle, 129, 257, 363
A Treasury of American Folklore (Botkin), 86
Trichromes (musical group), 389
"Trio for Two Cats and a Trombone" (Sitwell), 56
Trios, 382
Trist, Alan, 54, 83–84, 121, 228, 380
Tristram Shandy (Sterne), 337
Triumph of Death, 201
Troilus and Criseyde (Chaucer), 109
"Trooper and Maid" (Sharp #299), 83
Trouper's Club (Los Angeles), 15
Troy, Sandy, 174
"Truckin'" (Koehler, Bloom), 131
Trumbauer, Frankie, 184

Tubman, Harriet, 79
Tucker, Sophie, 385
Tuolumne County, California, 113
"Turn On Your Love Light" (Bland), 40
Turner, Ike and Tina, 364
Turtle Island, 266
Tuscaloosa, Alabama. *See* Memorial Coliseum
Twain, Mark, 125, 196
Tweeter Center (Mansfield, Massachusetts), 398
"The Twelve Days of Christmas" (traditional), 59
Twelve Flags of the American Revolution, 104
20,000 Leagues Under the Sea (Verne), 334
"The Two Sisters" (Child #10; Sharp #5), 76
2001: A Space Odyssey, 196
Tyler, Wat, 169

U
Uganda, 74
Uncle Dave Macon (musical group), 165
Uncle Sam, 218–219
Unfamiliar Territory (Sandoz), 34
Union Pacific Railroad, 145
Uniondale, New York, 211, 215, 422
United Artists, 192
University of Alabama, 278
University of California, Berkeley, 29, 324
University of Cincinnati, 115
University of Colorado, Colorado Springs, xxx
University of Connecticut, 106, 425
University of Michigan, 425
University of Minnesota, 166, 169, 170, 173, 175, 182
University of Vermont, 321
University of Virginia, 29, 123
The Unstrung Harp: Or, Mr. Earbrass Writes a Novel (Gorey), 126–127

"Up Around the Bend" (Creedence Clearwater Revival), 339
"Upon the Loss of His Mistresses" (Herrick), 369
Upper Limbo, 125
Utah, 111–112, 113

V
"A Valentine" (Poe), 189
La Vallée (Obscured by Clouds), 388
Van Allsburg, Chris, 127
Van Ronk, Dave, 255
Vancouver, British Columbia, 232
Vanport floods (Washington state), 205
Vatican, 246
Vaughn, Stevie Ray, 125
Velvet Underground (musical group), 133
Veneta, Oregon, 310, 311
Venice, California, 88
Venus (goddess), 42, 43, 44, 267–268
Verizon Wireless Amphitheater (Indianapolis, Indiana), 390
Verizon Wireless Amphitheater (Virginia Beach, Virginia), 394
Vermont, 76, 321
Verne, Jules, 334
"A Very Cellular Song" (Incredible String Band), 60
Vesey, Denmark, 179
"Viola Lee Blues" (Cannon's Jug Stompers), xxiii, 21
Virgil (poet), 265
Virgin Mary, 43, 350
Virginia, 10, 29, 123, 139, 394
Vlad V of Wallachia (Vlad the Impaler), 5
Voltaire, Francois-Marie Arouet, 352
Vonnegut, Kurt, 185, 247

W

Wade in the Water (Jones), 79, 178–179
"Wade in the Water" (traditional), 78–80
Wake Up Dead Man (Jackson), 11
Waldman, Anne, 263
Walker, Jerry Jeff, 305
Wallace, George, 107
"The Wanderer" (Williams), 333
"Wang Dang Doodle" (Taylor/Dixon), 373
Ward, Samuel A., 168
Warfield (San Francisco), 207
Warhol, Andy, 197
Warlocks (musical group), xxii, 204. *See also* Grateful
  Dead
Warren, Harry, 133, 184
"Was There a Time" (Thomas), 172
Washington (state), 205, 274
Washington, George, 98, 107, 219
Wasserman, Rob, 382
The Wasteland (Eliot), 213, 420
Watson, Burton, 56
Watson, John F., 160
Watson, R.P., 229
Wavy Gravy, 67
Webster's Dictionary, 169
Weill, Kurt, 415
Weir, Bob. *See also* Ratdog
  about, 424
  Cassady visions by, 44–45, 46
  "Cassidy" comments by, 228
  "Easy Answers" comments by, 382
  "Equinox" comments by, 279
  Graham's collaboration with, 426
  Haight-Ashbury room of, 46
  Hunter v., 119, 174
  Kingfish collaboration with, 48, 251
  living with, 225–226, 227
  "Looks Like Rain" comments by, 188
  as lyricist, xxi, xxii, 5, 31, 32, 44–45, 170, 174,
      186, 190, 405, 415
  "Me and My Uncle" notes from, 31
  Pessis collaboration with, 400
  "Picasso Moon" comments by, 357
  presidents cited by, 174
  as singer, 20, 34, 119, 133, 142, 148, 169, 190,
      316, 366, 395, 422
  solo and side project albums of, 227 *see also*
      Kingfish, Ratdog
    Ace, 143, 144, 148, 149, 170, 186, 190, 227,
      228
    Weir Here, 382
  "ten thousand" preferred by, 143
  touring memories of, 133
  Uncle Sam viewed by, 218–219
  "Victim or the Crime" comments by, 336–337
  Young's collaboration with, 382
Weir, Frankie, 226
Weir, Roberta, 152
Welch, Lew, xxiii
Weller, Sheila, 302
Wellesley College (Wellesley, Massachusetts), 168
Welnick, Vince, 366
WERE radio station (Cleveland, Ohio), 180
Wesleyan College (Middletown, Connecticut), 424
West, August (song character), 150, 152
West Springfield, Massachusetts, 77
Wharf Rats (Deadhead group), 150
"What'll We Do With the Baby?" (Sharp #228), 90
Wheeler, Mary, 285
"White Rabbit" (Jefferson Airplane), 5
White, T. H., 100
Whitman, Slim, 179
Whitman, Walt, 129, 378
The Who (musical group), 46, 347, 403

"Whole Lotta Shakin'" (Lewis/Williams, Hall), 378
Wilder, Alec, 178, 231, 290
Williams, Alfred, 219
Williams, Dave, 378
Williams, Hank, xvi, 22
Williams, J. M., 368
Williams, Spencer, 184, 377
Williams, Tennessee, 169, 192, 195
Williams, William Carlos, 333
Williamson, Robin, 60
Wind in the Willows (Grahame), 230–231
"Winin' Boy Blues" (Morton), 209, 363
Winnemucca, 420
Winterland Arena (San Francisco), xxxi
    closing of, 365
    performances, 35, 47, 120, 139, 184, 186, 220,
        221, 223, 243, 244, 247, 273–274
Wisconsin, 84
    performances in, 339, 340, 343, 345
Wodehouse, P. G., 184, 313
Woden (god), 92
Wolf Man, 181
Wolfe, Tom, 29, 45, 46, 197
Wolfman Jack (radio personality), 181, 402
Wollstonecraft, Mary, 181
Womack, David, 51
Wong, Bernard P., 183
Wood, Randy, 180
Woodstock (music festival), 225
"Woolly Bully" (Samudio), 157
Works and Days (Hesiod), 212
Wray, Fay, 251

Wright, Harold Bell, 203
Wrubel, Allie, 89
Wyler, William, 251
Wyoming, 227, 421, 424. *See also* Cora, Wyoming

X

Xanadu (mythological place), 90–92
XERF radio station (Mexico), 181

Y

Yale Bowl (Yale University, New Haven,
    Connecticut), 158, 161
Yeats, William Butler, 126, 173, 235, 417
Yevtushenko, Yevgeny, 197
"You Send Me" (Cooke), 408
Youmans, Vincent, 231
Young, Joe, 124
Young, Nathan, 286
Young, Neil, 31, 304, 317, 382
"You're the Top" (Porter), 384

Z

"Zekiel Saw De Wheel" (traditional), 258, 271–272
Zemba Queca (Brazilian dance), 384
Zen Buddhism, 55
Zero (musical group), 425
Zevon, Warren, 56, 347
Zimels, Peter Richard, xxi—xxii, xxiii, 425
Zodiac Killer, 84

index of songs

(Bold page numbers indicate main entries for songs)

A

"Alabama Getaway" (Garcia/Hunter), 128, **304–305**

"Alice D. Millionaire" (Grateful Dead), **28–29**

All I know is something like a bird within her sang, 153

"All New Minglewood Blues." See "New, New Minglewood Blues"

All of my friends come to see me last night, 100

"All That We Are" (Lesh), 390

All the years combine, 194

"Alligator" (McKernan, Lesh/Hunter, McKernan), xxii, **36–38,** 52, 126, 413

"Althea" (Garcia/Hunter), 38, 107, **293–297**

"And We Bid You Goodnight" (traditional), 48, **60**

Annie laid her head down in the roses, 221

"Antwerp's Placebo" (Kreutzmann/Hart), 414

"Apollo at the Ritz" (Garcia, Hart, Kreutzmann, Lesh, Branford Marsalis, Mydland, Weir), 416

Arabian wind, 239

As I was walkin' 'round Grosvenor Square, 229

As we rode out to Fennario, 217

"At a Siding" (Hart/Hunter). See "Terrapin Station"

"Attics of My Life" (Garcia/Hunter), **116–117,** 306, 362

B

"Baba Jingo" (Hart/Hunter), **403–404**

Baba Jingo, Baba Jingo, voices in the wind, 403

"The Banyan Tree" (Hart, Weir/Hunter), **396–397**

"Beat It On Down the Line" (Fuller), **13–14**

"Believe It Or Not" (Garcia/Hunter), **344–345**

"Bertha" (Garcia/Hunter), **141**

"Bird Song" (Garcia/Hunter), **153–154**

Black book of night, 390

"Black Muddy River" (Garcia/Hunter), 109, 139, **331–333**

"Black Peter" (Garcia/Hunter), **100–101**

"Black-Throated Wind" (Weir/Barlow), 143, **185–187,** 227

"Blow Away" (Mydland/Barlow), **340**

Blue light rain, whoa, unbroken chain, 236
"Blues for Allah" (Garcia/Hunter), 38, 75, 76, 92,
    93, **239–241**
"Bob Star." See "Little Star"
Boots were of leather, 68
"Born Cross-Eyed" (Weir), xxii, **48**, 51
"Box of Rain" (Lesh/Hunter), xvi, xx, xxii,
    137–140, 236, 339
Bringing me down, 185
"Brokedown Palace" (Garcia/Hunter), xviii, 121,
    122–123
"Brown-Eyed Women" (Garcia/Hunter), 108,
    162–163
"Built to Last" (Garcia/Hunter), **348–349**

C

"Candyman" (Garcia/Hunter), **114–115**, 158, 285
"Can't Come Down" (Grateful Dead/Garcia), **3–5**,
    410
"Cardboard Cowboy" (Lesh), **23–24**
Carve your name, 338
"Casey Jones" (Garcia/Hunter), xxiii, **86–89**, 96,
    108, 362, 364
"Cassidy" (Weir/Barlow), **224–228**
"Caution (Do Not Stop on Tracks)" (McKernan),
    6–7
Cérise was brushing her long hair gently down, 360
"Childhood's End" (Lesh), 23, **387–388**
"China Cat Sunflower" (Garcia/Hunter), xxii, 5, 52,
    55–57, 59, 92, 365, 410
"China Doll" (Garcia/Hunter), **200–201**
"Chinatown Shuffle" (McKernan), **183–184**
Chopped olive sandwiches, roses, and wine, 53
"Clementine" (Lesh/Hunter), **53–54**
Cold iron shackles and a ball and chain, 165
Cold mountain water, 74

"Cold Rain and Snow" (traditional), **10**
Come all you pretty women, 114
Comes a time, 172
"Comes a Time" (Garcia/Hunter), 5, 34, 132,
    172–173, 340
Compass card is spinning, 298
"Confusion's Prince." See "Mindbender"
"Corrina" (Weir, Hart/Hunter), 13, 76, **368–370**
Corrina . . . Wake it up baby, 368
"Cosmic Charlie" (Garcia/Hunter), 38, 64, **66–67**,
    67
Cosmic Charlie, how do you do?, 66
"Crazy Fingers" (Garcia/Hunter), 44, 122, **242–243**
"Cream Puff War" (Garcia), **16–17**
"Crowd Sculpture" (Bralove), 416
"Cryptical Envelopment" (Garcia). See "That's It for
    the Other One"
"Cumberland Blues" (Garcia, Lesh/Hunter), **97–99**

D

"Dark Star" (Garcia, Kreutzmann, Lesh, McKernan,
    Weir/Hunter), **49–52**, 182, 251, 365, 413
Dark star crashes, 49
"Days Between" (Garcia/Hunter), **380–381**
"Deal" (Garcia/Hunter), **155**, 337
"Delia Delyon and Staggerlee." See "Stagger Lee"
"Dire Wolf" (Garcia/Hunter), 77, **82–85**
"Doin' That Rag" (Garcia/Hunter), 37, **78–81**, 135,
    241, 316
Don't ease, don't ease, 22
"Don't Ease Me In" (traditional), **22**
"Don't Need Love" (Mydland), **326**
"Down the Road" (Hart/Hunter), 5, **410–412**
Down the road to Union Station running through the
    fog, 410
"Dupree's Diamond Blues" (Garcia/Hunter), **70–73**

E

F

G

H

I

I don't need love anymore, 326

I had a hard run, 141

I have seen where the wolf has slept by the silver stream, 224

I know these rails we're on like I know my lady's smile, 327

"I Know You Rider" (traditional), **11**, 57

I know you rider, gonna miss me when I'm gone, 11

I lit out from Reno, 111

"I Need a Miracle" (Weir/Barlow), **280**

I need a woman 'bout twice my age, 280

I take a little powder, 156

I told Althea I was feeling lost, 293

I turn and walk away, 259

I wanna tell you how it's gonna be, 65

I was born in a desert, raised in a lion's den, 20

I was standing on the corner, wondering what's become of me, 25

I went down one day, 6

I went down to the mountain, I was drinking some wine, 174

I will never get out in one piece, 391

"I Will Take You Home" (Mydland/Barlow), 129, **341–343**

I woke today . . ., 188

If I could only be less blind, 8

If I had a gun for every ace I've drawn, 145

If I had my way, 254

If I had the world to give, 288

"If I Had the World to Love" (Garcia/Hunter), **288**

If my words did glow, 126

"If the Shoe Fits" (Lesh/Charles), 315, **386**

If you wanna know what time it is, you don't have to ask, 15

"Iko Iko" (traditional), **276–277**

I'm flying down deserted streets, 3

I'm lookin' out my window, 373

In another time's forgotten space, 245

In the attics of my life, 116

In the timbers of Fennario, 82

"Infrared Roses" (Garcia, Lesh, Mydland, Weir, Bralove), 235, 416–417

Inside you're burning, 307

Inspiration move me brightly, 263

"It Must Have Been the Roses" (Hunter), **221**, 333

It's three a.m. in the combat zone, 346

I've been searching in sectors both private and dark, 398

J

"Jack Straw" (Weir/Hunter), xxv, **167–169**

"Jock-o-Mo." See "Iko Iko"

Julie catch a rabbit by his hair, 209

"Just a Little Light" (Mydland/Barlow), 214, **354–356**

Just like Jack the Ripper, 176

K

"KC Moan" (traditional), 363–364

"Keep Rolling By" (Grateful Dead), **26–27**

"Keep Your Day Job" (Garcia/Hunter), **309–310**

"King Solomon's Marbles" (Lesh, Hart, Kreutzmann), 414, 416

L

"Lady With a Fan" (Garcia/Hunter). See "Terrapin Station"

Laid back in an old saloon, with peso in my hand, 170

Last leaf fallen, 34

Lay down my dear brothers, lay down and take your rest, 60

Lazy lightnin', 251

"New Potato Caboose" (Lesh/Petersen), xxii, **34**

"New Speedway Boogie" (Garcia/Hunter), **109–110**

"Night of a Thousand Stars" (Lesh, Haynes/Hunter), **392–393**

1940 Xmas eve with a full moon over town, 281

"No Left Turn Unstoned." See "Cardboard Cowboy"

"No More Do I" (Lesh/Hunter), **394**

No more time to tell how, 58

No, no, she can't take your mind and leave, 16

"No Time to Cry." See "Alice D. Millionaire"

"Not Fade Away" (Petty, Holly), **65**

O

"October Queen" (Weir, Ratdog/Pessis), **400–401**

Oh I know there is no place you can go to, 9

Oh my darling tell me where I'm bound, 26

Old man down, 150

On the day that I was born, 198

"One More Saturday Night" (Weir), **174–175**

One or two moments, 344

"Only the Strange Remain" (Hart/Hunter), **398–399**

"The Only Time Is Now" (Grateful Dead/Garcia), **9**

"Operator" (McKernan), **124–125**, 196

Operator, can you help me?, 124

The other day they waited, the sky was dark and faded, 42

"The Other One." See "That's It for the Other One"

Out on the edge of the empty highway, 233

P

Paradise waits, 244

"Parallelogram" (Hart, Kreutzmann), 416

"Passenger" (Lesh/Monk), **278**

Patience runs out on the junkie, 336

"Peggy-O" (traditional), xx, **217**

"Picasso Moon" (Weir/Barlow, Bralove), 346, **357–359**

Picture a bright blue ball, just spinning, spinning free, 316

A pistol shot at five o'clock, 200

"Playing in the Band" (Weir, Hart/Hunter), xxv, **148–149**, 251, 316

Please don't dominate the rap, Jack, 109

"Post-Modern Highrise Table Top Stomp" (Garcia, Willie Green III, Hart, Kreutzmann, Lesh, Mydland, Weir), 416

"Prelude/Epilogue" (Grateful Dead), 414

"Pride of Cucamonga" (Lesh/Petersen), **233–235**, 417

Promises made in the dark dissolve by light of day, 382

"Pump Song." See "Greatest Story Every Told"

Q

"Quadlibet for Tenderfeet" (Grateful Dead), 413, **415–416**

R

"Ramble on Rose" (Garcia/Hunter), 37, 146, **176–182**, 242

Rat in a drain ditch, 192

Red and white / blue suede shoes, 218

"Reuben and Cérise" (Garcia/Hunter), 93, 302, **360–362**

"Revolutionary Hamstrung Blues" (Lesh/Petersen), **329–330**

"Rhythm Devils" (Kreutzmann, Hart), 414

Right outside this lazy summer home, 202

"Ripple" (Garcia/Hunter), xvi, xviii, 54, 91, 116, 121, **126–130**, 332, 340, 343, 378

"River of Nine Sorrows" (Hart, Kreutzmann,

Well, I spend my tomcat nights in New Orleans, 400

Well, I was drinking last night with a biker, 324

Well it was early in the morning, 18

Well look what's going down the river now, 248

Well she's coming down the stairs, combing back her yellow hair, 10

Well, the first days are the hardest days, don't you worry anymore, 102

Well, there ain't nobody safer than someone who doesn't care, 354

Well this job I got is just a little too hard, 13

Went to see the captain, 222

"West L.A. Fadeaway" (Garcia/Hunter), **311–312**

"Wharf Rat" (Garcia/Hunter), **150–152**, 340, 347, 371

What are they seeing, when they look in each other's eyes?, 191

"What's Become of the Baby?" (Garcia/Hunter), 44, 75, **90–93**, 119, 240

"The Wheel" (Garcia, Kreutzmann/Hunter), 251, **256–258**, 272

The wheel is turning, 256

When I was hoppin' freights and makin' payments on the farm, 387

When I was just a little young boy, 70

"When Push Comes to Shove" (Garcia/Hunter), 334–335

When the cardboard cowboy dreams and his cornucopia, 23

When the last rose of summer pricks my finger, 331

When they come to take you down, 159

While you were gone, 264

Who—do you think you are?, 371

Will your high hopes get you there, 386

Winter rain, now tell me why, 211

Without a warning, you broke my heart, 39

Y

"You Don't Have to Ask" (Grateful Dead), **15**

"You Remind Me" (Hart, Haynes/Hunter), **408–409**

You remind me of feather pillows, 408

You say you want to try again, 306

You say you're living in a world of trouble, 28

You see a broken heart, 12

"You See a Broken Heart" (McKernan), **12**

You tell me this town ain't got no heart, 290

You told me good-bye, 94

Your rain falls like crazy fingers, 242